TOMARE!

You're going the wrong way!

Manga is a completely different type of reading experience.

To start at the *beginning*, go to the *end*!

That's right! Authentic manga is read the traditional Japanese way—from right to left. Exactly the opposite of how American books are read. It's easy to follow: Just go to the other end of the book, and read each page—and each panel—from right side to left side, starting at the top right. Now you're experiencing manga as it was meant to be!

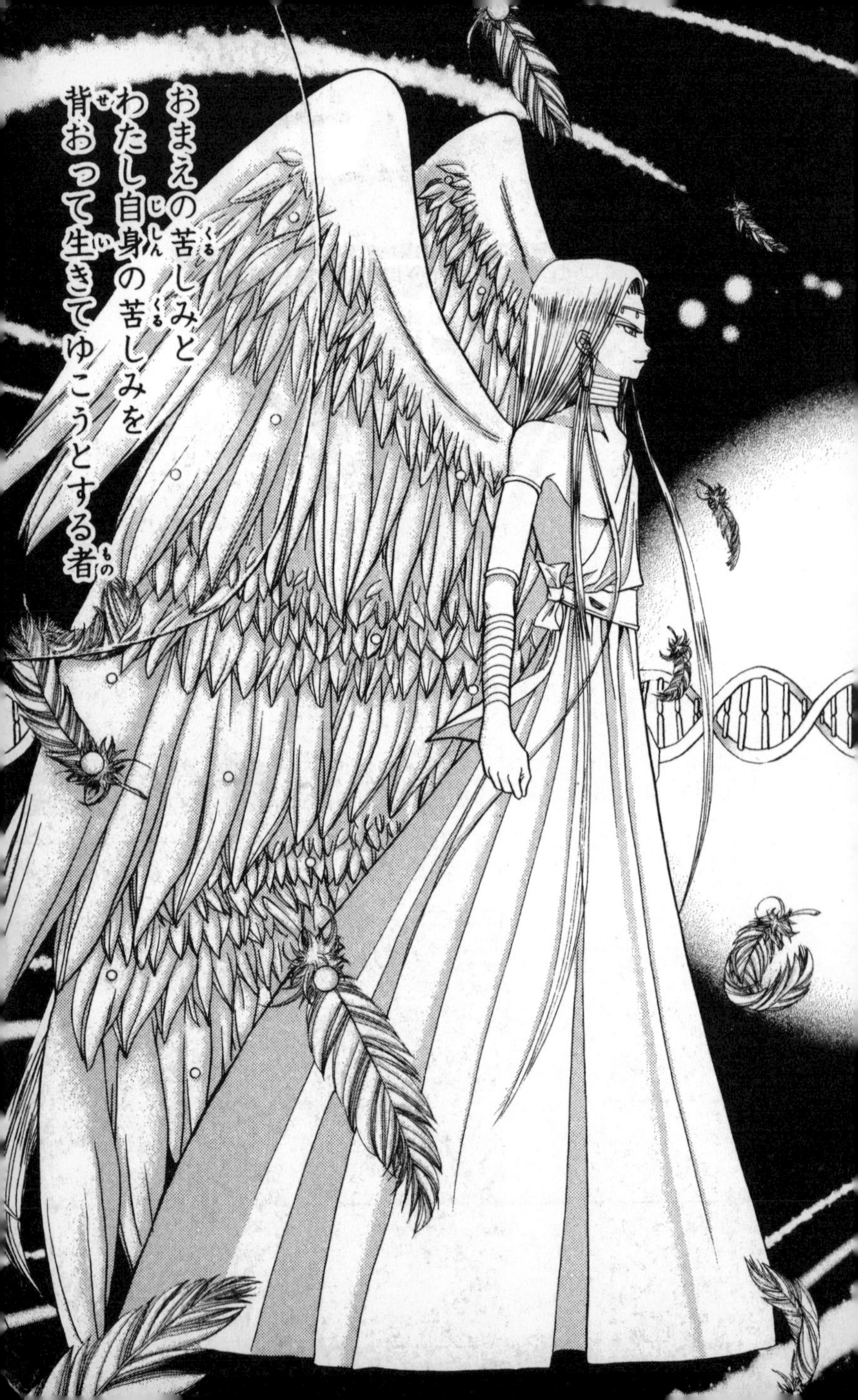
おまえの苦しみと
わたし自身の苦しみを
背おって生きてゆこうとする者

Pichi Pichi Pitch 5

MANGA BY PINK HANAMORI
SCENARIO BY MICHIKO YOKOTE

Translated and adapted by William Flanagan
Lettered by Min Choi

BALLANTINE BOOKS • NEW YORK

A Del Rey Trade Paperback Original

Pichi Pichi Pitch copyright © 2004 by Pink Hanamori, Michiko Yokote, Kodansha Ltd., and We've.

English translation copyright © 2007 by Pink Hanamori, Michiko Yokote, Kodansha Ltd., and We've.
All rights reserved.

Published in the United States by Del Rey Books, an imprint of The Random House Publishing Group, a division of Random House, Inc., New York.

DEL REY is a registered trademark and the Del Rey colophon is a trademark of Random House, Inc.

Publication rights arranged through Kodansha Ltd.

First published in Japan in 2004 by Kodansha Ltd., Tokyo.

ISBN 978-0-345-49200-5

Printed in the United States of America

www.delreymanga.com

9 8 7 6 5 4 3 2 1

Translator/Adaptor—William Flanagan
Lettering—Min Choi
Original cover design—Akiko Omo

Contents

Honorifics Explained

Throughout the Del Rey Manga books, you will find Japanese honorifics left intact in the translations. For those not familiar with how the Japanese use honorifics and, more important, how they differ from American honorifics, we present this brief overview.

Politeness has always been a critical facet of Japanese culture. Ever since the feudal era, when Japan was a highly stratified society, use of honorifics—which can be defined as polite speech that indicates relationship or status—has played an essential role in the Japanese language. When addressing someone in Japanese, an honorific usually takes the form of a suffix attached to one's name (example: "Asuna-san"), or as a title at the end of one's name, or in place of the name itself (example: "Negi-sensei," or simply "Sensei!").

Honorifics can be expressions of respect or endearment. In the context of manga and anime, honorifics give insight into the nature of the relationship between characters. Many English translations leave out these important honorifics, and therefore distort the feel of the original Japanese. Because Japanese honorifics contain nuances that English honorifics lack, it is our policy at Del Rey not to translate them. Here, instead, is a guide to some of the honorifics you may encounter in Del Rey Manga.

-san: This is the most common honorific, and is equivalent to Mr., Miss, Ms., or Mrs. It is the all-purpose honorific and can be used in any situation where politeness is required.

-sama: This is one level higher than "-san" and is used to confer great respect.

-dono: This comes from the word "tono," which means "lord." It is an even higher level than "-sama" and confers utmost respect.

-kun: This suffix is used at the end of boys' names to express familiarity or endearment. It is also sometimes used by men among friends, or when addressing someone younger or of a lower station.

-chan: This is used to express endearment, mostly toward girls. It is also used for little boys, pets, and even among lovers. It gives a sense of childish cuteness.

Bozu: This is an informal way to refer to a boy, similar to the English terms "kid" or "squirt."

Sempai/: This title suggests that the addressee is one's senior in a group
Senpai or organization. It is most often used in a school setting, where underclassmen refer to their upperclassmen as "sempai." It can also be used in the workplace, such as when a newer employee addresses an employee who has seniority in the company.

Kohai: This is the opposite of "-sempai," and is used toward underclassmen in school or newcomers in the workplace. It connotes that the addressee is of a lower station.

Sensei: Literally meaning "one who has come before," this title is used for teachers, doctors, or masters of any profession or art.

[blank]: This is usually forgotten in these lists, but it is perhaps the most significant difference between Japanese and English. The lack of honorific means that the speaker has permission to address the person in a very intimate way. Usually, only family, spouses, or very close friends have this kind of permission. Known as *yobisute,* it can be gratifying when someone who has earned the intimacy starts to call one by one's name without an honorific. But when that intimacy hasn't been earned, it can be very insulting.

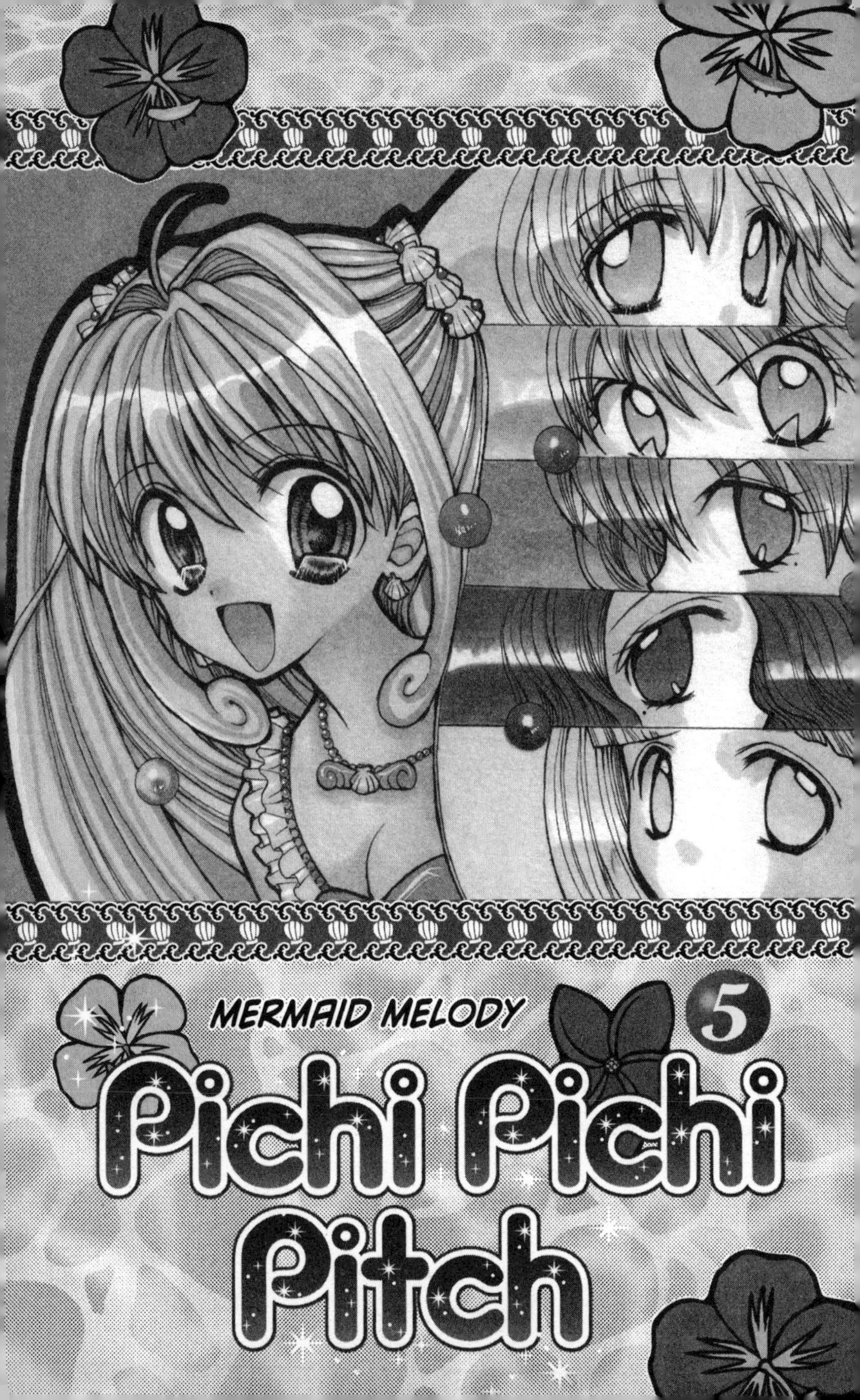
MERMAID MELODY
5
Pichi Pichi Pitch

PEARL BATHS ♥

LUCIA'S BATH-WORKER DIARY

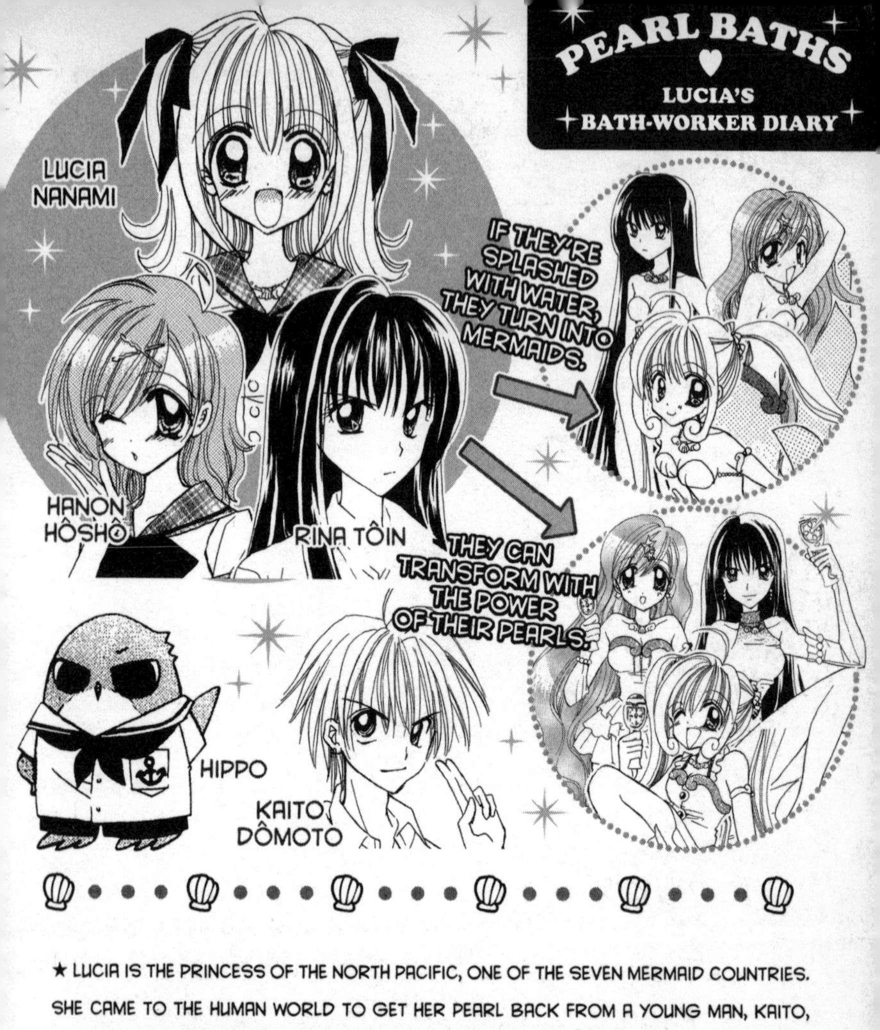
IF THEY'RE SPLASHED WITH WATER, THEY TURN INTO MERMAIDS.
THEY CAN TRANSFORM WITH THE POWER OF THEIR PEARLS.
LUCIA NANAMI
HANON HÔSHÔ
RINA TÔIN
HIPPO
KAITO DÔMOTO

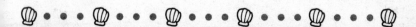

★ LUCIA IS THE PRINCESS OF THE NORTH PACIFIC, ONE OF THE SEVEN MERMAID COUNTRIES. SHE CAME TO THE HUMAN WORLD TO GET HER PEARL BACK FROM A YOUNG MAN, KAITO, WHOM SHE SAVED FROM DROWNING SEVEN YEARS AGO. BUT THAT WAS THE BEGINNING OF A BATTLE AGAINST GACKTO, WHO WANTED TO RULE THE SEAS!

★ GACKTO HAD THE ORANGE MERMAID PRINCESS SARA AS HIS ALLY, AND IT TURNS OUT THAT KAITO WAS HIS TWIN BROTHER. BUT IN THE END, THE FEELINGS INSIDE LUCIA'S HEART GOT THROUGH TO SARA, AND THEY DEFEATED GACKTO'S AMBITIONS. AND FINALLY KAITO REALIZES THAT LUCIA WAS THE MERMAID HE FELL IN LOVE WITH SO MANY YEARS AGO. ♡♡

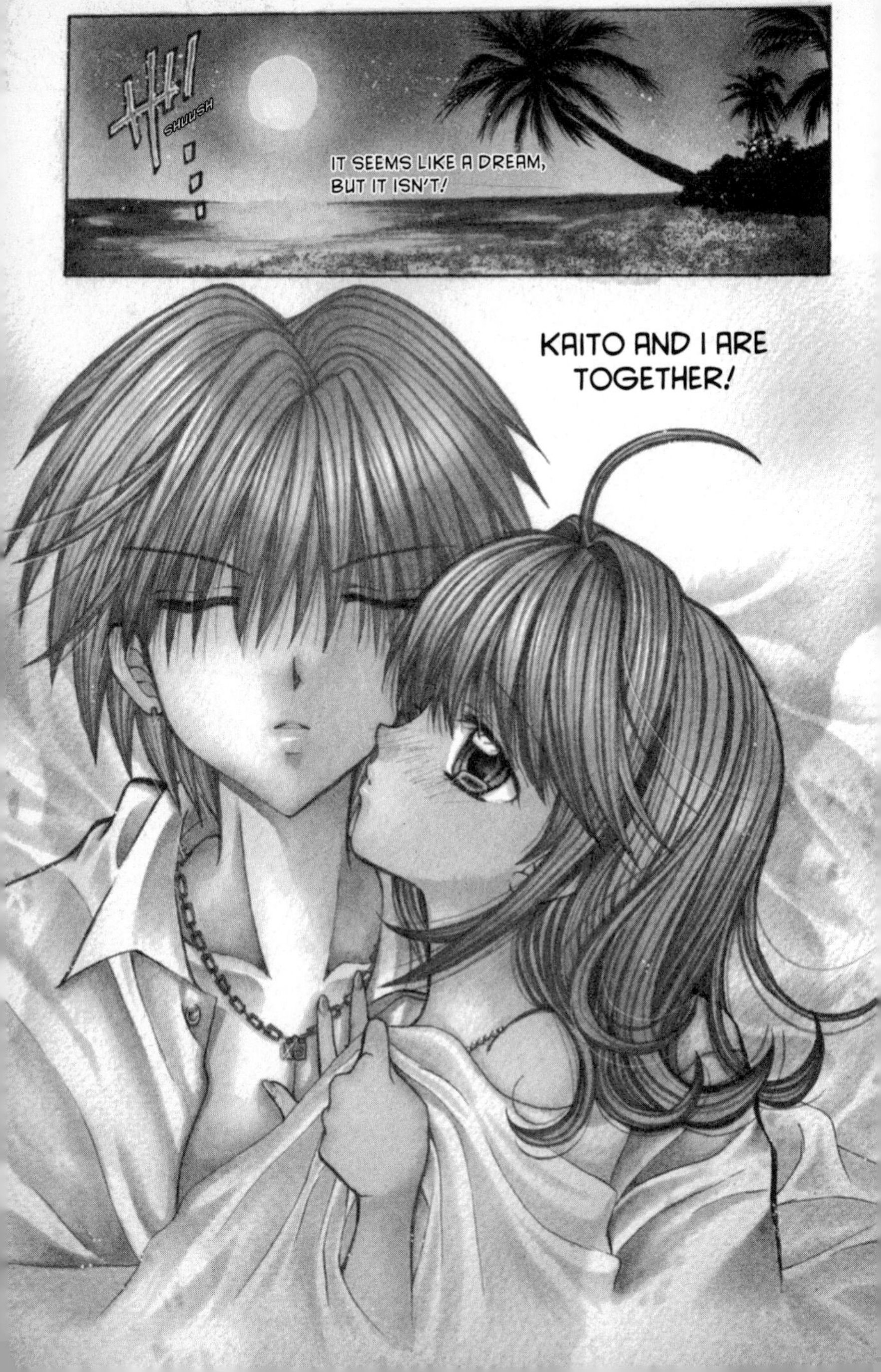
IT SEEMS LIKE A DREAM, BUT IT ISN'T!
SHUUSH
KAITO AND I ARE TOGETHER!

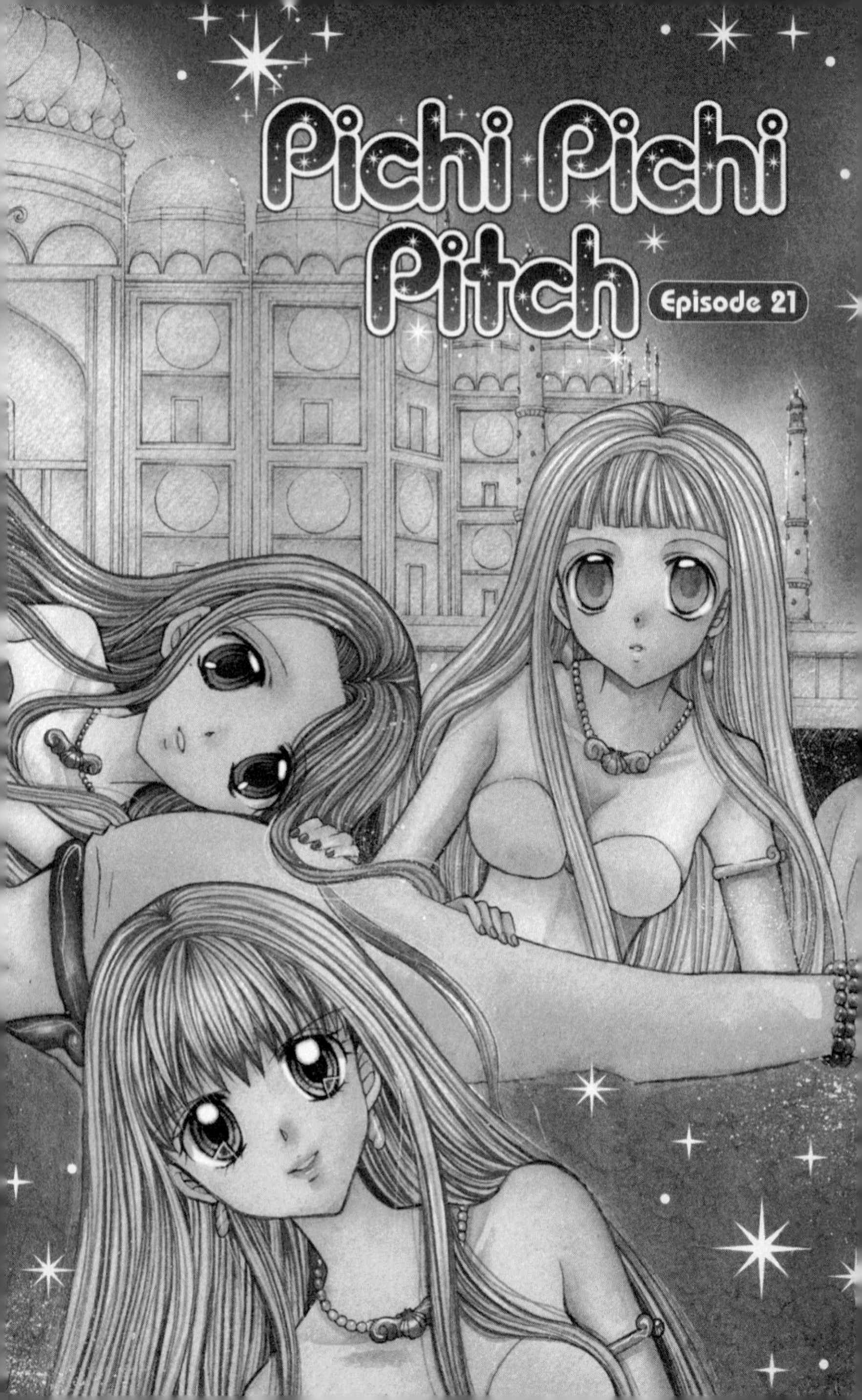
Pichi Pichi Pitch
Episode 21

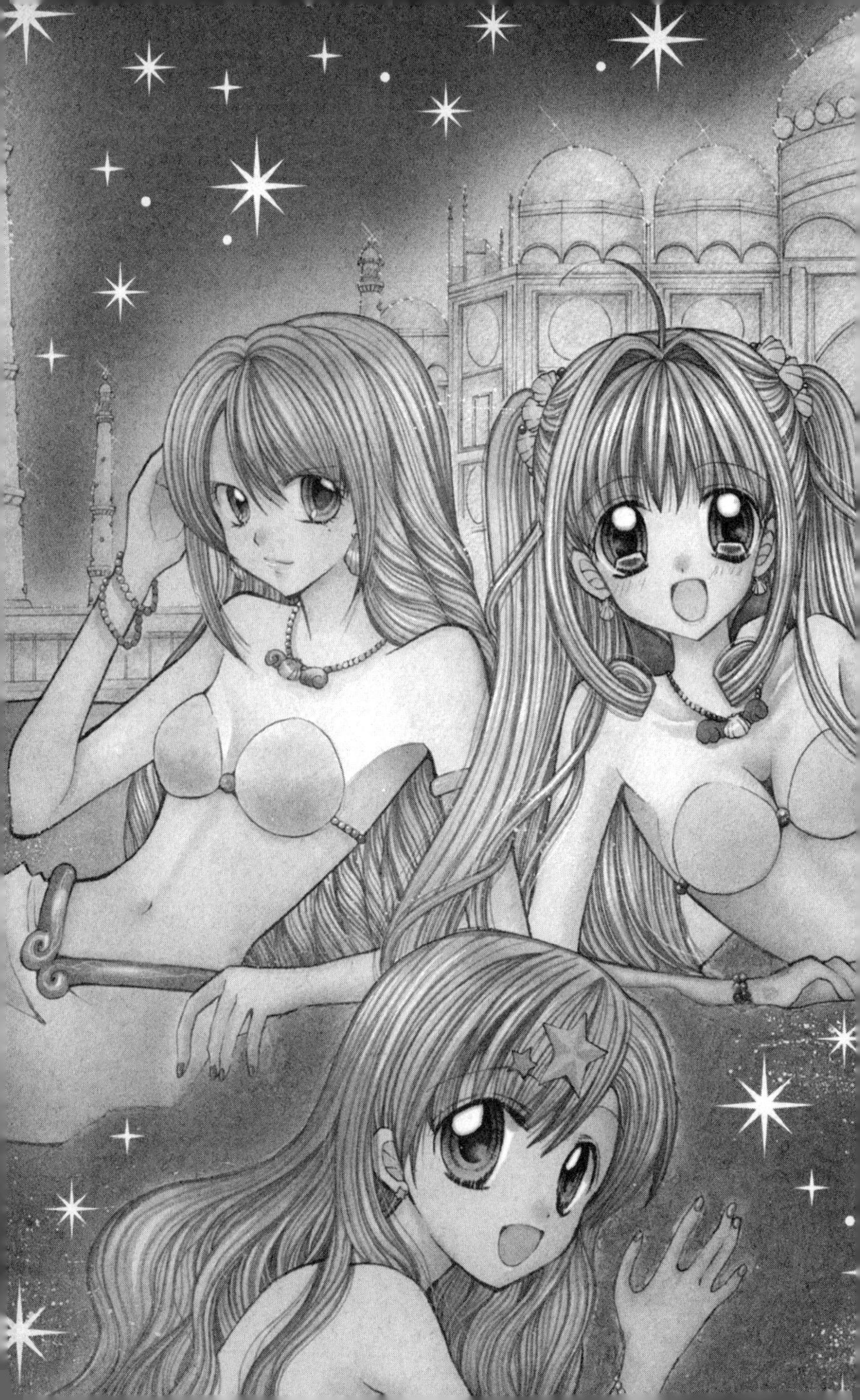

GREETINGS!

LIPS

HELLO TO THE PEOPLE COMING BACK AFTER SO LONG, AND TO THOSE READING FOR THE FIRST TIME! MY NAME IS PINK HANAMORI.

THE 5TH VOLUME IS IN YOUR HANDS.

PLEASE, PLEASE! ENJOY IT, OKAY?

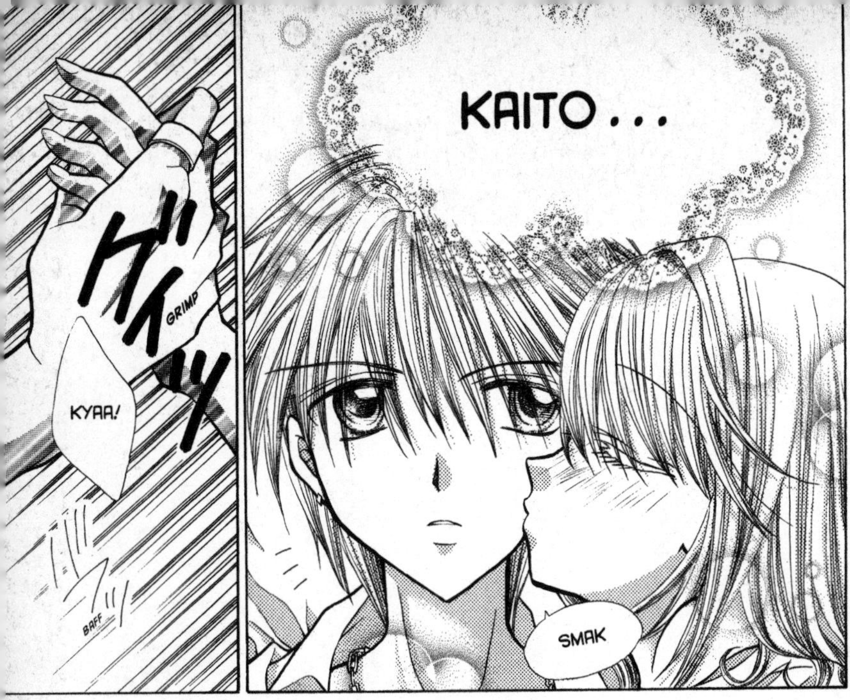
KAITO . . .
SMAK
GRIMP
KYAA!
BAFF

<EPISODE 21>

THIS IS THE EPISODE THAT STARTS THE NEW SERIES.
IT WAS FUN TO DRAW THE ROMANTIC SCENES WITH KAITO AND LUCIA. YEAH, I LOVE DRAWING LOVE SCENES THE BEST! KAITO WENT TO HAWAII, BUT I'VE NEVER BEEN THERE MYSELF . . . I WANNA GO!!
THIS EPISODE IS SIXTY-THREE PAGES, AND IT WAS SIXTY PAGES IN THE MAGAZINE, BUT I'LL ALWAYS REMEMBER THAT I HAD TO PRODUCE IT IN FIFTEEN DAYS. THAT'S A PACE WHERE I REALLY HAVE TO WORK AT IT! IN THE SECOND HALF, MY STRENGTH WAS REALLY CLOSE TO GIVING OUT. ON THE OTHER HAND, BECAUSE OF IT, I GET THE FEELING THAT I'VE GOTTEN A LITTLE FASTER IN MY DRAWING FROM THEN ON. BUT I USE UP ANY EXTRA TIME I GAINED BY SLEEPING, SO THE WHOLE THING TAKES ABOUT THE SAME AMOUNT OF TIME. ~

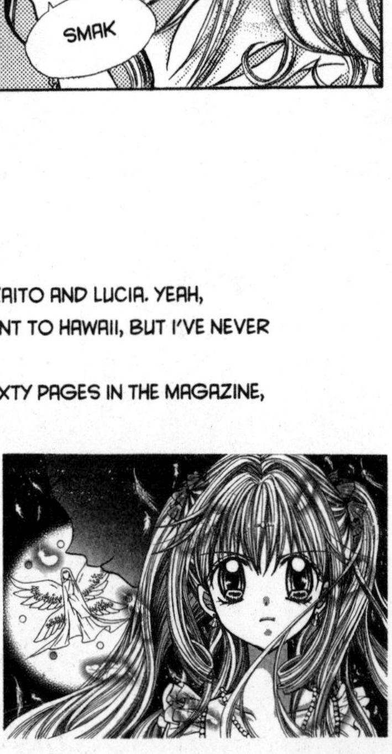

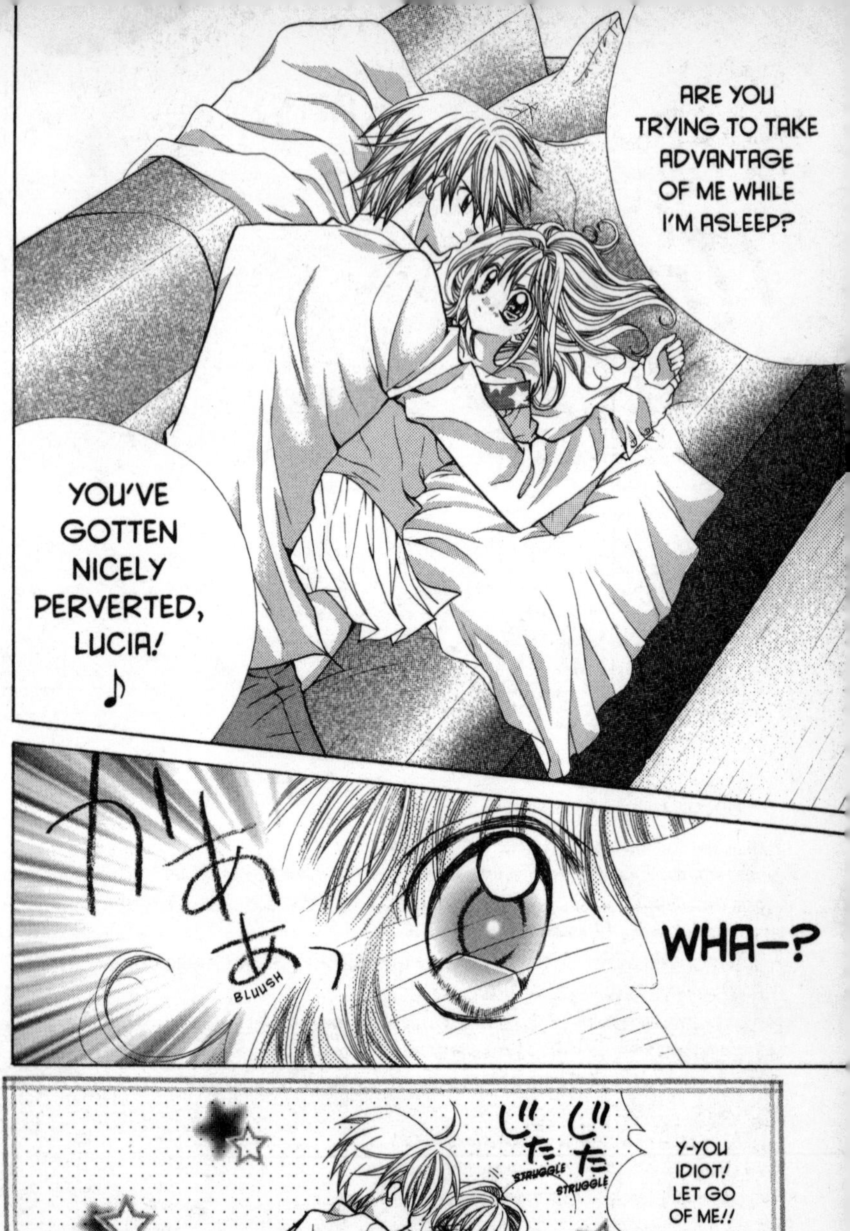
ARE YOU TRYING TO TAKE ADVANTAGE OF ME WHILE I'M ASLEEP?
YOU'VE GOTTEN NICELY PERVERTED, LUCIA! ♪
WHA-?
かああっ
BLUUSH
Y-YOU IDIOT! LET GO OF ME!!
じた
STRUGGLE
じた
STRUGGLE

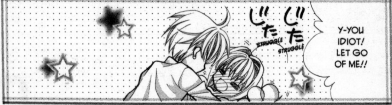

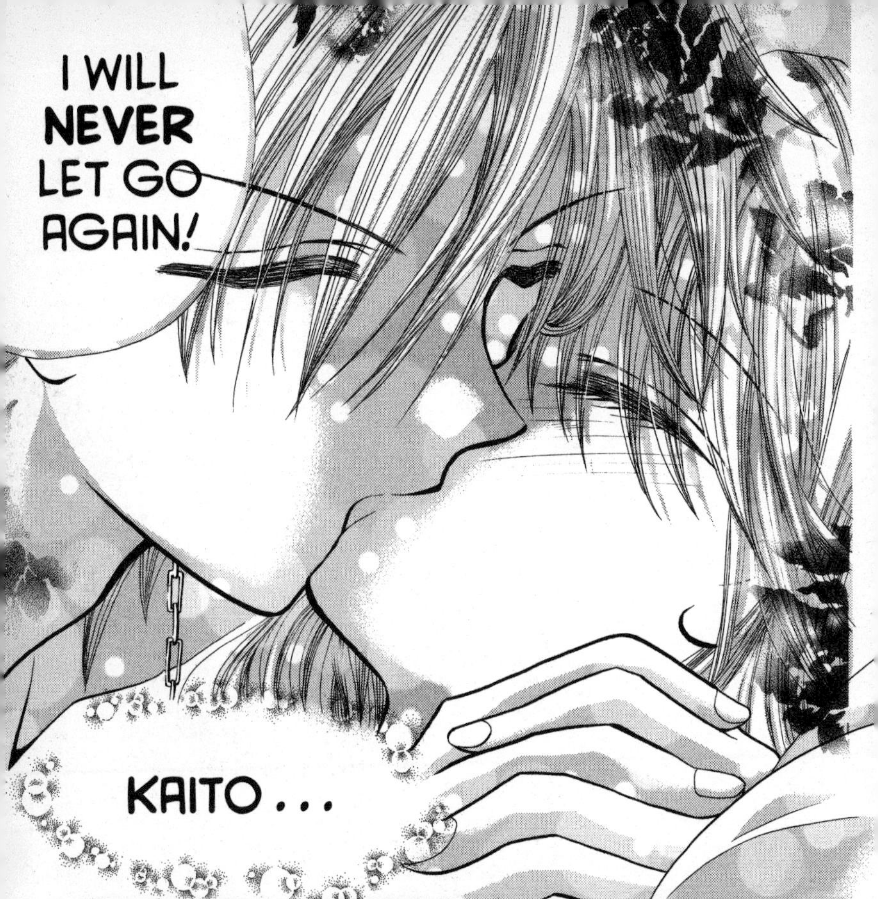
I WILL NEVER LET GO AGAIN!
KAITO . . .

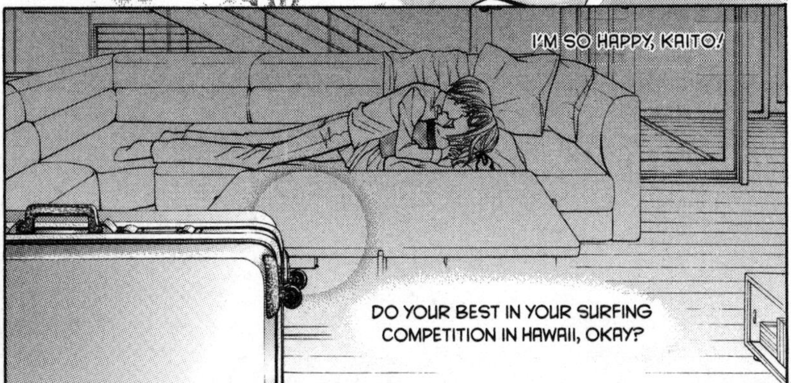
I'M SO HAPPY, KAITO!
DO YOUR BEST IN YOUR SURFING COMPETITION IN HAWAII, OKAY?

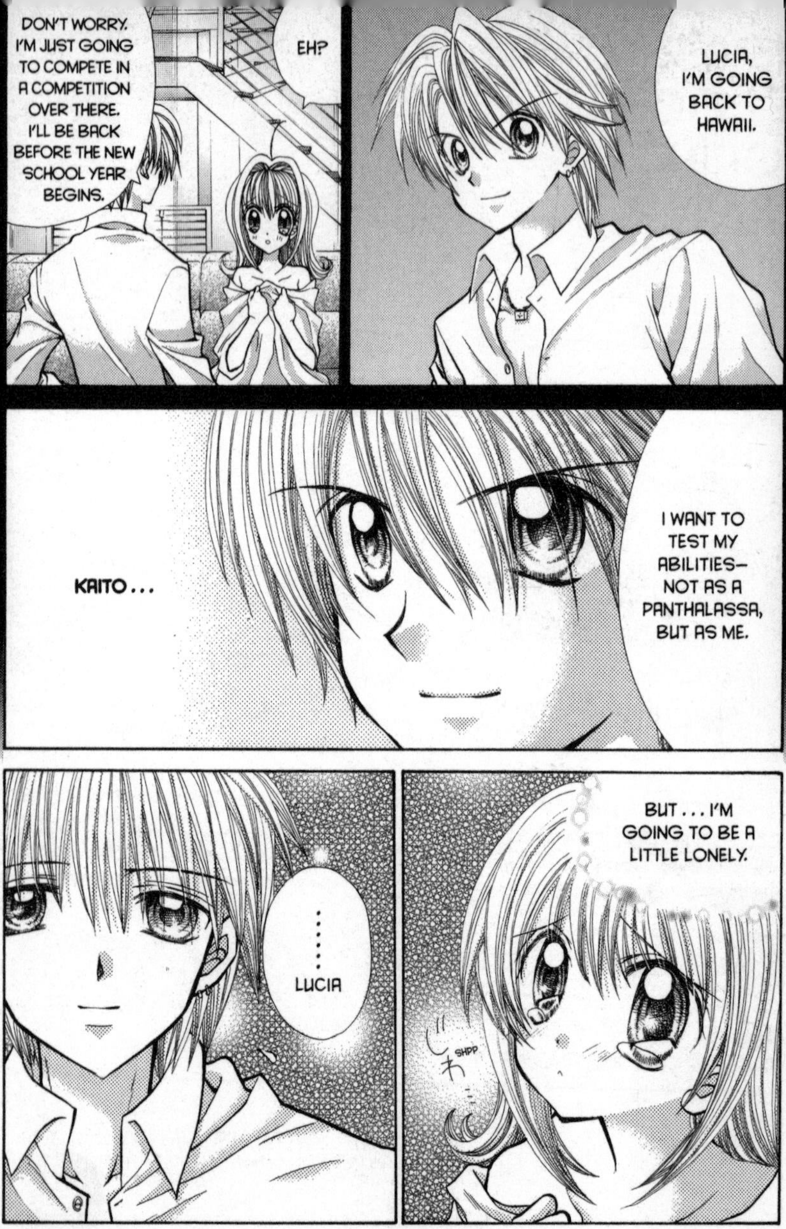
LUCIA, I'M GOING BACK TO HAWAII.
EH?
DON'T WORRY. I'M JUST GOING TO COMPETE IN A COMPETITION OVER THERE. I'LL BE BACK BEFORE THE NEW SCHOOL YEAR BEGINS.
I WANT TO TEST MY ABILITIES— NOT AS A PANTHALASSA, BUT AS ME.
KAITO . . .
BUT . . . I'M GOING TO BE A LITTLE LONELY.
SHPP
. . . . . . LUCIA

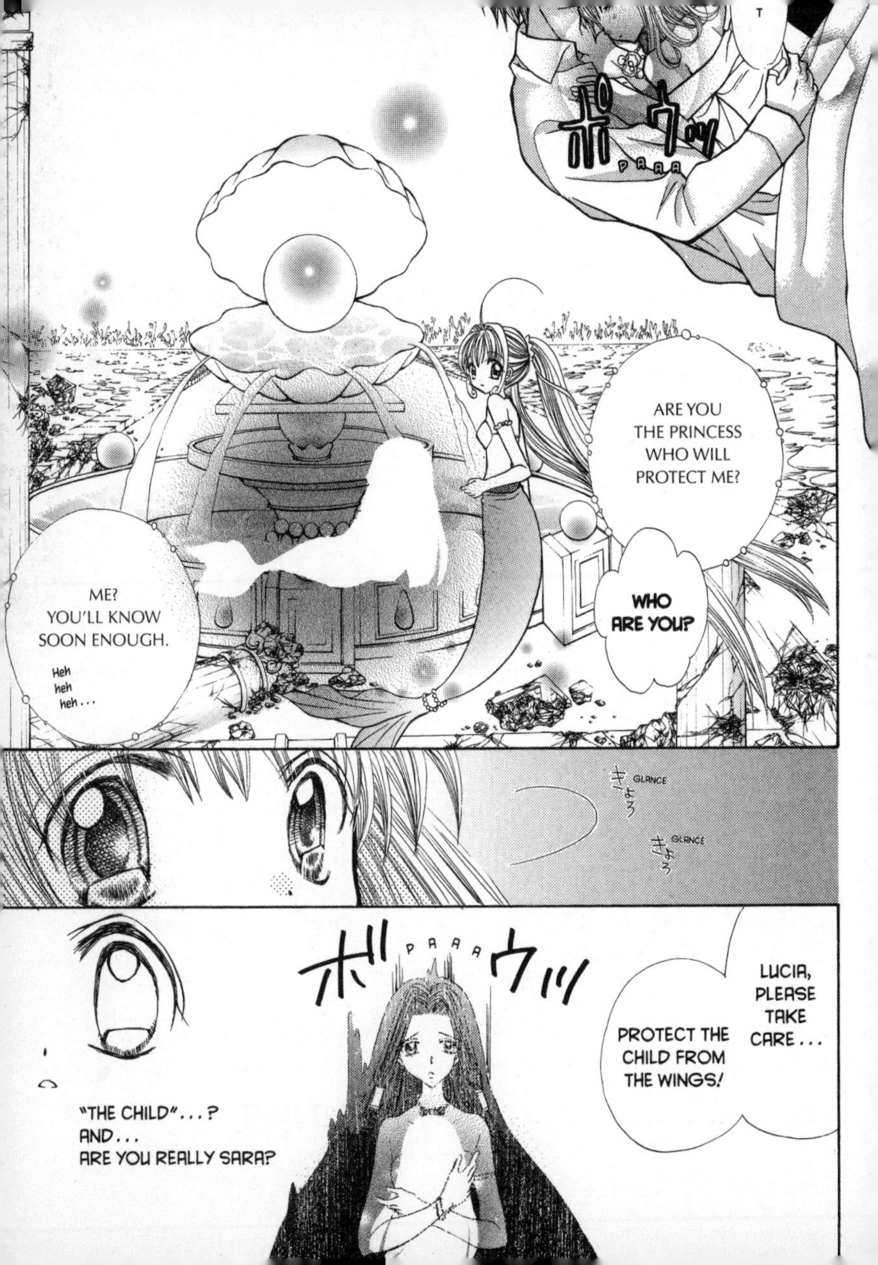
PAAA
ARE YOU THE PRINCESS WHO WILL PROTECT ME?
WHO ARE YOU?
ME? YOU'LL KNOW SOON ENOUGH.
Heh heh heh...
GLANCE
GLANCE
LUCIA, PLEASE TAKE CARE...
PROTECT THE CHILD FROM THE WINGS!
PAAA
"THE CHILD"...? AND... ARE YOU REALLY SARA?

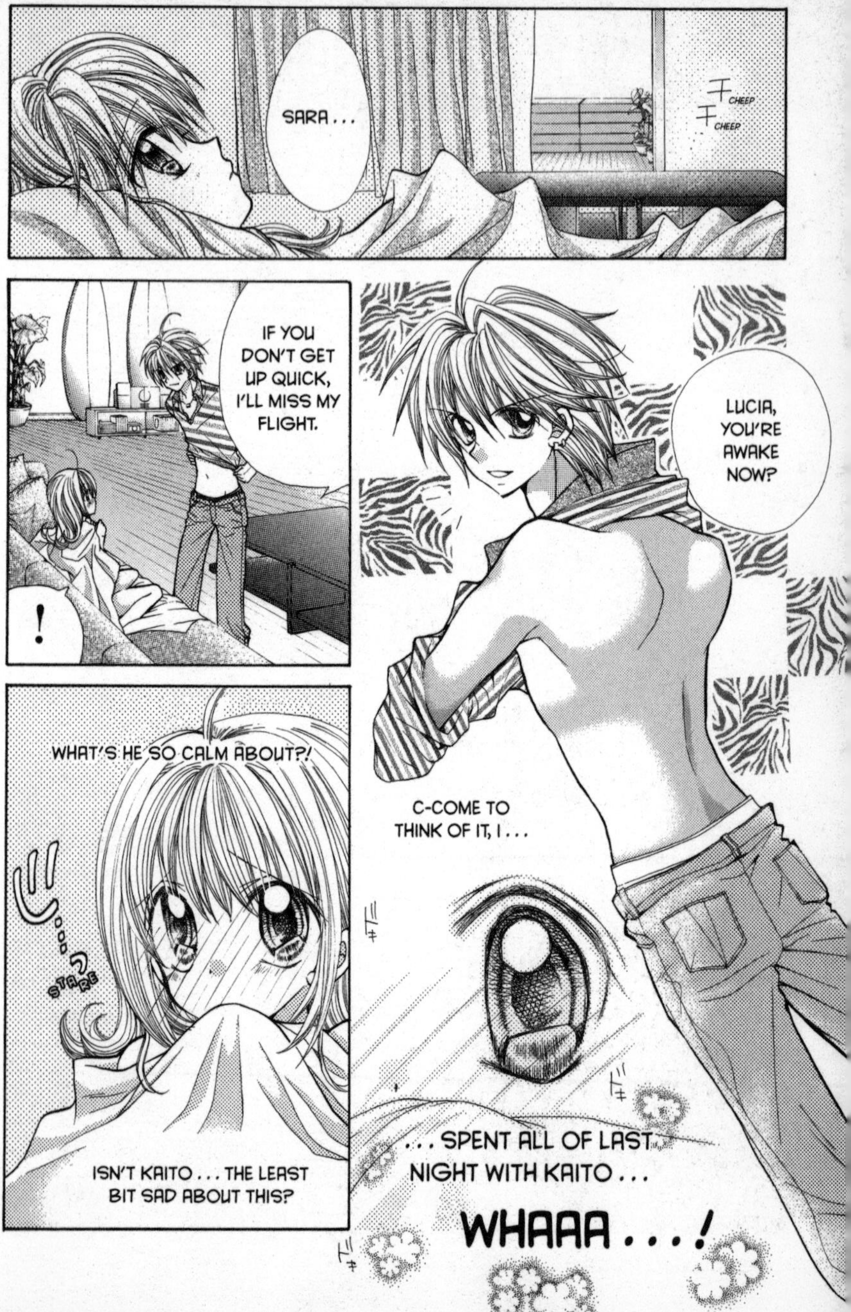
SARA . . .
CHEEP
CHEEP
LUCIA, YOU'RE AWAKE NOW?
C-COME TO THINK OF IT, I . . .
. . . SPENT ALL OF LAST NIGHT WITH KAITO . . .
WHAAA . . . !
IF YOU DON'T GET UP QUICK, I'LL MISS MY FLIGHT.
!
WHAT'S HE SO CALM ABOUT?!
STARE
ISN'T KAITO . . . THE LEAST BIT SAD ABOUT THIS?

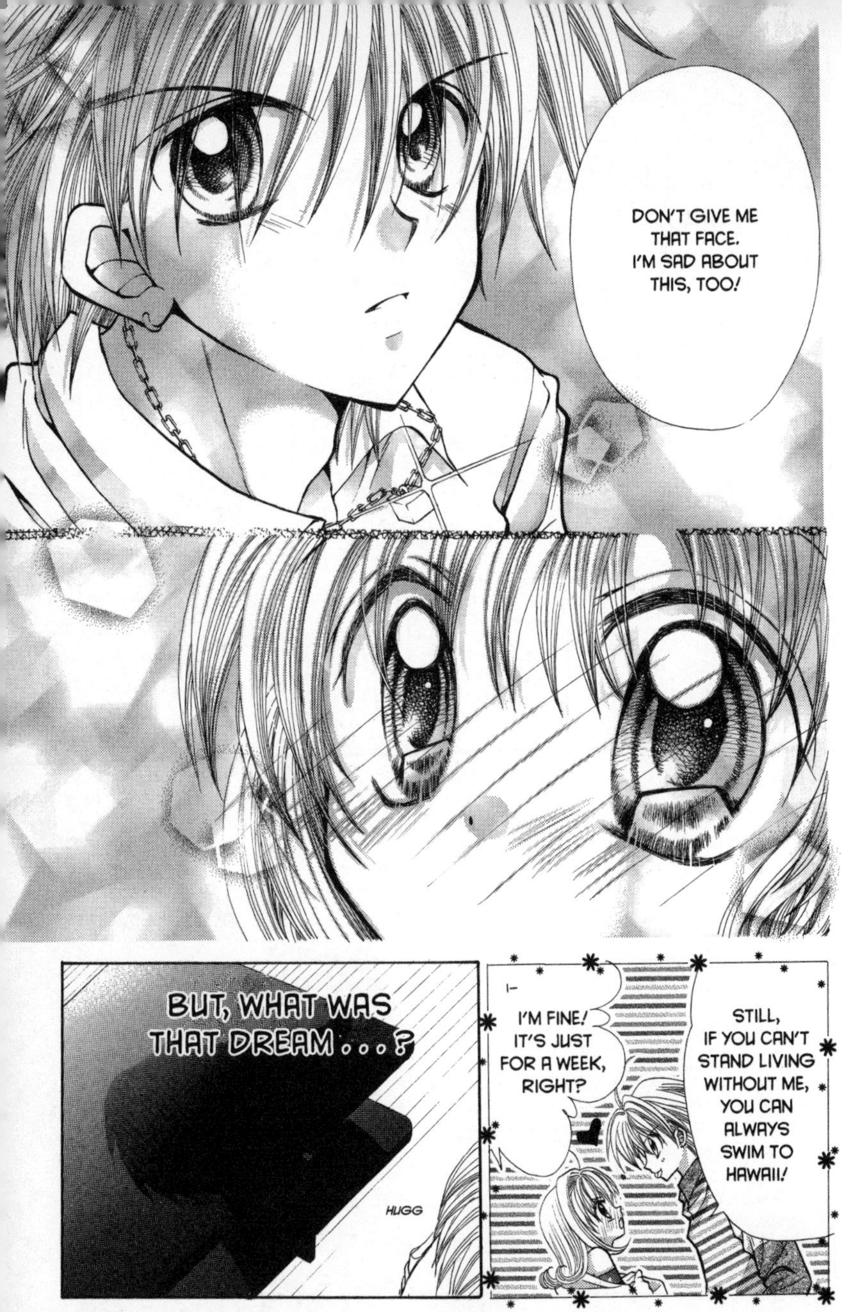
DON'T GIVE ME THAT FACE. I'M SAD ABOUT THIS, TOO!
STILL, IF YOU CAN'T STAND LIVING WITHOUT ME, YOU CAN ALWAYS SWIM TO HAWAII!
I–
I'M FINE! IT'S JUST FOR A WEEK, RIGHT?
BUT, WHAT WAS THAT DREAM . . . ?
HUGG

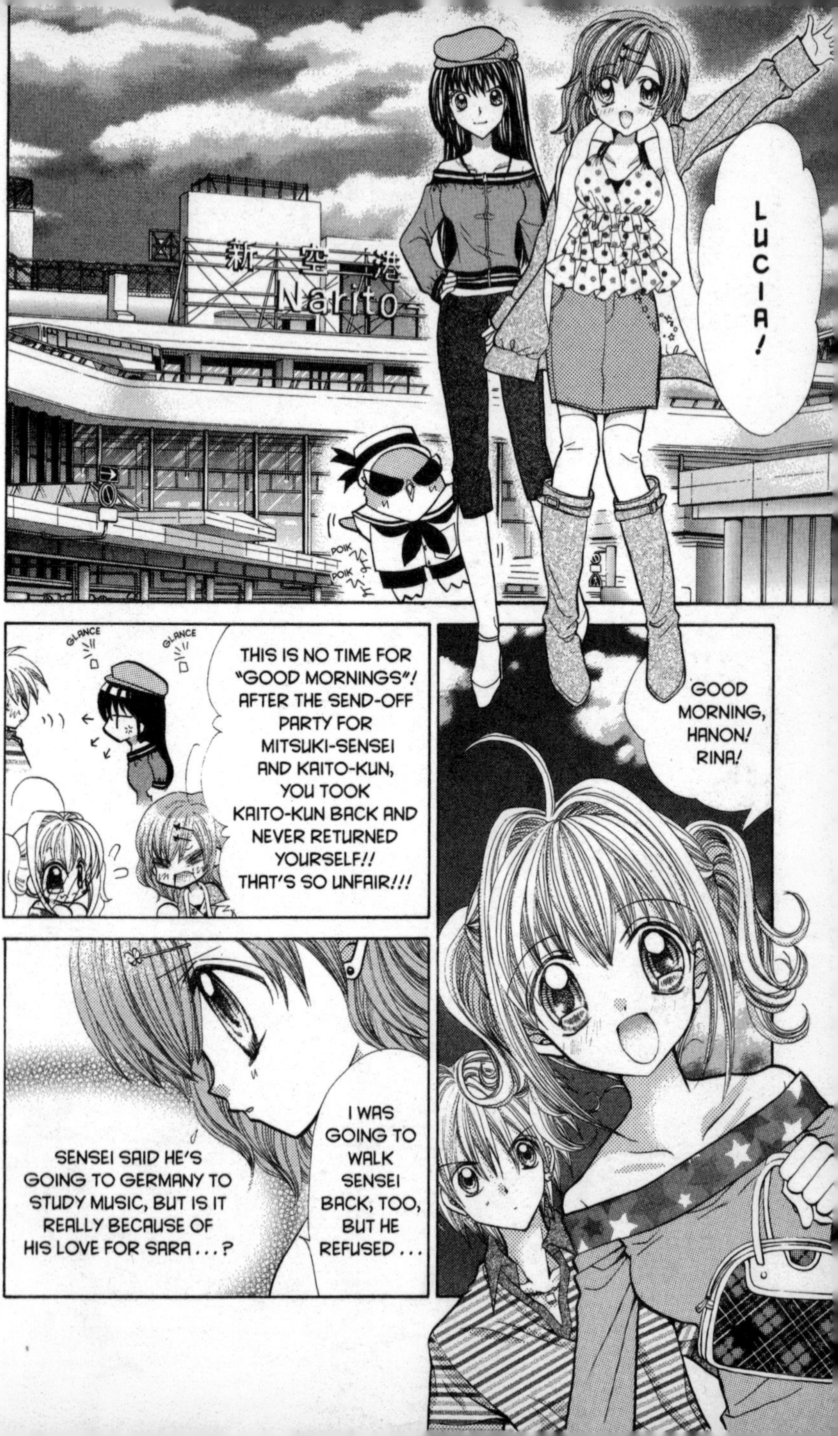
LUCIA!
新空港
Narito
POIK POIK
ぴよ ぴよ
GOOD MORNING, HANON! RINA!
GLANCE
GLANCE
THIS IS NO TIME FOR "GOOD MORNINGS"! AFTER THE SEND-OFF PARTY FOR MITSUKI-SENSEI AND KAITO-KUN, YOU TOOK KAITO-KUN BACK AND NEVER RETURNED YOURSELF!! THAT'S SO UNFAIR!!!
I WAS GOING TO WALK SENSEI BACK, TOO, BUT HE REFUSED . . .
SENSEI SAID HE'S GOING TO GERMANY TO STUDY MUSIC, BUT IS IT REALLY BECAUSE OF HIS LOVE FOR SARA . . . ?

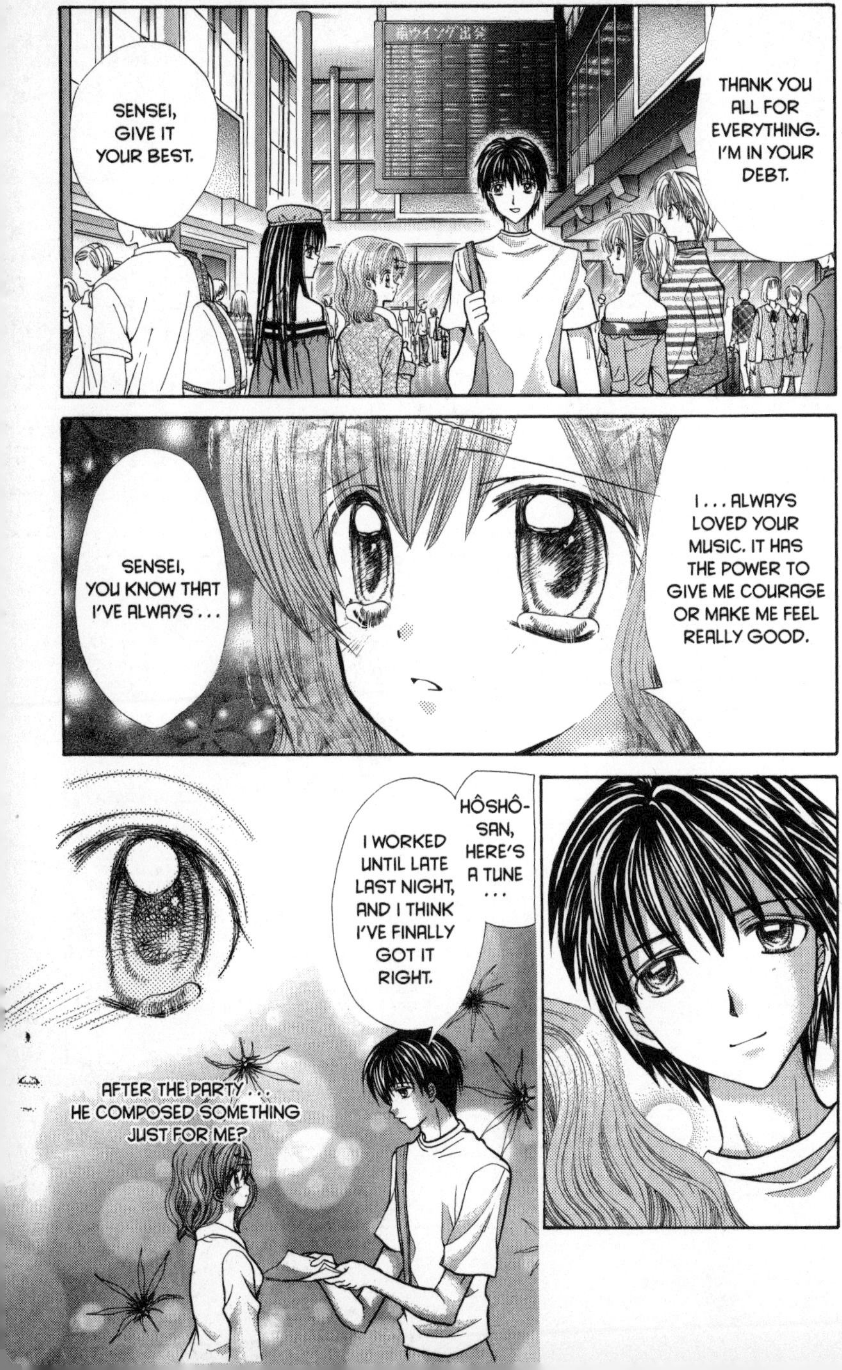
THANK YOU ALL FOR EVERYTHING. I'M IN YOUR DEBT.
SENSEI, GIVE IT YOUR BEST.
I . . . ALWAYS LOVED YOUR MUSIC. IT HAS THE POWER TO GIVE ME COURAGE OR MAKE ME FEEL REALLY GOOD.
SENSEI, YOU KNOW THAT I'VE ALWAYS . . .
HÔSHÔ-SAN, HERE'S A TUNE . . .
I WORKED UNTIL LATE LAST NIGHT, AND I THINK I'VE FINALLY GOT IT RIGHT.
AFTER THE PARTY . . . HE COMPOSED SOMETHING JUST FOR ME?

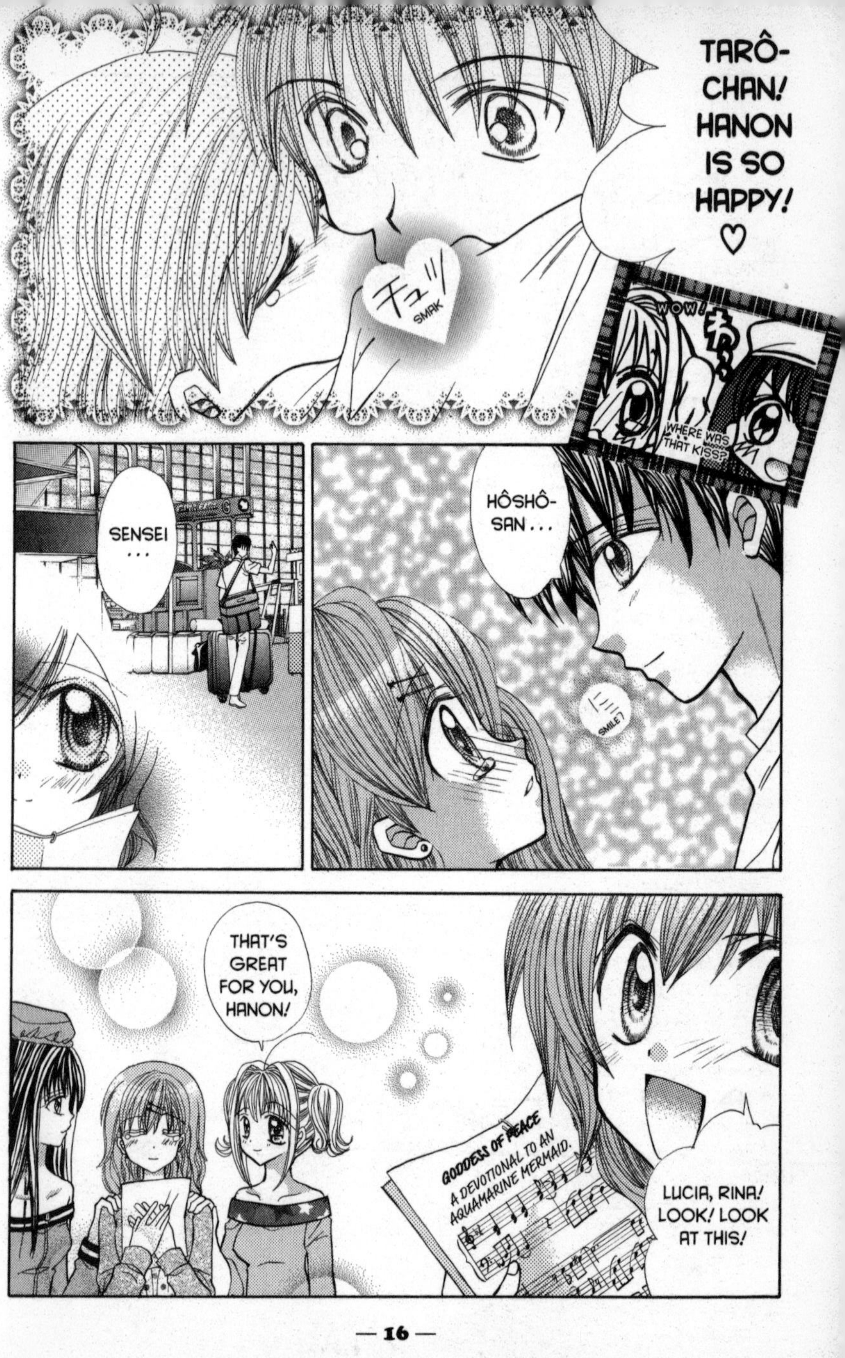
TARÔ-CHAN! HANON IS SO HAPPY! ♡
チュッ
SMAK
WOW!
わっ
WHERE WAS THAT KISS?
HÔSHÔ-SAN . . .
にこ
SMILE
SENSEI . . .
LUCIA, RINA! LOOK! LOOK AT THIS!
GODDESS OF PEACE
A DEVOTIONAL TO AN AQUAMARINE MERMAID.
THAT'S GREAT FOR YOU, HANON!

FAN LETTERS ♥

THANK YOU FOR ALL OF YOUR LETTERS AND E-MAIL TO MY HOME PAGE!! THEY ALWAYS CHEER ME UP! AND TO THOSE OF YOU WHO SENT ME PRESENTS, THANKS! I USE THEM ALL! SPEAKING OF PRESENTS, I'M SORRY FOR REPORTING THIS SO LATE, BUT DURING AN EVENT TO MARK WHEN THEY DECIDED TO ANIMATE THE SERIES, I RECEIVED A BOUQUET OF FLOWERS AND SOME HIGH-QUALITY CHOCOLATES! TO THE PERSON WHO GAVE THEM TO ME, ARE YOU READING THIS? THANK YOU SO MUCH!! TO TELL YOU THE TRUTH, I'M NOT REALLY FOND OF THE TERM "FAN LETTER." IT SEEMS SO PRESUMPTUOUS. JUST BECAUSE WE GET A LETTER DOESN'T NECESSARILY MEAN IT'S FROM A FAN, AND IT'S RUDE TO ASSUME THAT THEY ALL ARE. ON THE OTHER HAND, A CERTAIN CELEBRITY WOULD ONLY CALL FAN LETTERS SIMPLY LETTERS, BUT . . .

← TO BE CONTINUED ON PAGE 55!

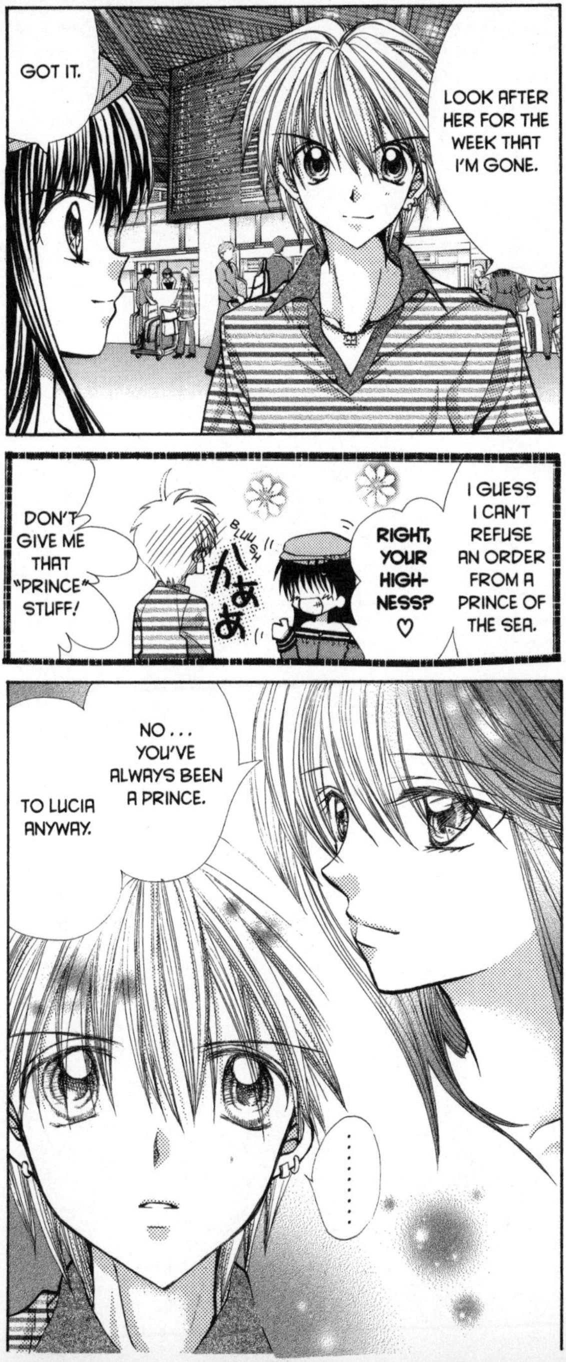
LOOK AFTER HER FOR THE WEEK THAT I'M GONE.
GOT IT.
I GUESS I CAN'T REFUSE AN ORDER FROM A PRINCE OF THE SEA.
RIGHT, YOUR HIGH-NESS? ♡
BLUUSH
かぁぁ
DON'T GIVE ME THAT "PRINCE" STUFF!
NO . . . YOU'VE ALWAYS BEEN A PRINCE.
TO LUCIA ANYWAY.
. . . .

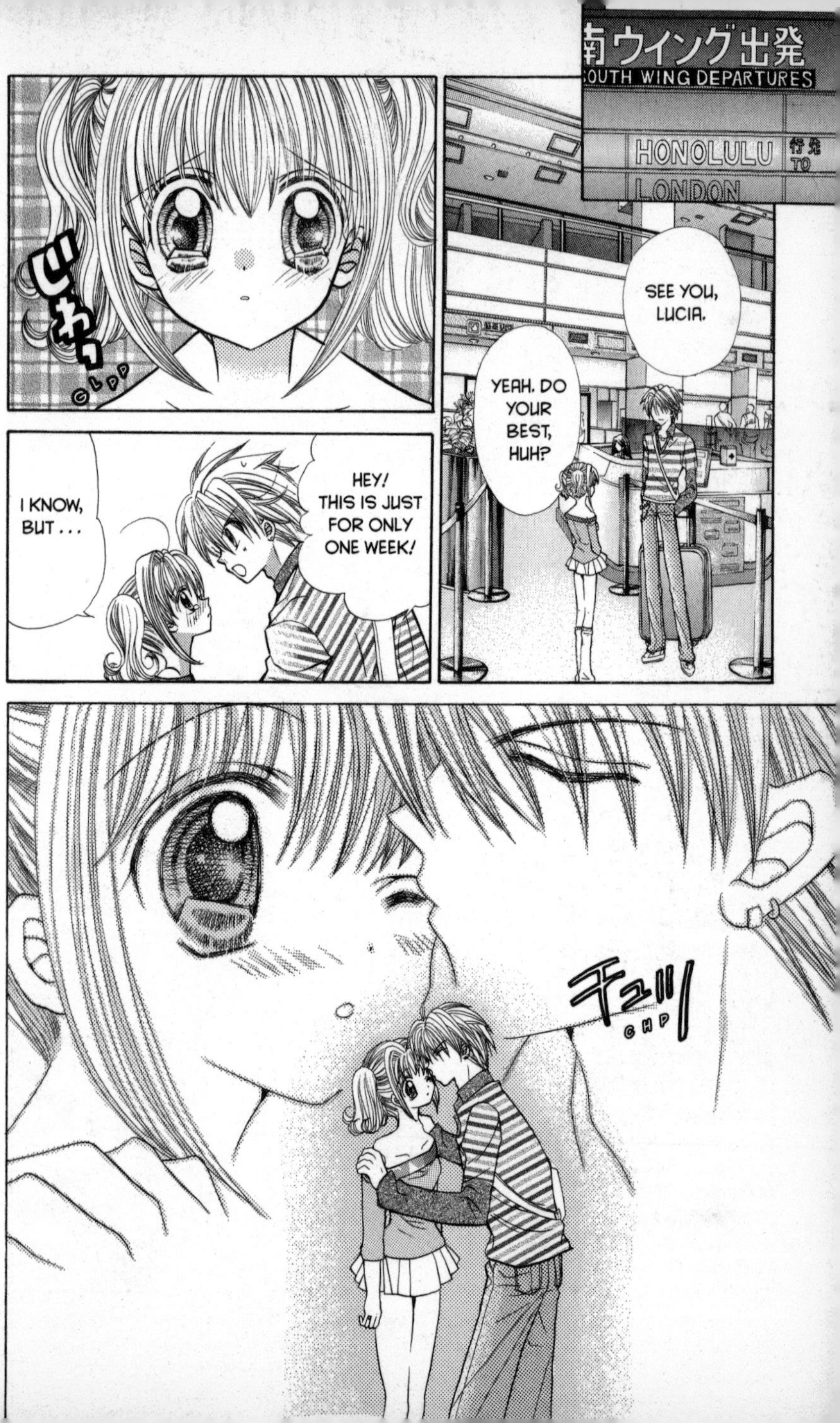

南ウィング出発
SOUTH WING DEPARTURES
HONOLULU 行先 TO
LONDON
SEE YOU, LUCIA.
YEAH. DO YOUR BEST, HUH?
じわっ
GLPP
HEY! THIS IS JUST FOR ONLY ONE WEEK!
I KNOW, BUT . . .
チュッ
CHP

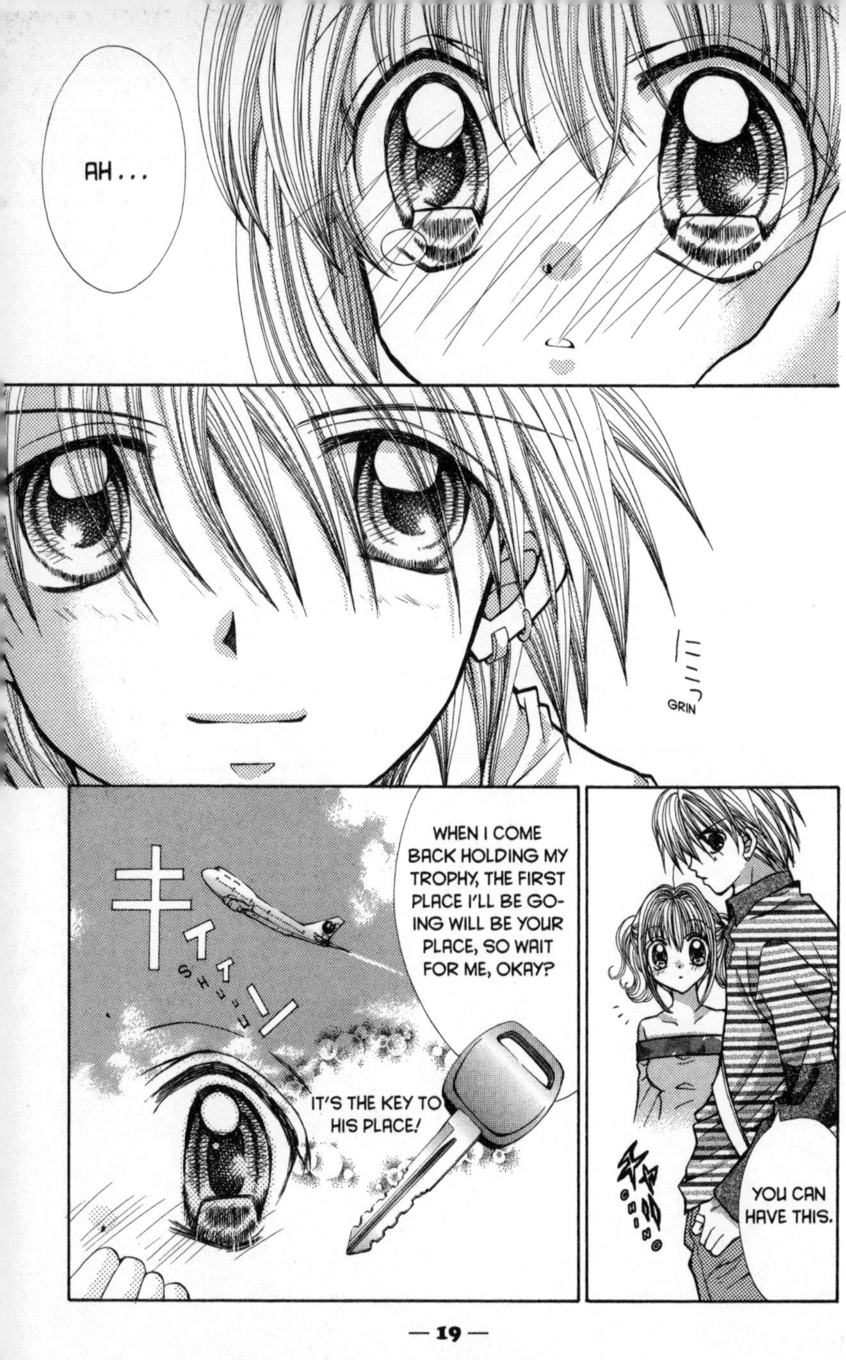
AH...
GRIN
YOU CAN HAVE THIS.
CHING
WHEN I COME BACK HOLDING MY TROPHY, THE FIRST PLACE I'LL BE GO-ING WILL BE YOUR PLACE, SO WAIT FOR ME, OKAY?
SHUUU
IT'S THE KEY TO HIS PLACE!

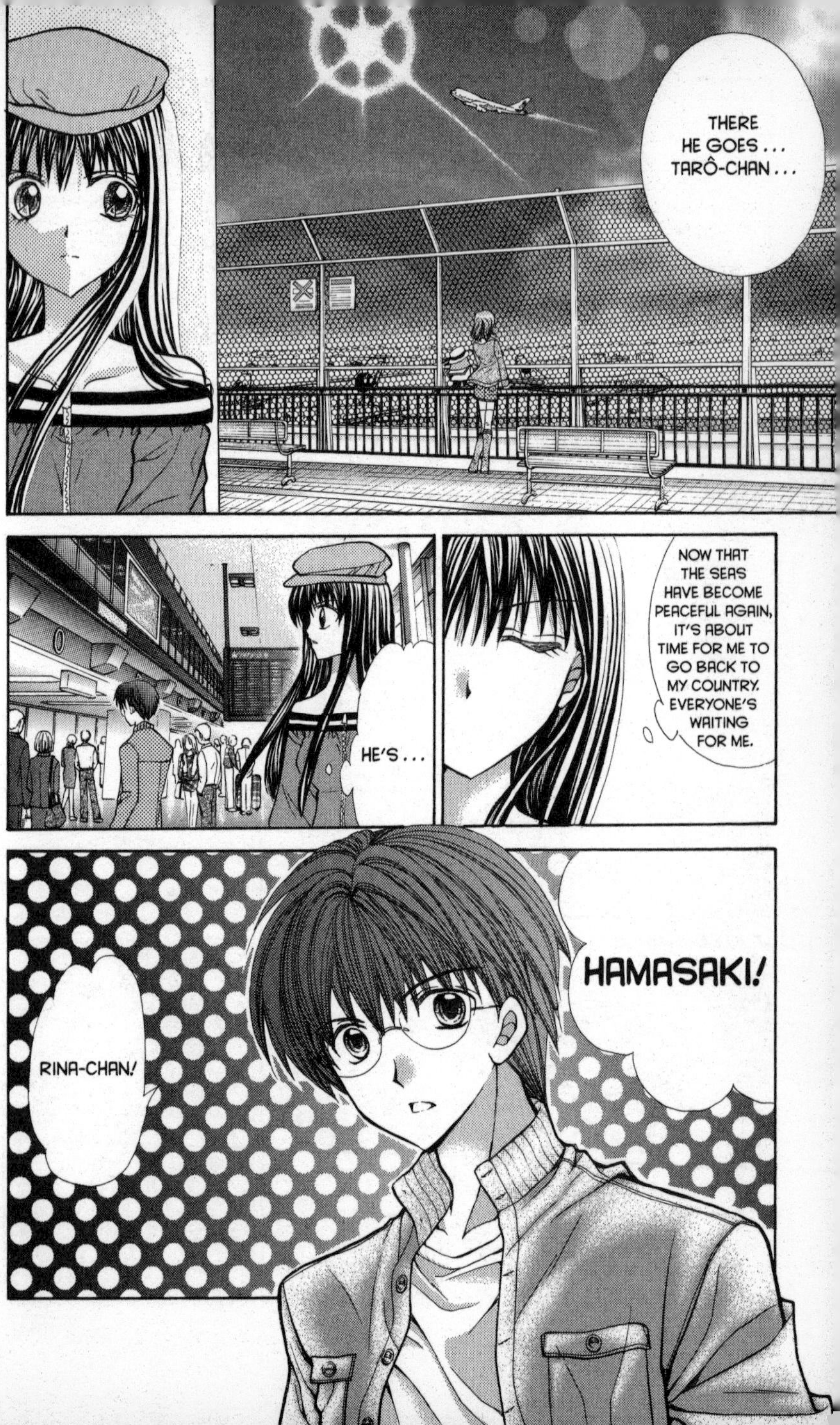
THERE HE GOES . . . TARÔ-CHAN . . .
NOW THAT THE SEAS HAVE BECOME PEACEFUL AGAIN, IT'S ABOUT TIME FOR ME TO GO BACK TO MY COUNTRY. EVERYONE'S WAITING FOR ME.
HE'S . . .
HAMASAKI!
RINA-CHAN!

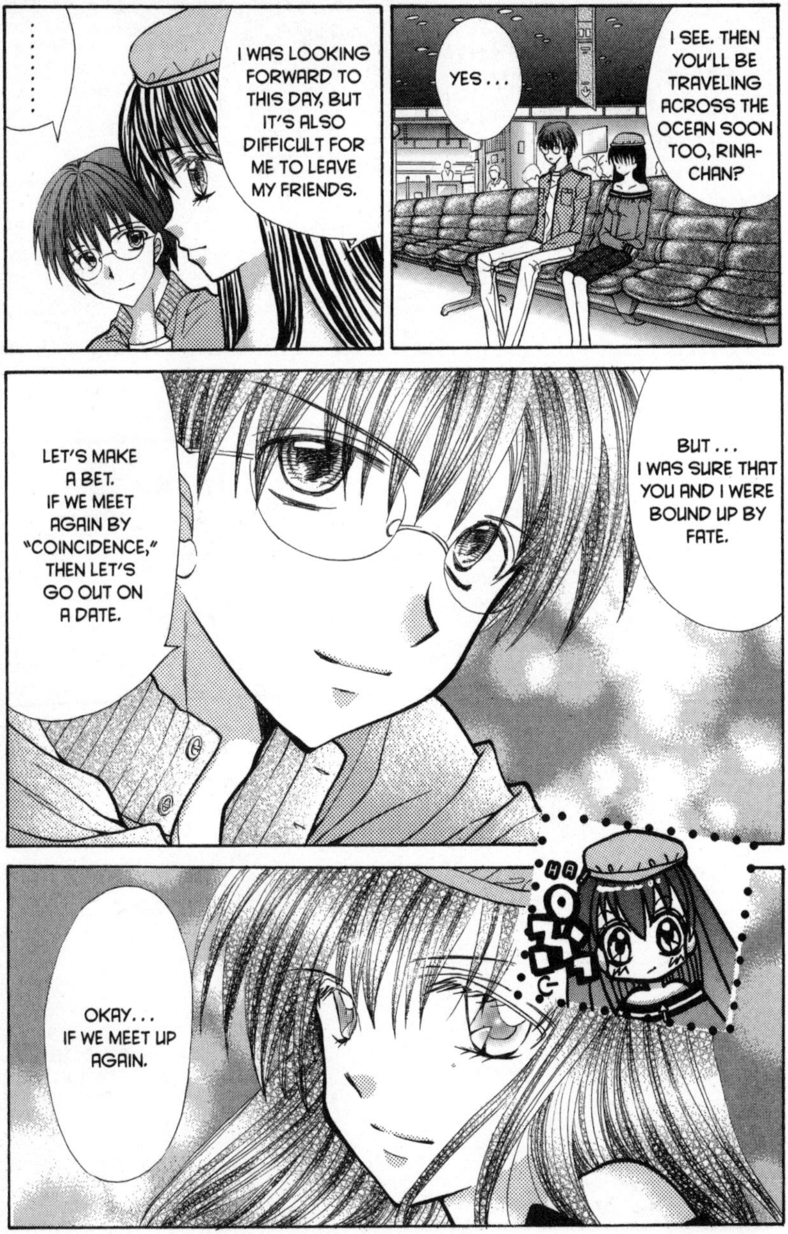
I SEE. THEN YOU'LL BE TRAVELING ACROSS THE OCEAN SOON TOO, RINA-CHAN?
YES . . .
I WAS LOOKING FORWARD TO THIS DAY, BUT IT'S ALSO DIFFICULT FOR ME TO LEAVE MY FRIENDS.
. . . . . .
BUT . . . I WAS SURE THAT YOU AND I WERE BOUND UP BY FATE.
LET'S MAKE A BET. IF WE MEET AGAIN BY "COINCIDENCE," THEN LET'S GO OUT ON A DATE.
OKAY . . . IF WE MEET UP AGAIN.

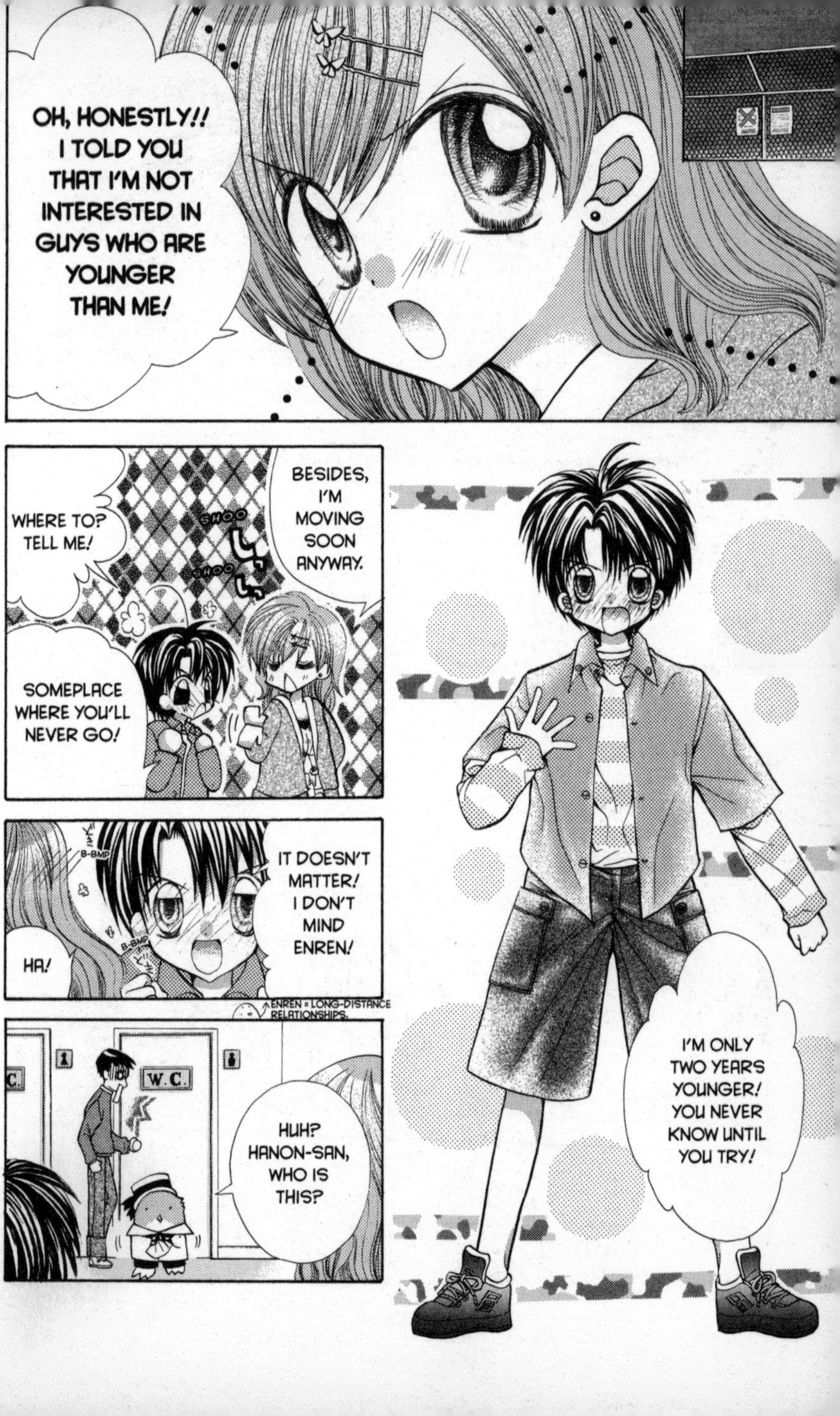
OH, HONESTLY!! I TOLD YOU THAT I'M NOT INTERESTED IN GUYS WHO ARE YOUNGER THAN ME!
I'M ONLY TWO YEARS YOUNGER! YOU NEVER KNOW UNTIL YOU TRY!
BESIDES, I'M MOVING SOON ANYWAY.
SHOO
SHOO
WHERE TO? TELL ME!
SOMEPLACE WHERE YOU'LL NEVER GO!
IT DOESN'T MATTER! I DON'T MIND ENREN!
B-BMP
B-BMP
HA!
ENREN = LONG-DISTANCE RELATIONSHIPS.
HUH? HANON-SAN, WHO IS THIS?
W.C.
C.

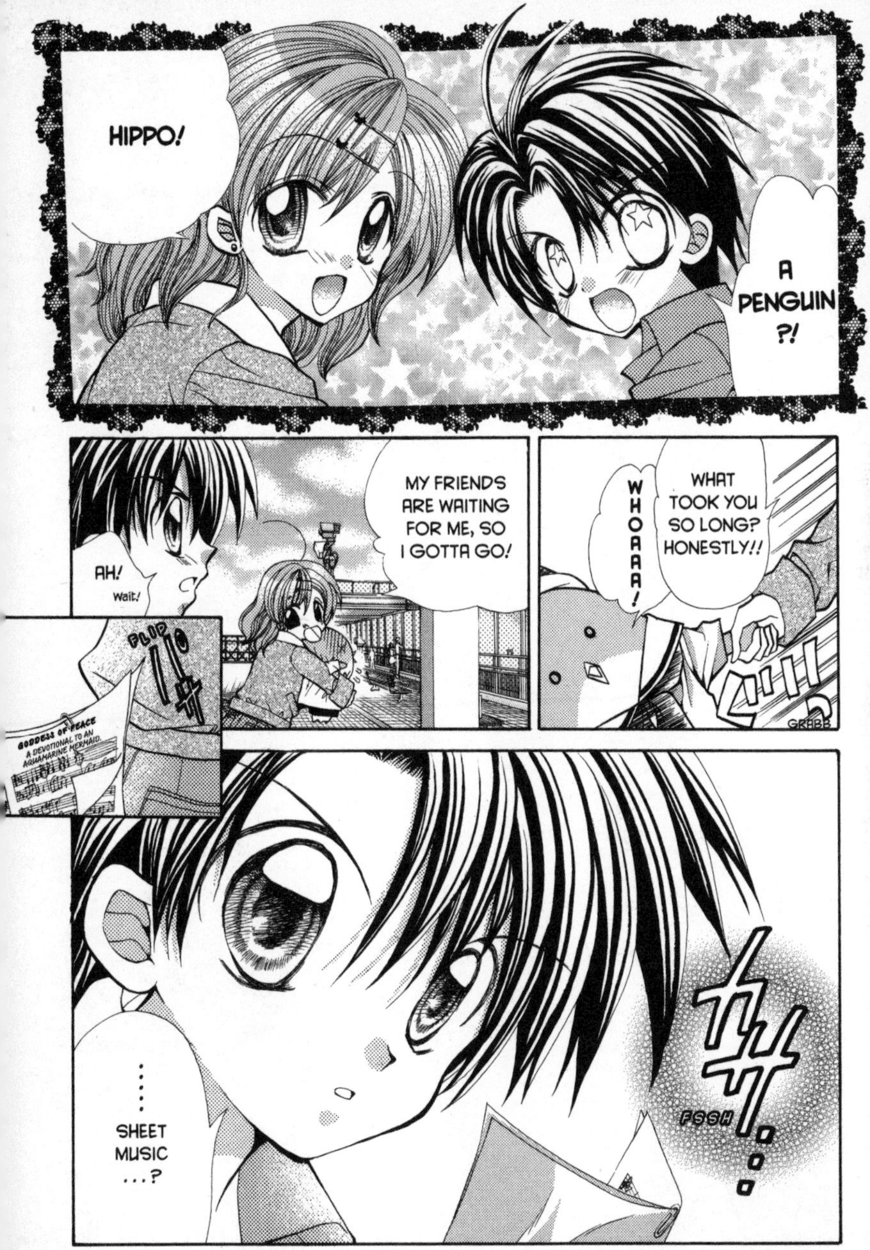

A PENGUIN ?!
HIPPO!
WHAT TOOK YOU SO LONG? HONESTLY!!
WHOAAAA!
GRABB
MY FRIENDS ARE WAITING FOR ME, SO I GOTTA GO!
AH!
Wait!
FLIP
GODDESS OF PEACE
A DEVOTIONAL TO AN AQUAMARINE MERMAID.
FSSH
..... SHEET MUSIC ...?

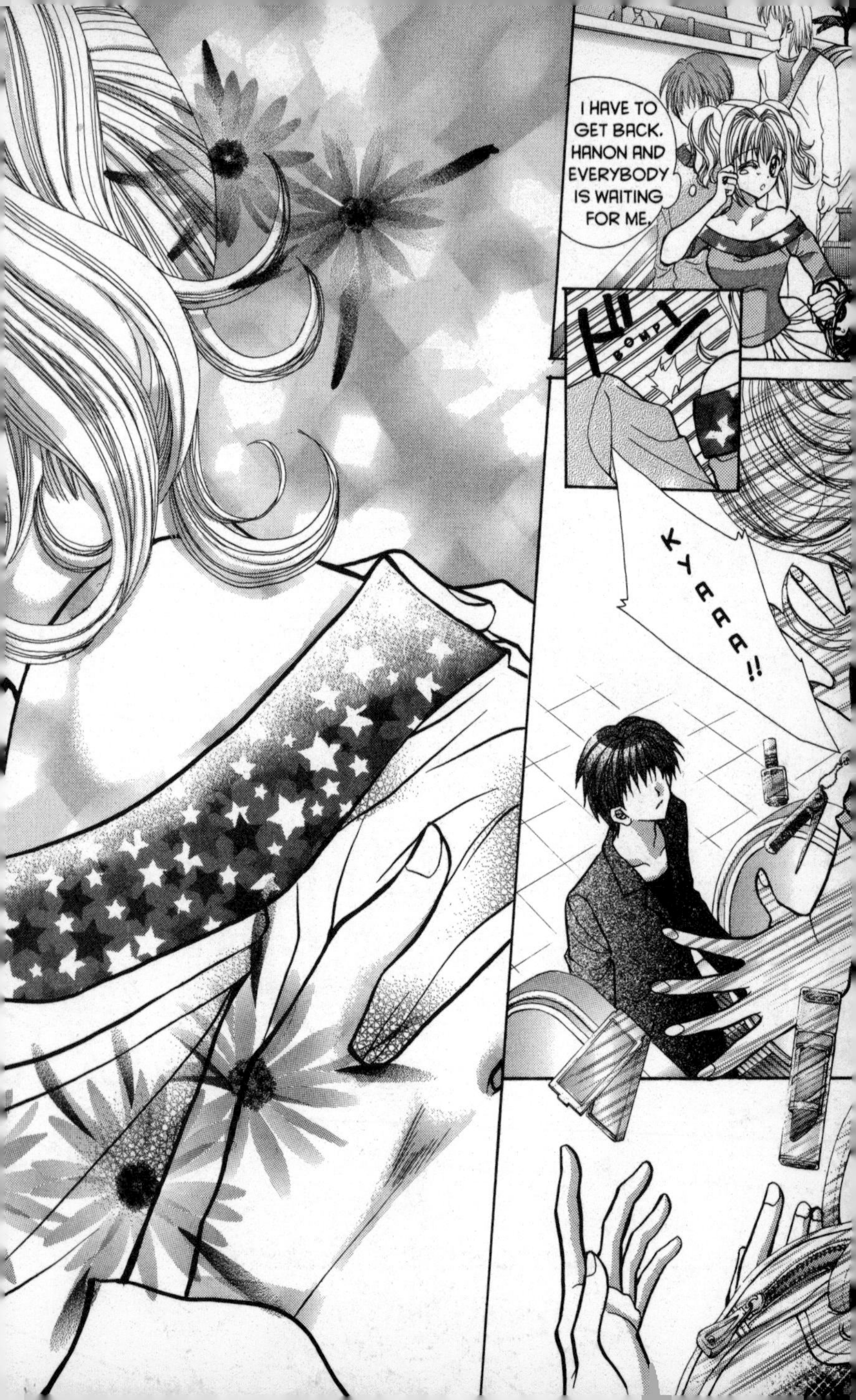
I HAVE TO GET BACK. HANON AND EVERYBODY IS WAITING FOR ME.
BOMP
KYAAAA!!

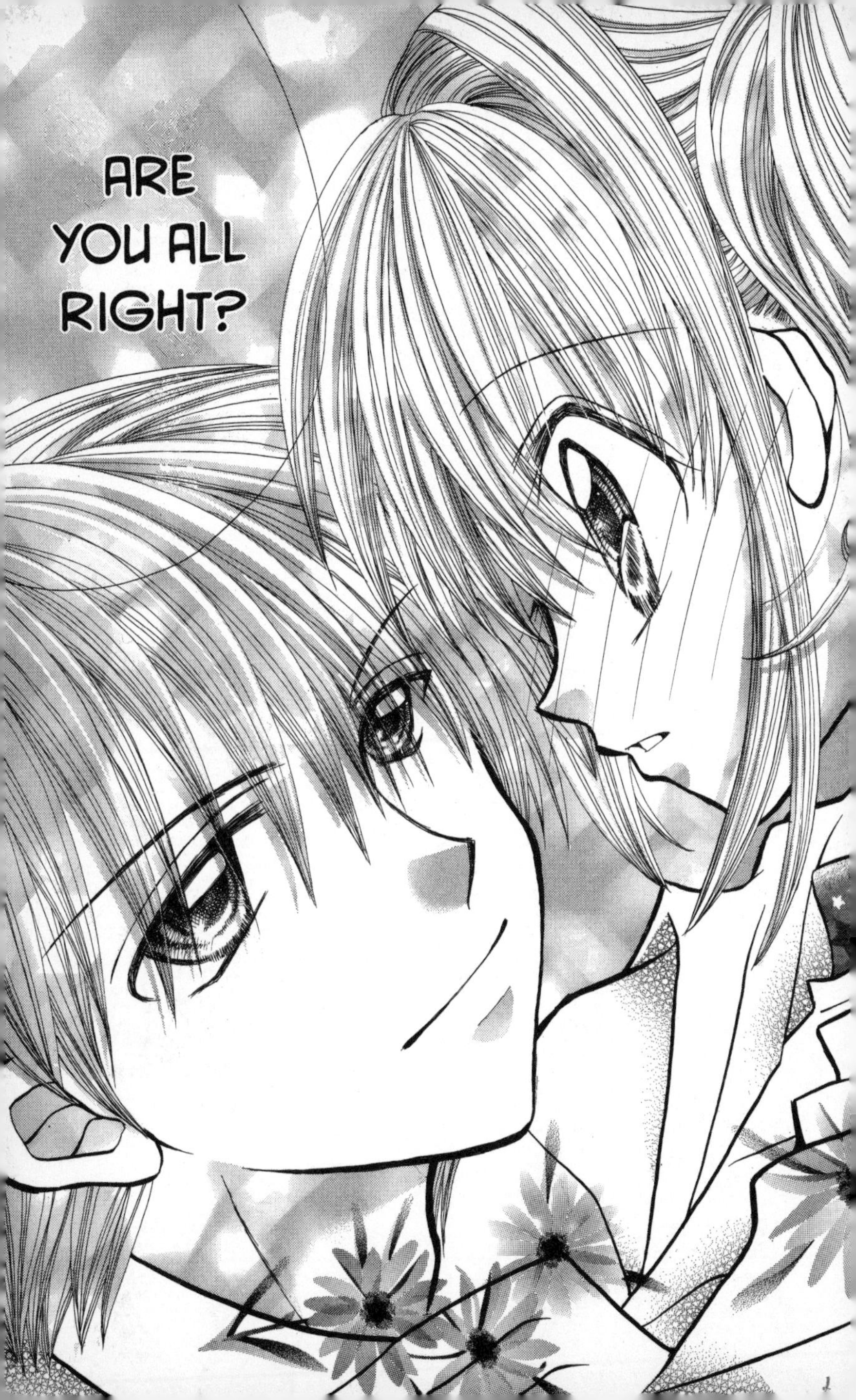
ARE YOU ALL RIGHT?

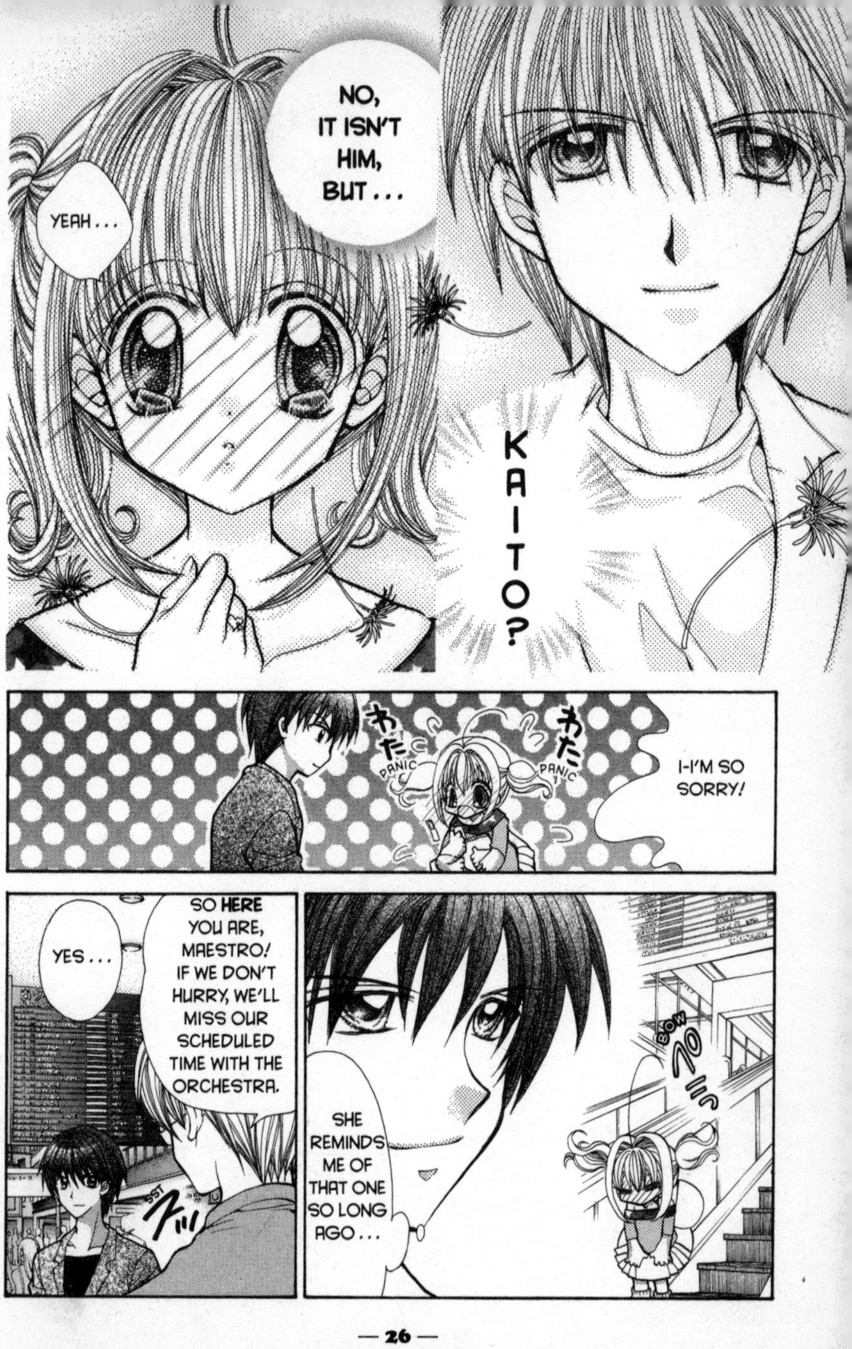
KAITO?
NO, IT ISN'T HIM, BUT . . .
YEAH . . .
I-I'M SO SORRY!
わた PANIC
わた PANIC
BOW
SHE REMINDS ME OF THAT ONE SO LONG AGO . . .
SO HERE YOU ARE, MAESTRO! IF WE DON'T HURRY, WE'LL MISS OUR SCHEDULED TIME WITH THE ORCHESTRA.
YES . . .
SST

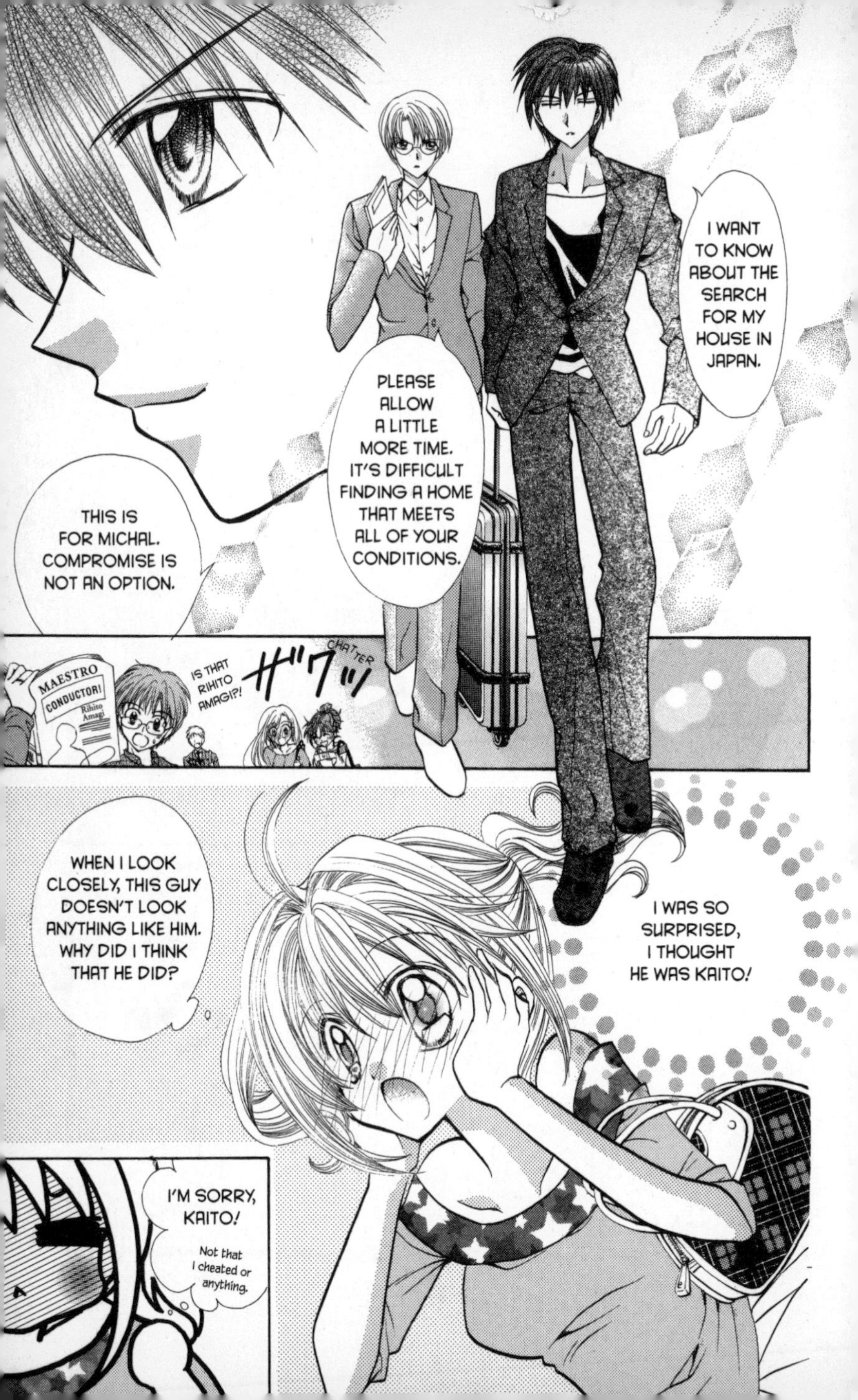
I WANT TO KNOW ABOUT THE SEARCH FOR MY HOUSE IN JAPAN.
PLEASE ALLOW A LITTLE MORE TIME. IT'S DIFFICULT FINDING A HOME THAT MEETS ALL OF YOUR CONDITIONS.
THIS IS FOR MICHAL. COMPROMISE IS NOT AN OPTION.
ザワッ
CHATTER
IS THAT RIHITO AMAGI?!
MAESTRO
CONDUCTOR!
Rihito Amagi
I WAS SO SURPRISED, I THOUGHT HE WAS KAITO!
WHEN I LOOK CLOSELY, THIS GUY DOESN'T LOOK ANYTHING LIKE HIM. WHY DID I THINK THAT HE DID?
I'M SORRY, KAITO!
Not that I cheated or anything.

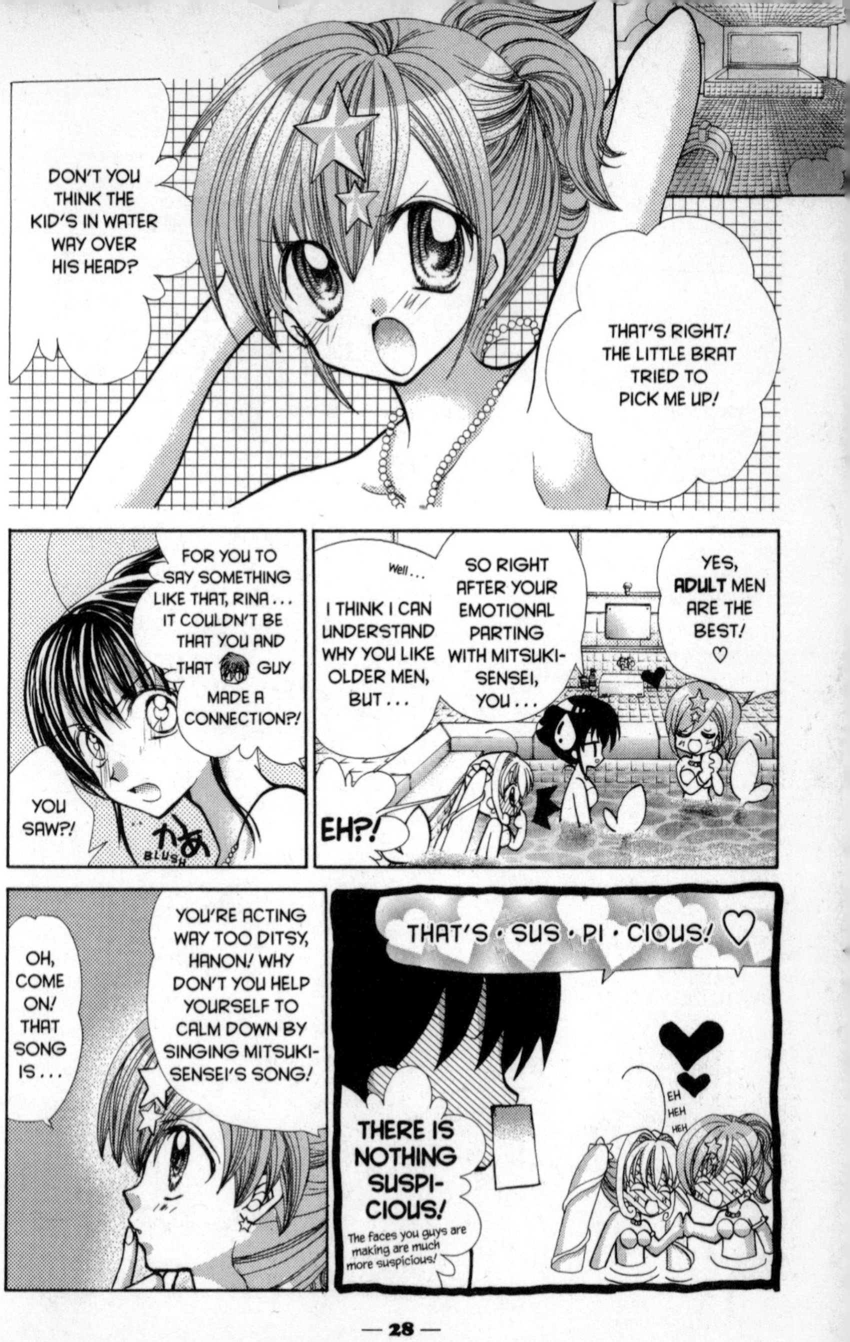
DON'T YOU THINK THE KID'S IN WATER WAY OVER HIS HEAD?
THAT'S RIGHT! THE LITTLE BRAT TRIED TO PICK ME UP!
YES, ADULT MEN ARE THE BEST! ♡
SO RIGHT AFTER YOUR EMOTIONAL PARTING WITH MITSUKI-SENSEI, YOU...
Well... I THINK I CAN UNDERSTAND WHY YOU LIKE OLDER MEN, BUT...
EH?!
FOR YOU TO SAY SOMETHING LIKE THAT, RINA... IT COULDN'T BE THAT YOU AND THAT GUY MADE A CONNECTION?!
YOU SAW?!
BLUSH
THAT'S · SUS · PI · CIOUS! ♡
EH HEH HEH
THERE IS NOTHING SUSPICIOUS!
The faces you guys are making are much more suspicious!
YOU'RE ACTING WAY TOO DITSY, HANON! WHY DON'T YOU HELP YOURSELF TO CALM DOWN BY SINGING MITSUKI-SENSEI'S SONG!
OH, COME ON! THAT SONG IS...

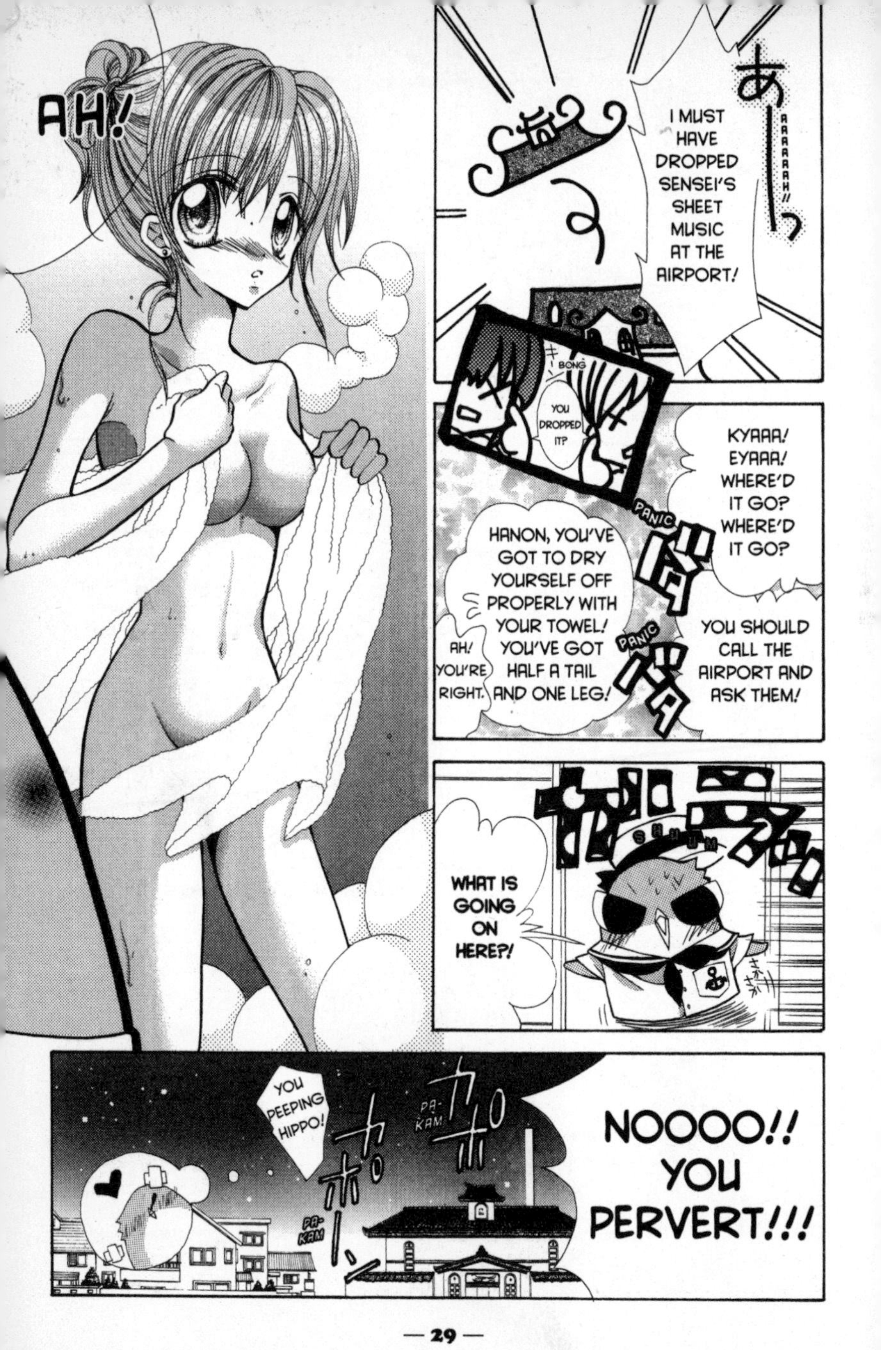
あーっ
AAAAAAH!!
I MUST HAVE DROPPED SENSEI'S SHEET MUSIC AT THE AIRPORT!
BONG
YOU DROPPED IT?
KYAAA! EYAAA! WHERE'D IT GO? WHERE'D IT GO?
PANIC
HANON, YOU'VE GOT TO DRY YOURSELF OFF PROPERLY WITH YOUR TOWEL! YOU'VE GOT HALF A TAIL AND ONE LEG!
PANIC
AH! YOU'RE RIGHT.
YOU SHOULD CALL THE AIRPORT AND ASK THEM!
SHUUM
WHAT IS GOING ON HERE?!
AH!
NOOOO!! YOU PERVERT!!!
PA-KAM
YOU PEEPING HIPPO!
PA-KAM

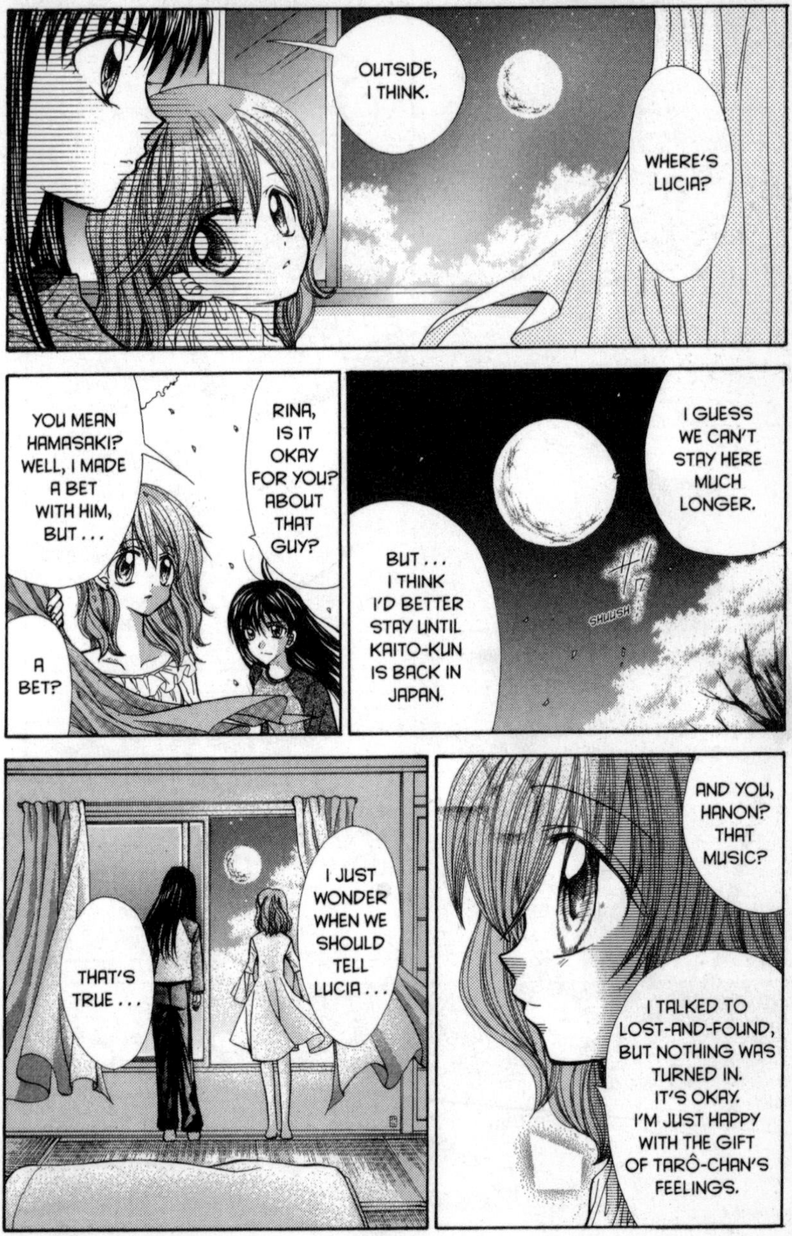
WHERE'S LUCIA?
OUTSIDE, I THINK.
I GUESS WE CAN'T STAY HERE MUCH LONGER.
SHUUSH
BUT . . . I THINK I'D BETTER STAY UNTIL KAITO-KUN IS BACK IN JAPAN.
RINA, IS IT OKAY FOR YOU? ABOUT THAT GUY?
YOU MEAN HAMASAKI? WELL, I MADE A BET WITH HIM, BUT . . .
A BET?
AND YOU, HANON? THAT MUSIC?
I TALKED TO LOST-AND-FOUND, BUT NOTHING WAS TURNED IN. IT'S OKAY. I'M JUST HAPPY WITH THE GIFT OF TARÔ-CHAN'S FEELINGS.
I JUST WONDER WHEN WE SHOULD TELL LUCIA . . .
THAT'S TRUE . . .

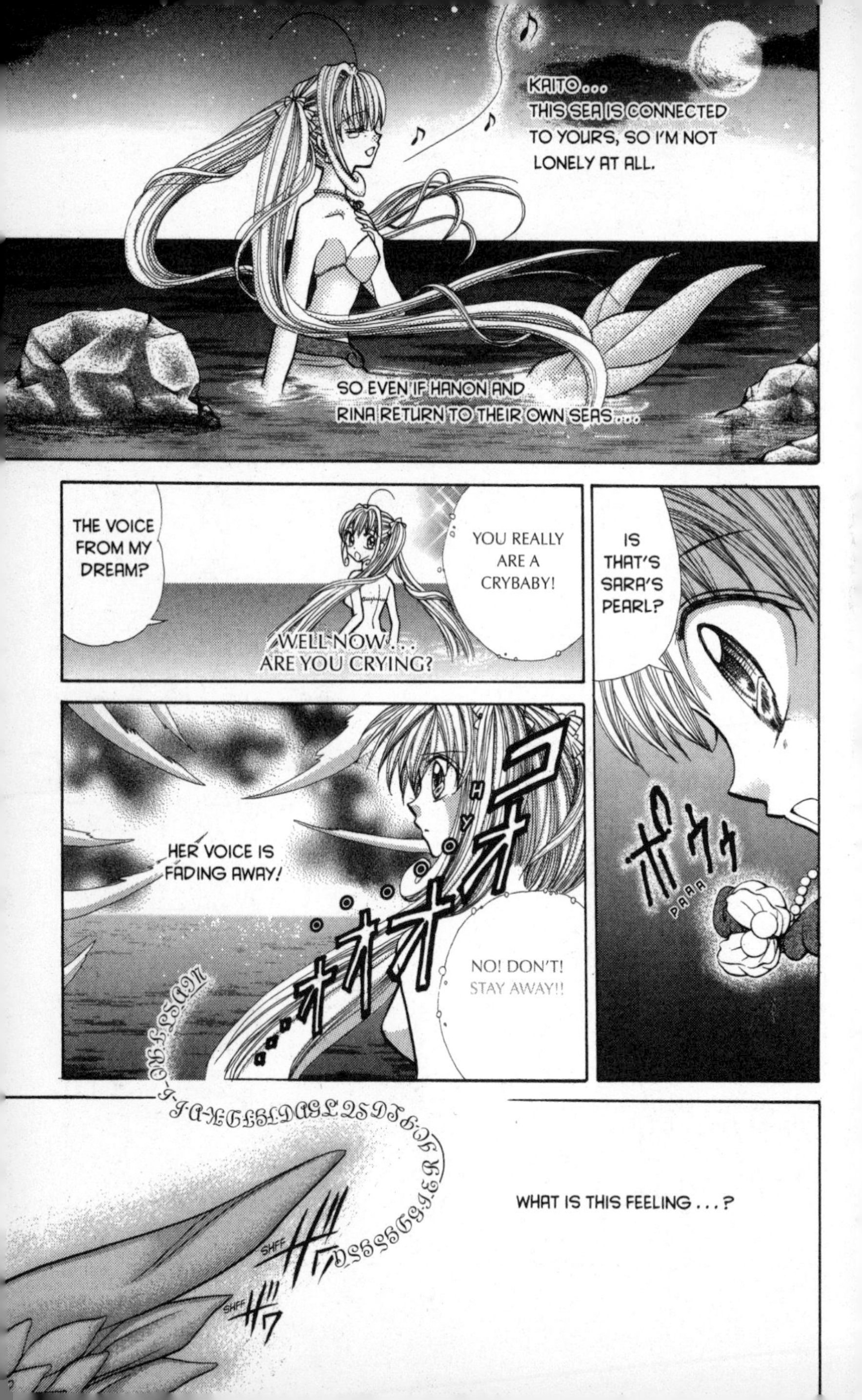
KAITO...
THIS SEA IS CONNECTED TO YOURS, SO I'M NOT LONELY AT ALL.
SO EVEN IF HANON AND RINA RETURN TO THEIR OWN SEAS...
IS THAT'S SARA'S PEARL?
PAAA
YOU REALLY ARE A CRYBABY!
THE VOICE FROM MY DREAM?
WELL NOW... ARE YOU CRYING?
HYU
NO! DON'T! STAY AWAY!!
HER VOICE IS FADING AWAY!
WHAT IS THIS FEELING...?
SHFF
SHFF

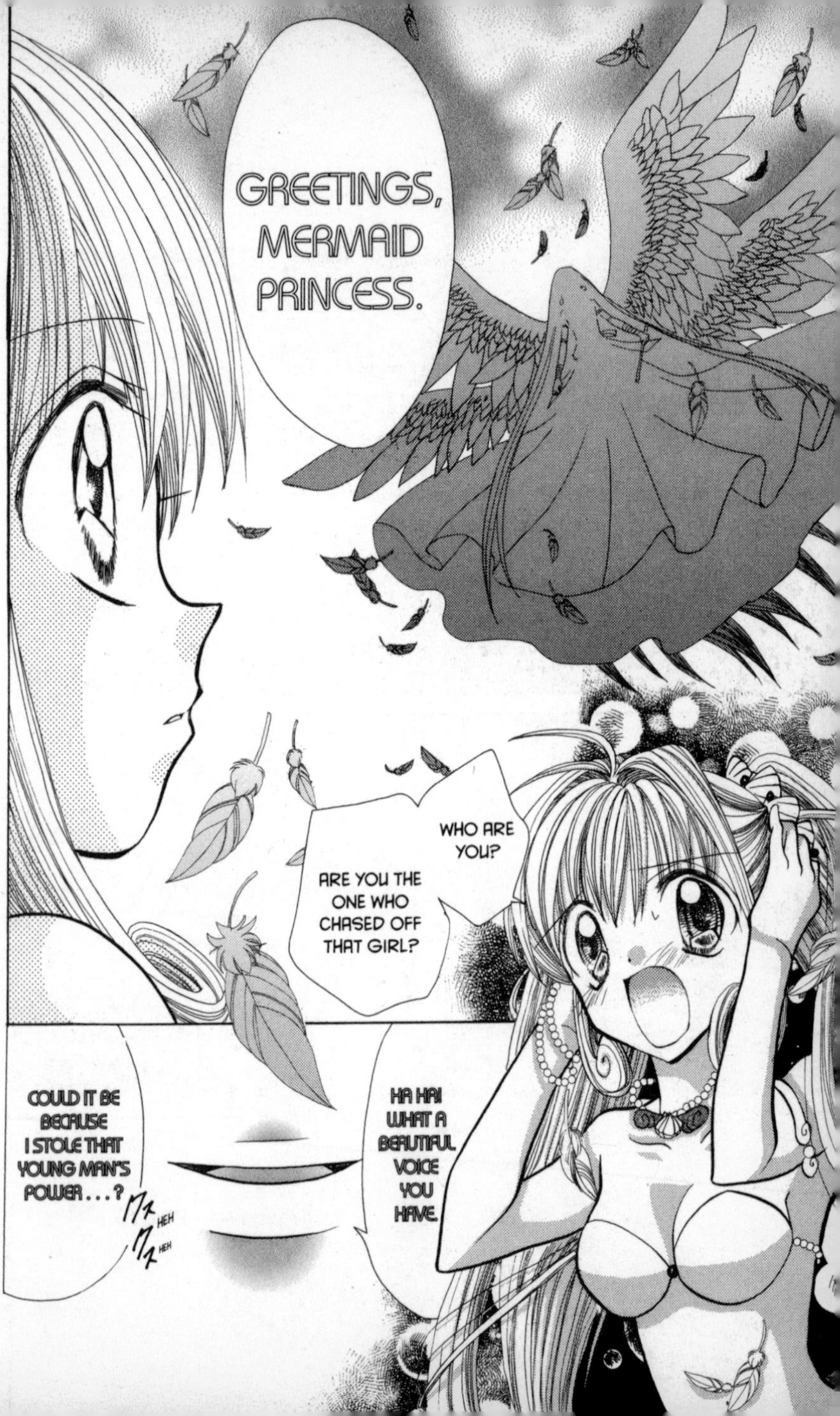
GREETINGS, MERMAID PRINCESS.
WHO ARE YOU?
ARE YOU THE ONE WHO CHASED OFF THAT GIRL?
HA HA! WHAT A BEAUTIFUL VOICE YOU HAVE.
COULD IT BE BECAUSE I STOLE THAT YOUNG MAN'S POWER...?
HEH HEH

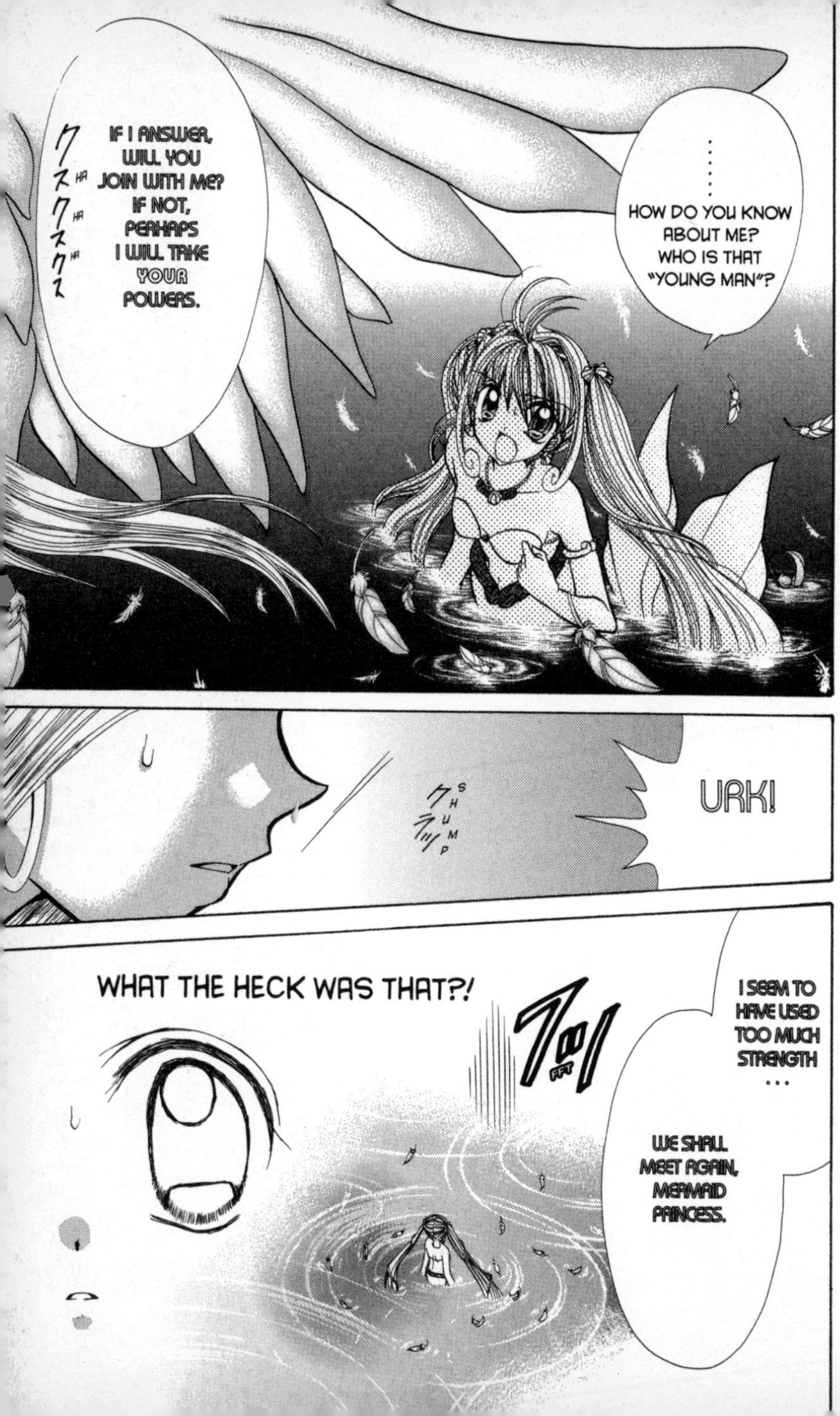
......
HOW DO YOU KNOW ABOUT ME? WHO IS THAT "YOUNG MAN"?
IF I ANSWER, WILL YOU JOIN WITH ME? IF NOT, PERHAPS I WILL TAKE YOUR POWERS.
クスクスクス
HA HA HA
URK!
SHUMP
I SEEM TO HAVE USED TOO MUCH STRENGTH ...
WE SHALL MEET AGAIN, MERMAID PRINCESS.
FFT
WHAT THE HECK WAS THAT?!

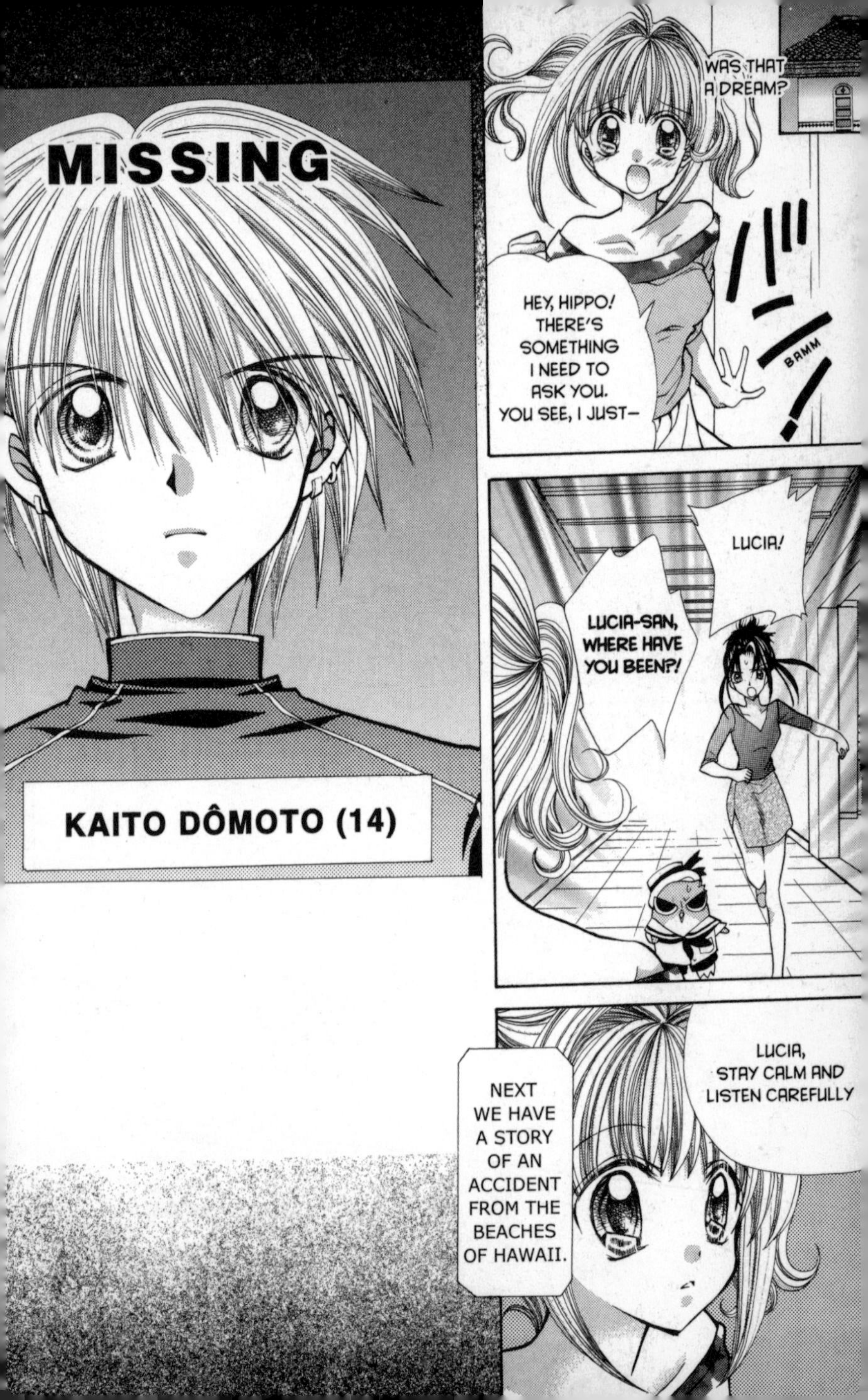
WAS THAT A DREAM?
BAMM
HEY, HIPPO! THERE'S SOMETHING I NEED TO ASK YOU. YOU SEE, I JUST—
LUCIA!
LUCIA-SAN, WHERE HAVE YOU BEEN?!
LUCIA, STAY CALM AND LISTEN CAREFULLY
NEXT WE HAVE A STORY OF AN ACCIDENT FROM THE BEACHES OF HAWAII.
MISSING
KAITO DÔMOTO (14)

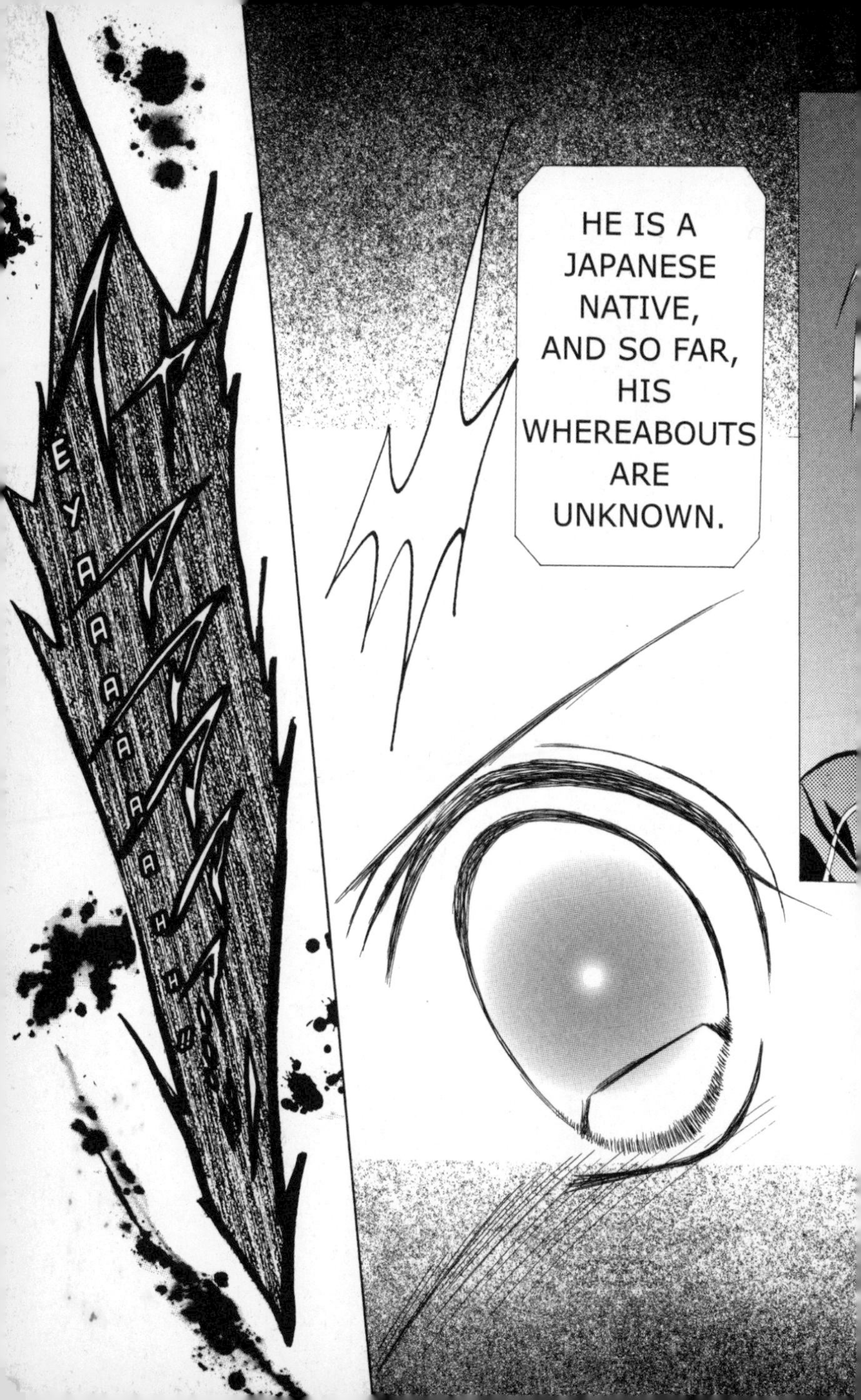
HE IS A JAPANESE NATIVE, AND SO FAR, HIS WHEREABOUTS ARE UNKNOWN.
EYAAAAAAHH!!

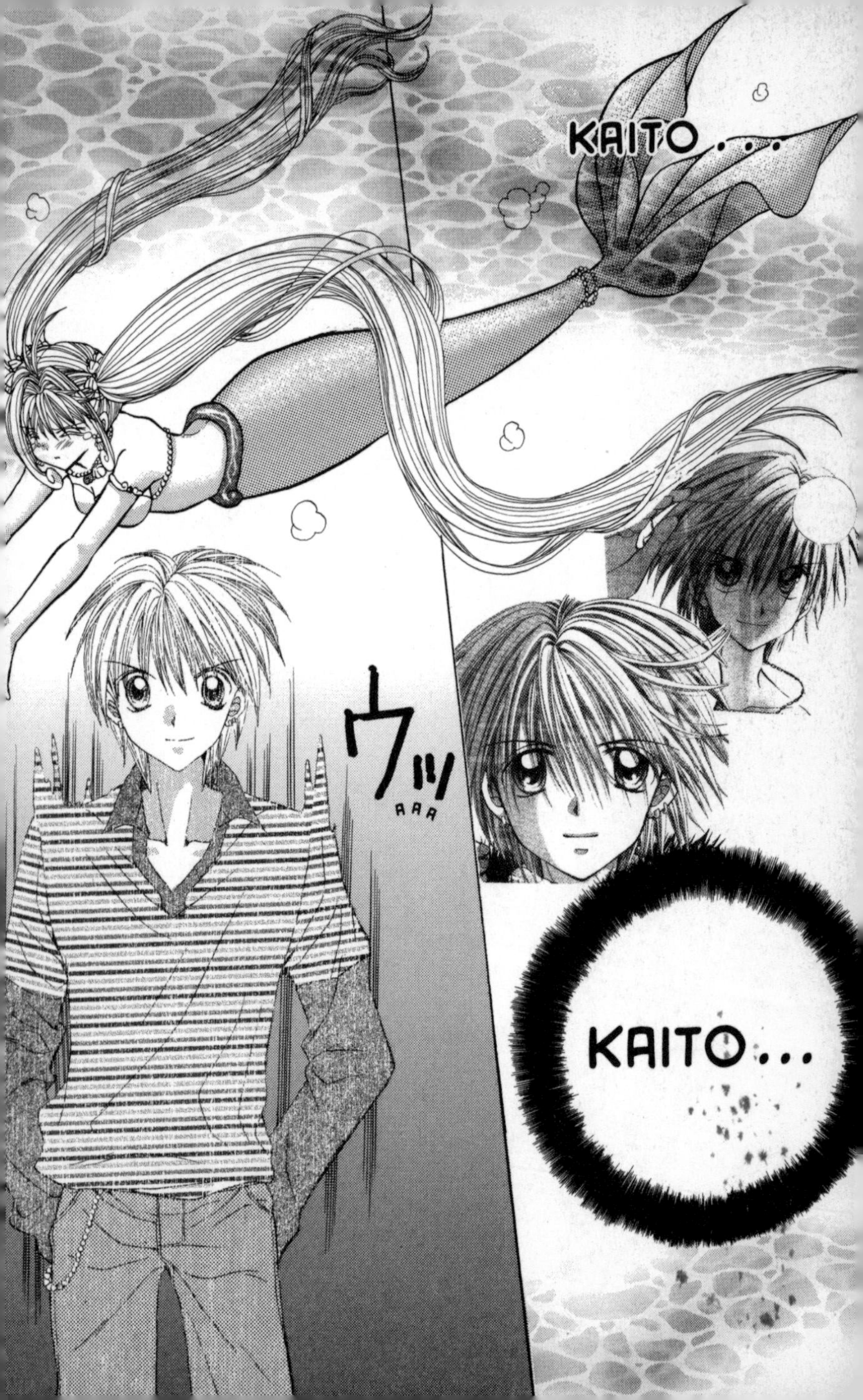
KAITO . . .
KAITO...
ウッ

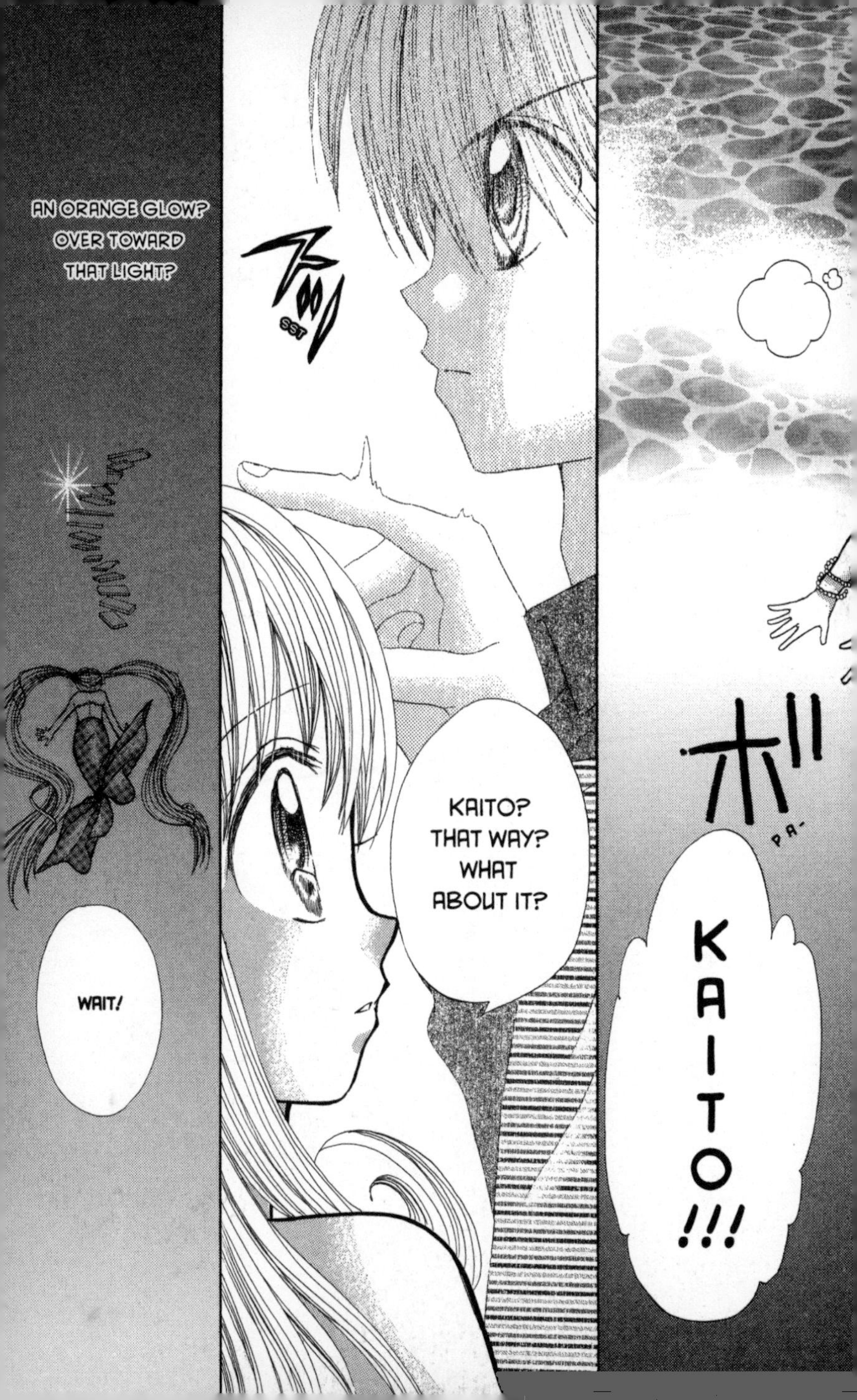
ボ
PA-
KAITO!!!
スッ
SST
KAITO? THAT WAY? WHAT ABOUT IT?
AN ORANGE GLOW? OVER TOWARD THAT LIGHT?
WAIT!

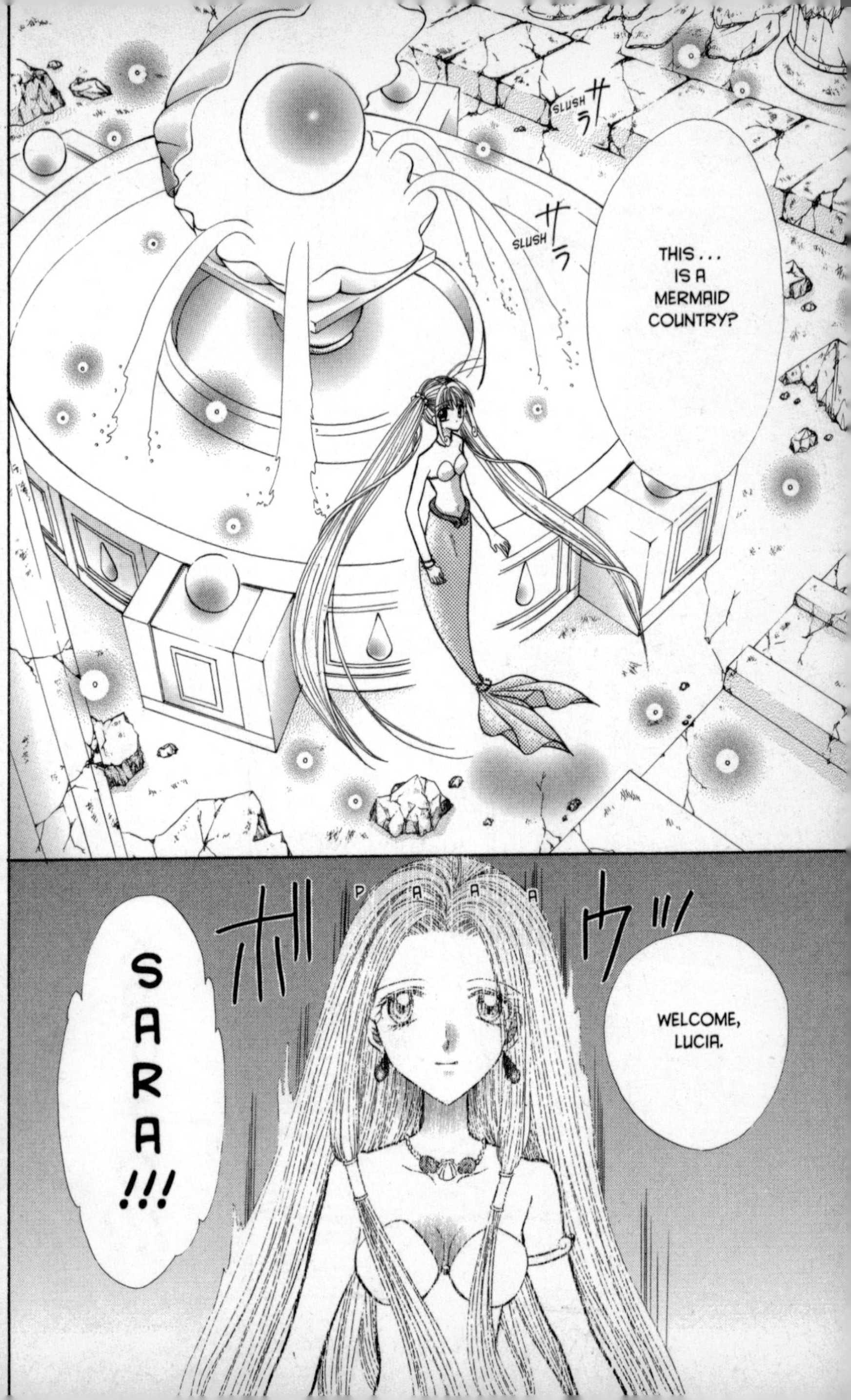
SLUSH
SLUSH
THIS . . . IS A MERMAID COUNTRY?
WELCOME, LUCIA.
P A A A
SARA!!!

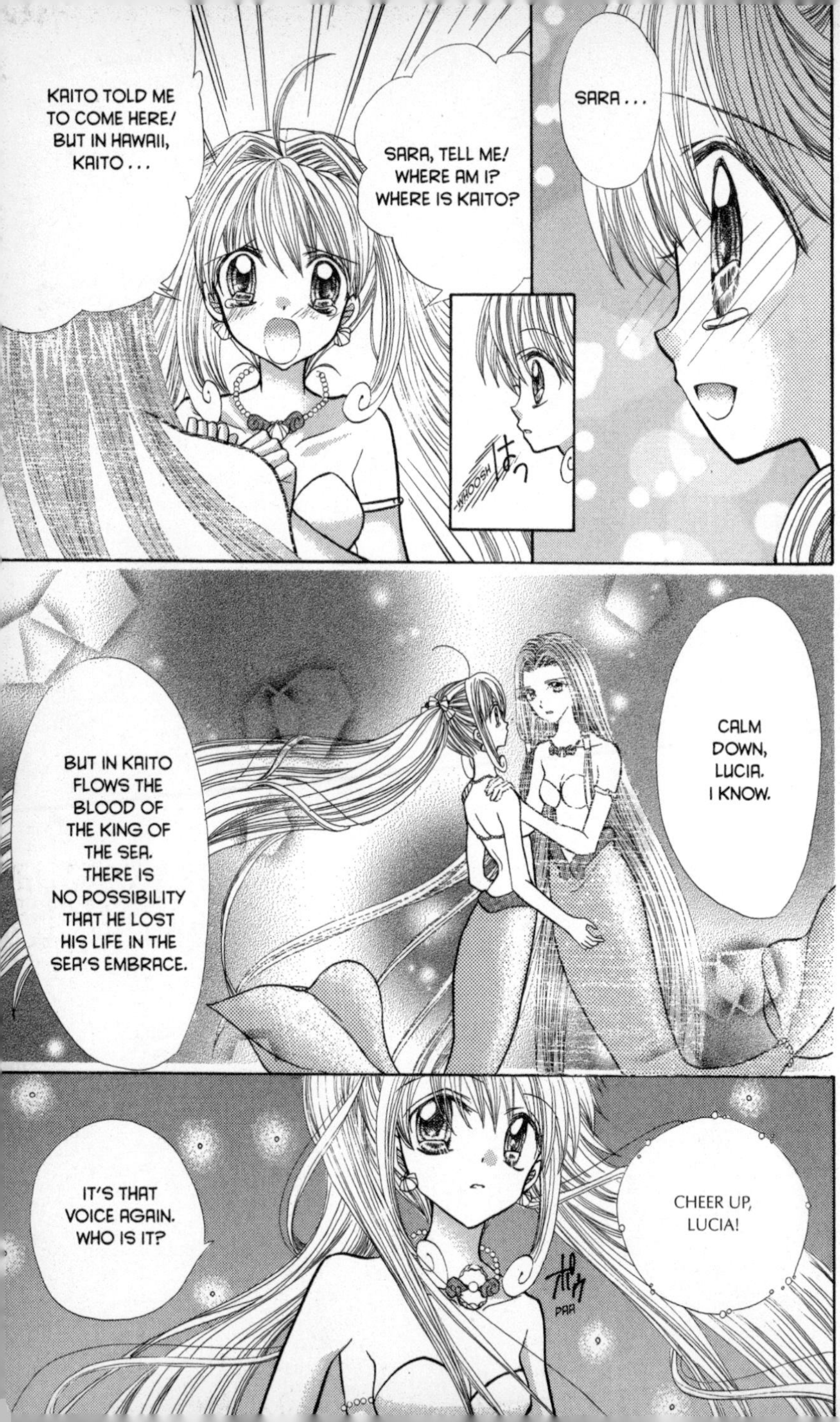
SARA . . .
WHOOSH
はっ
SARA, TELL ME! WHERE AM I? WHERE IS KAITO?
KAITO TOLD ME TO COME HERE! BUT IN HAWAII, KAITO . . .
CALM DOWN, LUCIA. I KNOW.
BUT IN KAITO FLOWS THE BLOOD OF THE KING OF THE SEA. THERE IS NO POSSIBILITY THAT HE LOST HIS LIFE IN THE SEA'S EMBRACE.
CHEER UP, LUCIA!
PAA
IT'S THAT VOICE AGAIN. WHO IS IT?

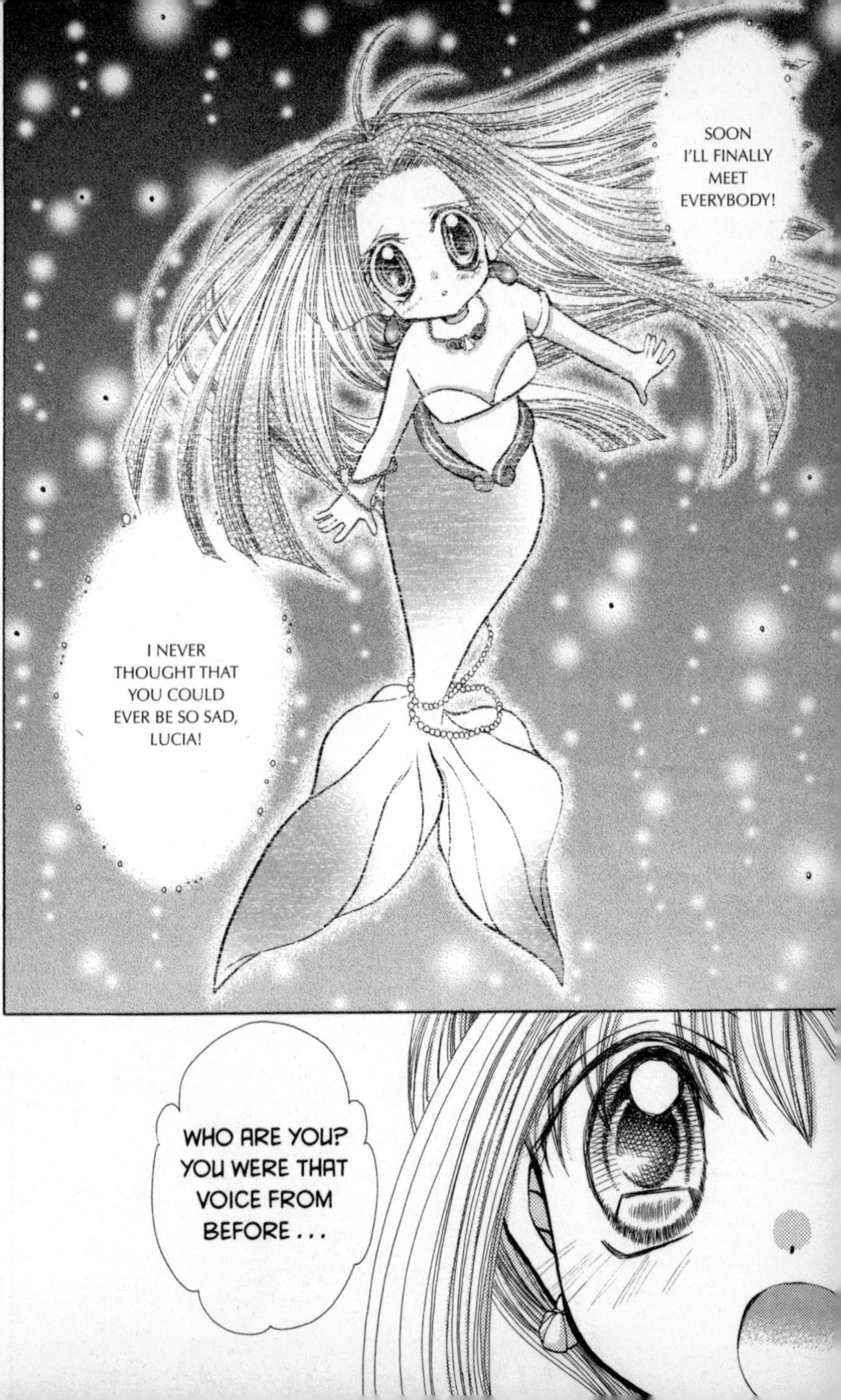
SOON I'LL FINALLY MEET EVERYBODY!
I NEVER THOUGHT THAT YOU COULD EVER BE SO SAD, LUCIA!
WHO ARE YOU? YOU WERE THAT VOICE FROM BEFORE . . .

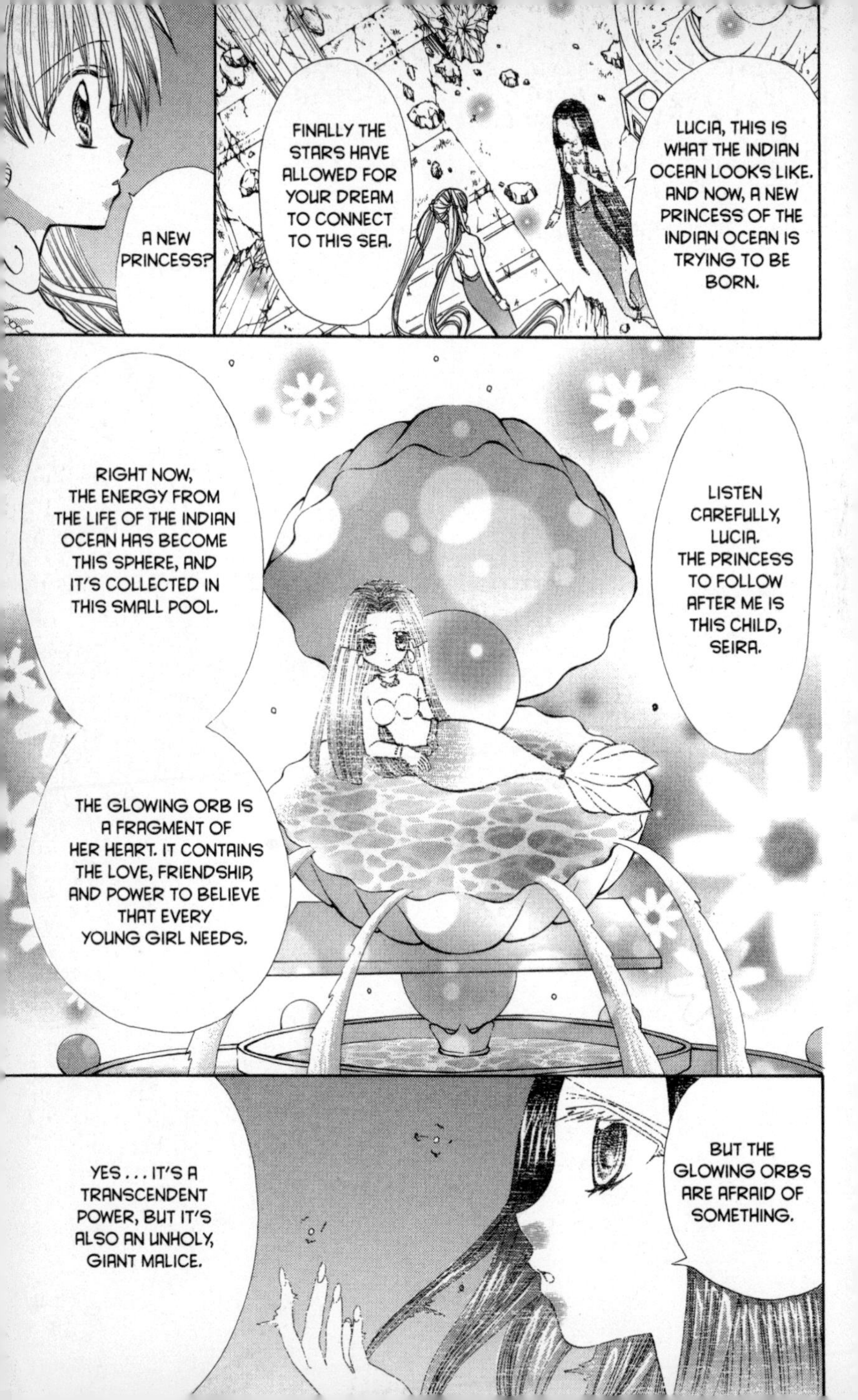
LUCIA, THIS IS WHAT THE INDIAN OCEAN LOOKS LIKE. AND NOW, A NEW PRINCESS OF THE INDIAN OCEAN IS TRYING TO BE BORN.
FINALLY THE STARS HAVE ALLOWED FOR YOUR DREAM TO CONNECT TO THIS SEA.
A NEW PRINCESS?
LISTEN CAREFULLY, LUCIA. THE PRINCESS TO FOLLOW AFTER ME IS THIS CHILD, SEIRA.
RIGHT NOW, THE ENERGY FROM THE LIFE OF THE INDIAN OCEAN HAS BECOME THIS SPHERE, AND IT'S COLLECTED IN THIS SMALL POOL.
THE GLOWING ORB IS A FRAGMENT OF HER HEART. IT CONTAINS THE LOVE, FRIENDSHIP, AND POWER TO BELIEVE THAT EVERY YOUNG GIRL NEEDS.
BUT THE GLOWING ORBS ARE AFRAID OF SOMETHING.
YES . . . IT'S A TRANSCENDENT POWER, BUT IT'S ALSO AN UNHOLY, GIANT MALICE.

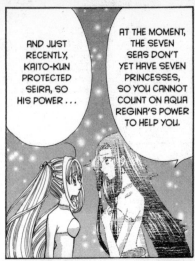

GIANT MALICE?
"COULD IT BE BECAUSE I STOLE THAT YOUNG MAN'S POWER . . . ?"
GREETINGS, MERMAID PRINCESS.
ZHAAN
WHEN HE SAID "YOUNG MAN," HE COULDN'T HAVE MEANT KAITO, COULD HE?
AT THE MOMENT, THE SEVEN SEAS DON'T YET HAVE SEVEN PRINCESSES, SO YOU CANNOT COUNT ON AQUA REGINA'S POWER TO HELP YOU.
AND JUST RECENTLY, KAITO-KUN PROTECTED SEIRA, SO HIS POWER . . .
OH, NO!!
LUCIA, HURRY AND PUT THAT PEARL IN THE POND!
EH?
IT FEELS LIKE THAT TIME . . .
IT LOOKS LIKE THE STORM IS HERE.
SHAA
AHH . . .

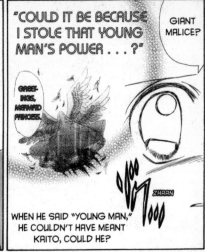

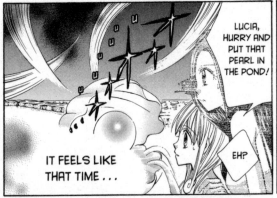

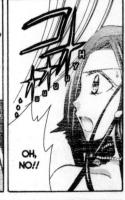

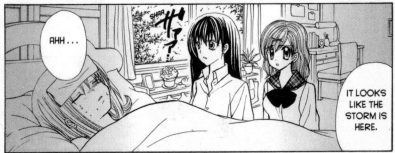

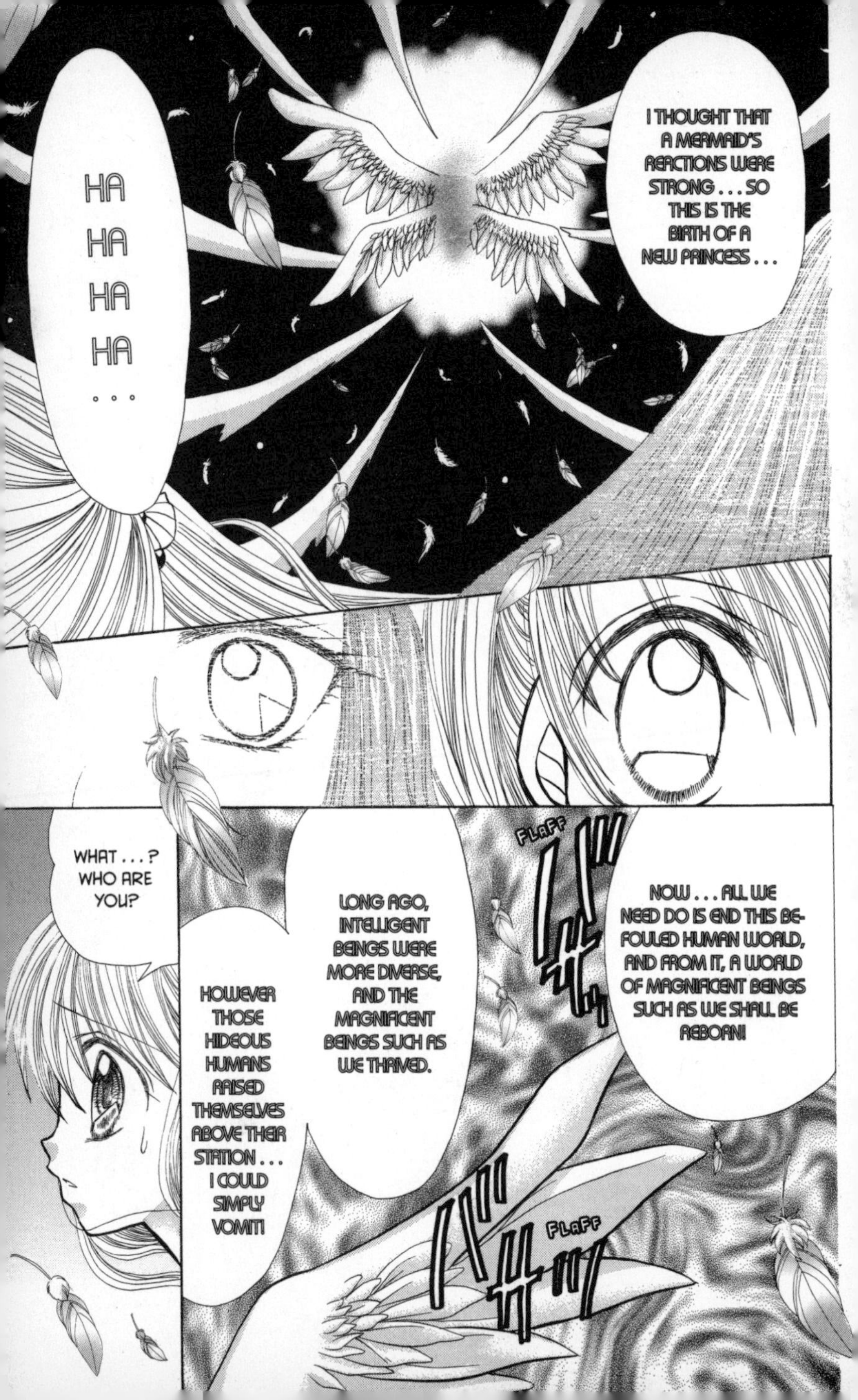
I THOUGHT THAT A MERMAID'S REACTIONS WERE STRONG . . . SO THIS IS THE BIRTH OF A NEW PRINCESS . . .
HA HA HA HA . . .
FLAFF
NOW . . . ALL WE NEED DO IS END THIS BE-FOULED HUMAN WORLD, AND FROM IT, A WORLD OF MAGNIFICENT BEINGS SUCH AS WE SHALL BE REBORN!
WHAT . . . ? WHO ARE YOU?
LONG AGO, INTELLIGENT BEINGS WERE MORE DIVERSE, AND THE MAGNIFICENT BEINGS SUCH AS WE THRIVED.
HOWEVER THOSE HIDEOUS HUMANS RAISED THEMSELVES ABOVE THEIR STATION . . . I COULD SIMPLY VOMIT!
FLAFF

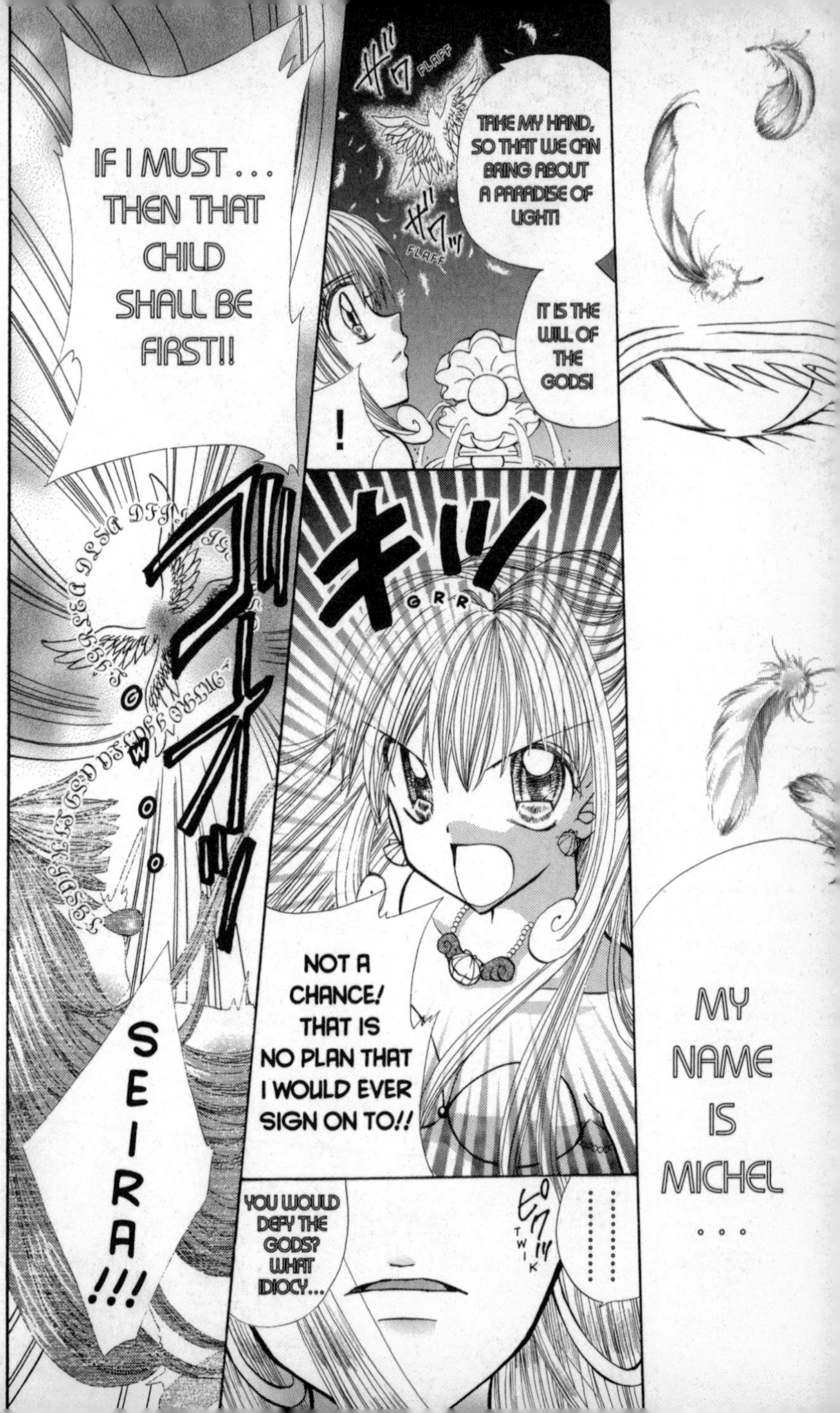
MY NAME IS MICHEL . . .
FLAFF
FLAFF
TAKE MY HAND, SO THAT WE CAN BRING ABOUT A PARADISE OF LIGHT!
IT IS THE WILL OF THE GODS!
!
GRR
NOT A CHANCE! THAT IS NO PLAN THAT I WOULD EVER SIGN ON TO!!
TWIK
YOU WOULD DEFY THE GODS? WHAT IDIOCY...
....
IF I MUST . . . THEN THAT CHILD SHALL BE FIRST!!
SEIRA!!!

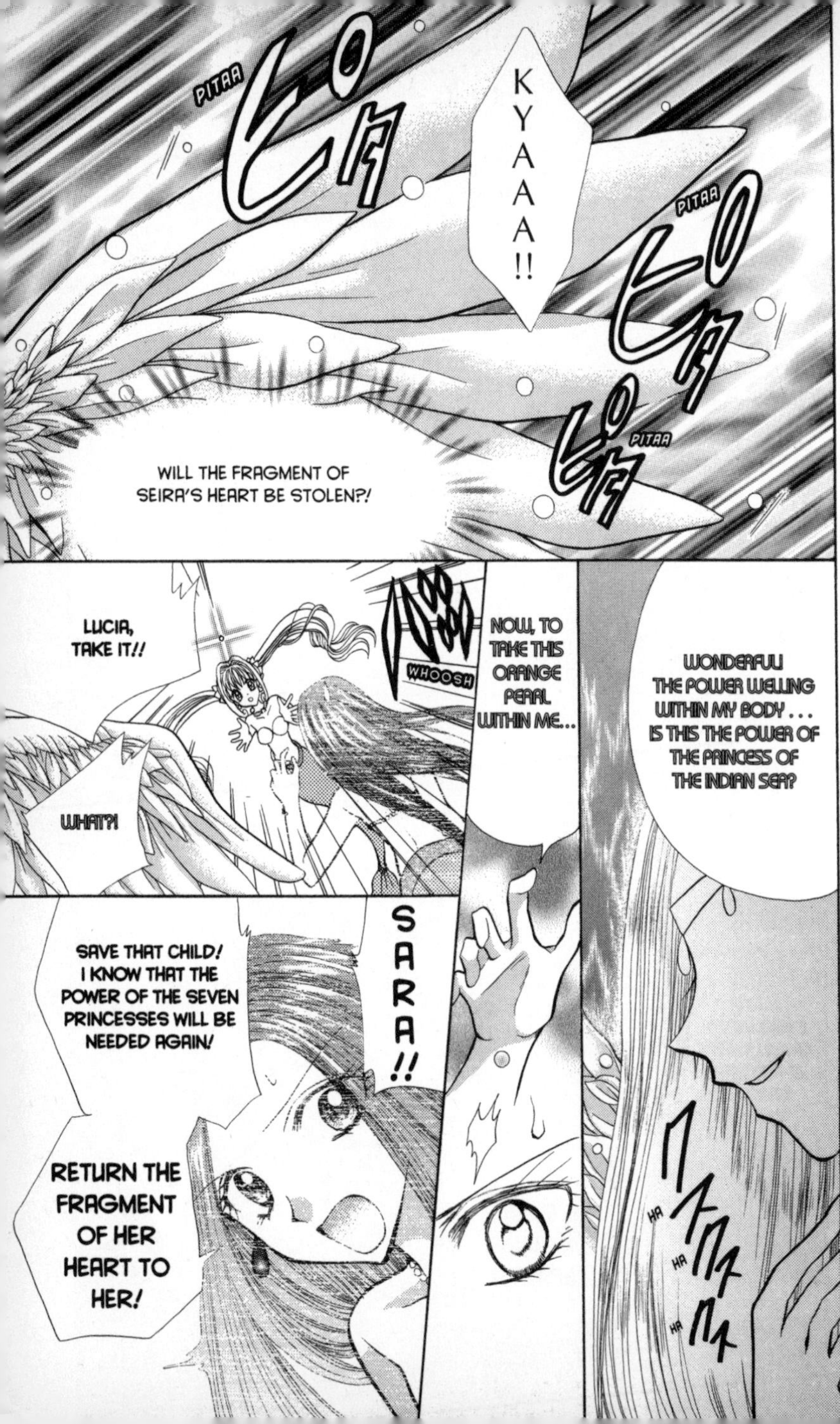
KYAAAA!!
PITAA
PITAA
PITAA
WILL THE FRAGMENT OF SEIRA'S HEART BE STOLEN?!
WONDERFUL! THE POWER WELLING WITHIN MY BODY . . . IS THIS THE POWER OF THE PRINCESS OF THE INDIAN SEA?
HA
HA
HA
NOW, TO TAKE THIS ORANGE PEARL WITHIN ME...
WHOOSH
LUCIA, TAKE IT!!
WHAT?!
SARA!!
SAVE THAT CHILD! I KNOW THAT THE POWER OF THE SEVEN PRINCESSES WILL BE NEEDED AGAIN!
RETURN THE FRAGMENT OF HER HEART TO HER!

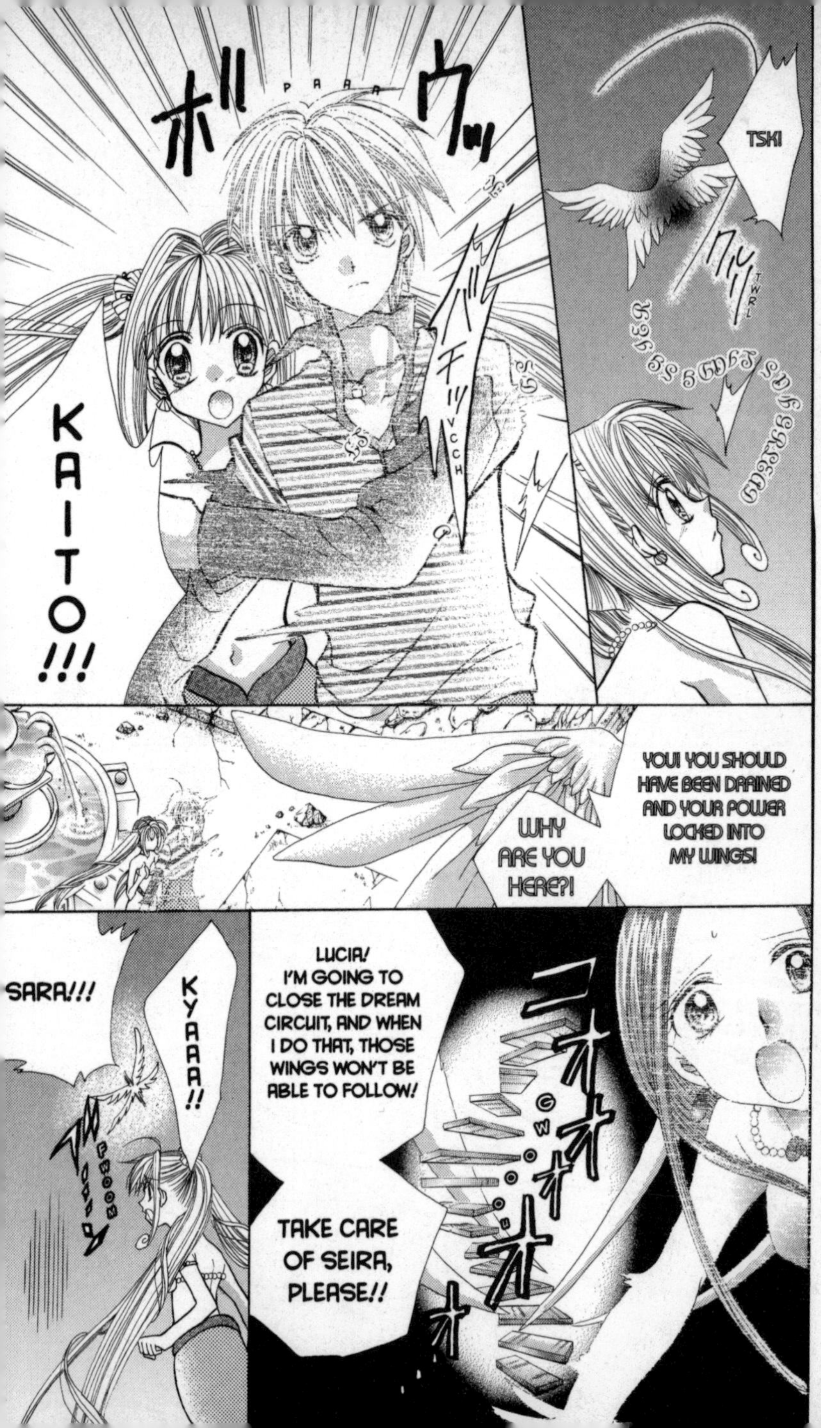
TSK!
TWRL
PAAA
VCCH
KAITO!!!
YOU! YOU SHOULD HAVE BEEN DRAINED AND YOUR POWER LOCKED INTO MY WINGS!
WHY ARE YOU HERE?!
LUCIA! I'M GOING TO CLOSE THE DREAM CIRCUIT, AND WHEN I DO THAT, THOSE WINGS WON'T BE ABLE TO FOLLOW!
GWOOOU
TAKE CARE OF SEIRA, PLEASE!!
SARA!!!
KYAAAA!!
FWOOM

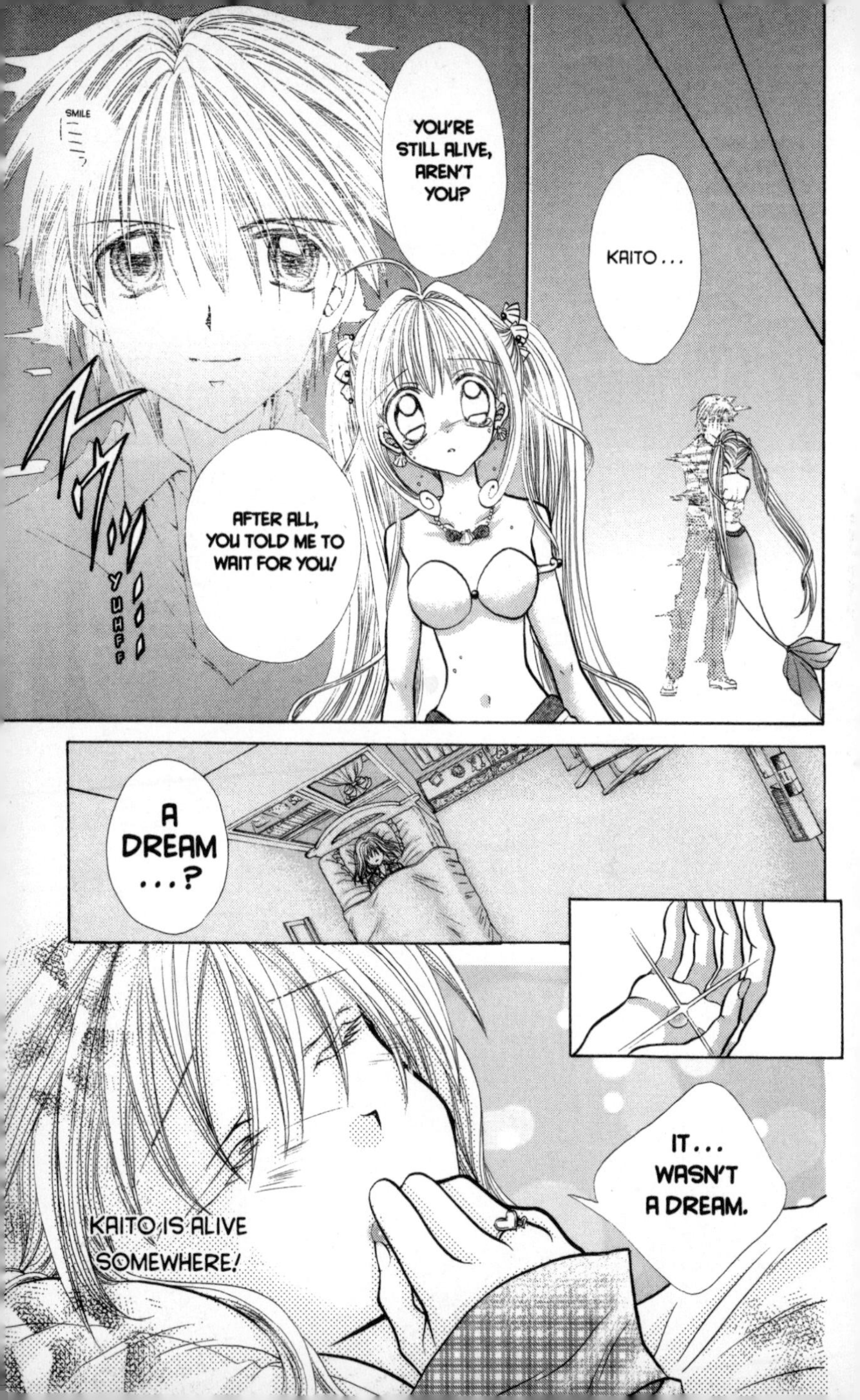
KAITO . . .
YOU'RE STILL ALIVE, AREN'T YOU?
SMILE
AFTER ALL, YOU TOLD ME TO WAIT FOR YOU!
YUHFF
A DREAM . . . ?
IT . . . WASN'T A DREAM.
KAITO IS ALIVE SOMEWHERE!

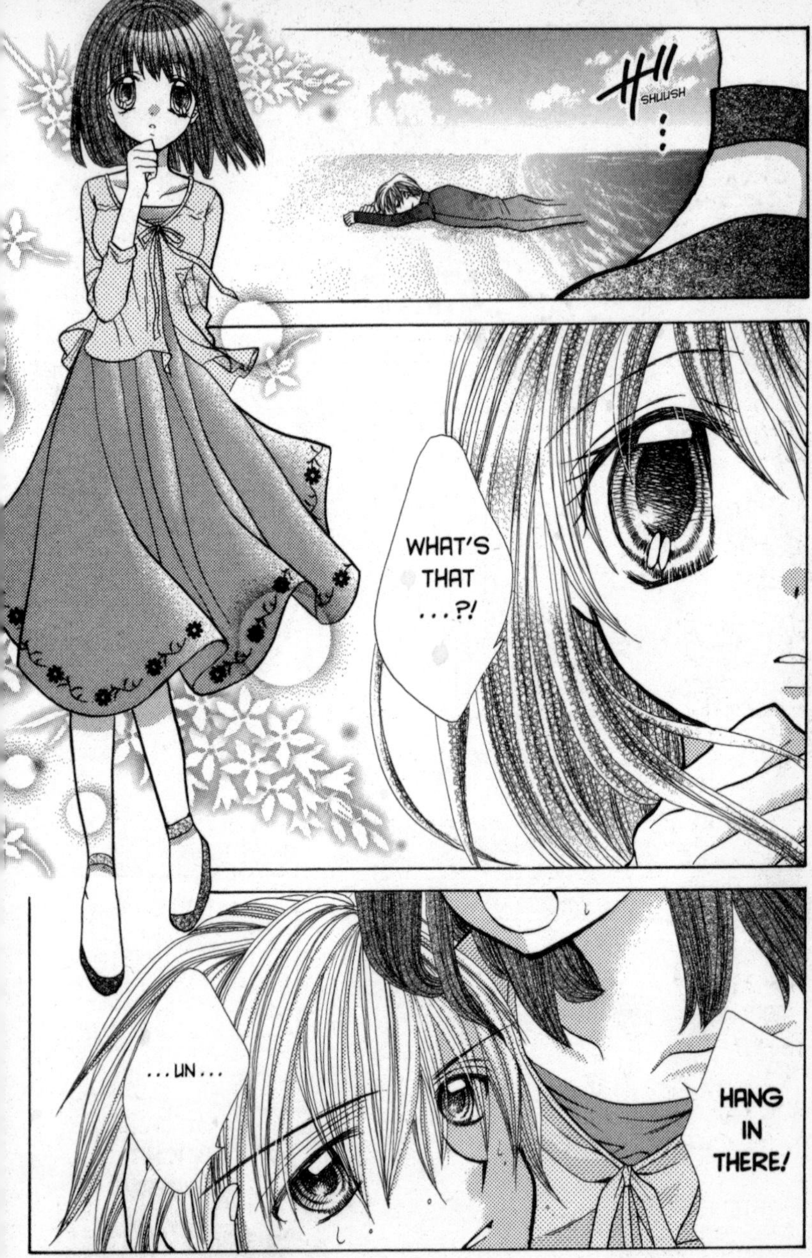
SHUUSH
...
WHAT'S THAT ...?!
HANG IN THERE!
...UN...

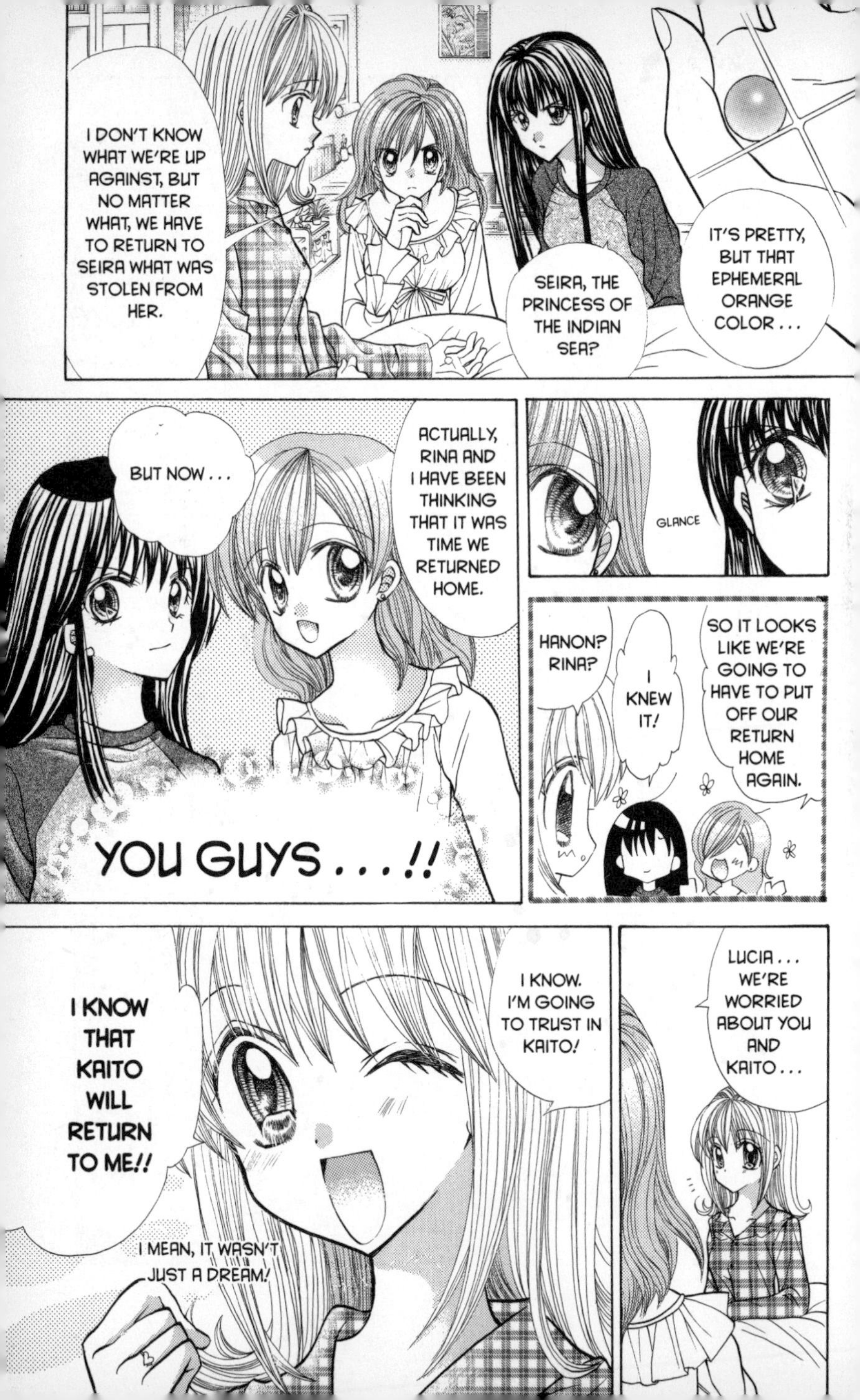
IT'S PRETTY, BUT THAT EPHEMERAL ORANGE COLOR . . .
SEIRA, THE PRINCESS OF THE INDIAN SEA?
I DON'T KNOW WHAT WE'RE UP AGAINST, BUT NO MATTER WHAT, WE HAVE TO RETURN TO SEIRA WHAT WAS STOLEN FROM HER.
GLANCE
SO IT LOOKS LIKE WE'RE GOING TO HAVE TO PUT OFF OUR RETURN HOME AGAIN.
I KNEW IT!
HANON? RINA?
ACTUALLY, RINA AND I HAVE BEEN THINKING THAT IT WAS TIME WE RETURNED HOME.
BUT NOW . . .
YOU GUYS . . . !!
LUCIA . . . WE'RE WORRIED ABOUT YOU AND KAITO . . .
I KNOW. I'M GOING TO TRUST IN KAITO!
I KNOW THAT KAITO WILL RETURN TO ME!!
I MEAN, IT WASN'T JUST A DREAM!

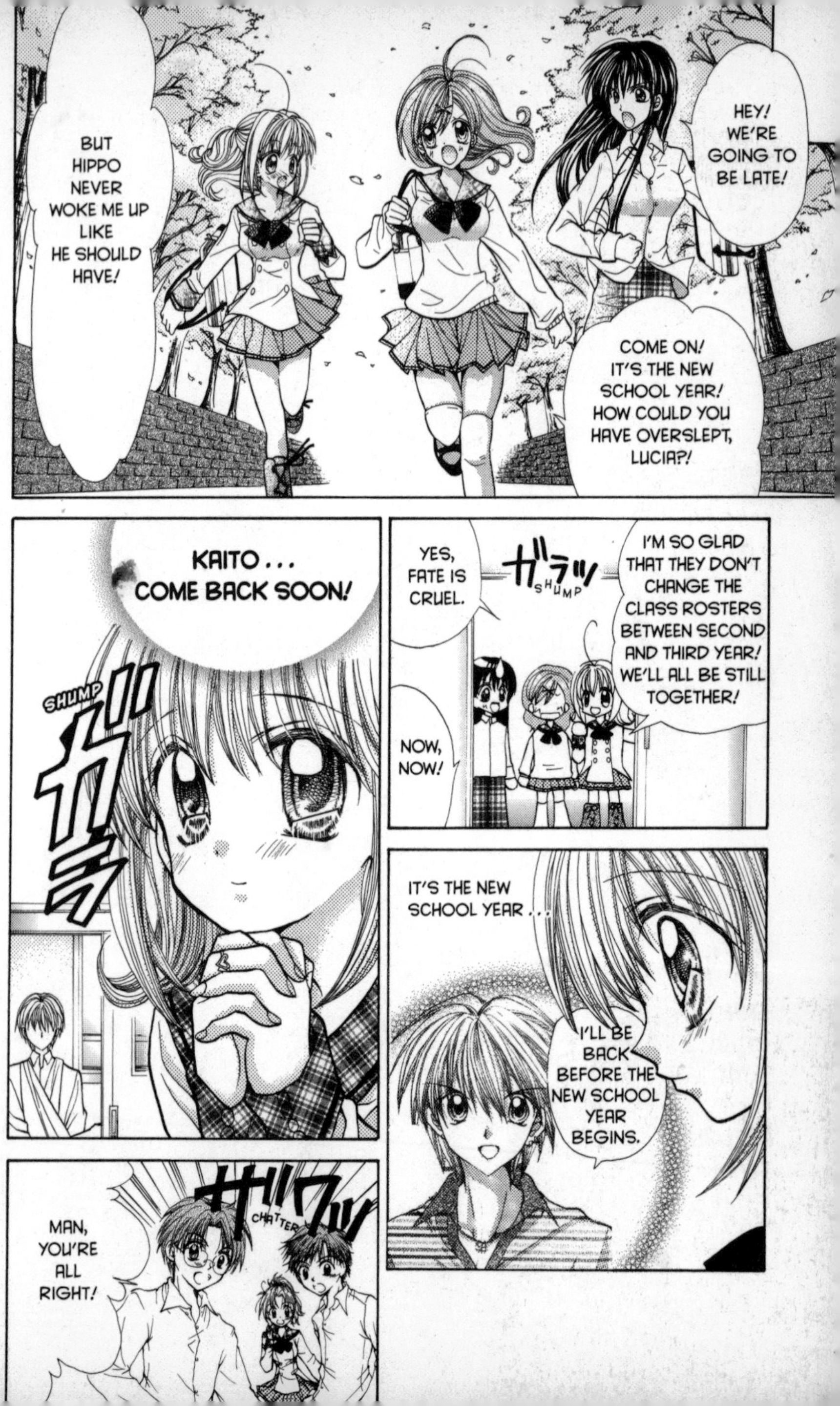
HEY! WE'RE GOING TO BE LATE!
COME ON! IT'S THE NEW SCHOOL YEAR! HOW COULD YOU HAVE OVERSLEPT, LUCIA?!
BUT HIPPO NEVER WOKE ME UP LIKE HE SHOULD HAVE!
ガラッ
SHUMP
I'M SO GLAD THAT THEY DON'T CHANGE THE CLASS ROSTERS BETWEEN SECOND AND THIRD YEAR! WE'LL ALL BE STILL TOGETHER!
YES, FATE IS CRUEL.
NOW, NOW!
IT'S THE NEW SCHOOL YEAR...
I'LL BE BACK BEFORE THE NEW SCHOOL YEAR BEGINS.
KAITO... COME BACK SOON!
SHUMP
ガラ
ザワッ
CHATTER
MAN, YOU'RE ALL RIGHT!

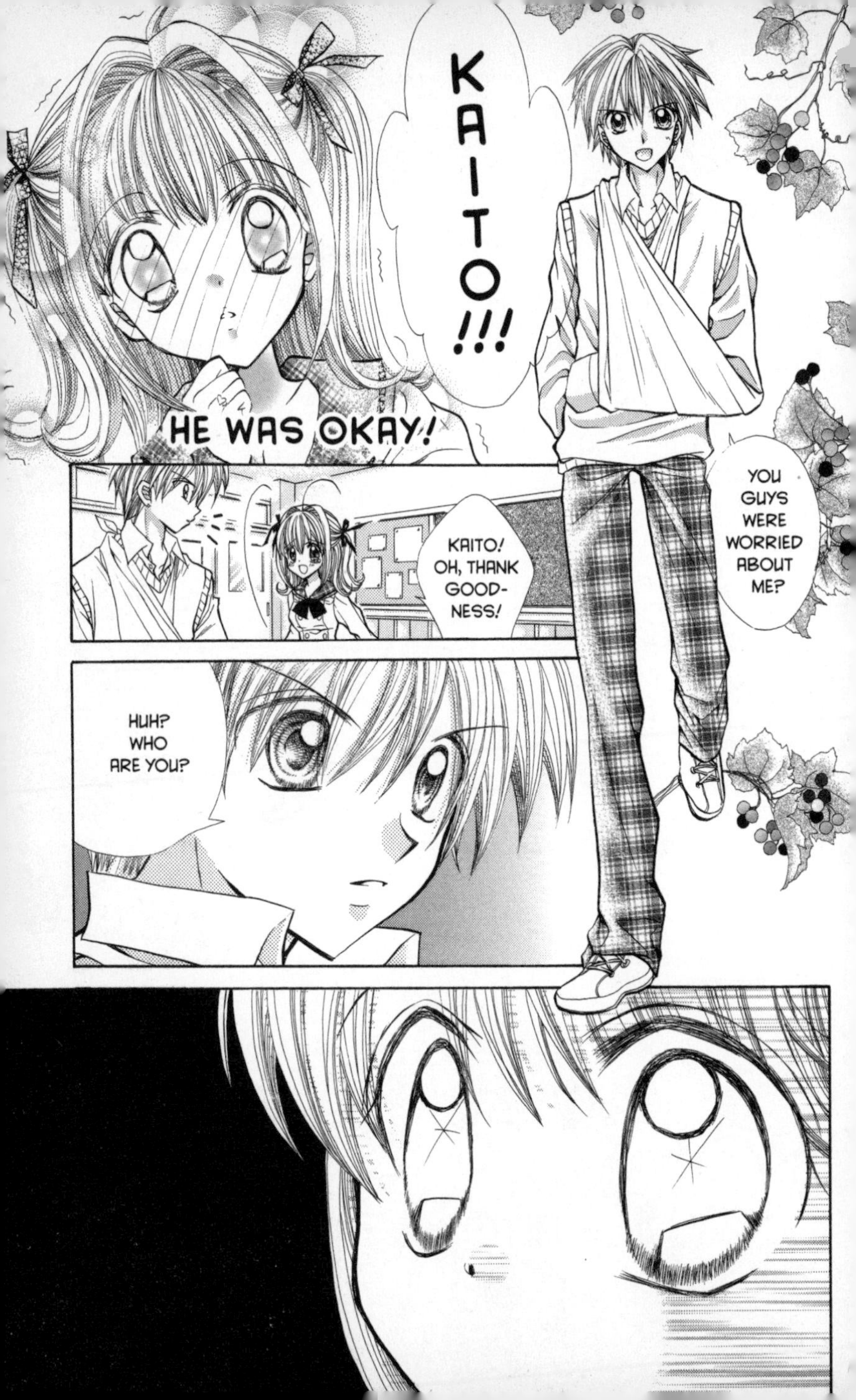
KAITO!!!
HE WAS OKAY!
YOU GUYS WERE WORRIED ABOUT ME?
KAITO! OH, THANK GOODNESS!
HUH? WHO ARE YOU?

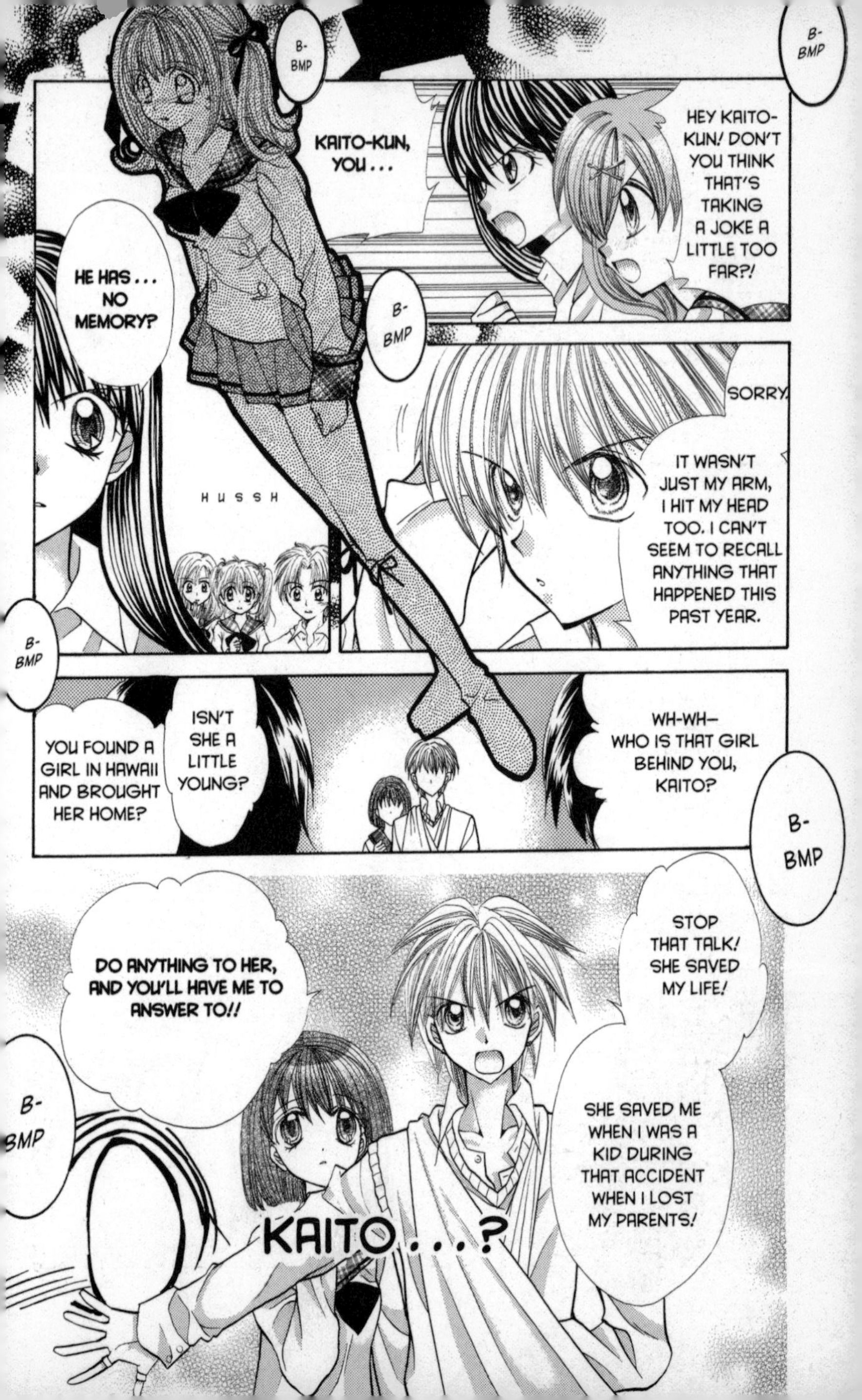
B-BMP
HEY KAITO-KUN! DON'T YOU THINK THAT'S TAKING A JOKE A LITTLE TOO FAR?!
KAITO-KUN, YOU...
B-BMP
SORRY.
IT WASN'T JUST MY ARM, I HIT MY HEAD TOO. I CAN'T SEEM TO RECALL ANYTHING THAT HAPPENED THIS PAST YEAR.
B-BMP
HE HAS... NO MEMORY?
HUSSH
B-BMP
B-BMP
WH-WH- WHO IS THAT GIRL BEHIND YOU, KAITO?
ISN'T SHE A LITTLE YOUNG?
YOU FOUND A GIRL IN HAWAII AND BROUGHT HER HOME?
STOP THAT TALK! SHE SAVED MY LIFE!
SHE SAVED ME WHEN I WAS A KID DURING THAT ACCIDENT WHEN I LOST MY PARENTS!
DO ANYTHING TO HER, AND YOU'LL HAVE ME TO ANSWER TO!!
B-BMP
KAITO...?

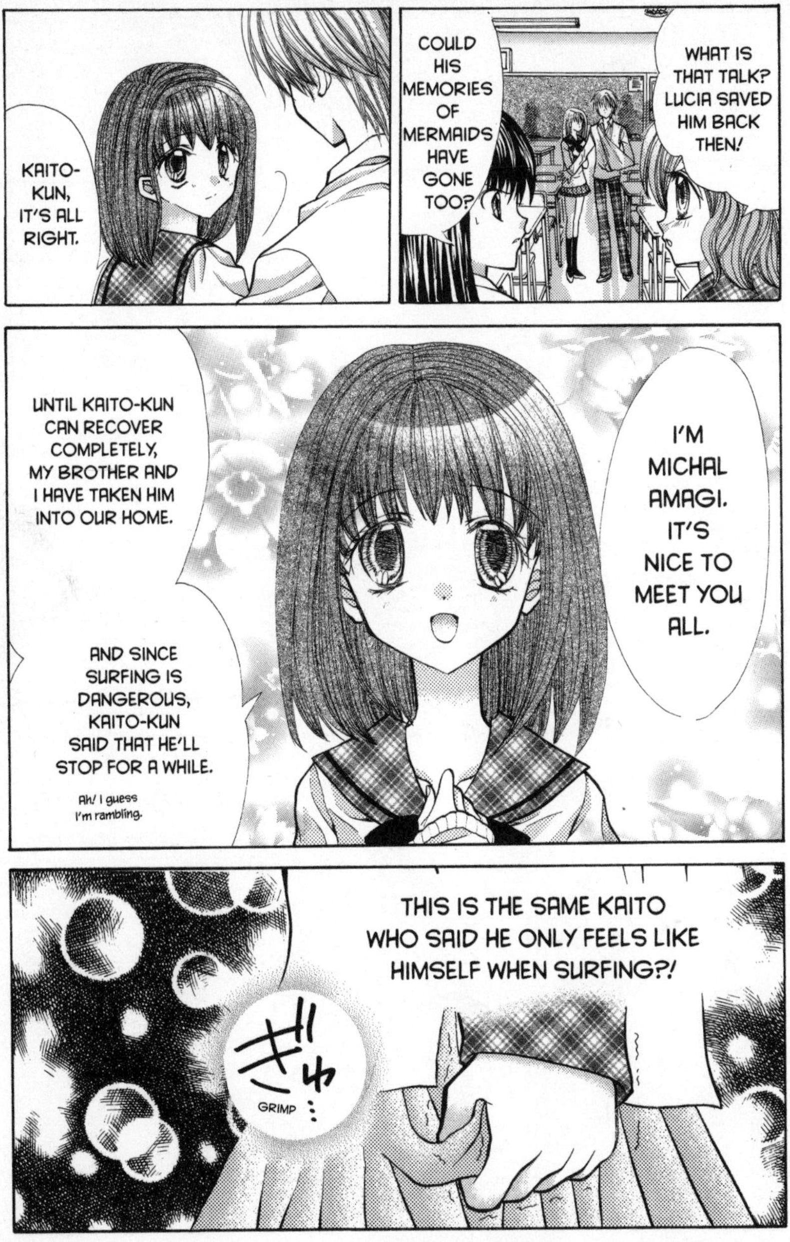
WHAT IS THAT TALK? LUCIA SAVED HIM BACK THEN!
COULD HIS MEMORIES OF MERMAIDS HAVE GONE TOO?
KAITO-KUN, IT'S ALL RIGHT.
I'M MICHAL AMAGI. IT'S NICE TO MEET YOU ALL.
UNTIL KAITO-KUN CAN RECOVER COMPLETELY, MY BROTHER AND I HAVE TAKEN HIM INTO OUR HOME.
AND SINCE SURFING IS DANGEROUS, KAITO-KUN SAID THAT HE'LL STOP FOR A WHILE.
Ah! I guess I'm rambling.
THIS IS THE SAME KAITO WHO SAID HE ONLY FEELS LIKE HIMSELF WHEN SURFING?!
ぎゅ
GRIMP

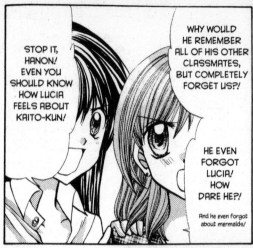

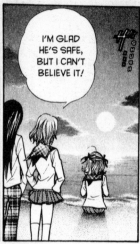

I'M GLAD HE'S SAFE, BUT I CAN'T BELIEVE IT!
SHUSH
WHY WOULD HE REMEMBER ALL OF HIS OTHER CLASSMATES, BUT COMPLETELY FORGET US?!
HE EVEN FORGOT LUCIA! HOW DARE HE?!
And he even forgot about mermaids!
STOP IT, HANON! EVEN YOU SHOULD KNOW HOW LUCIA FEELS ABOUT KAITO-KUN!
I DON'T SEE WHY YOU TWO ARE SO ANGRY . . .
IT'S PERFECTLY FINE WITH ME.
?
AFTER ALL, KAITO IS ALL RIGHT!
THERE'S NOTHING THAT MAKES ME MORE HAPPY THAN THAT!
LUCIA!!
SLUSS

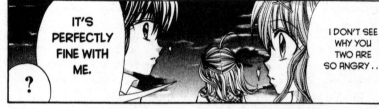

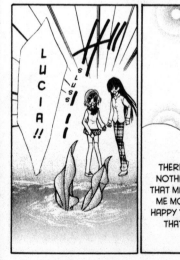

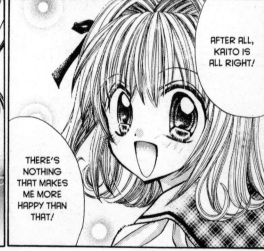

CONTINUED FROM PAGE 17

. . . I CAN ONLY FEEL THAT WHEN I WROTE FAN LETTERS, THEY WEREN'T "JUST LETTERS" TO ME! (A LONG TIME AGO, I WROTE FAN LETTERS TO SOME CELEBRITIES THAT I REALLY LOVED.) NOW, I SORT OF GET THE FEELING THAT THIS RECENT CELEBRITY WAS CRITICIZING THE FANS, AND I THOUGHT THAT WAS SAD. STILL I THINK THE PERSON WAS TRYING TO BE HUMBLE ABOUT IT.
BUT I DON'T WANT MY FANS TO FEEL THE WAY I FELT BACK THEN, SO SOMETIMES I WILL BE SO BOLD AS TO CALL THEM FAN LETTERS.
IF THAT CAUSES ANY DISCOMFORT TO PEOPLE WHO AREN'T FANS AND SENT LETTERS, THEN I APOLOGIZE.
I'D RATHER MAKE PEOPLE ANGRY THAN HURT THEM. SO IF THERE ARE ANY ATTACKS TO BE MADE, I'D RATHER BE ATTACKED THAN HAVE ME DO THE ATTACKING.

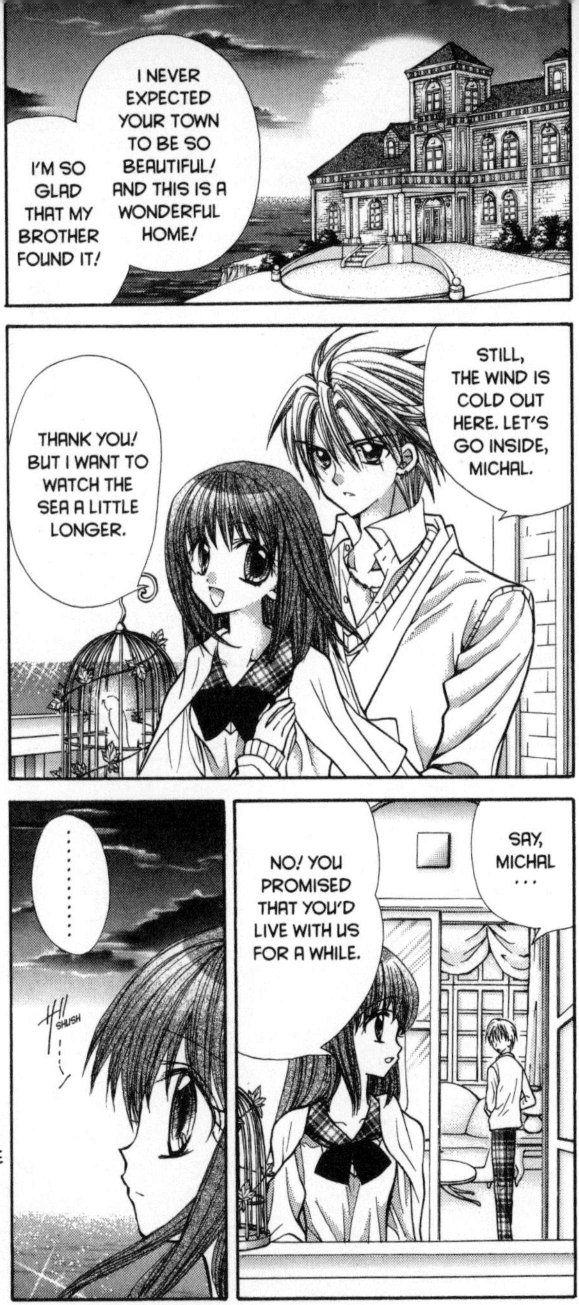
I NEVER EXPECTED YOUR TOWN TO BE SO BEAUTIFUL! AND THIS IS A WONDERFUL HOME!
I'M SO GLAD THAT MY BROTHER FOUND IT!
STILL, THE WIND IS COLD OUT HERE. LET'S GO INSIDE, MICHAL.
THANK YOU! BUT I WANT TO WATCH THE SEA A LITTLE LONGER.
SAY, MICHAL . . .
NO! YOU PROMISED THAT YOU'D LIVE WITH US FOR A WHILE.
. . . .
SHUSH

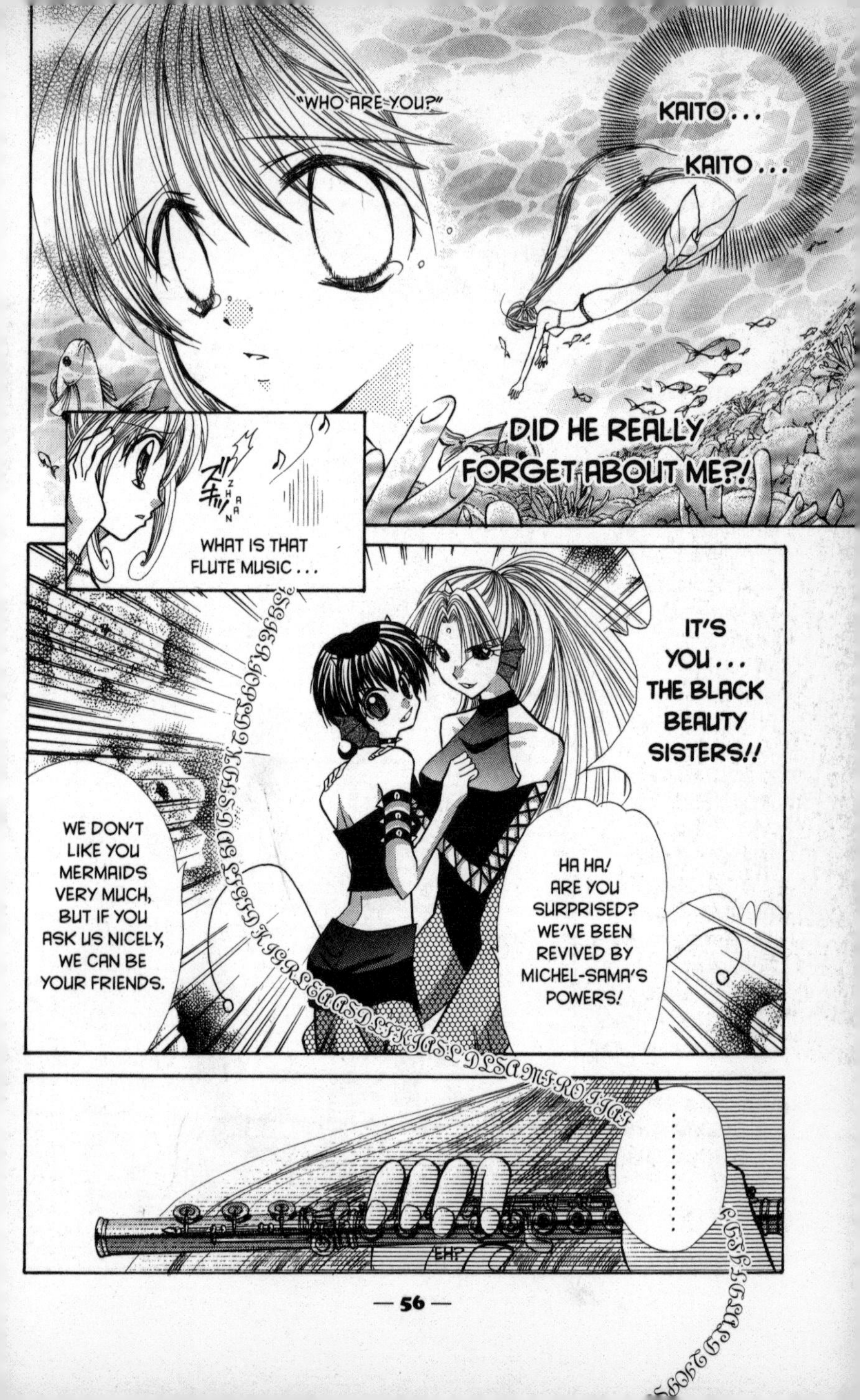
KAITO . . .
KAITO . . .
"WHO ARE YOU?"
DID HE REALLY FORGET ABOUT ME?!
ZHAAN
WHAT IS THAT FLUTE MUSIC . . .
IT'S YOU . . . THE BLACK BEAUTY SISTERS!!
HA HA! ARE YOU SURPRISED? WE'VE BEEN REVIVED BY MICHEL-SAMA'S POWERS!
WE DON'T LIKE YOU MERMAIDS VERY MUCH, BUT IF YOU ASK US NICELY, WE CAN BE YOUR FRIENDS.
. . . .
EH?

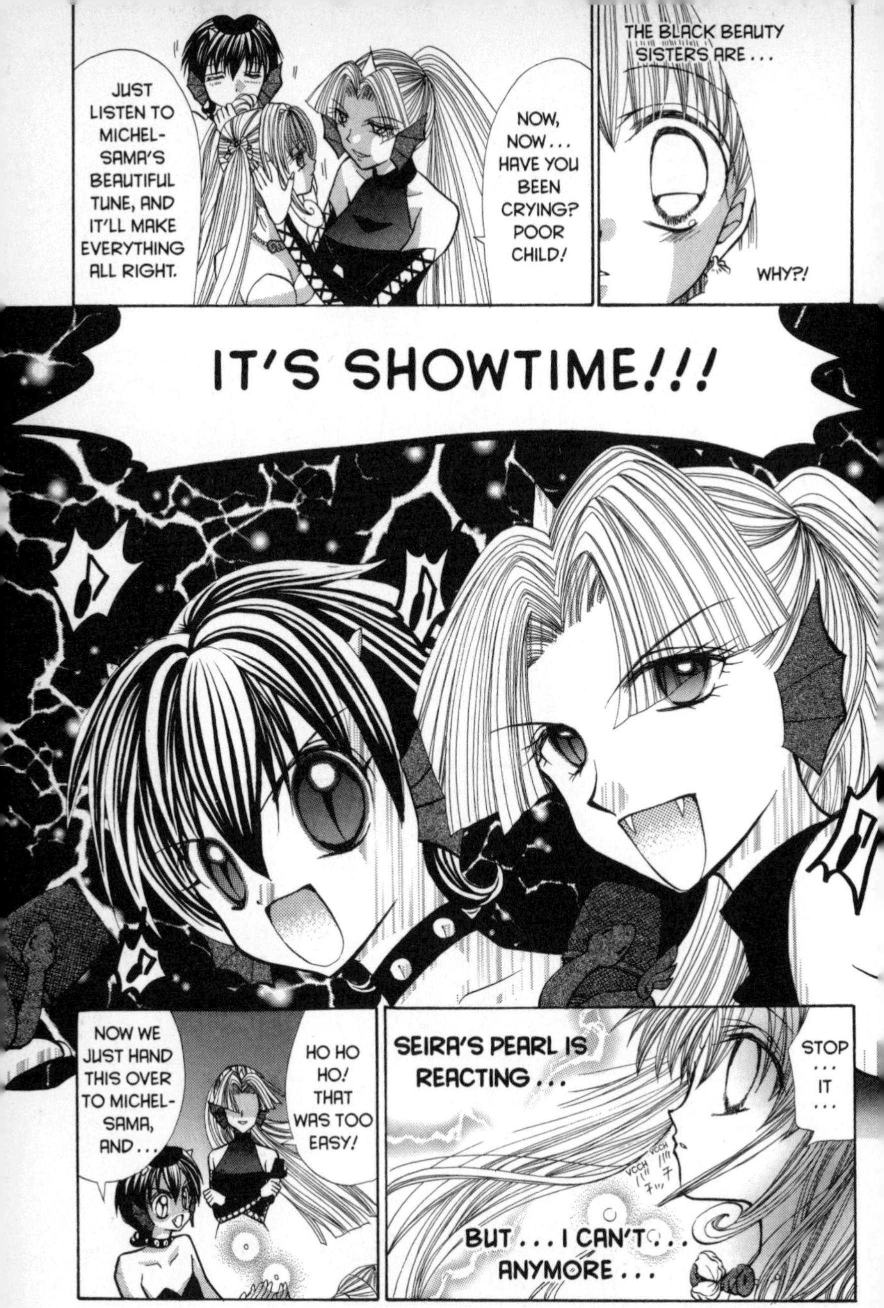
THE BLACK BEAUTY SISTERS ARE . . .
WHY?!
NOW, NOW . . . HAVE YOU BEEN CRYING? POOR CHILD!
JUST LISTEN TO MICHEL-SAMA'S BEAUTIFUL TUNE, AND IT'LL MAKE EVERYTHING ALL RIGHT.
IT'S SHOWTIME!!!
STOP . . . IT . . .
SEIRA'S PEARL IS REACTING . . .
VCCH VCCH
BUT . . . I CAN'T . . . ANYMORE . . .
HO HO HO! THAT WAS TOO EASY!
NOW WE JUST HAND THIS OVER TO MICHEL-SAMA, AND . . .

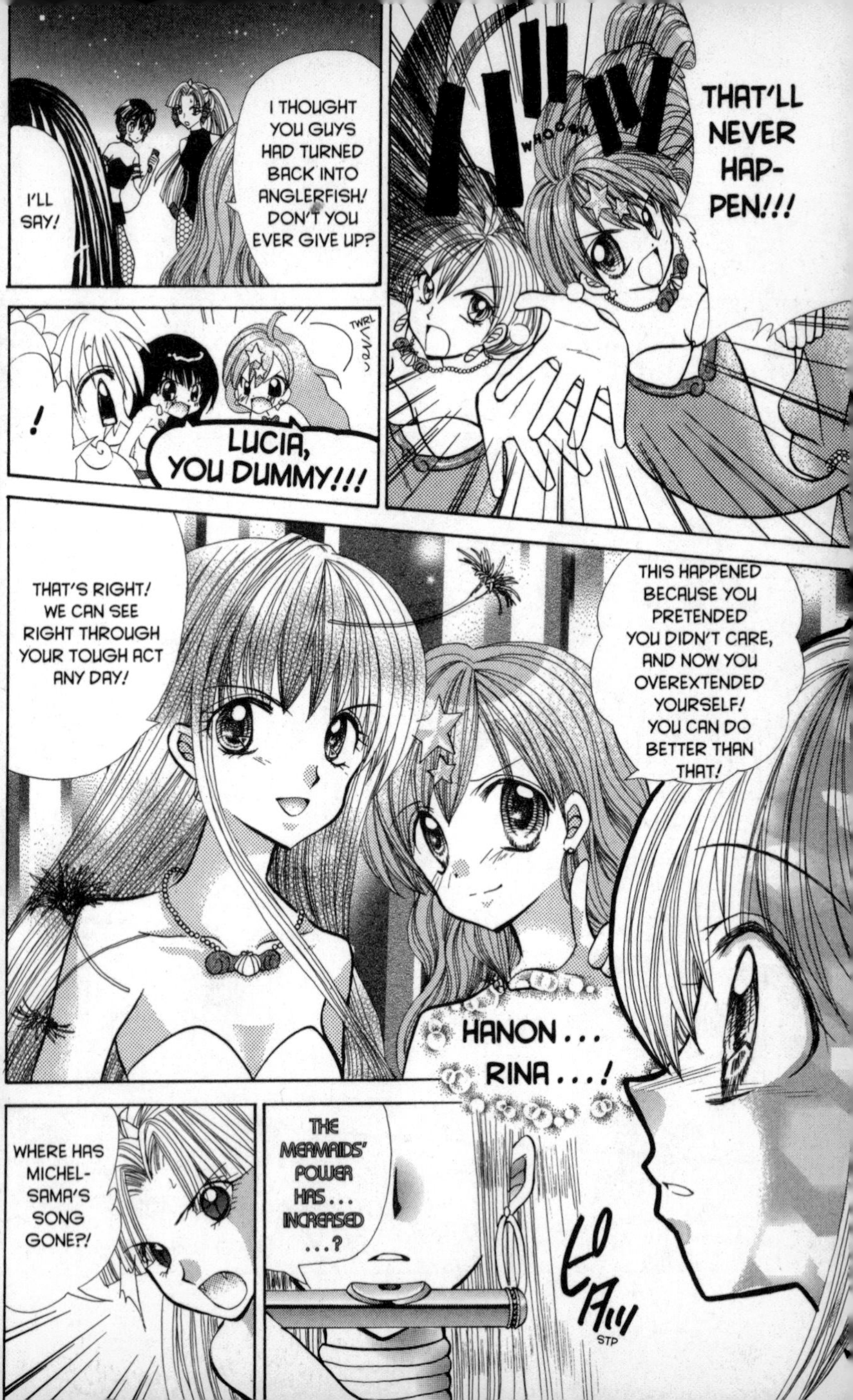
WHOOSH
THAT'LL NEVER HAP-PEN!!!
I THOUGHT YOU GUYS HAD TURNED BACK INTO ANGLERFISH! DON'T YOU EVER GIVE UP?
I'LL SAY!
TWRL
!
LUCIA, YOU DUMMY!!!
THIS HAPPENED BECAUSE YOU PRETENDED YOU DIDN'T CARE, AND NOW YOU OVEREXTENDED YOURSELF! YOU CAN DO BETTER THAN THAT!
THAT'S RIGHT! WE CAN SEE RIGHT THROUGH YOUR TOUGH ACT ANY DAY!
HANON... RINA...!
STP
THE MERMAIDS' POWER HAS... INCREASED...?
WHERE HAS MICHEL-SAMA'S SONG GONE?!

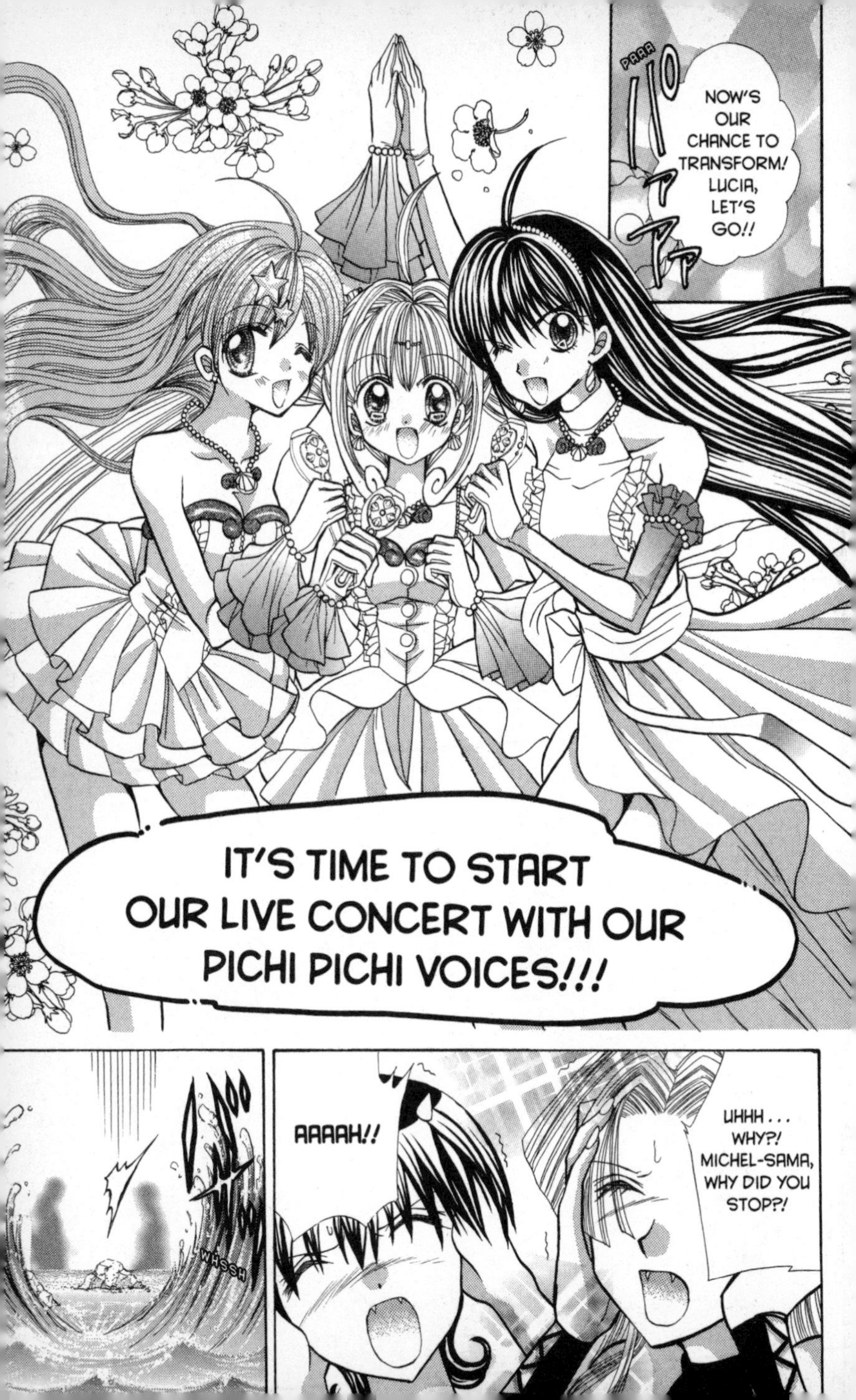
PAAA
NOW'S OUR CHANCE TO TRANSFORM! LUCIA, LET'S GO!!
IT'S TIME TO START OUR LIVE CONCERT WITH OUR PICHI PICHI VOICES!!!
UHHH . . . WHY?! MICHEL-SAMA, WHY DID YOU STOP?!
AAAAH!!
WHSSH

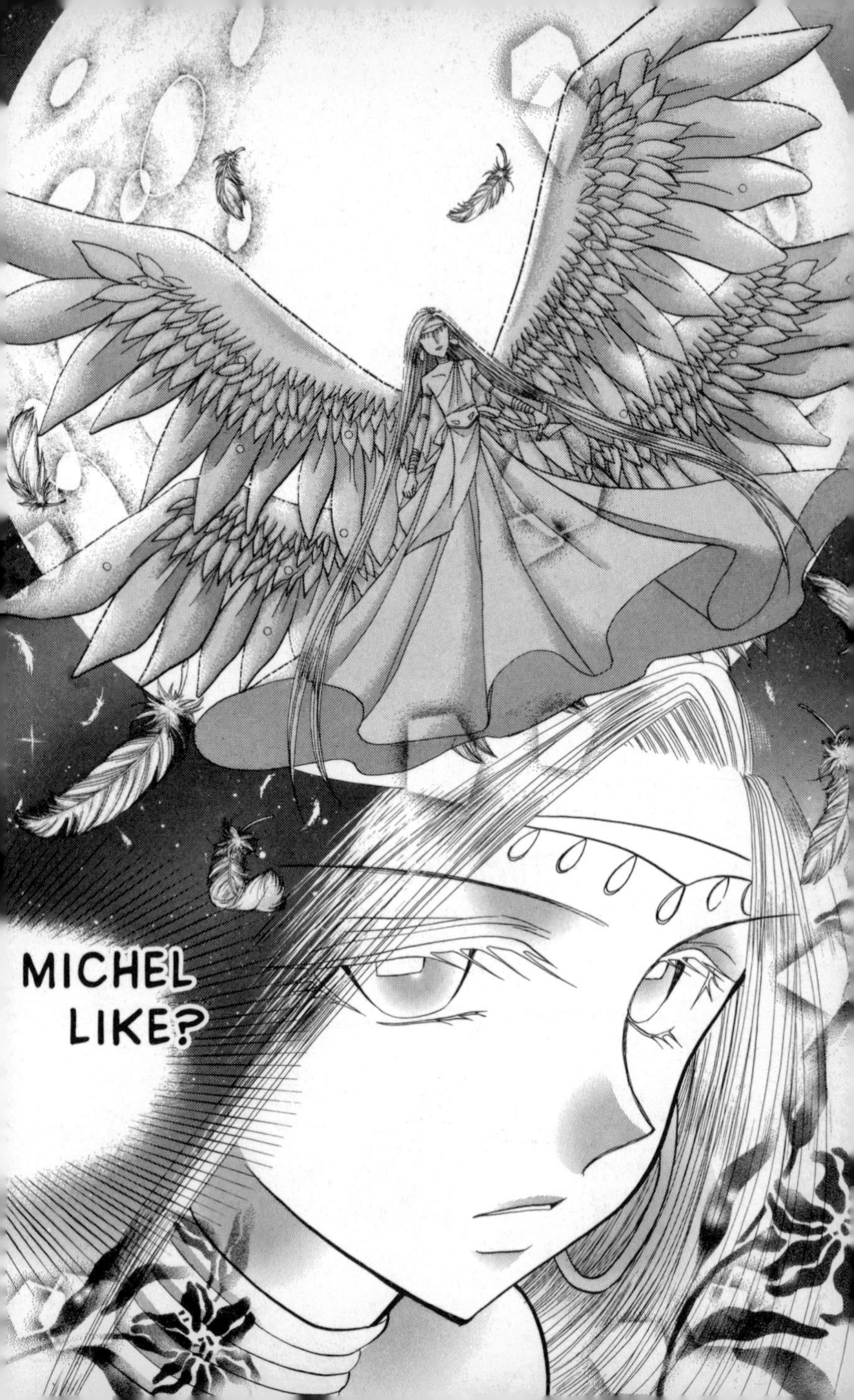
MICHEL
LIKE?

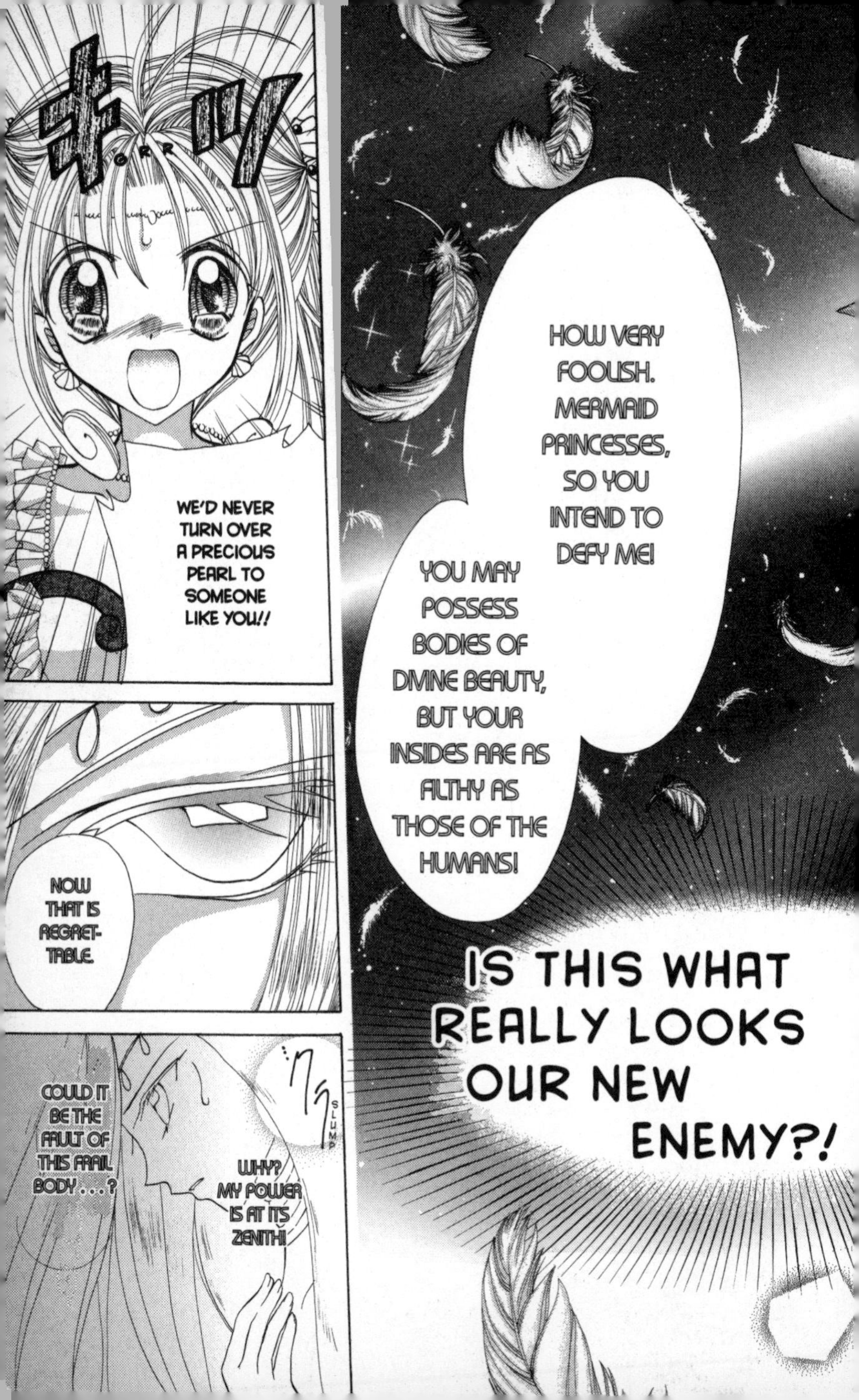
HOW VERY FOOLISH. MERMAID PRINCESSES, SO YOU INTEND TO DEFY ME!
YOU MAY POSSESS BODIES OF DIVINE BEAUTY, BUT YOUR INSIDES ARE AS FILTHY AS THOSE OF THE HUMANS!
IS THIS WHAT REALLY LOOKS OUR NEW ENEMY?!
GRR
WE'D NEVER TURN OVER A PRECIOUS PEARL TO SOMEONE LIKE YOU!!
NOW THAT IS REGRET-TABLE.
SLUMP
WHY? MY POWER IS AT ITS ZENITH!
COULD IT BE THE FAULT OF THIS FRAIL BODY . . . ?

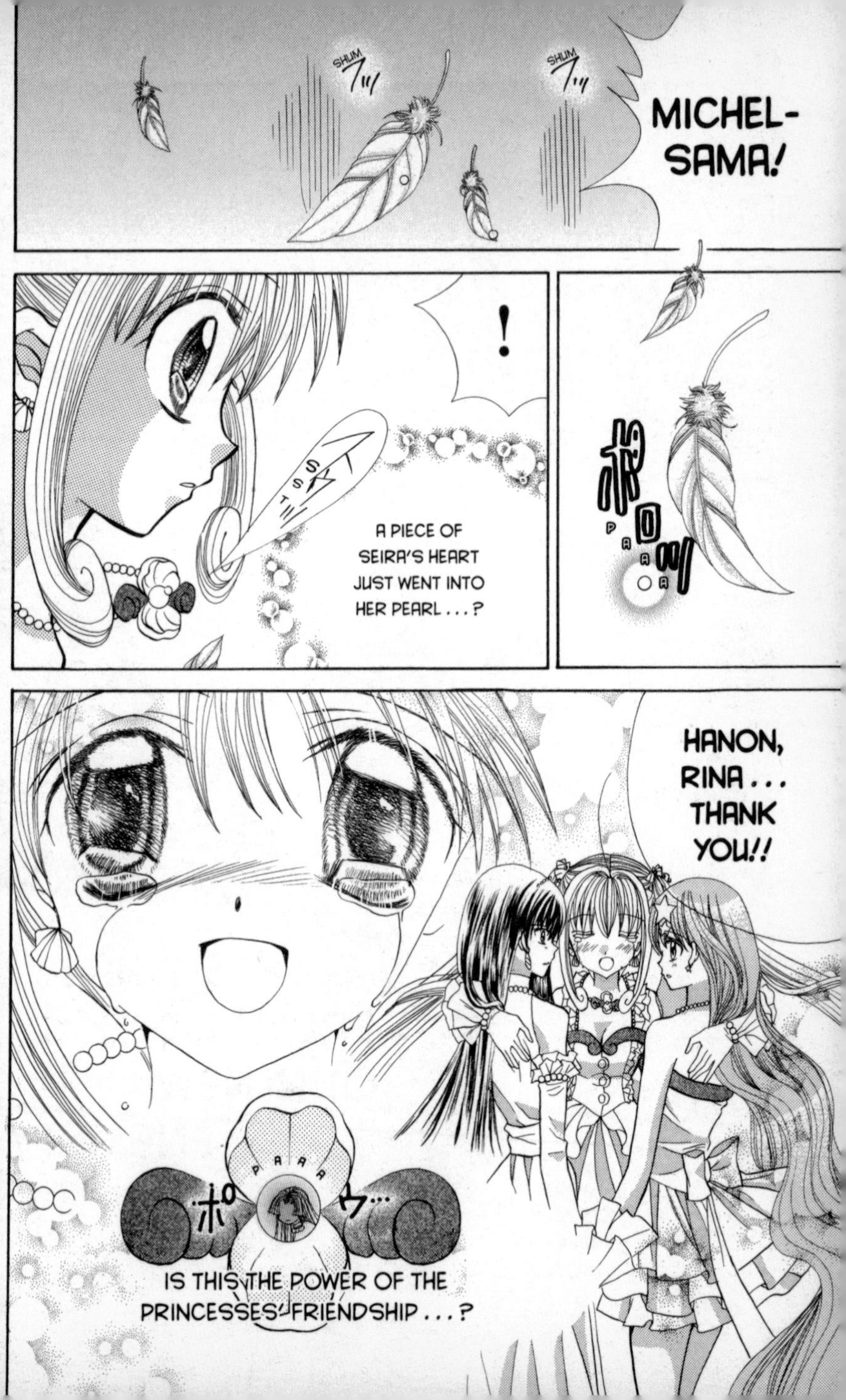
SHUM
フッ
SHUM
フッ
MICHEL-SAMA!
PAAA
!
SSST
A PIECE OF SEIRA'S HEART JUST WENT INTO HER PEARL . . . ?
HANON, RINA . . . THANK YOU!!
PAAA
IS THIS THE POWER OF THE PRINCESSES' FRIENDSHIP . . . ?

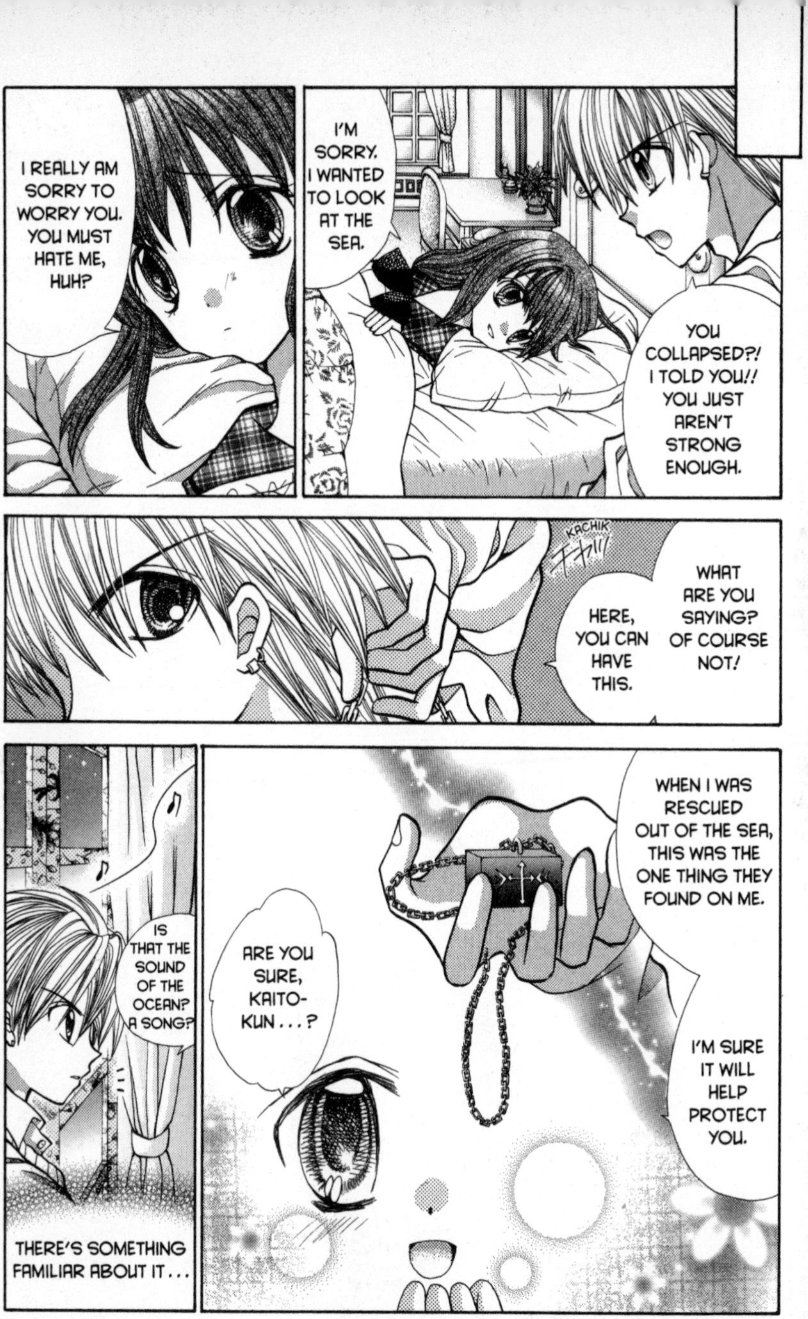
YOU COLLAPSED?! I TOLD YOU!! YOU JUST AREN'T STRONG ENOUGH.
I'M SORRY. I WANTED TO LOOK AT THE SEA.
I REALLY AM SORRY TO WORRY YOU. YOU MUST HATE ME, HUH?
KACHIK
WHAT ARE YOU SAYING? OF COURSE NOT!
HERE, YOU CAN HAVE THIS.
WHEN I WAS RESCUED OUT OF THE SEA, THIS WAS THE ONE THING THEY FOUND ON ME.
I'M SURE IT WILL HELP PROTECT YOU.
ARE YOU SURE, KAITO-KUN . . . ?
IS THAT THE SOUND OF THE OCEAN? A SONG?
THERE'S SOMETHING FAMILIAR ABOUT IT . . .

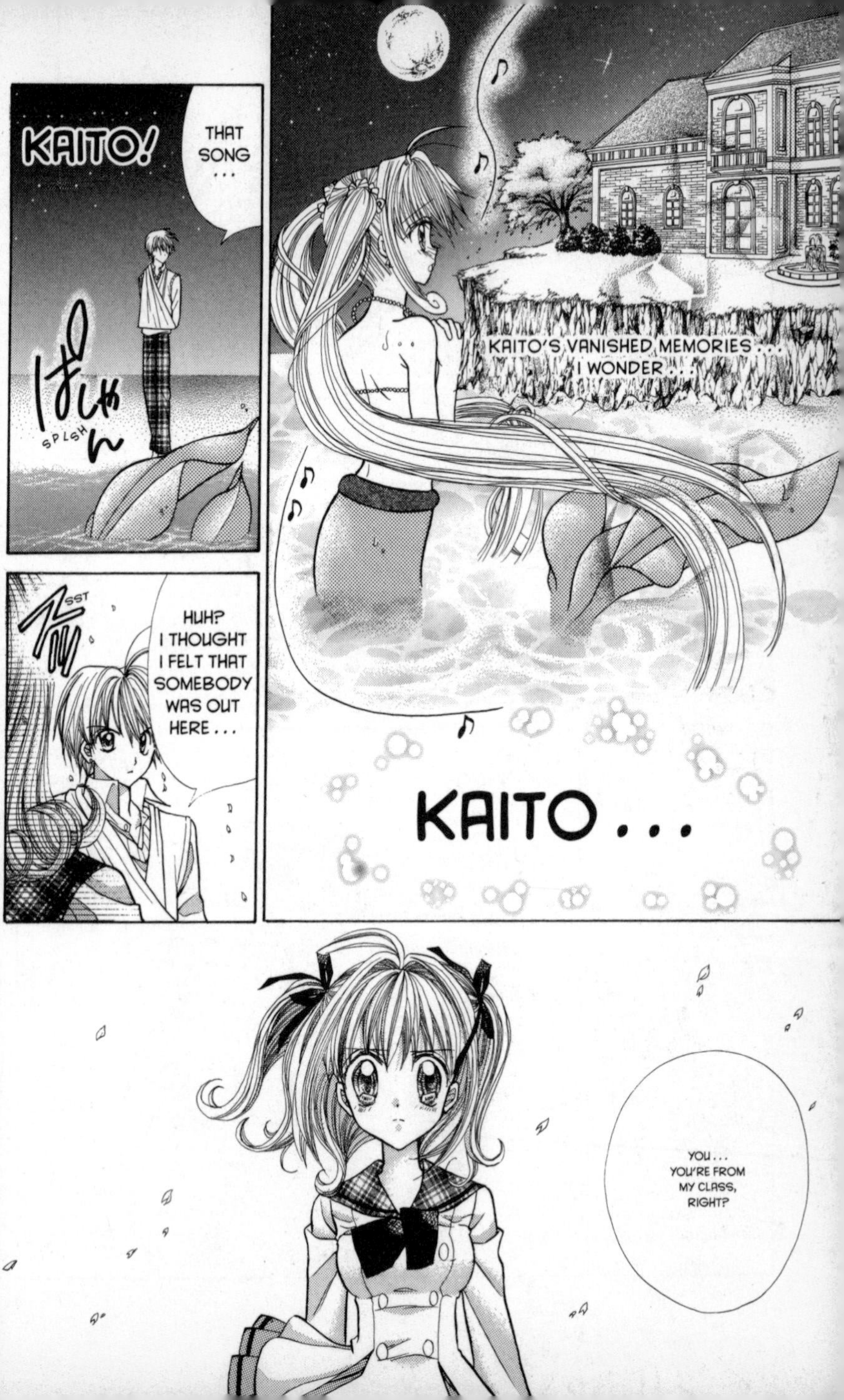
KAITO'S VANISHED MEMORIES . . .
I WONDER . . .
KAITO . . .
THAT SONG . . .
KAITO!
SPLSH
SST
HUH? I THOUGHT I FELT THAT SOMEBODY WAS OUT HERE . . .
YOU . . . YOU'RE FROM MY CLASS, RIGHT?

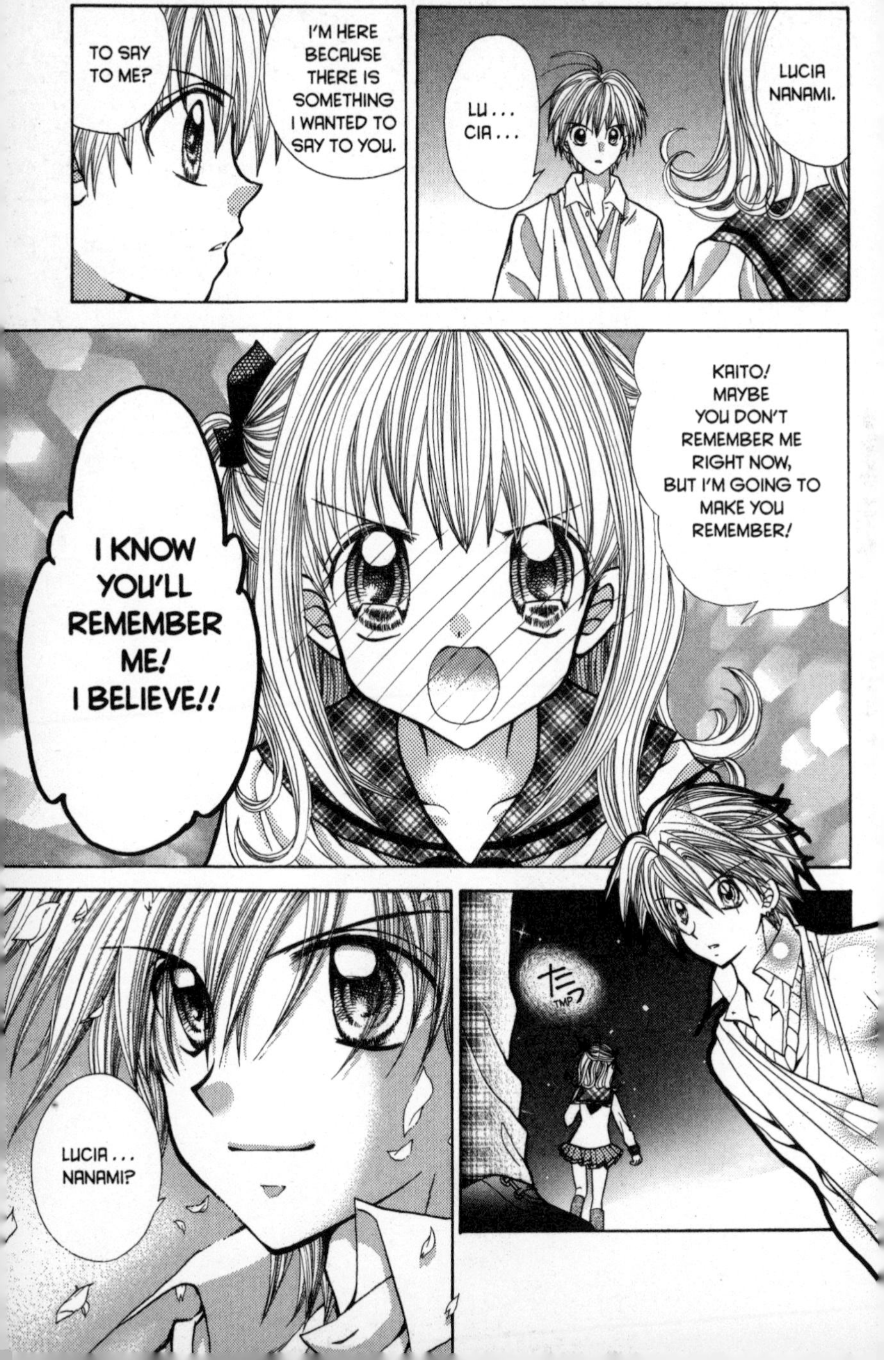
LUCIA NANAMI.
LU... CIA...
I'M HERE BECAUSE THERE IS SOMETHING I WANTED TO SAY TO YOU.
TO SAY TO ME?
KAITO! MAYBE YOU DON'T REMEMBER ME RIGHT NOW, BUT I'M GOING TO MAKE YOU REMEMBER!
I KNOW YOU'LL REMEMBER ME! I BELIEVE!!
たっ
TMP
LUCIA... NANAMI?

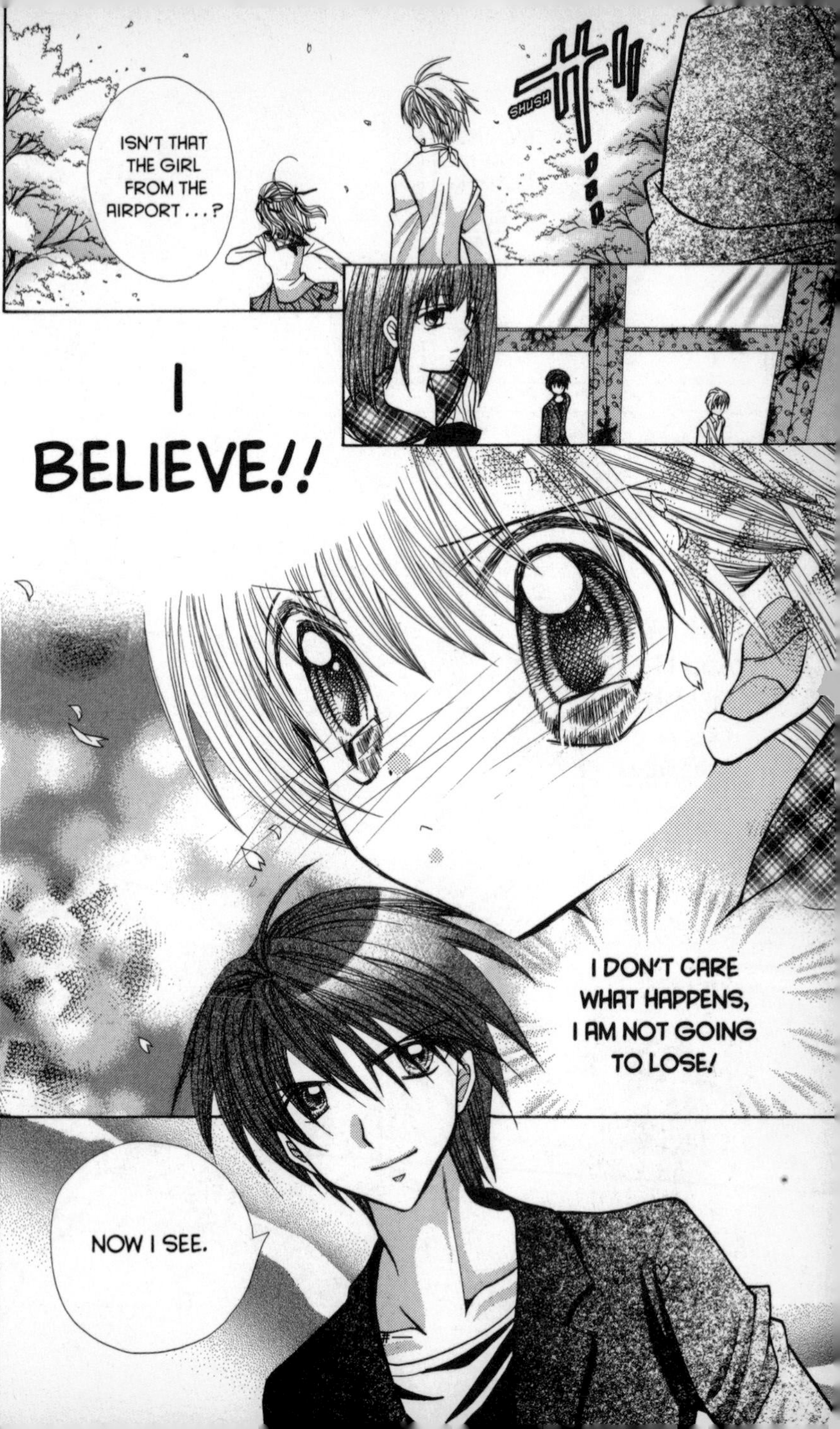
SHUSH
ISN'T THAT THE GIRL FROM THE AIRPORT . . . ?
I BELIEVE!!
I DON'T CARE WHAT HAPPENS, I AM NOT GOING TO LOSE!
NOW I SEE.

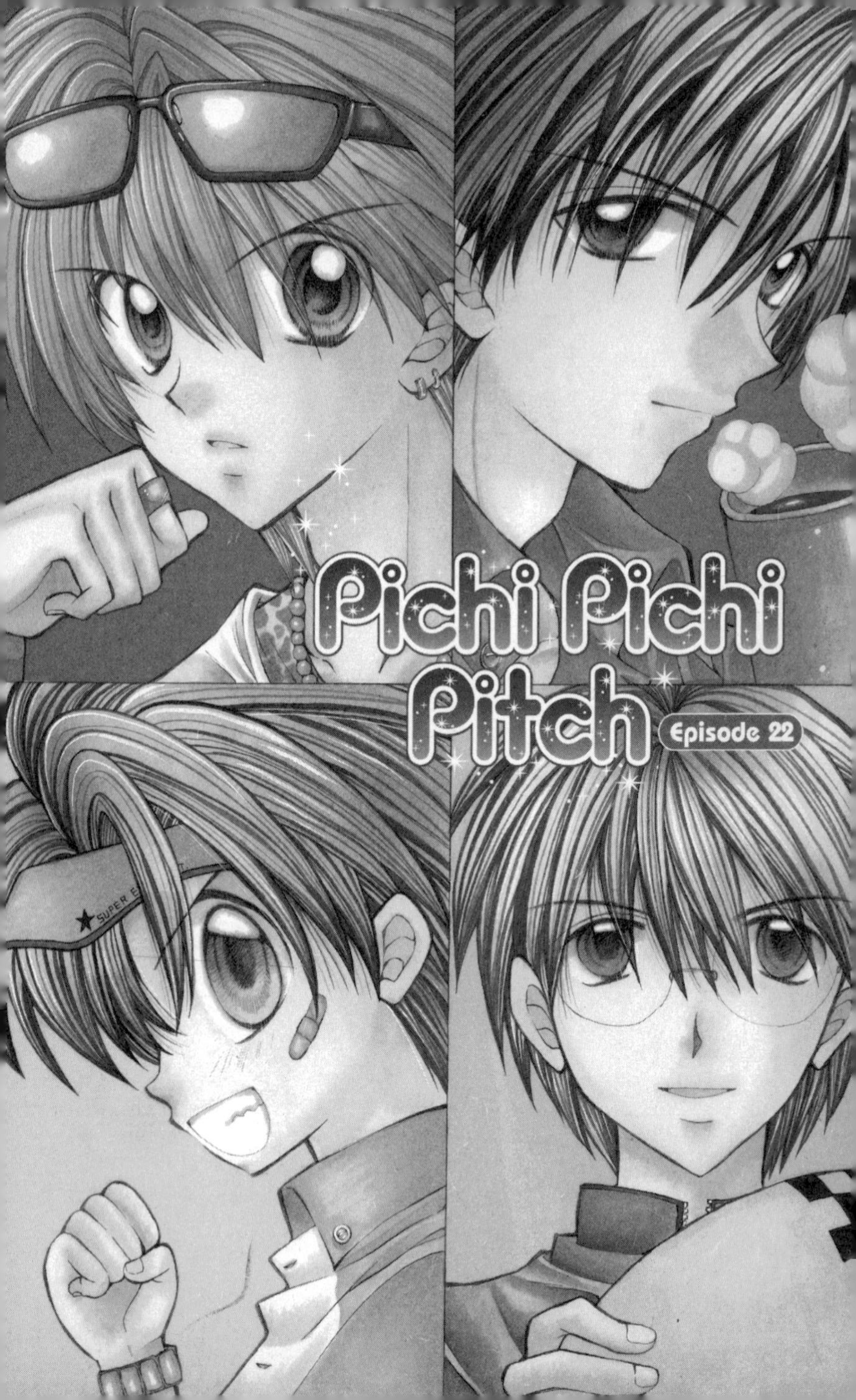
Pichi Pichi Pitch
Episode 22

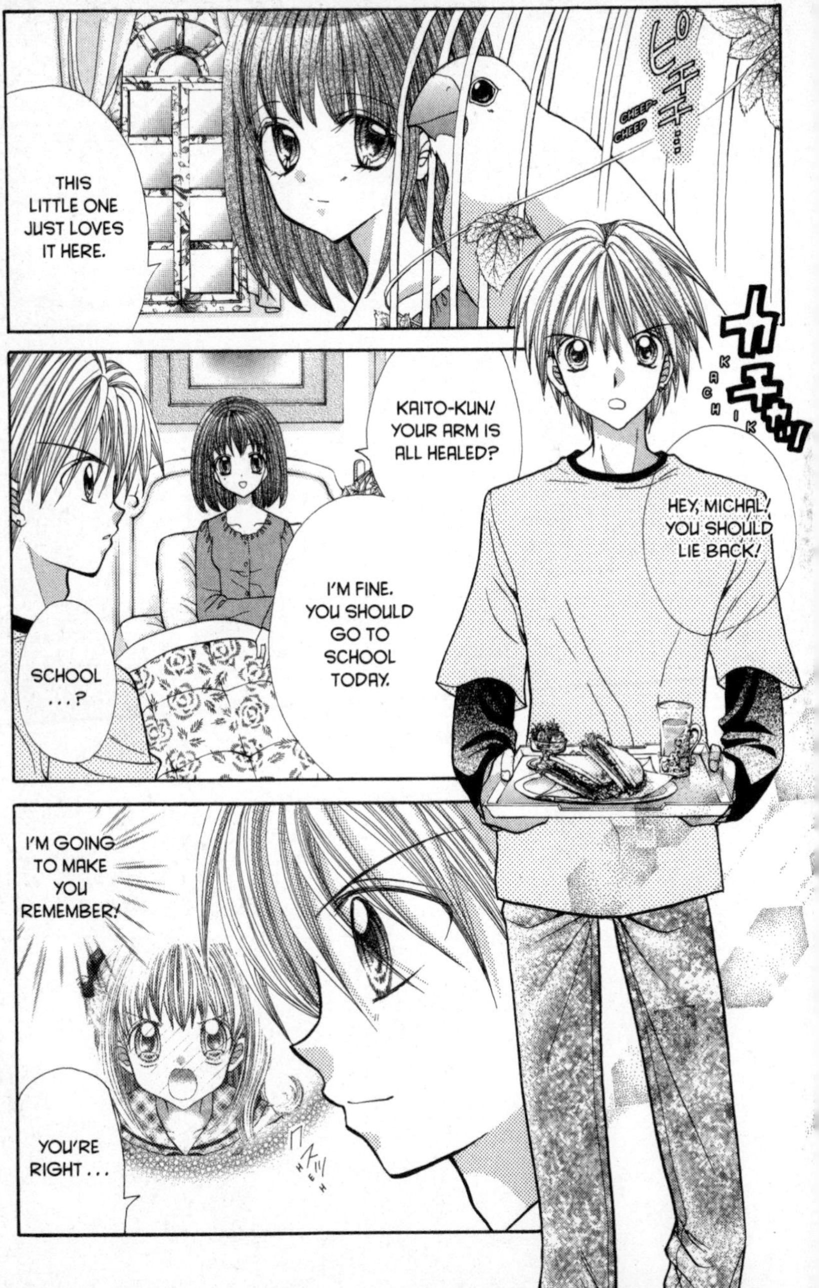
ピチチ…
CHEEP-CHEEP
THIS LITTLE ONE JUST LOVES IT HERE.
KACHIK
HEY, MICHAL! YOU SHOULD LIE BACK!
KAITO-KUN! YOUR ARM IS ALL HEALED?
I'M FINE. YOU SHOULD GO TO SCHOOL TODAY.
SCHOOL . . . ?
I'M GOING TO MAKE YOU REMEMBER!
HEH
YOU'RE RIGHT . . .

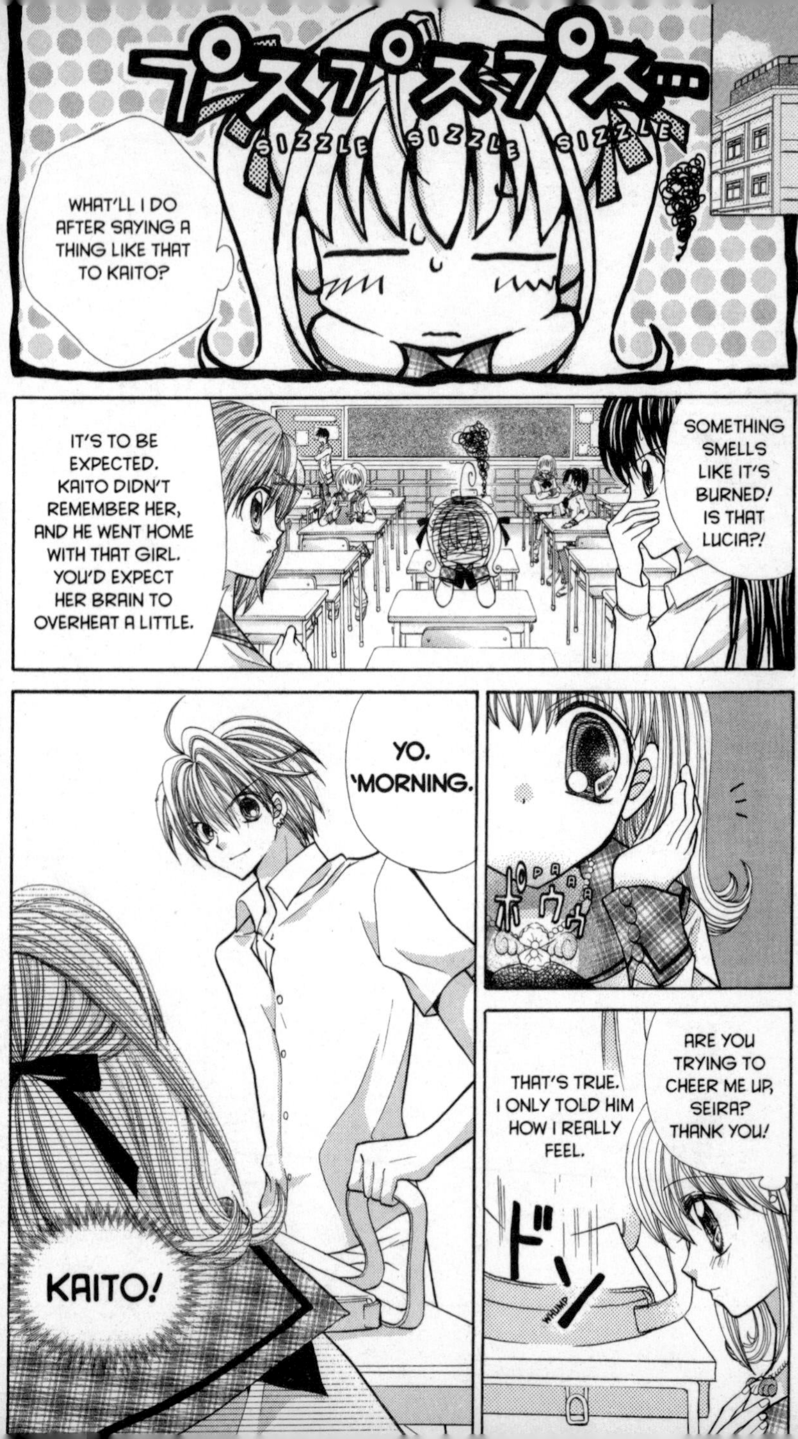
ぷスぷスぷス…
SIZZLE SIZZLE SIZZLE
WHAT'LL I DO AFTER SAYING A THING LIKE THAT TO KAITO?
SOMETHING SMELLS LIKE IT'S BURNED! IS THAT LUCIA?!
IT'S TO BE EXPECTED. KAITO DIDN'T REMEMBER HER, AND HE WENT HOME WITH THAT GIRL. YOU'D EXPECT HER BRAIN TO OVERHEAT A LITTLE.
ポウゥ
PAAAA
ARE YOU TRYING TO CHEER ME UP, SEIRA? THANK YOU!
THAT'S TRUE. I ONLY TOLD HIM HOW I REALLY FEEL.
ドン
WHUMP
YO. 'MORNING.
KAITO!

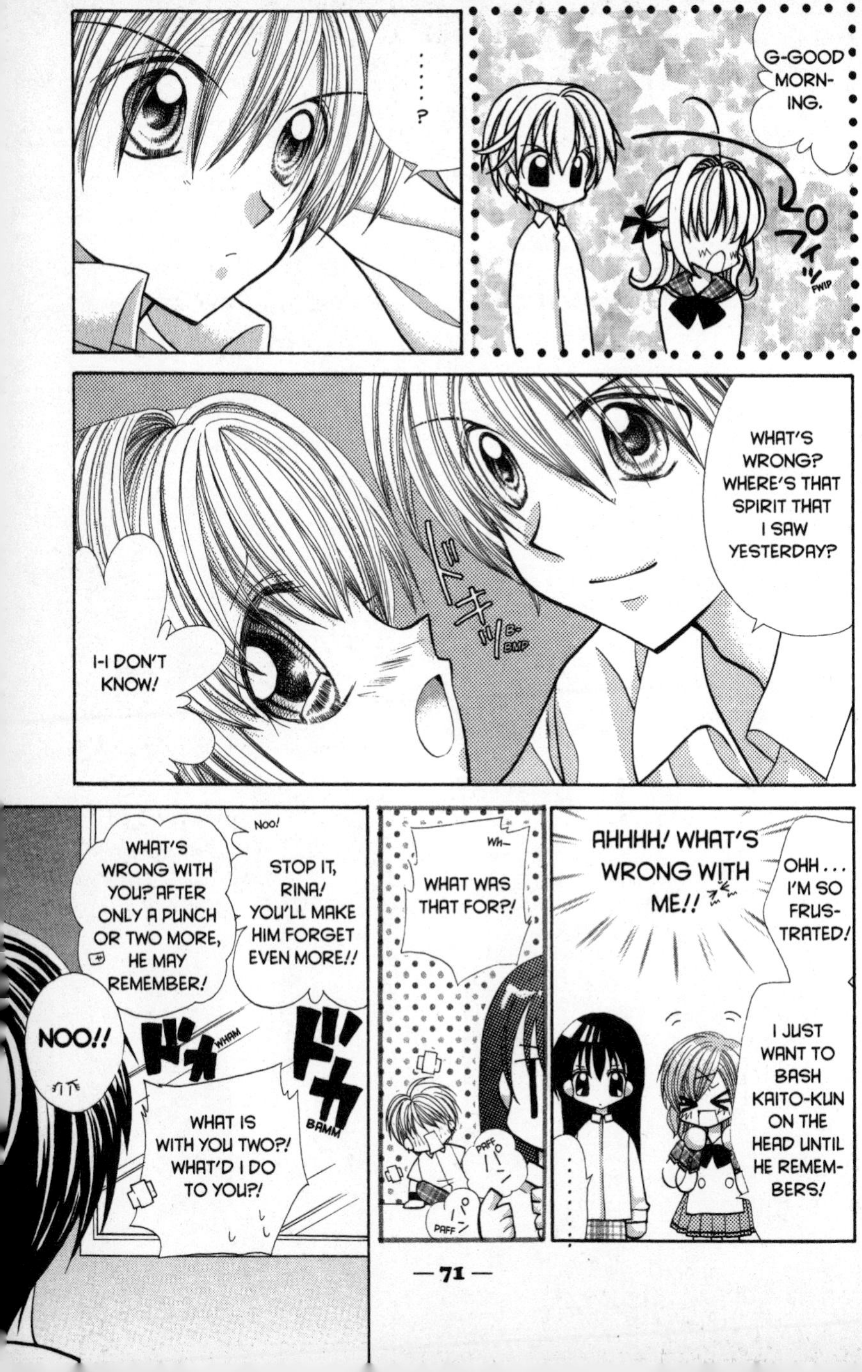
G-GOOD MORNING.
FWIP
. . . . ?
WHAT'S WRONG? WHERE'S THAT SPIRIT THAT I SAW YESTERDAY?
B-BMP
I-I DON'T KNOW!
AHHHH! WHAT'S WRONG WITH ME!!
OHH . . . I'M SO FRUS-TRATED!
I JUST WANT TO BASH KAITO-KUN ON THE HEAD UNTIL HE REMEM-BERS!
WH—
WHAT WAS THAT FOR?!
PAFF
PAFF
Noo!
STOP IT, RINA! YOU'LL MAKE HIM FORGET EVEN MORE!!
WHAT'S WRONG WITH YOU? AFTER ONLY A PUNCH OR TWO MORE, HE MAY REMEMBER!
BAMM
WHAM
NOO!!
WHAT IS WITH YOU TWO?! WHAT'D I DO TO YOU?!

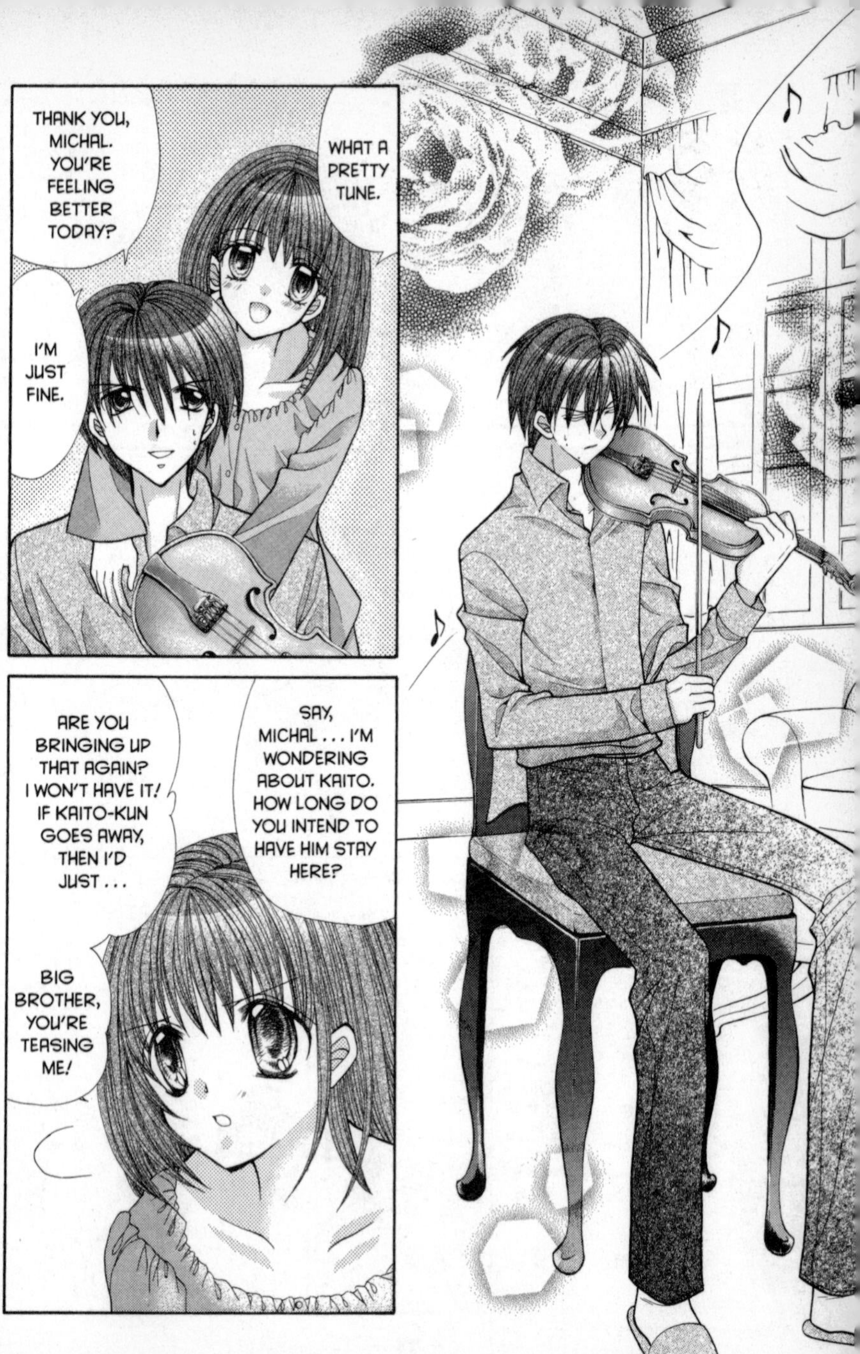
WHAT A PRETTY TUNE.
THANK YOU, MICHAL. YOU'RE FEELING BETTER TODAY?
I'M JUST FINE.
SAY, MICHAL . . . I'M WONDERING ABOUT KAITO. HOW LONG DO YOU INTEND TO HAVE HIM STAY HERE?
ARE YOU BRINGING UP THAT AGAIN? I WON'T HAVE IT! IF KAITO-KUN GOES AWAY, THEN I'D JUST . . .
BIG BROTHER, YOU'RE TEASING ME!

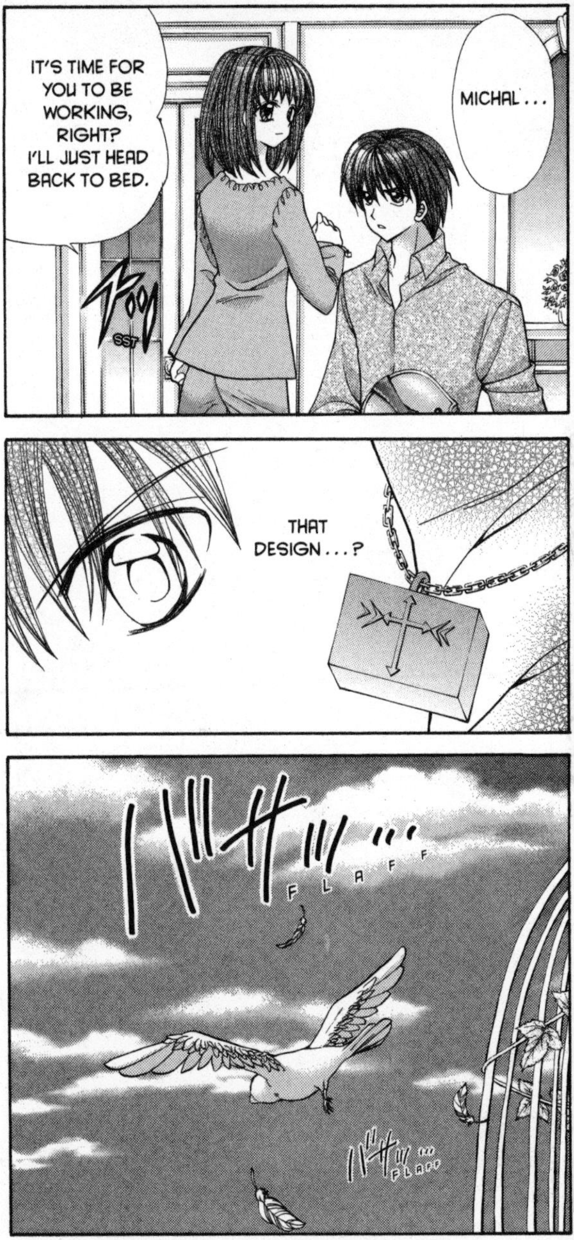
MICHAL . . .
IT'S TIME FOR YOU TO BE WORKING, RIGHT? I'LL JUST HEAD BACK TO BED.
SST
THAT DESIGN . . . ?
FLAFF
FLAFF

DOGS

I LOVE DOGS!
I LOVE CATS ALSO.
I LOVE BIRDS AS WELL.

I LOVE ANY LIVING BEING THAT'S FLUFFY!

IF I START TALKING ABOUT DOGS, I'LL NEVER STOP.
AHH . . . DOGS!
VIVA DOGS!!
DOGS ARE THE BEST!

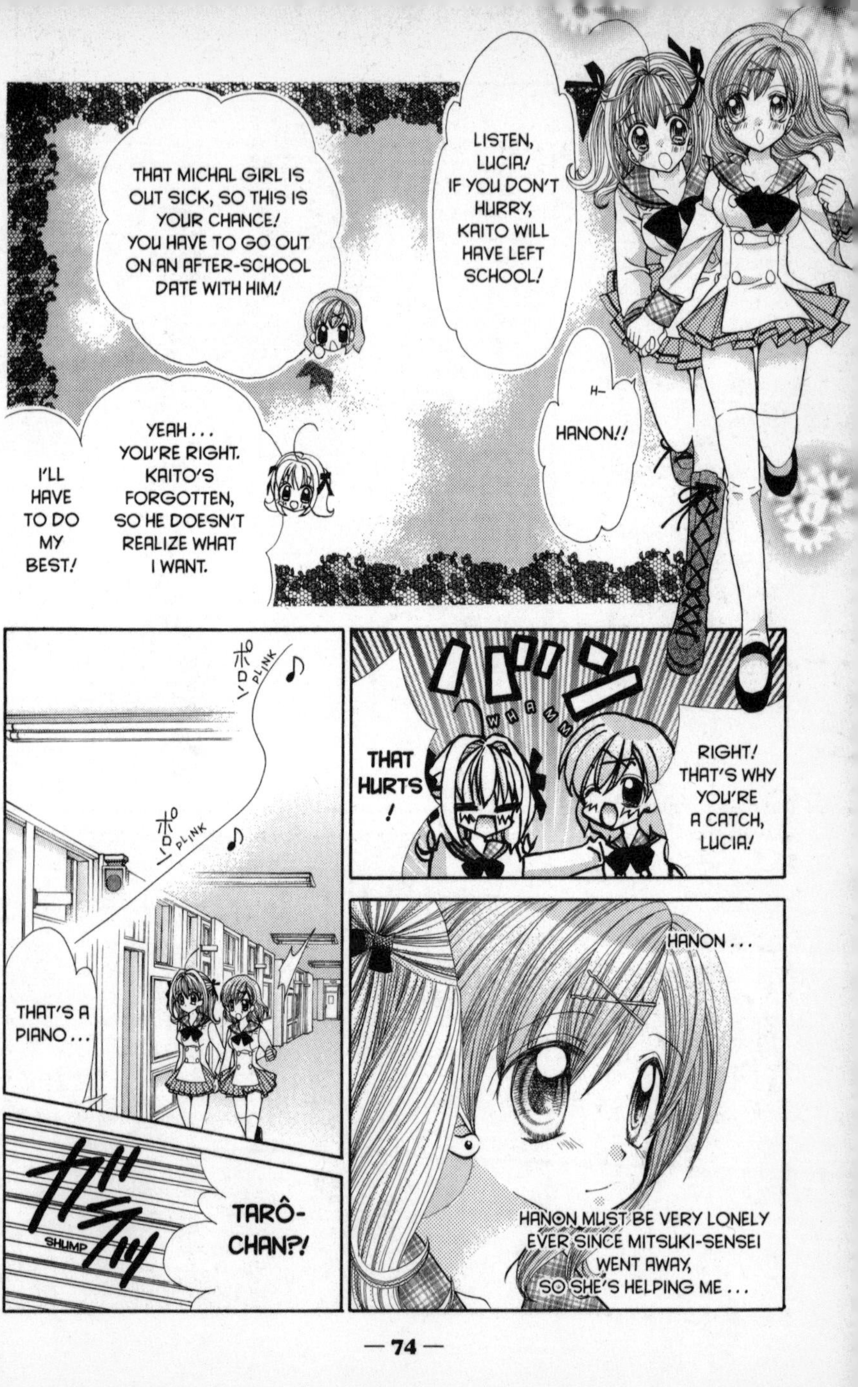
LISTEN, LUCIA! IF YOU DON'T HURRY, KAITO WILL HAVE LEFT SCHOOL!
H– HANON!!
THAT MICHAL GIRL IS OUT SICK, SO THIS IS YOUR CHANCE! YOU HAVE TO GO OUT ON AN AFTER-SCHOOL DATE WITH HIM!
YEAH . . . YOU'RE RIGHT. KAITO'S FORGOTTEN, SO HE DOESN'T REALIZE WHAT I WANT.
I'LL HAVE TO DO MY BEST!
RIGHT! THAT'S WHY YOU'RE A CATCH, LUCIA!
バシン
WHAM
THAT HURTS!
HANON . . .
HANON MUST BE VERY LONELY EVER SINCE MITSUKI-SENSEI WENT AWAY, SO SHE'S HELPING ME . . .
ポロ PLINK
ポロ PLINK
THAT'S A PIANO . . .
ガシャ
SHUMP
TARÔ-CHAN?!

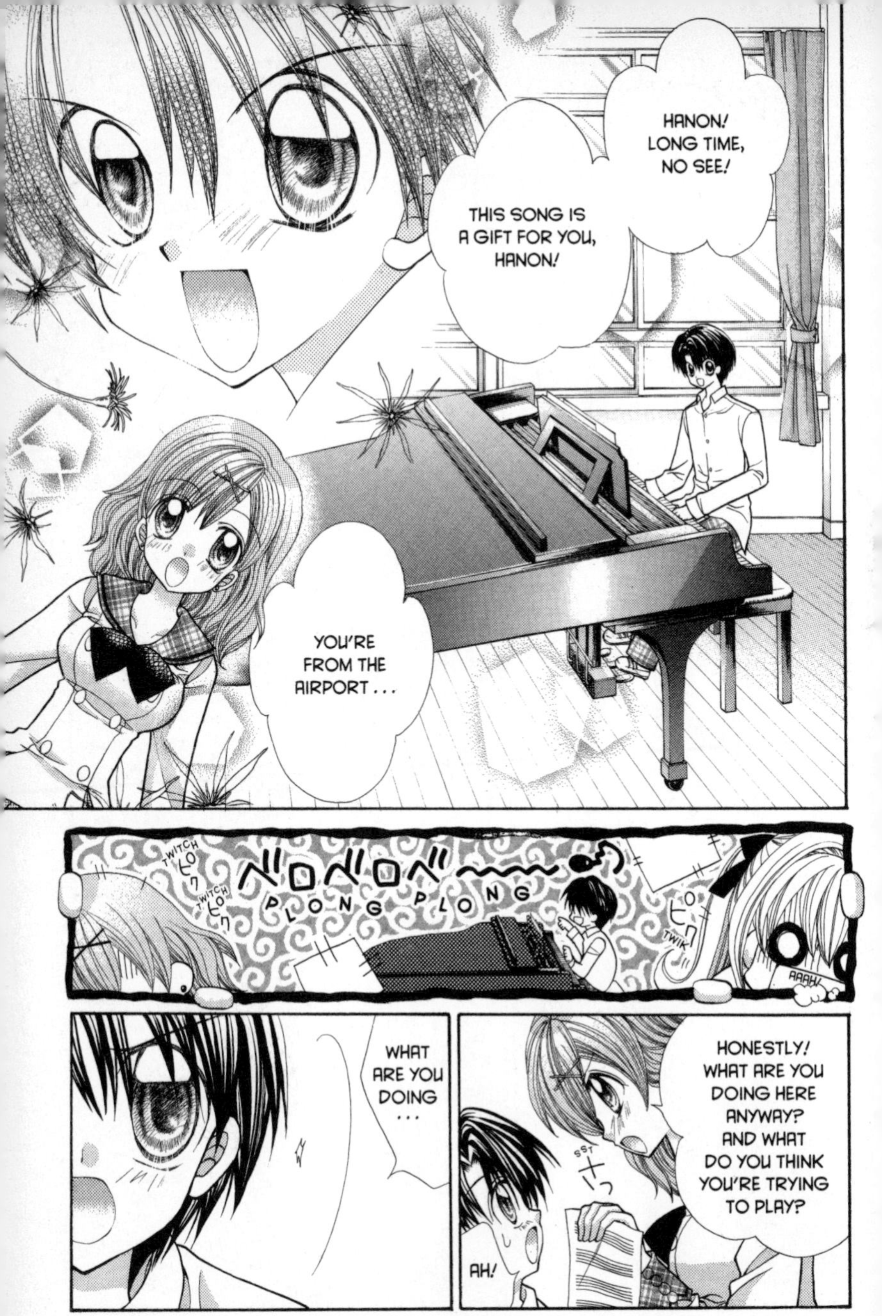
HANON! LONG TIME, NO SEE!
THIS SONG IS A GIFT FOR YOU, HANON!
YOU'RE FROM THE AIRPORT . . .
TWIK
AAAH!
PLONG PLONG
TWITCH
TWITCH
HONESTLY! WHAT ARE YOU DOING HERE ANYWAY? AND WHAT DO YOU THINK YOU'RE TRYING TO PLAY?
SST
AH!
WHAT ARE YOU DOING . . .

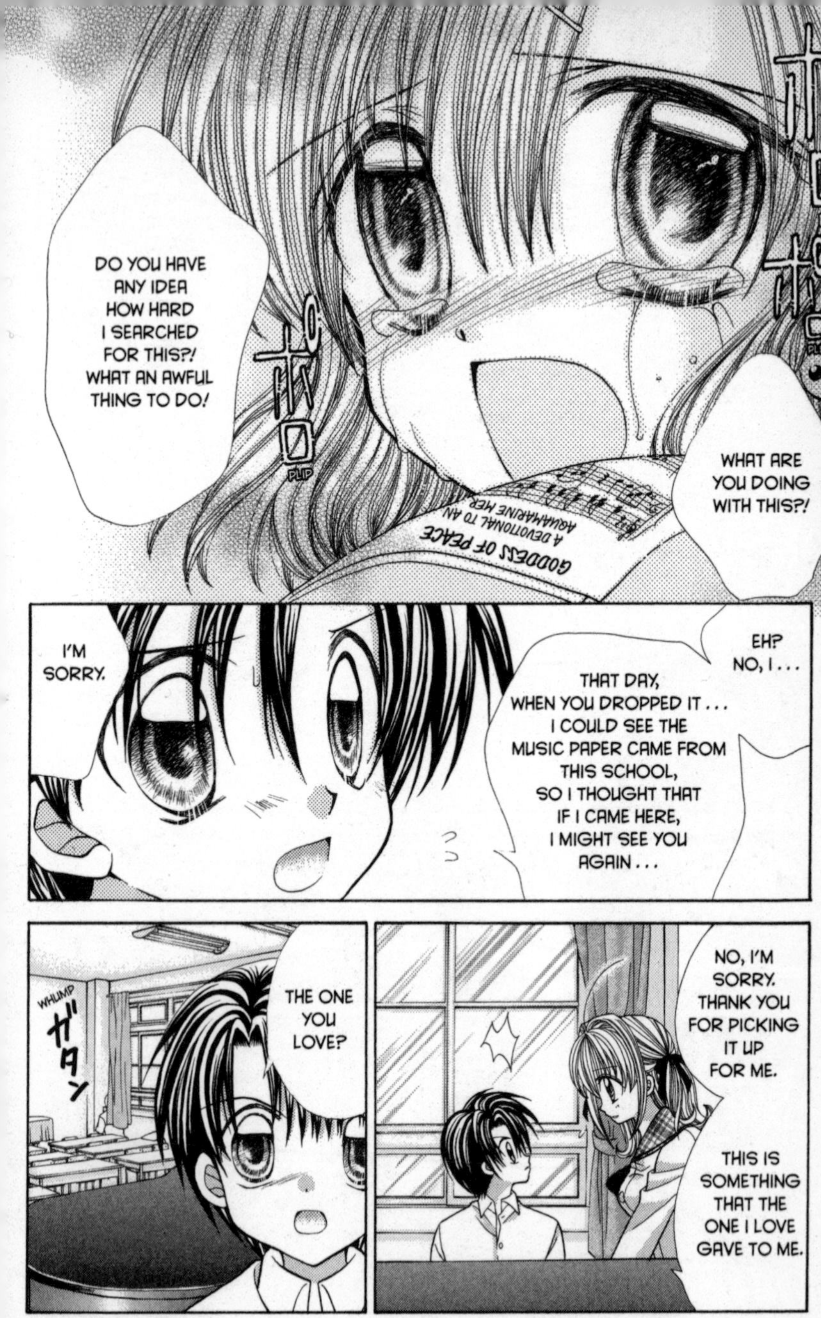
PLIP
PLIP
WHAT ARE YOU DOING WITH THIS?!
PLIP
DO YOU HAVE ANY IDEA HOW HARD I SEARCHED FOR THIS?! WHAT AN AWFUL THING TO DO!
GODDESS OF PEACE
A DEVOTIONAL TO AN AQUAMARINE MER
EH? NO, I . . .
THAT DAY, WHEN YOU DROPPED IT . . . I COULD SEE THE MUSIC PAPER CAME FROM THIS SCHOOL, SO I THOUGHT THAT IF I CAME HERE, I MIGHT SEE YOU AGAIN . . .
I'M SORRY.
NO, I'M SORRY. THANK YOU FOR PICKING IT UP FOR ME.
THIS IS SOMETHING THAT THE ONE I LOVE GAVE TO ME.
THE ONE YOU LOVE?
WHUMP

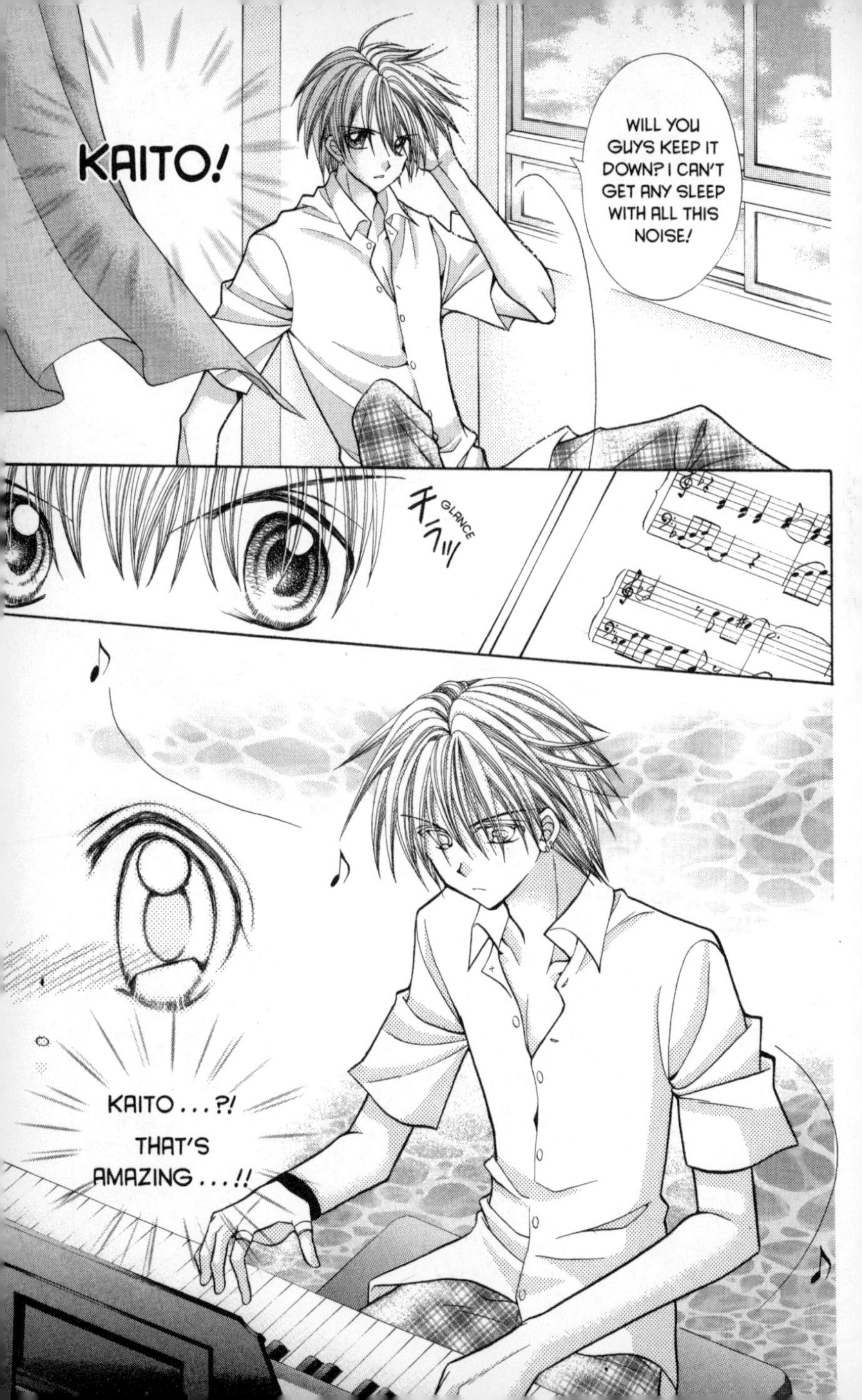
WILL YOU GUYS KEEP IT DOWN? I CAN'T GET ANY SLEEP WITH ALL THIS NOISE!
KAITO!
GLANCE
KAITO . . . ?!
THAT'S AMAZING . . . !!

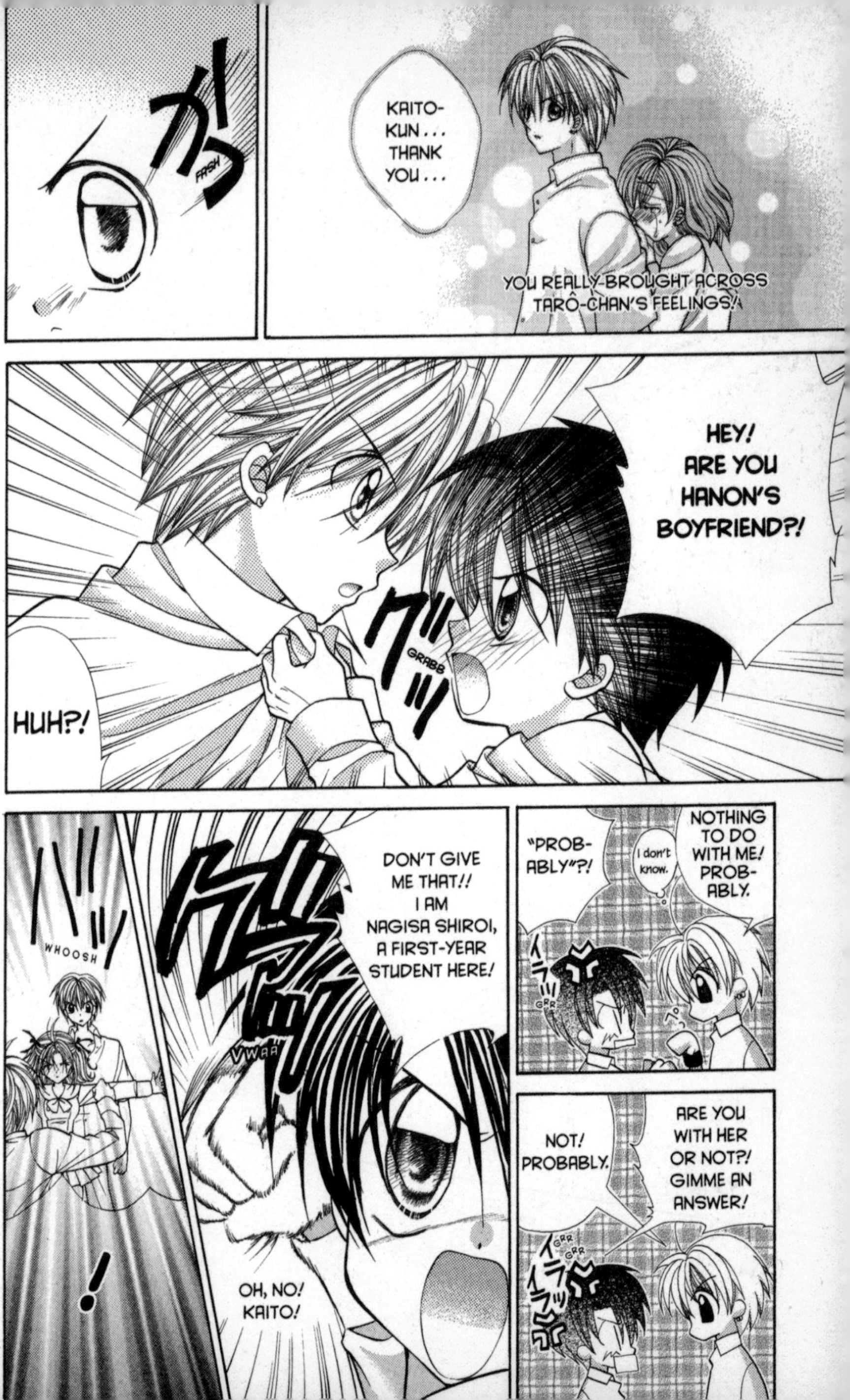
KAITO-KUN . . . THANK YOU . . .
YOU REALLY BROUGHT ACROSS TARÔ-CHAN'S FEELINGS!
FASH
HEY! ARE YOU HANON'S BOYFRIEND?!
GRABB
HUH?!
NOTHING TO DO WITH ME! PROBABLY.
I don't know.
"PROB-ABLY"?!
GRR
ARE YOU WITH HER OR NOT?! GIMME AN ANSWER!
NOT! PROBABLY.
GRR GRR
DON'T GIVE ME THAT!! I AM NAGISA SHIROI, A FIRST-YEAR STUDENT HERE!
VWAA
OH, NO! KAITO!
WHOOSH

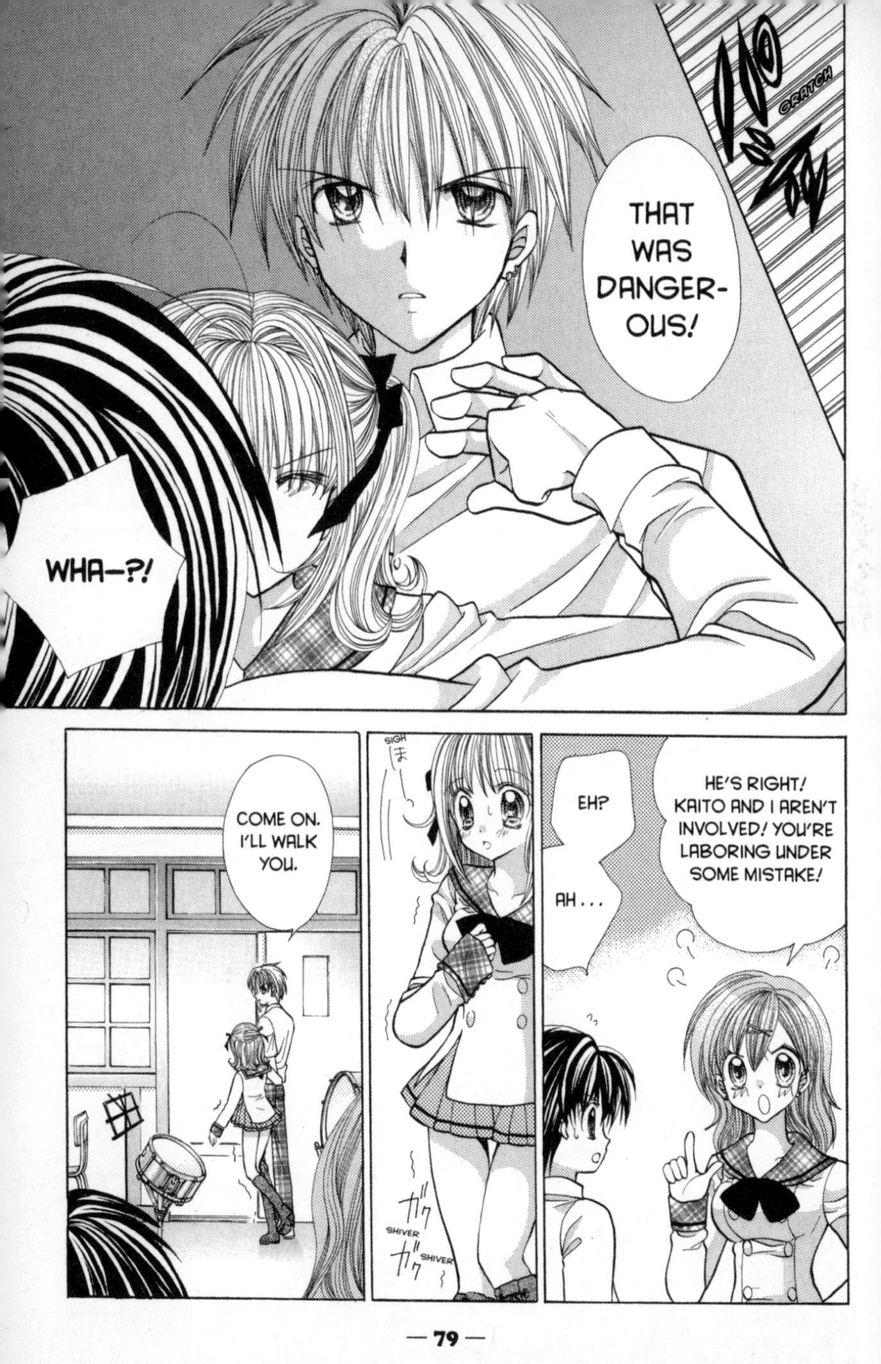
SCRATCH
THAT WAS DANGER-OUS!
WHA–?!
HE'S RIGHT! KAITO AND I AREN'T INVOLVED! YOU'RE LABORING UNDER SOME MISTAKE!
EH?
AH . . .
SIGH
SHIVER
SHIVER
COME ON. I'LL WALK YOU.

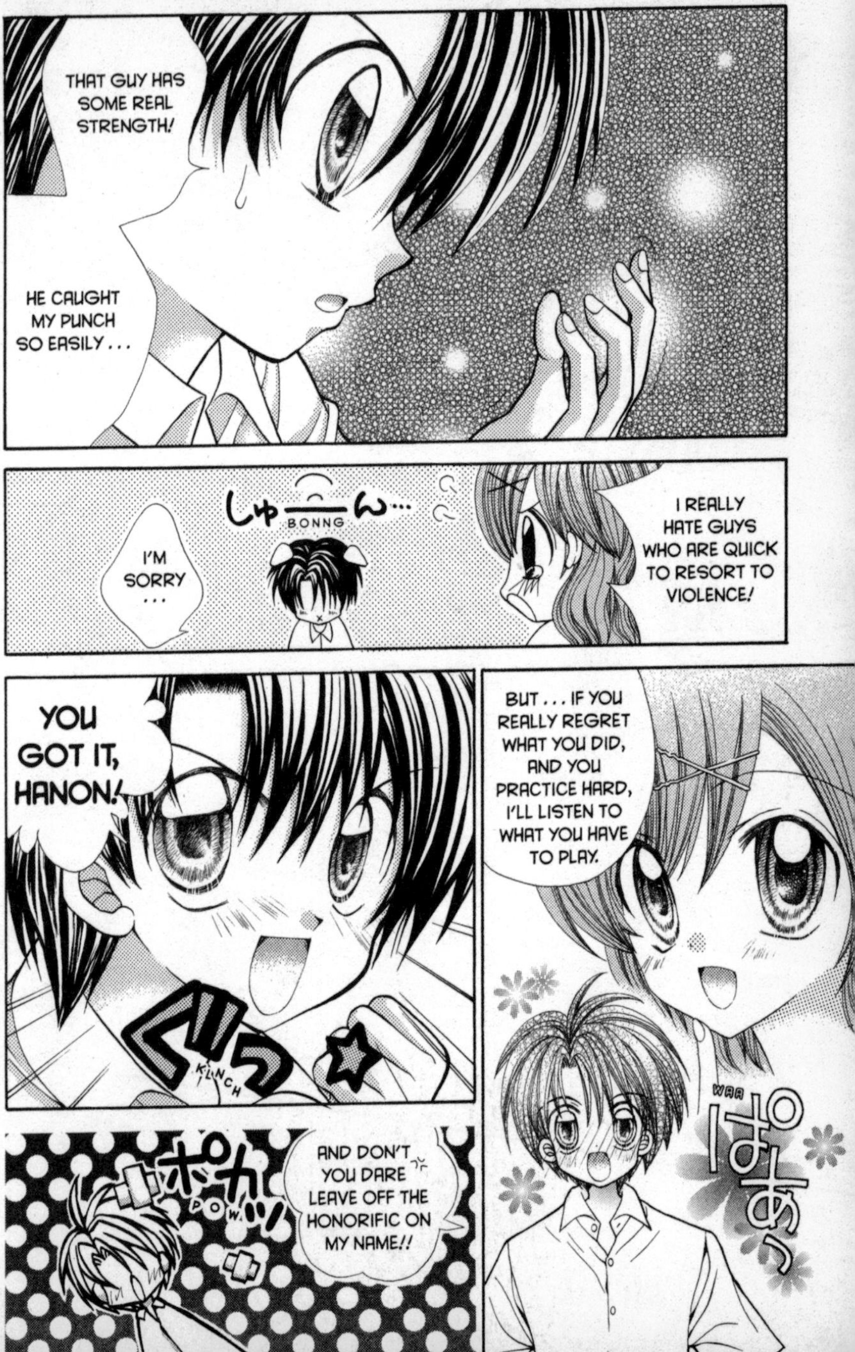
THAT GUY HAS SOME REAL STRENGTH!
HE CAUGHT MY PUNCH SO EASILY . . .
I REALLY HATE GUYS WHO ARE QUICK TO RESORT TO VIOLENCE!
しゅーん… BONNG
I'M SORRY . . .
BUT . . . IF YOU REALLY REGRET WHAT YOU DID, AND YOU PRACTICE HARD, I'LL LISTEN TO WHAT YOU HAVE TO PLAY.
ぱあっ WAA
YOU GOT IT, HANON!
ぐっ KLINCH
AND DON'T YOU DARE LEAVE OFF THE HONORIFIC ON MY NAME!!
ポカッ POW

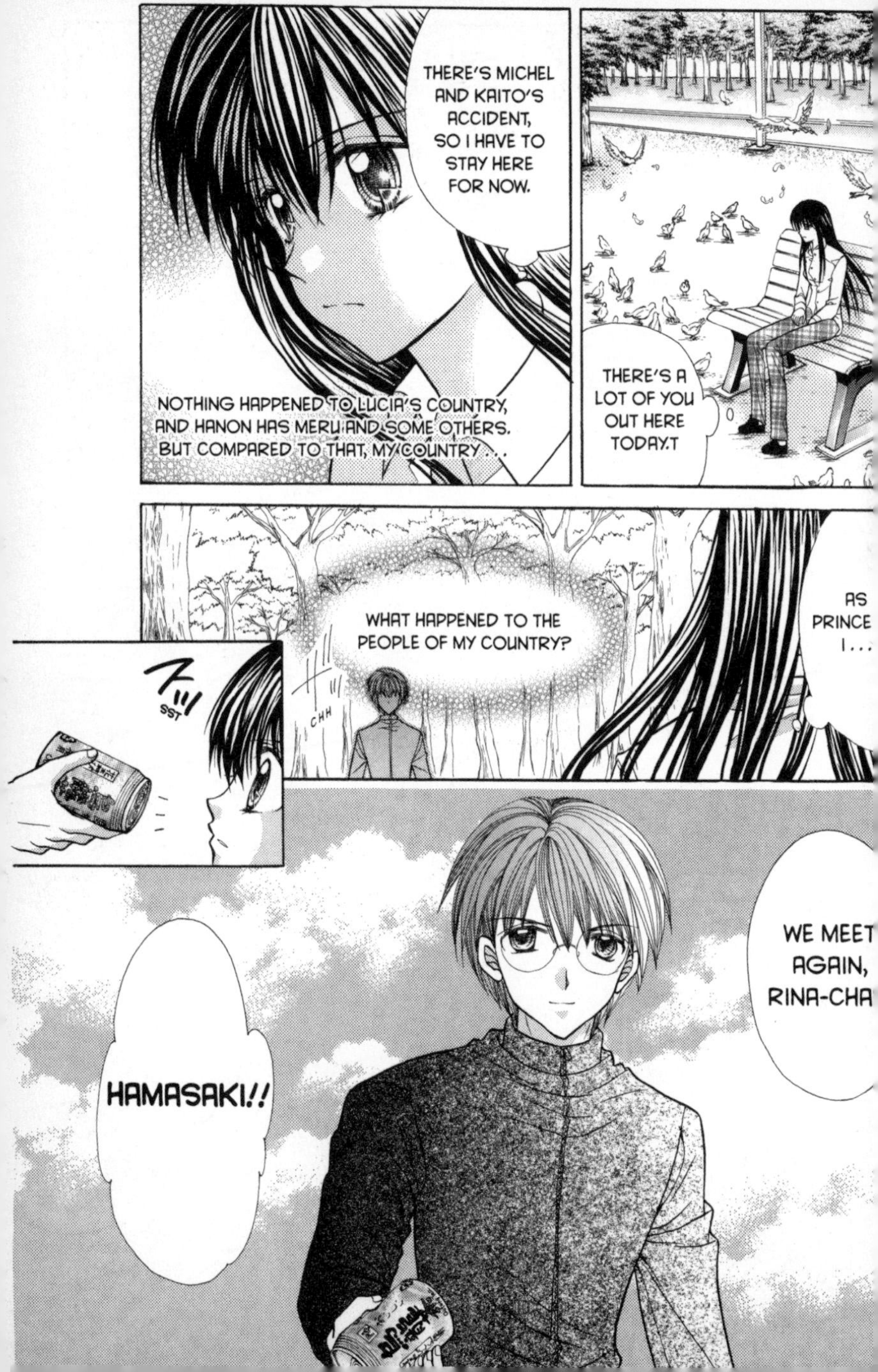

THERE'S A LOT OF YOU OUT HERE TODAY.T
THERE'S MICHEL AND KAITO'S ACCIDENT, SO I HAVE TO STAY HERE FOR NOW.
NOTHING HAPPENED TO LUCIA'S COUNTRY, AND HANON HAS MERU AND SOME OTHERS. BUT COMPARED TO THAT, MY COUNTRY . . .
AS PRINCE I . . .
WHAT HAPPENED TO THE PEOPLE OF MY COUNTRY?
CHH
SST
WE MEET AGAIN, RINA-CHA
HAMASAKI!!

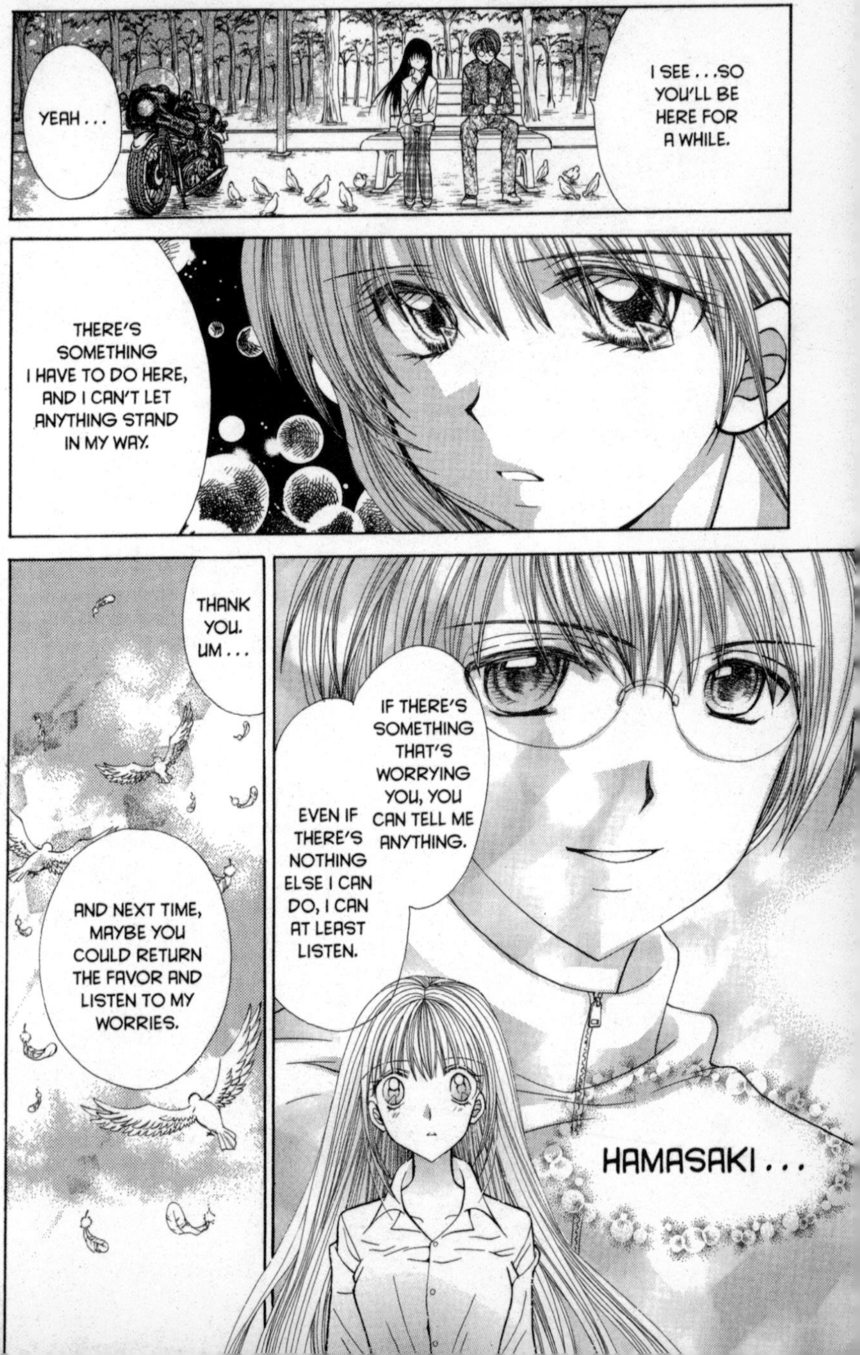
I SEE . . . SO YOU'LL BE HERE FOR A WHILE.
YEAH . . .
THERE'S SOMETHING I HAVE TO DO HERE, AND I CAN'T LET ANYTHING STAND IN MY WAY.
IF THERE'S SOMETHING THAT'S WORRYING YOU, YOU CAN TELL ME ANYTHING.
EVEN IF THERE'S NOTHING ELSE I CAN DO, I CAN AT LEAST LISTEN.
HAMASAKI . . .
THANK YOU. UM . . .
AND NEXT TIME, MAYBE YOU COULD RETURN THE FAVOR AND LISTEN TO MY WORRIES.

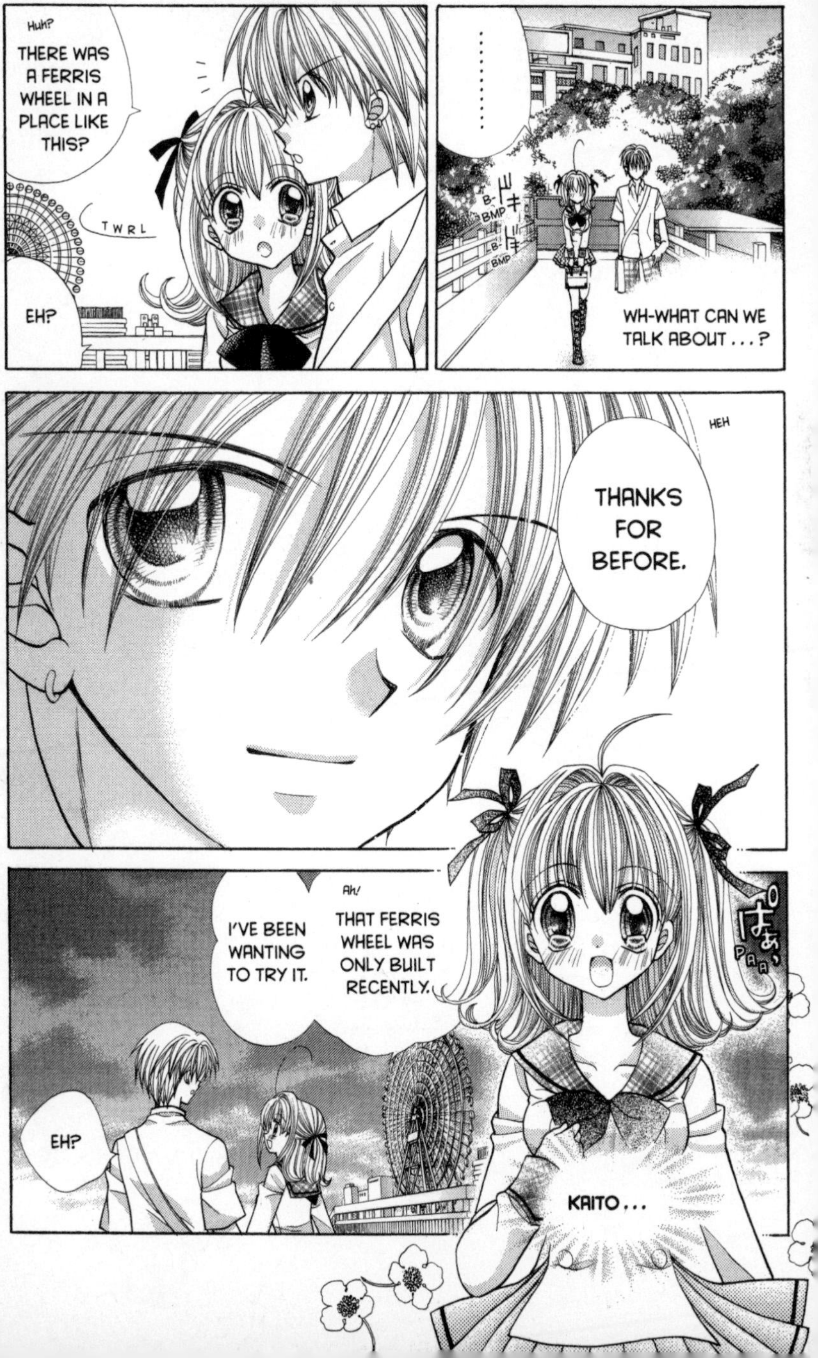
......
B-BMP
B-BMP
WH-WHAT CAN WE TALK ABOUT . . . ?
Huh?
THERE WAS A FERRIS WHEEL IN A PLACE LIKE THIS?
TWRL
EH?
HEH
THANKS FOR BEFORE.
ぱぁ
PAA
Ah!
THAT FERRIS WHEEL WAS ONLY BUILT RECENTLY.
I'VE BEEN WANTING TO TRY IT.
KAITO . . .
EH?

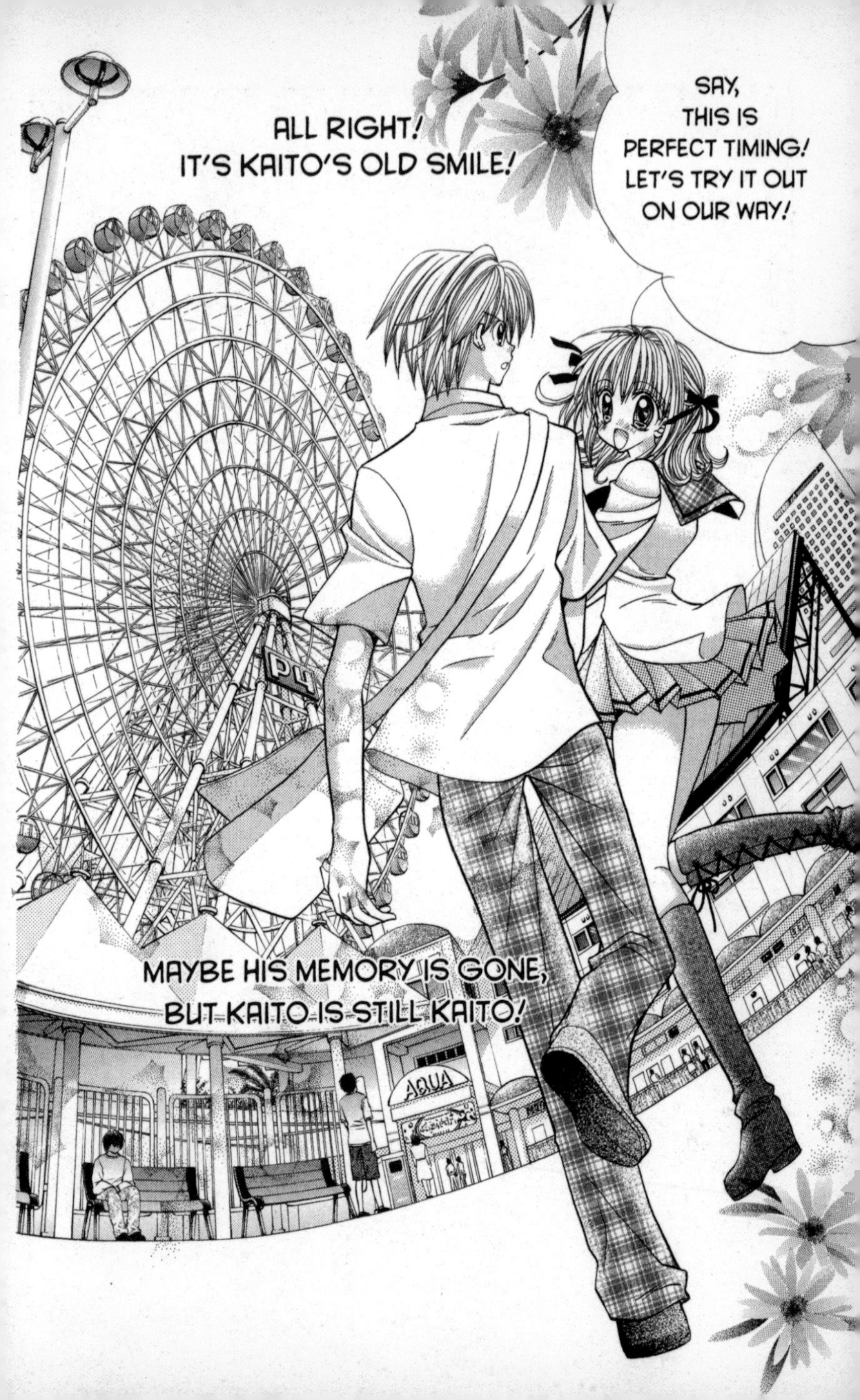
SAY, THIS IS PERFECT TIMING! LET'S TRY IT OUT ON OUR WAY!
ALL RIGHT! IT'S KAITO'S OLD SMILE!
MAYBE HIS MEMORY IS GONE, BUT KAITO IS STILL KAITO!
AQUA

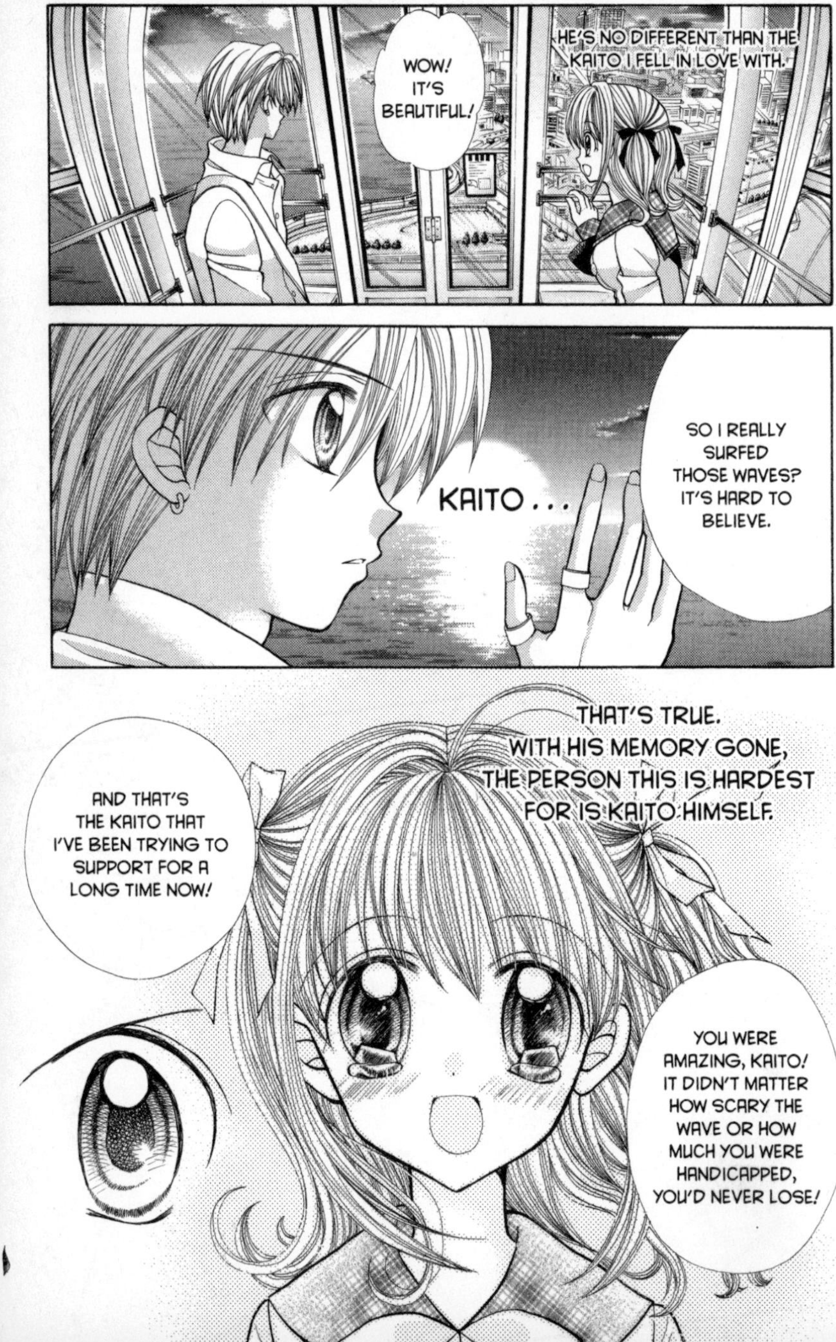
HE'S NO DIFFERENT THAN THE KAITO I FELL IN LOVE WITH.
WOW! IT'S BEAUTIFUL!
SO I REALLY SURFED THOSE WAVES? IT'S HARD TO BELIEVE.
KAITO . . .
THAT'S TRUE. WITH HIS MEMORY GONE, THE PERSON THIS IS HARDEST FOR IS KAITO HIMSELF.
YOU WERE AMAZING, KAITO! IT DIDN'T MATTER HOW SCARY THE WAVE OR HOW MUCH YOU WERE HANDICAPPED, YOU'D NEVER LOSE!
AND THAT'S THE KAITO THAT I'VE BEEN TRYING TO SUPPORT FOR A LONG TIME NOW!

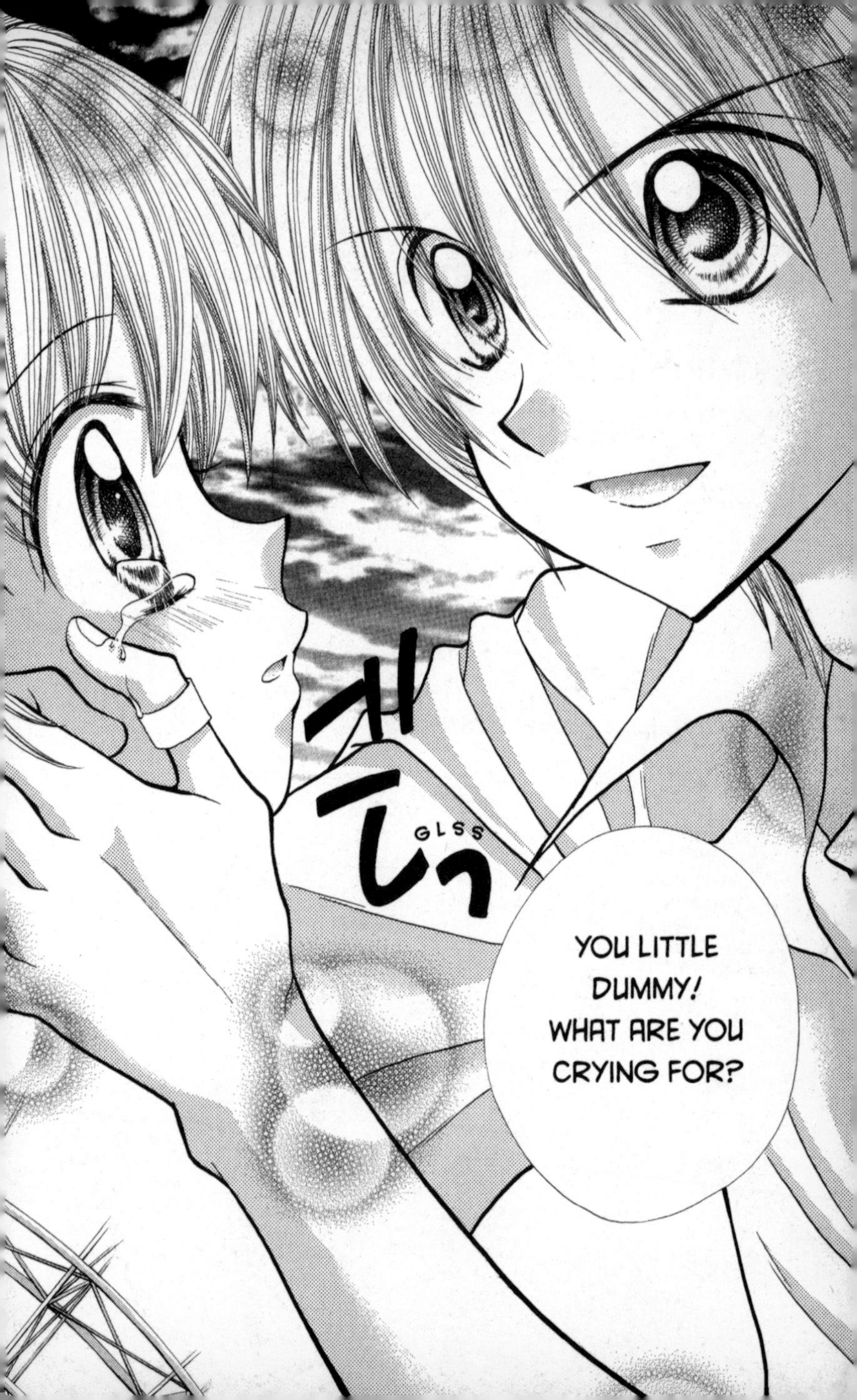
GLSS
YOU LITTLE DUMMY! WHAT ARE YOU CRYING FOR?

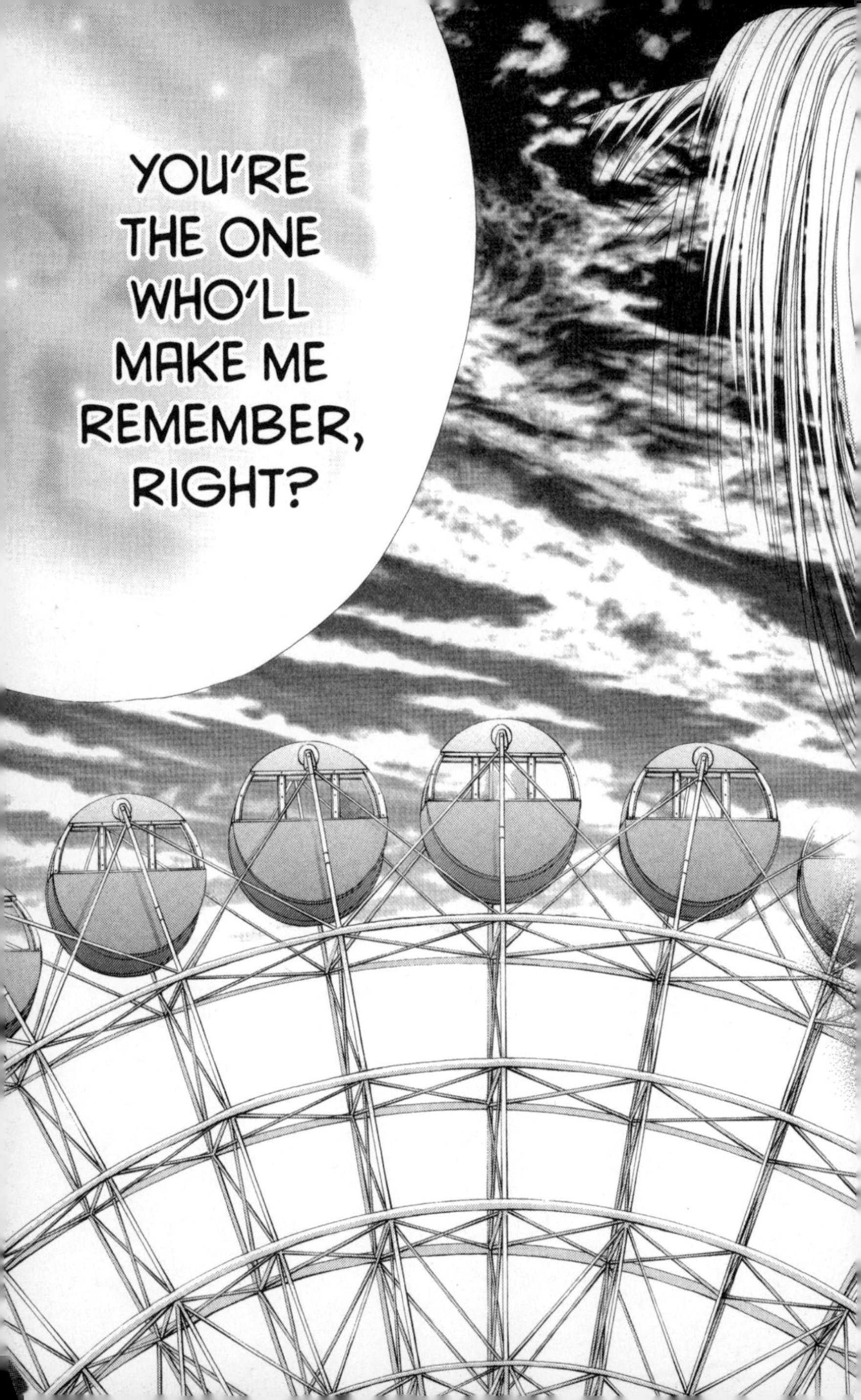
YOU'RE THE ONE WHO'LL MAKE ME REMEMBER, RIGHT?

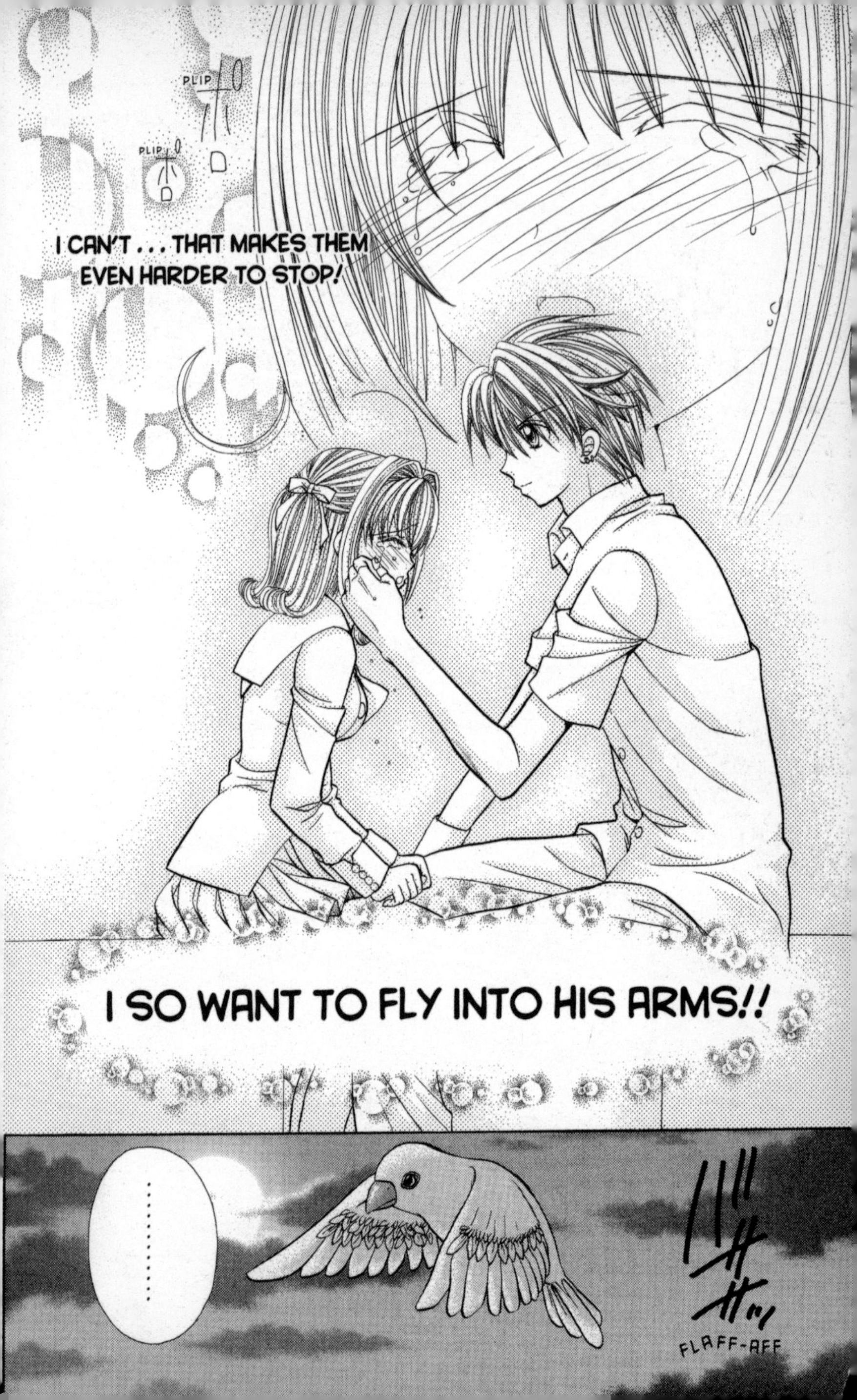
PLIP
PLIP
I CAN'T . . . THAT MAKES THEM EVEN HARDER TO STOP!
I SO WANT TO FLY INTO HIS ARMS!!
FLAFF-AFF
. . . .

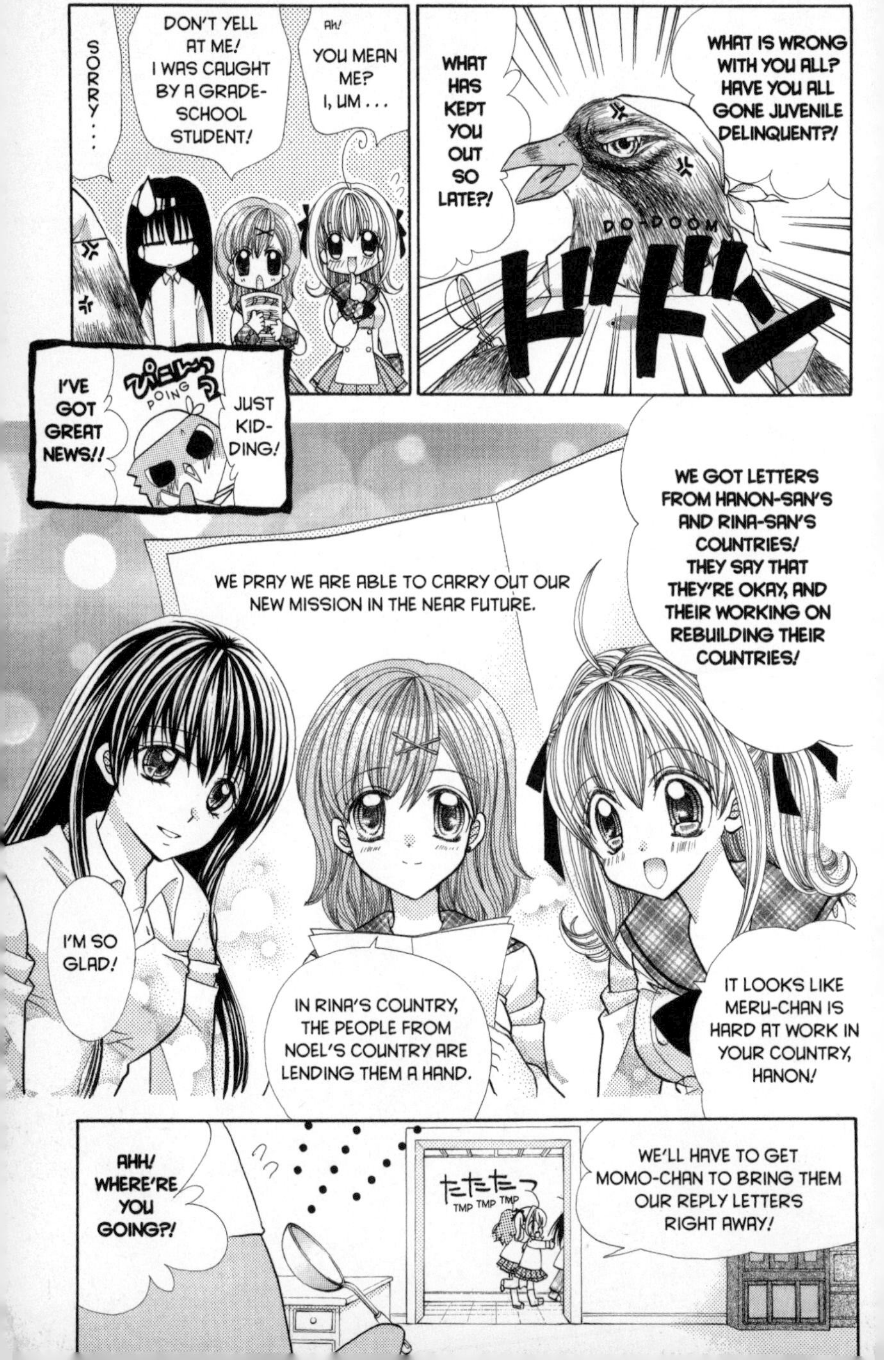
WHAT IS WRONG WITH YOU ALL? HAVE YOU ALL GONE JUVENILE DELINQUENT?!
WHAT HAS KEPT YOU OUT SO LATE?!
DO-DOOM
Ah!
YOU MEAN ME? I, UM . . .
DON'T YELL AT ME! I WAS CAUGHT BY A GRADE-SCHOOL STUDENT!
SORRY . . .
POING
JUST KID-DING!
I'VE GOT GREAT NEWS!!
WE GOT LETTERS FROM HANON-SAN'S AND RINA-SAN'S COUNTRIES! THEY SAY THAT THEY'RE OKAY, AND THEIR WORKING ON REBUILDING THEIR COUNTRIES!
WE PRAY WE ARE ABLE TO CARRY OUT OUR NEW MISSION IN THE NEAR FUTURE.
IT LOOKS LIKE MERU-CHAN IS HARD AT WORK IN YOUR COUNTRY, HANON!
IN RINA'S COUNTRY, THE PEOPLE FROM NOEL'S COUNTRY ARE LENDING THEM A HAND.
I'M SO GLAD!
WE'LL HAVE TO GET MOMO-CHAN TO BRING THEM OUR REPLY LETTERS RIGHT AWAY!
たたたっ
TMP TMP TMP
AHH! WHERE'RE YOU GOING?!

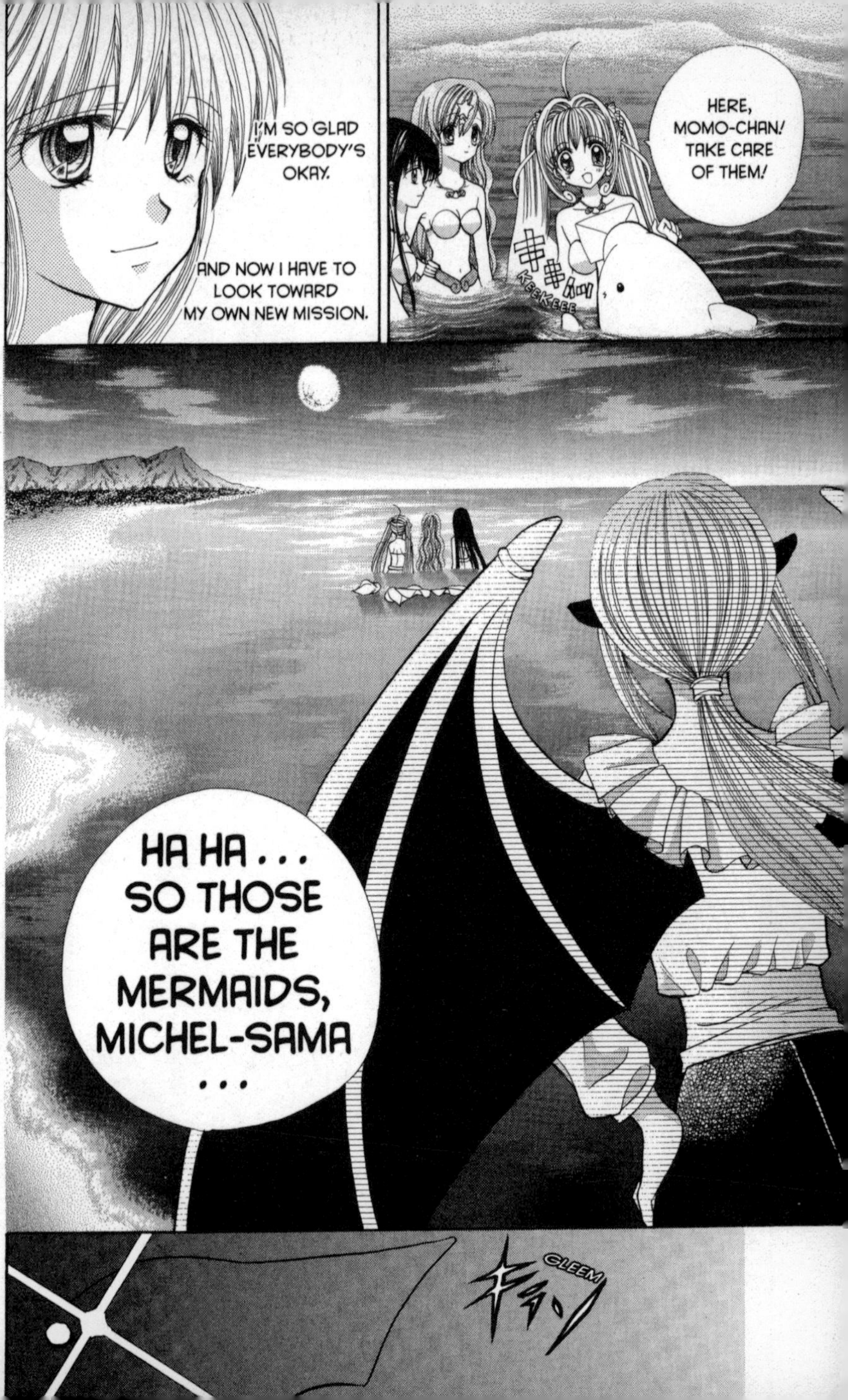
HERE, MOMO-CHAN! TAKE CARE OF THEM!
KEEKEEE
I'M SO GLAD EVERYBODY'S OKAY.
AND NOW I HAVE TO LOOK TOWARD MY OWN NEW MISSION.
HA HA . . . SO THOSE ARE THE MERMAIDS, MICHEL-SAMA . . .
GLEEM

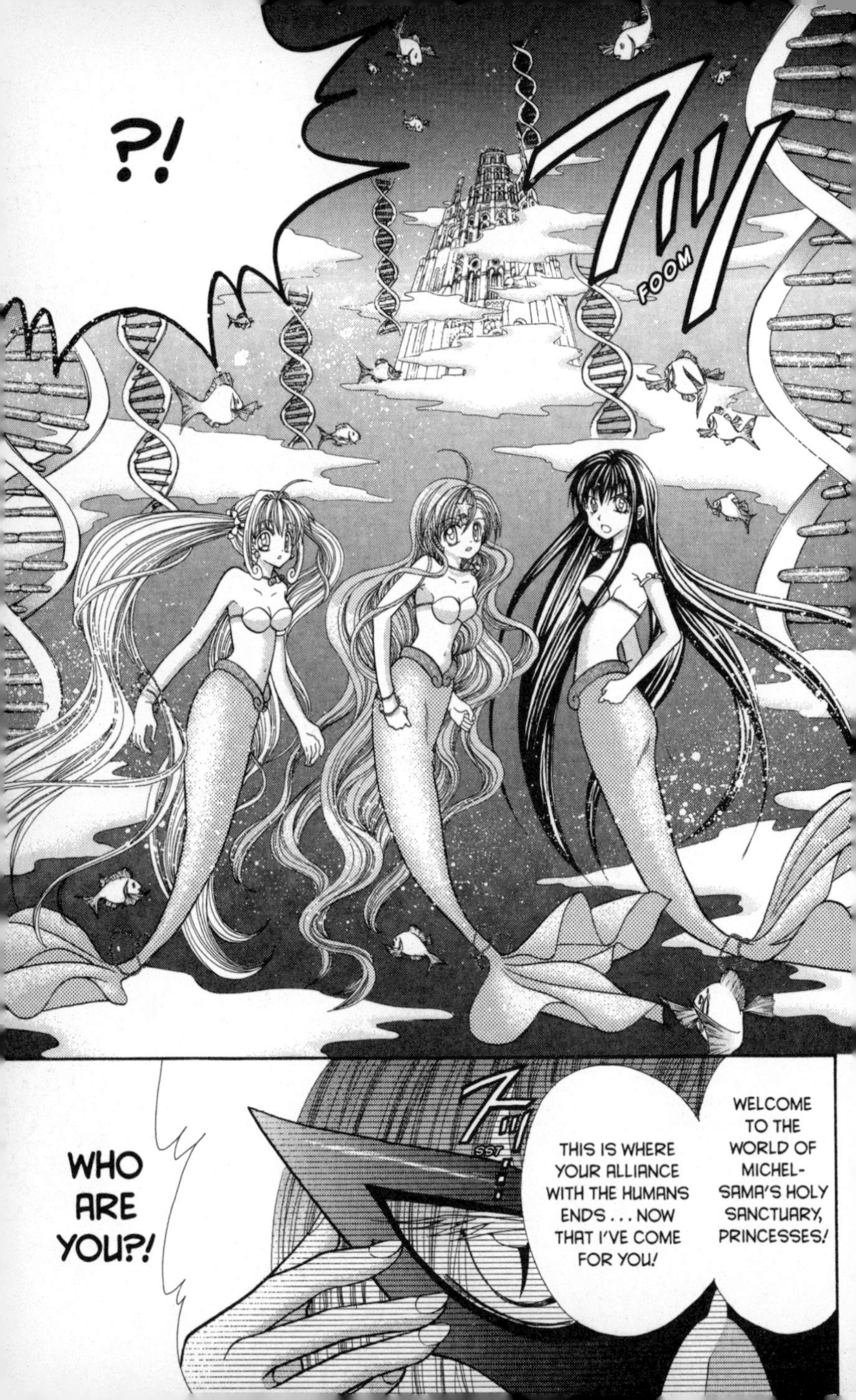
FOOM
?!
WELCOME TO THE WORLD OF MICHEL-SAMA'S HOLY SANCTUARY, PRINCESSES!
THIS IS WHERE YOUR ALLIANCE WITH THE HUMANS ENDS . . . NOW THAT I'VE COME FOR YOU!
SST
WHO ARE YOU?!

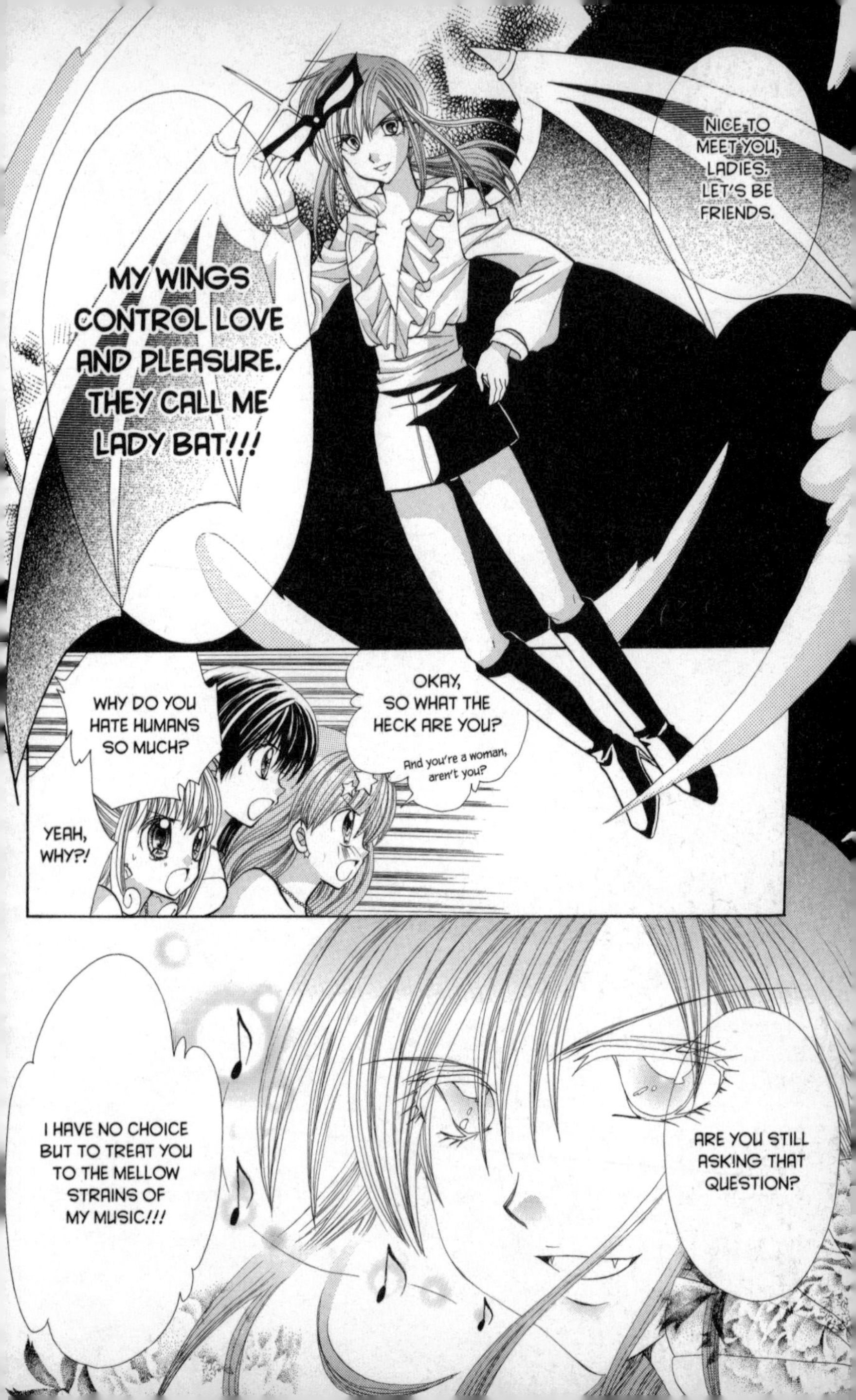
NICE TO MEET YOU, LADIES. LET'S BE FRIENDS.
MY WINGS CONTROL LOVE AND PLEASURE. THEY CALL ME LADY BAT!!!
OKAY, SO WHAT THE HECK ARE YOU?
And you're a woman, aren't you?
WHY DO YOU HATE HUMANS SO MUCH?
YEAH, WHY?!
ARE YOU STILL ASKING THAT QUESTION?
I HAVE NO CHOICE BUT TO TREAT YOU TO THE MELLOW STRAINS OF MY MUSIC!!!

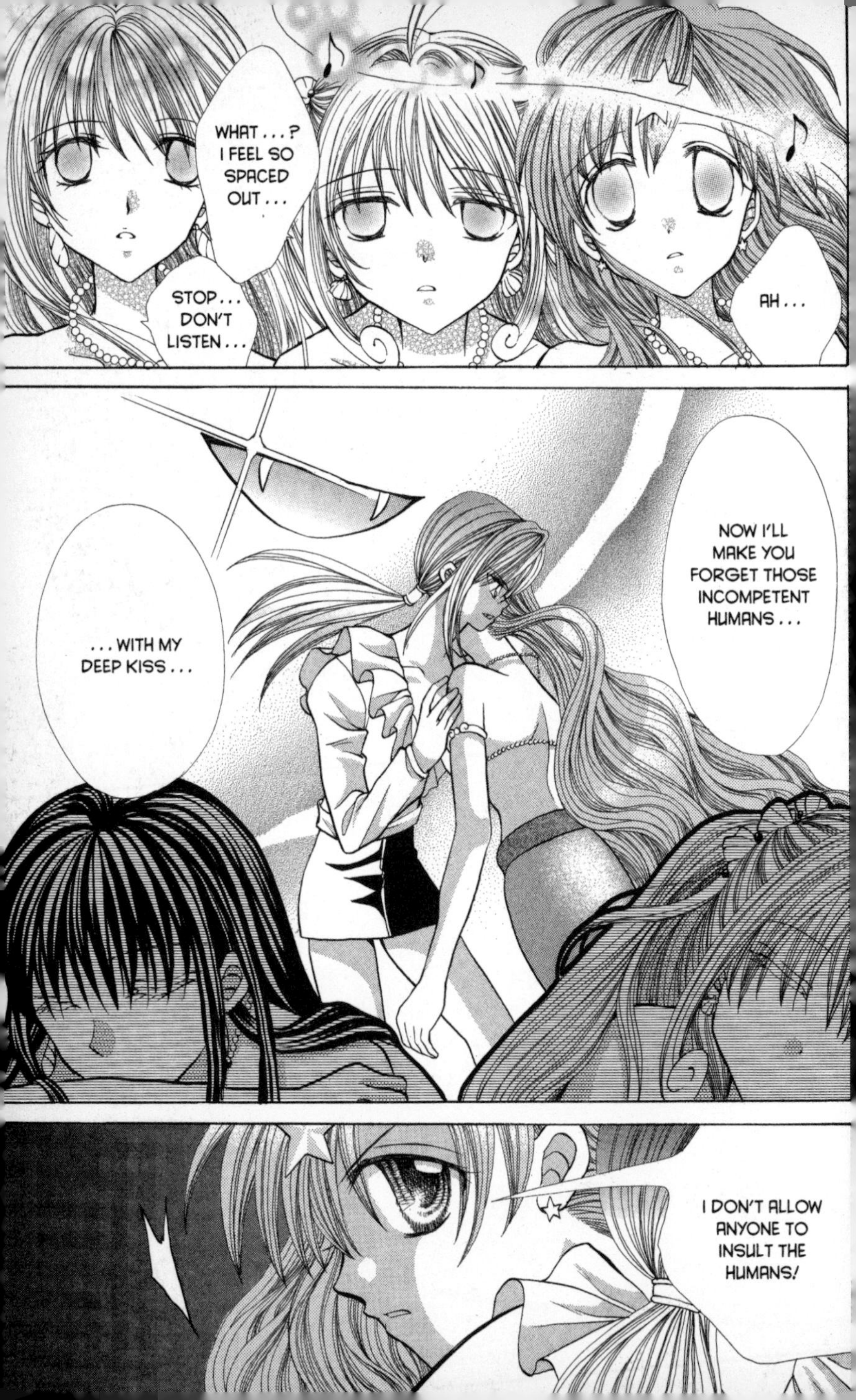
AH . . .
WHAT . . . ? I FEEL SO SPACED OUT . . .
STOP . . . DON'T LISTEN . . .
NOW I'LL MAKE YOU FORGET THOSE INCOMPETENT HUMANS . . .
. . . WITH MY DEEP KISS . . .
I DON'T ALLOW ANYONE TO INSULT THE HUMANS!

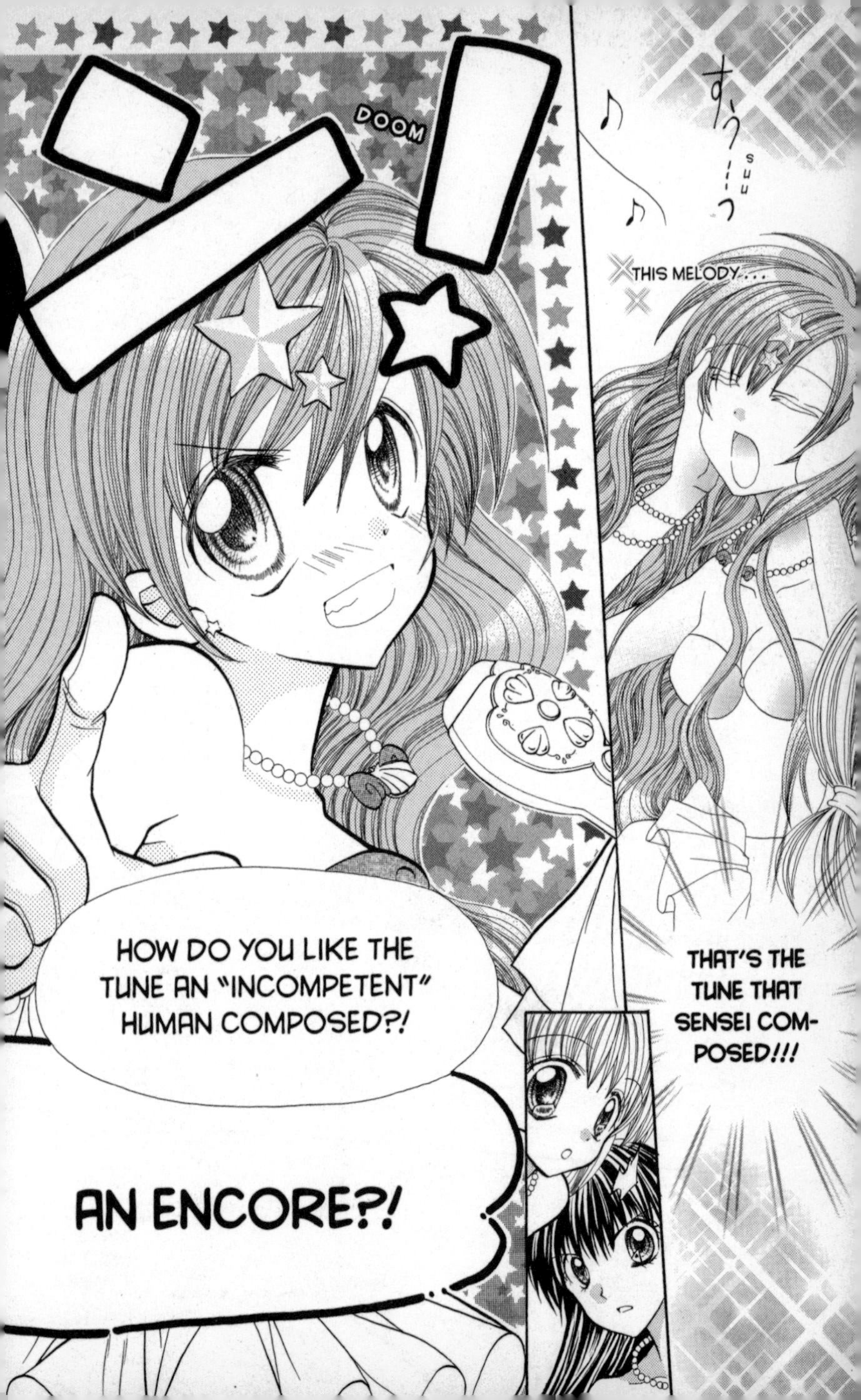
SUU
THIS MELODY...
THAT'S THE TUNE THAT SENSEI COMPOSED!!!
DOOM
HOW DO YOU LIKE THE TUNE AN "INCOMPETENT" HUMAN COMPOSED?!
AN ENCORE?!

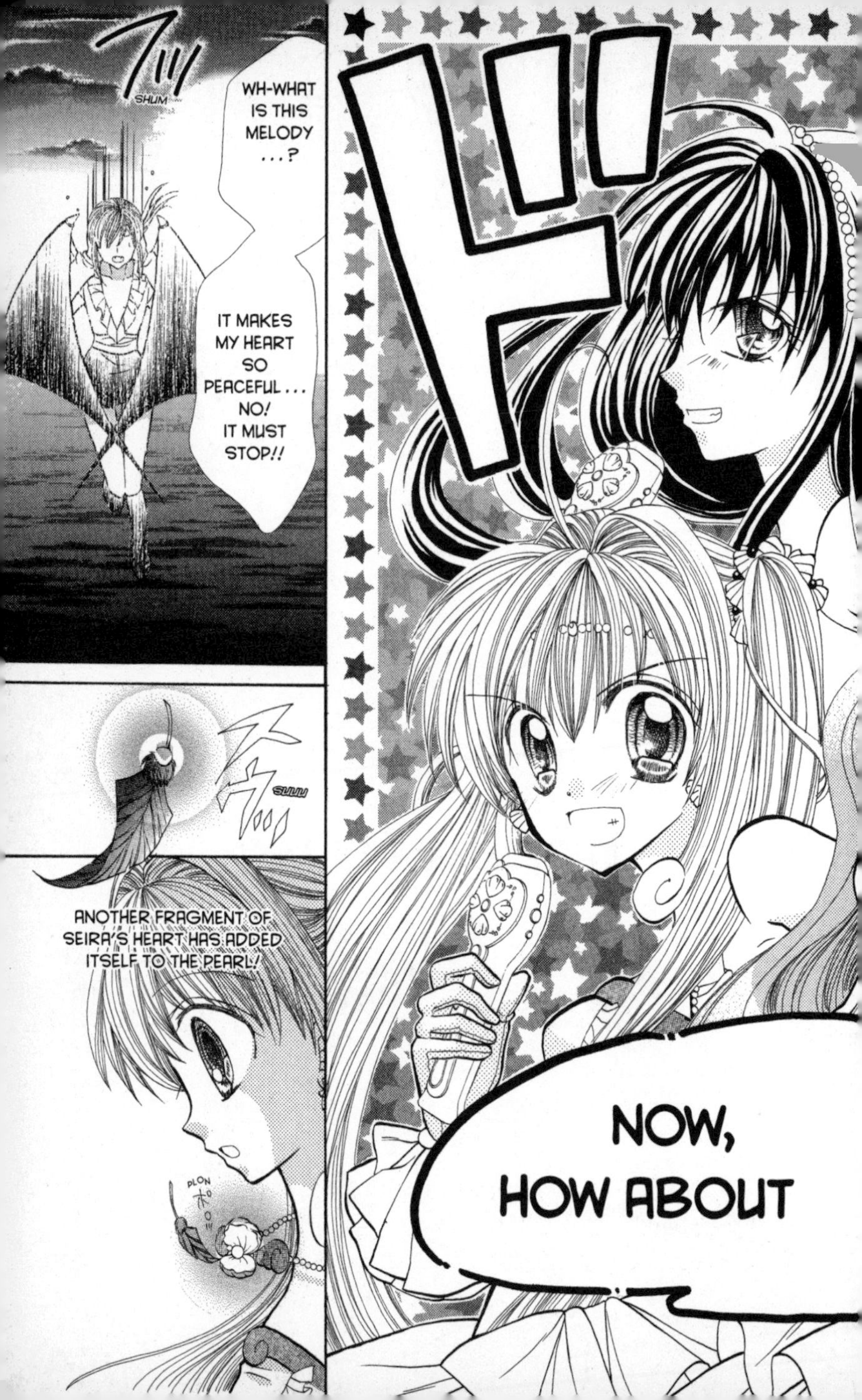
NOW, HOW ABOUT
SHUM
WH-WHAT IS THIS MELODY ...?
IT MAKES MY HEART SO PEACEFUL ... NO! IT MUST STOP!!
SUUU
ANOTHER FRAGMENT OF SEIRA'S HEART HAS ADDED ITSELF TO THE PEARL!
PLON

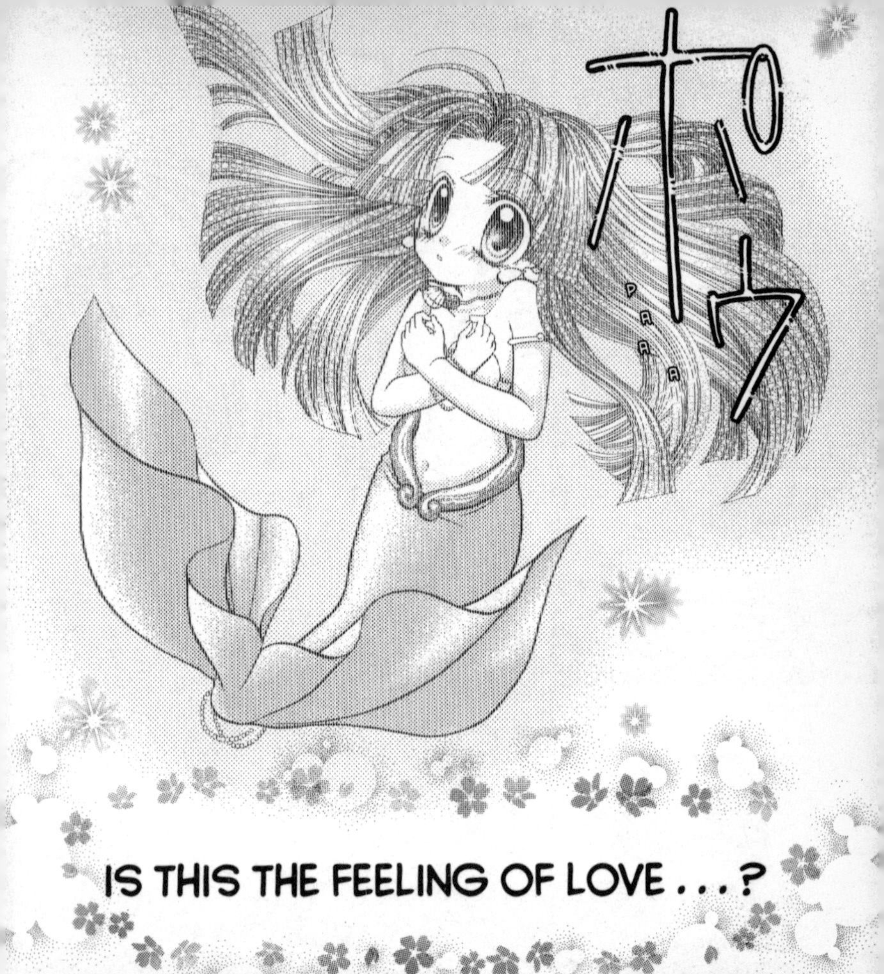
ポワ
PAAAA
IS THIS THE FEELING OF LOVE . . . ?

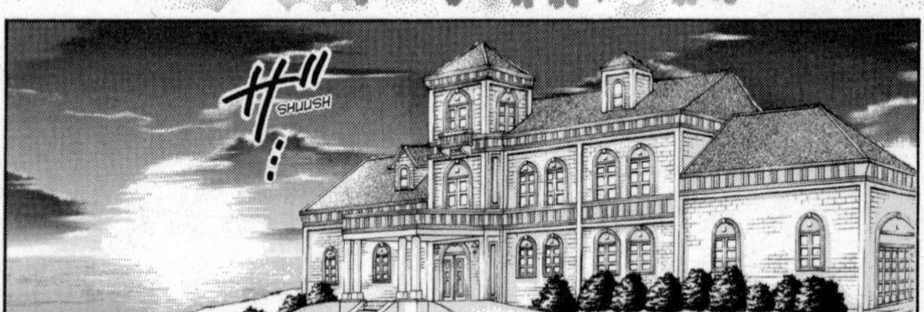
ザ…
SHUUSH

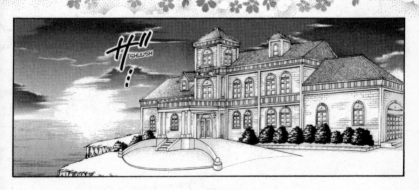

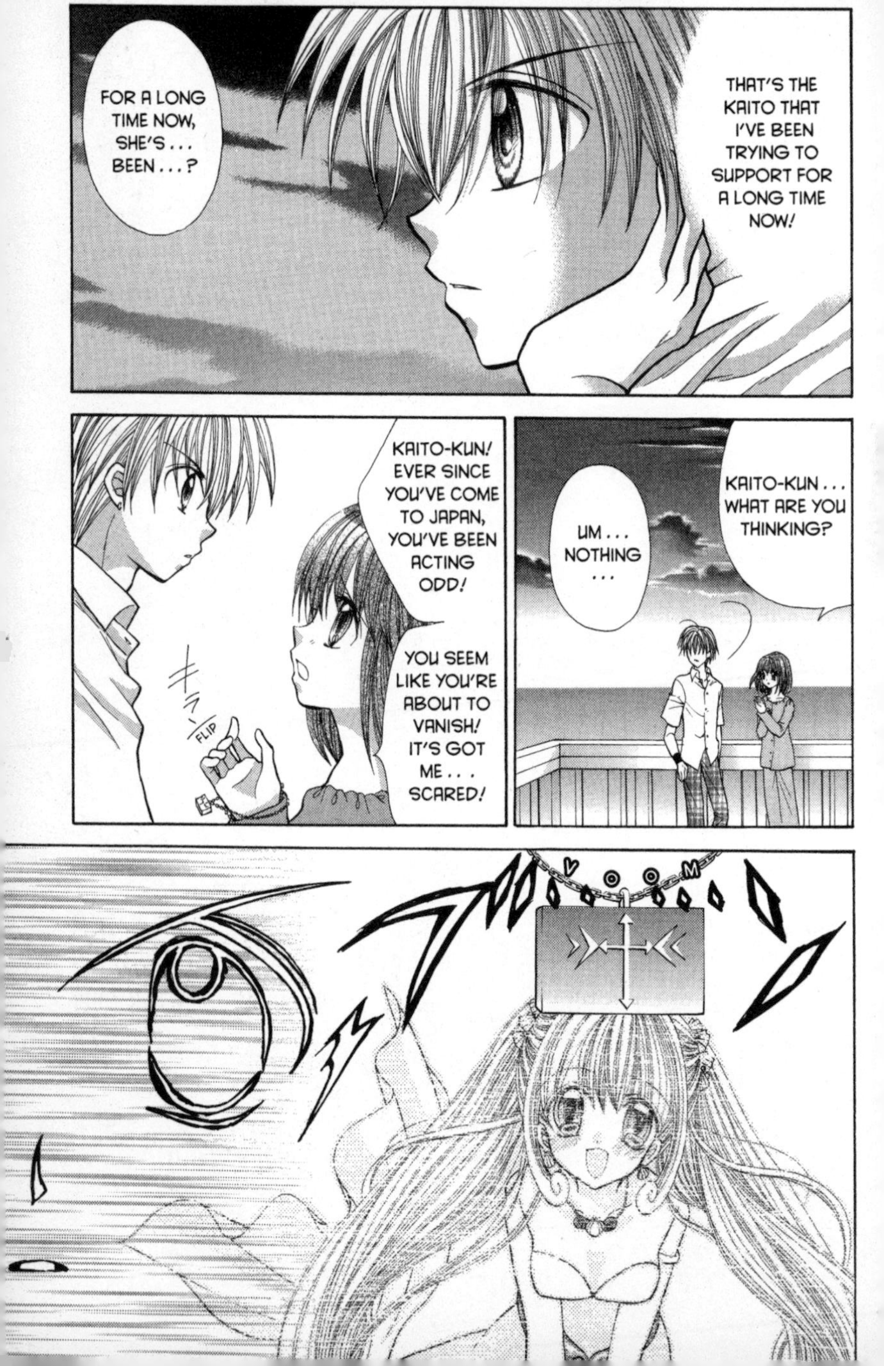
THAT'S THE KAITO THAT I'VE BEEN TRYING TO SUPPORT FOR A LONG TIME NOW!
FOR A LONG TIME NOW, SHE'S... BEEN...?
KAITO-KUN... WHAT ARE YOU THINKING?
UM... NOTHING...
KAITO-KUN! EVER SINCE YOU'VE COME TO JAPAN, YOU'VE BEEN ACTING ODD!
YOU SEEM LIKE YOU'RE ABOUT TO VANISH! IT'S GOT ME... SCARED!
FLIP
VOOM

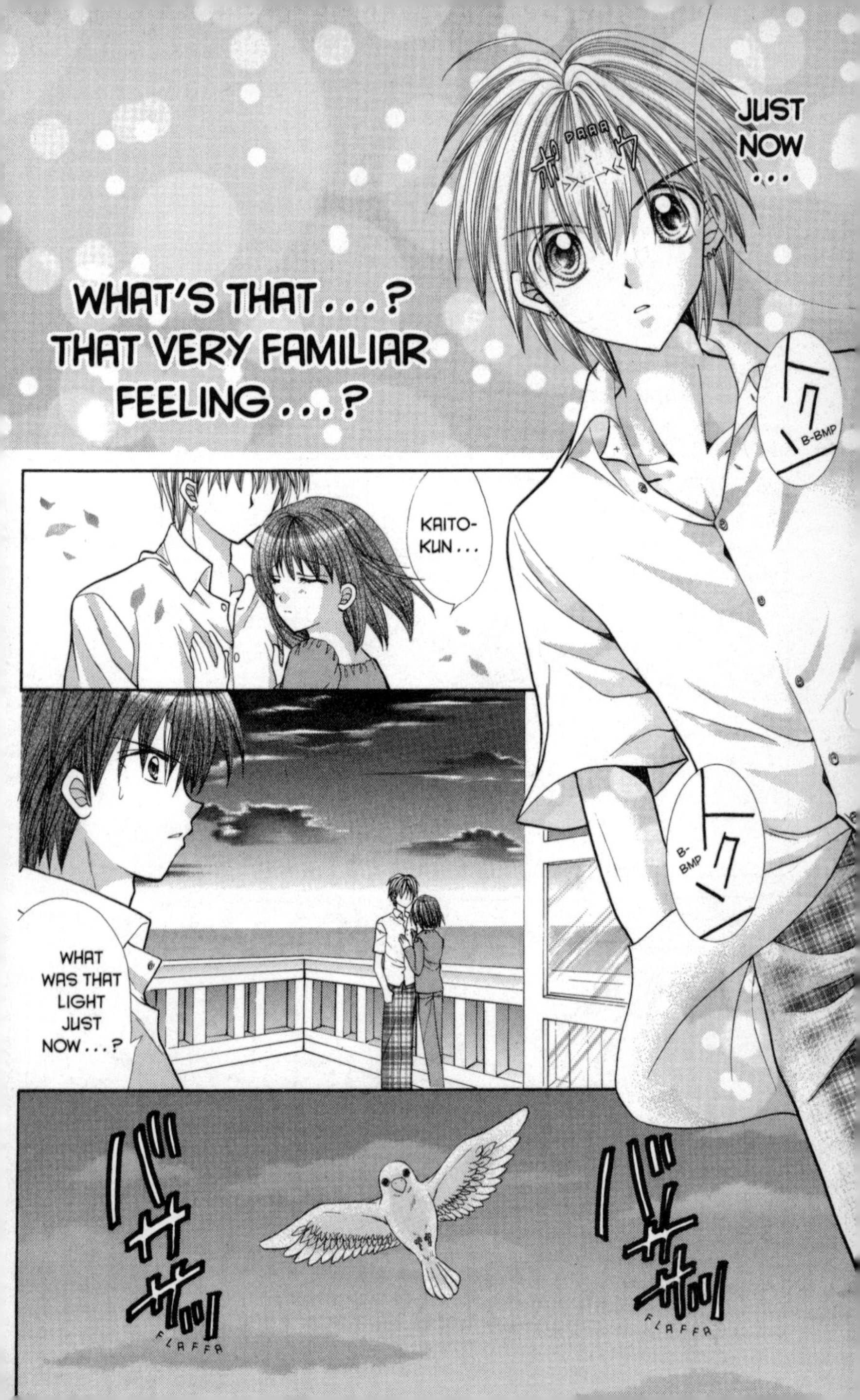
PAAAA
JUST NOW . . .
B-BMP
B-BMP
WHAT'S THAT . . . ? THAT VERY FAMILIAR FEELING . . . ?
KAITO-KUN . . .
WHAT WAS THAT LIGHT JUST NOW . . . ?
FLAFFA
FLAFFA

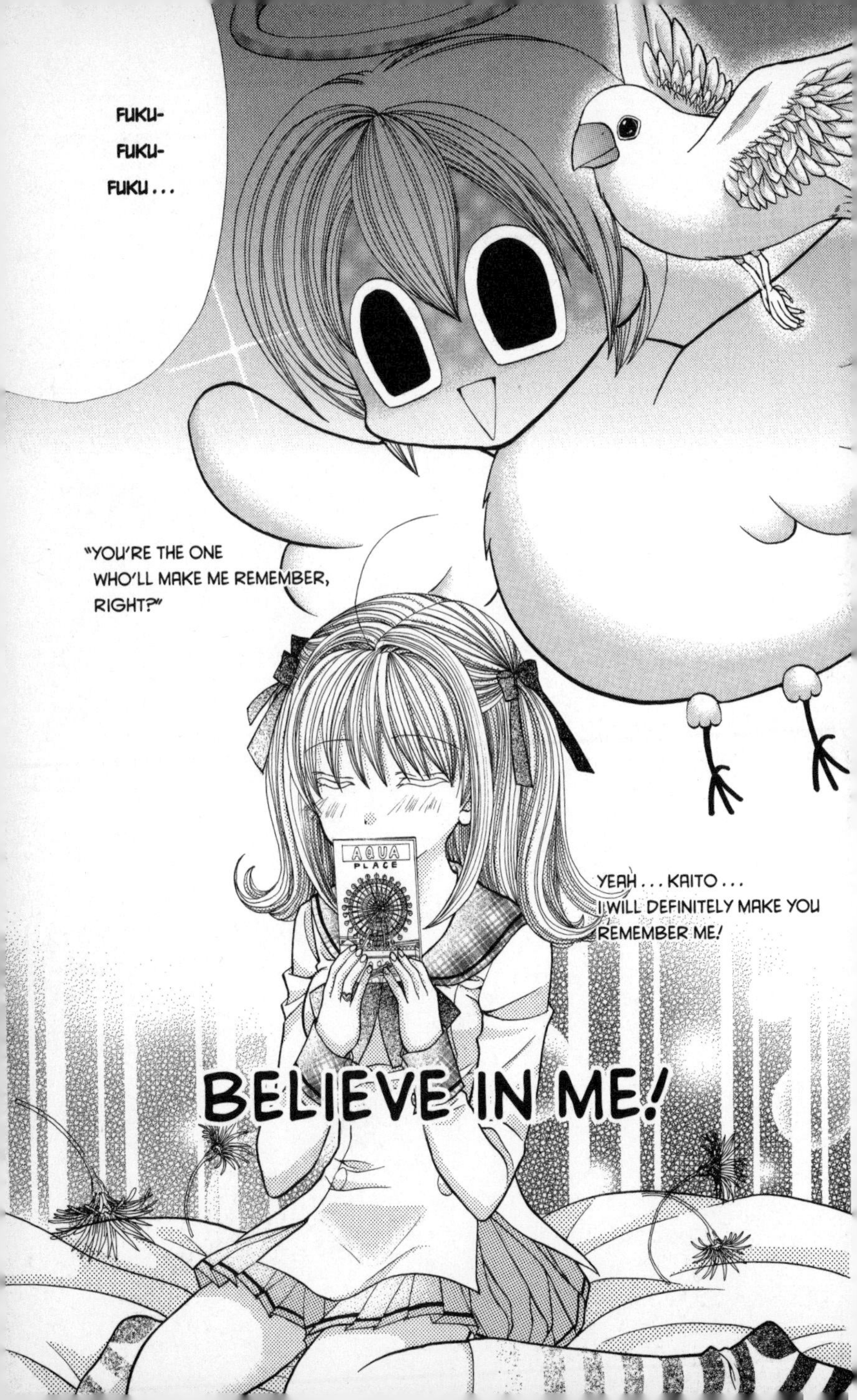
FUKU-
FUKU-
FUKU...
"YOU'RE THE ONE WHO'LL MAKE ME REMEMBER, RIGHT?"
AQUA PLACE
YEAH... KAITO... I WILL DEFINITELY MAKE YOU REMEMBER ME!
BELIEVE IN ME!

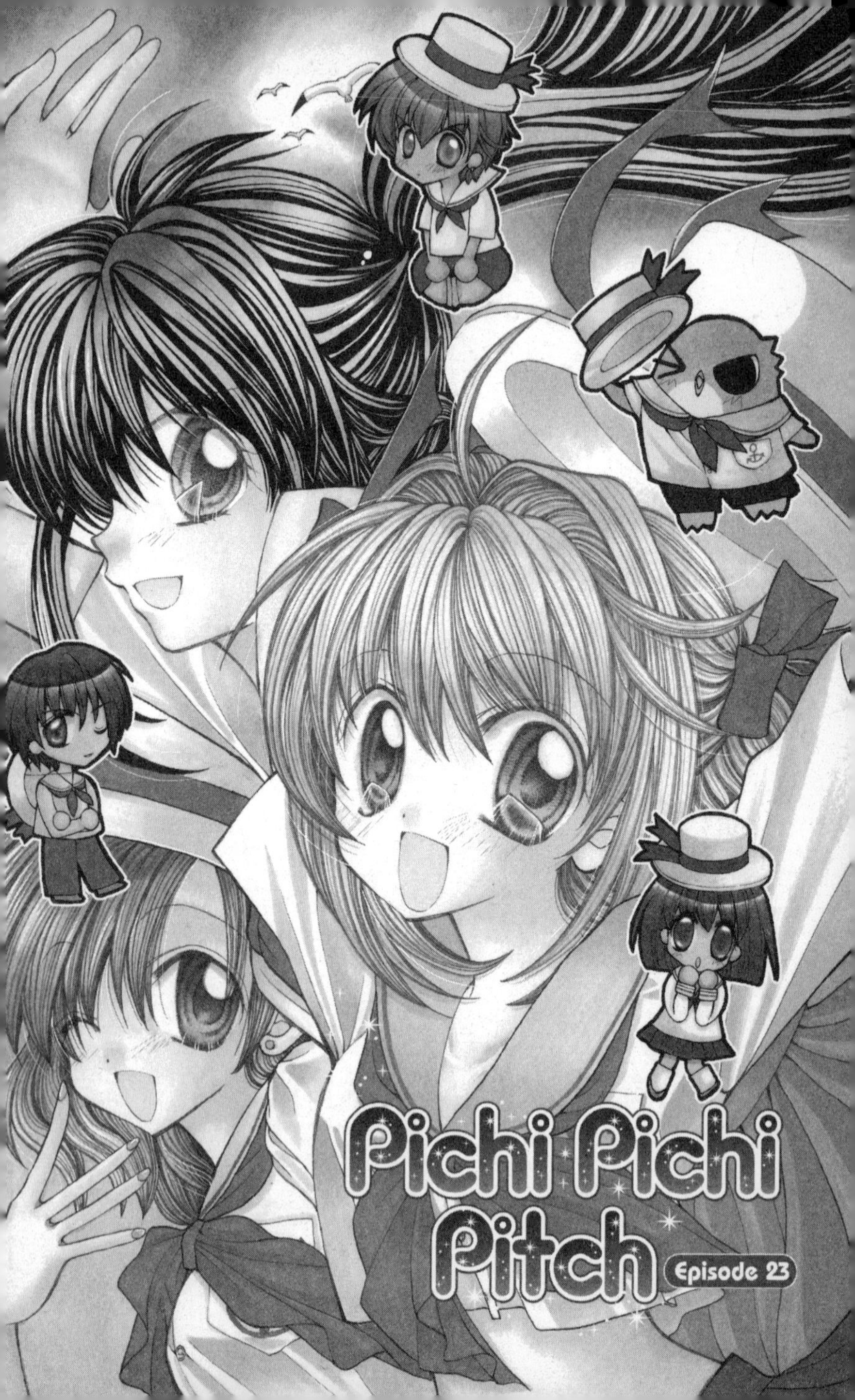
Pichi Pichi Pitch
Episode 23

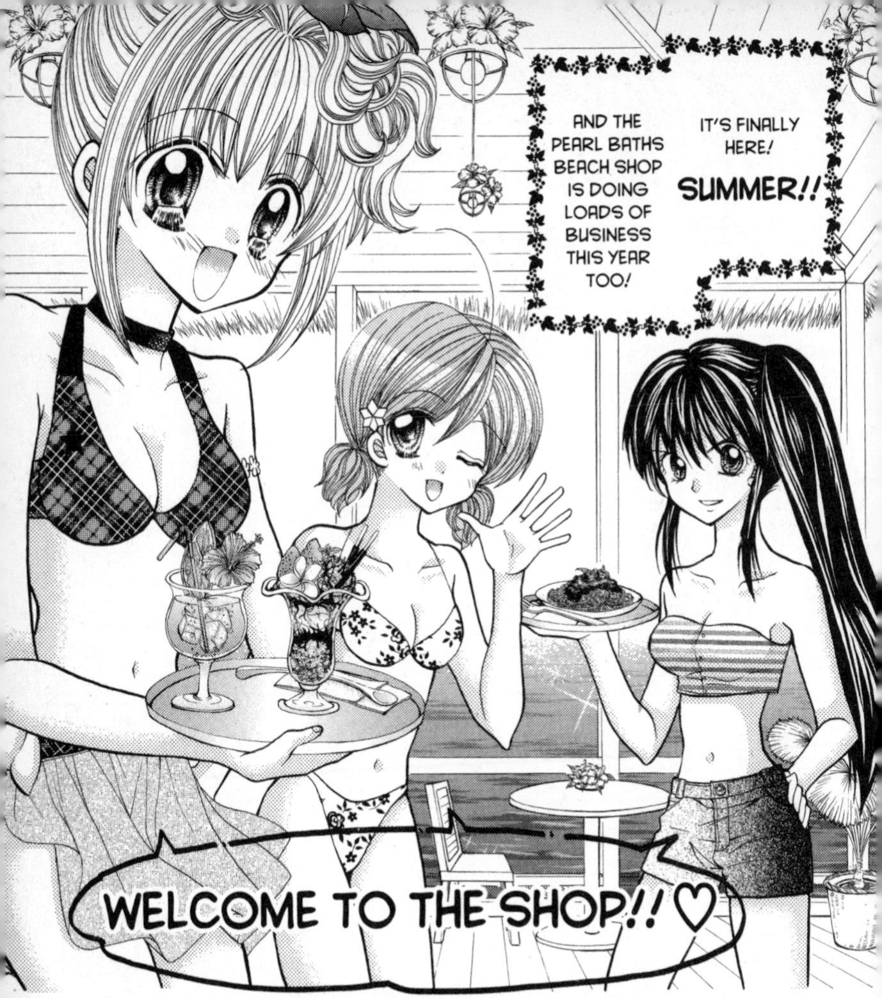
IT'S FINALLY HERE! SUMMER!!
AND THE PEARL BATHS BEACH SHOP IS DOING LOADS OF BUSINESS THIS YEAR TOO!
WELCOME TO THE SHOP!! ♡

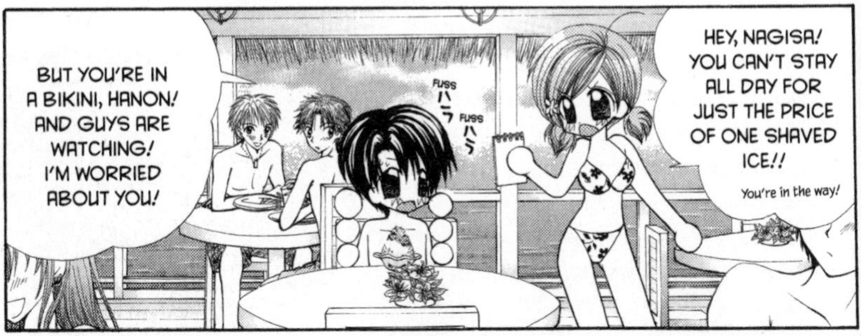
HEY, NAGISA! YOU CAN'T STAY ALL DAY FOR JUST THE PRICE OF ONE SHAVED ICE!!
You're in the way!
FUSS FUSS
BUT YOU'RE IN A BIKINI, HANON! AND GUYS ARE WATCHING! I'M WORRIED ABOUT YOU!

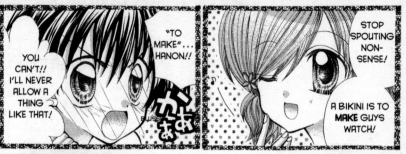

STOP SPOUTING NON-SENSE!
A BIKINI IS TO **MAKE** GUYS WATCH!
"TO MAKE"... HANON!!
YOU CAN'T!! I'LL NEVER ALLOW A THING LIKE THAT!
Ah ha!
NO MATTER WHAT HANON SAYS, THOSE TWO MAKE A GOOD COMBINATION.
GYAA
IT DOESN'T MATTER WHETHER A GRADE-SCHOOLER ALLOWS SOMETHING OR NOT!
WHAT WAS THAT?!
GYAA
SURE DO!

<EPISODE 22><EPISODE 23>

THE SPLASH PAGE FOR EPISODE 22 IS ALL GUYS.
COME TO THINK OF IT, WHENEVER I TURNED A SPLASH PAGE IN BEFORE, MY EDITOR K-SAN WOULD ALWAYS MAKE SOME KIND OF COMMENT, BUT THIS TIME, NOTHING. MEN JUST DON'T INTEREST ME!
MY THEORY IS THAT IT WAS ALL MEN, SO MY EDITOR WASN'T INTERESTED. → WOULD BE WHAT HE'D SAY. WHAT DO YOU THINK, K-SAN? I THOUGHT OF WHAT THE REAL HIPPO WOULD LOOK LIKE WHILE I WAS DRAWING, SO I DREW IT. EVERY NOW AND AGAIN I THINK THAT IT WOULD BE FUN TO DO THAT WITH OTHER CHARACTERS TOO!
BUT IF I ACTUALLY TRIED IT, IT MIGHT BE SCARY.
THE SPLASH PAGE FOR EPISODE 23 WAS TO PUT EVERYBODY IN HIPPO'S CLOTHES. I HAD WANTED TO DO THAT FOR A LONG TIME! ♥
WHEN LANHUA SPLIT HERSELF INTO ALL THOSE SMALL LANHUA, I'D DRAW AND DRAW AND NEVER GET FINISHED! I NEVER THOUGHT THAT A CHARACTER WHO USES THAT TECHNIQUE WOULD BE SO HARD...

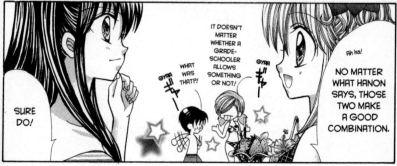

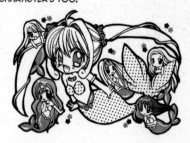

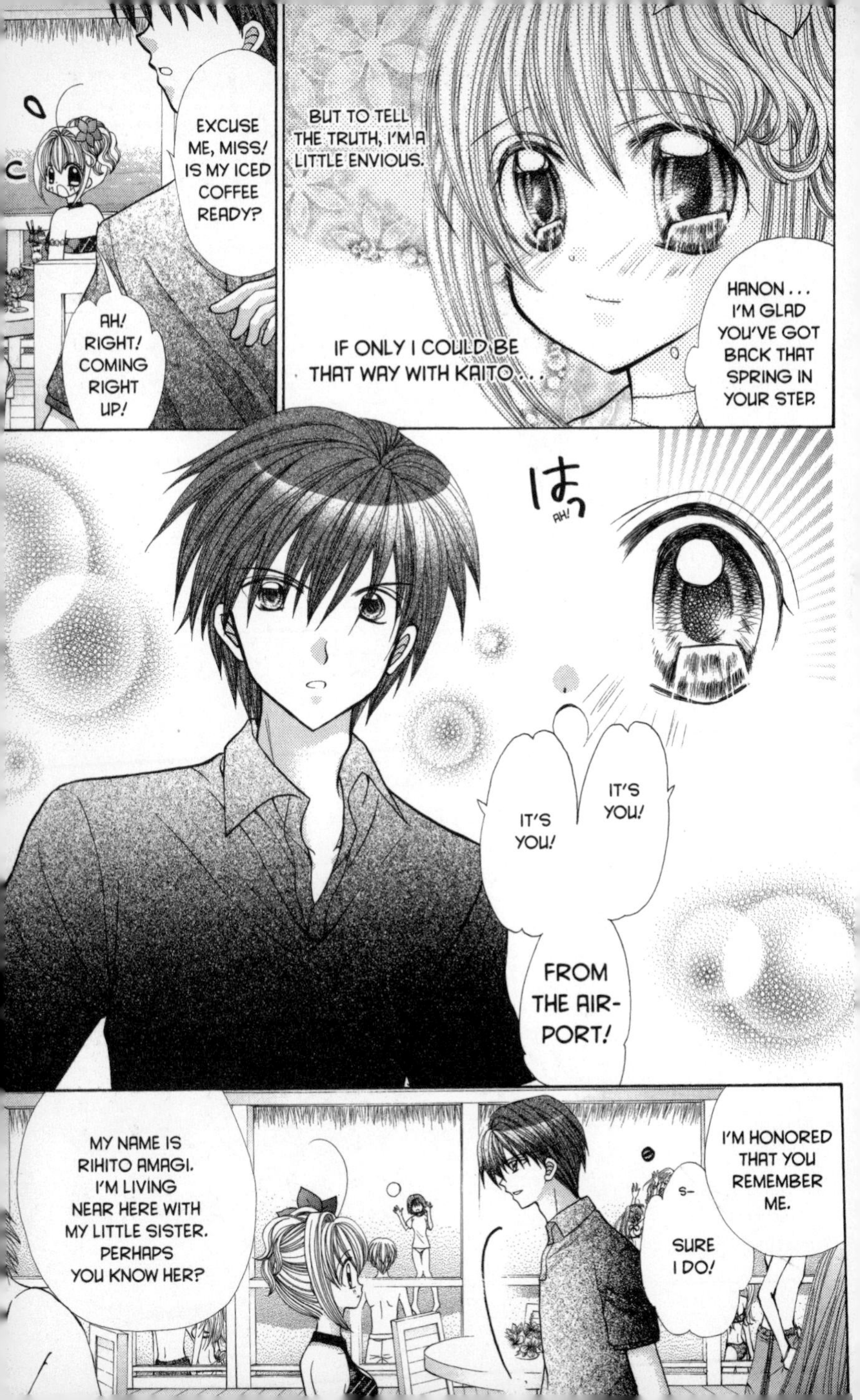
HANON . . . I'M GLAD YOU'VE GOT BACK THAT SPRING IN YOUR STEP.
BUT TO TELL THE TRUTH, I'M A LITTLE ENVIOUS.
IF ONLY I COULD BE THAT WAY WITH KAITO . . .
EXCUSE ME, MISS! IS MY ICED COFFEE READY?
AH! RIGHT! COMING RIGHT UP!
はっ
AH!
IT'S YOU!
IT'S YOU!
FROM THE AIR-PORT!
I'M HONORED THAT YOU REMEMBER ME.
S-
SURE I DO!
MY NAME IS RIHITO AMAGI. I'M LIVING NEAR HERE WITH MY LITTLE SISTER. PERHAPS YOU KNOW HER?

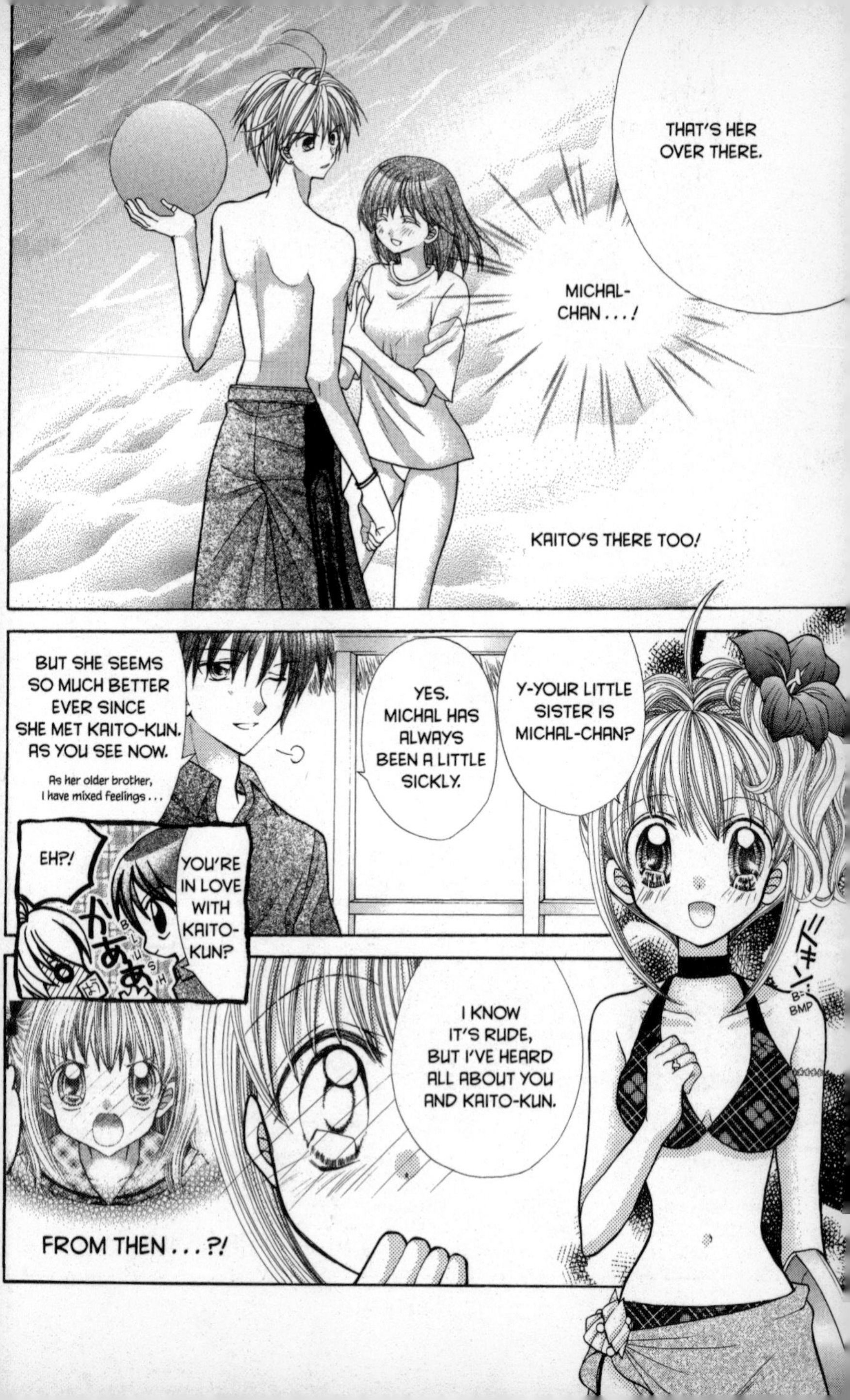
THAT'S HER OVER THERE.
MICHAL-CHAN . . . !
KAITO'S THERE TOO!
Y-YOUR LITTLE SISTER IS MICHAL-CHAN?
YES. MICHAL HAS ALWAYS BEEN A LITTLE SICKLY.
BUT SHE SEEMS SO MUCH BETTER EVER SINCE SHE MET KAITO-KUN. AS YOU SEE NOW.
As her older brother, I have mixed feelings . . .
BMP
YOU'RE IN LOVE WITH KAITO-KUN?
EH?!
BLUSH
I KNOW IT'S RUDE, BUT I'VE HEARD ALL ABOUT YOU AND KAITO-KUN.
FROM THEN . . . ?!

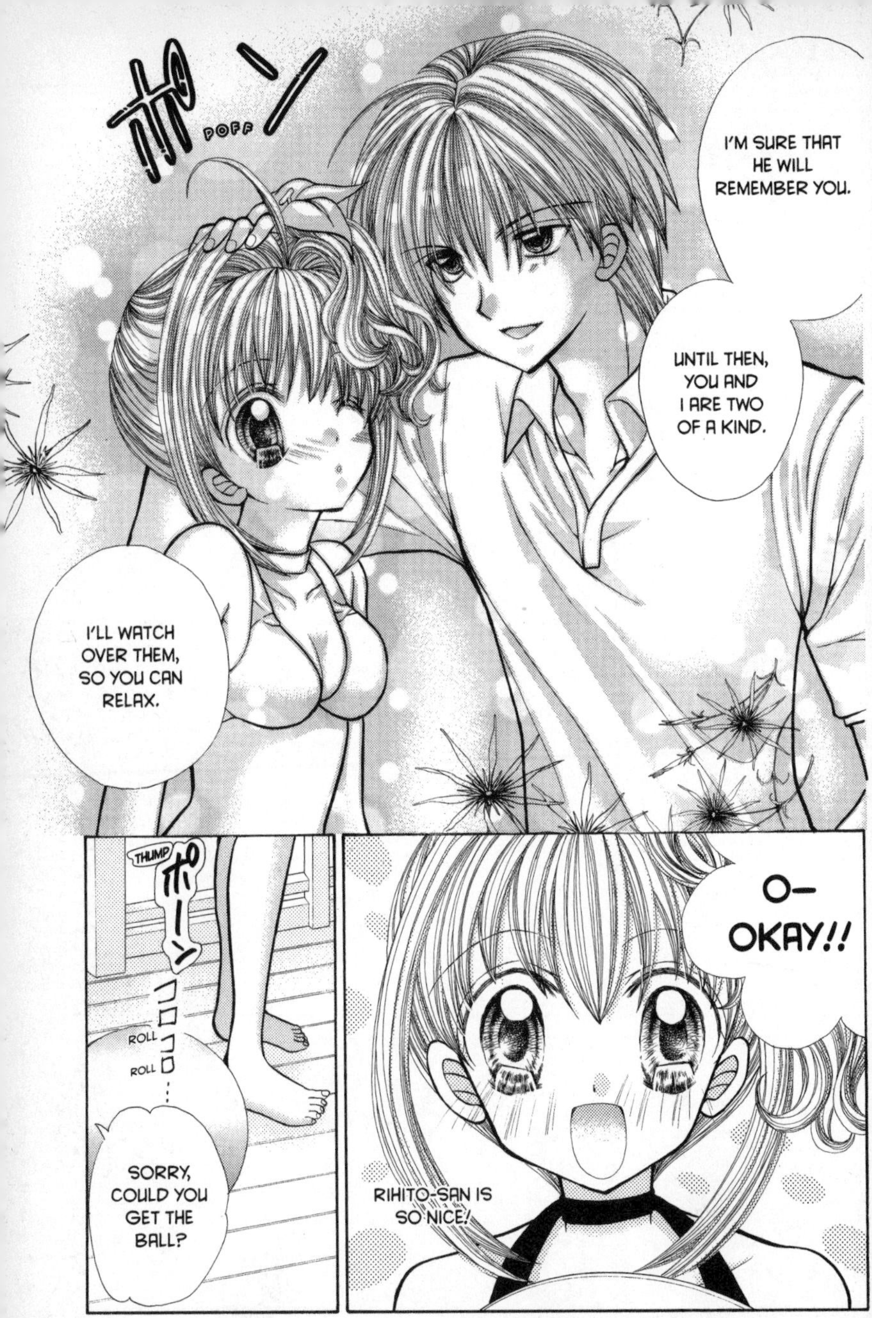

I'M SURE THAT HE WILL REMEMBER YOU.
UNTIL THEN, YOU AND I ARE TWO OF A KIND.
POFF
I'LL WATCH OVER THEM, SO YOU CAN RELAX.
O-OKAY!!
RIHITO-SAN IS SO NICE!
THUMP
ROLL
ROLL
SORRY, COULD YOU GET THE BALL?

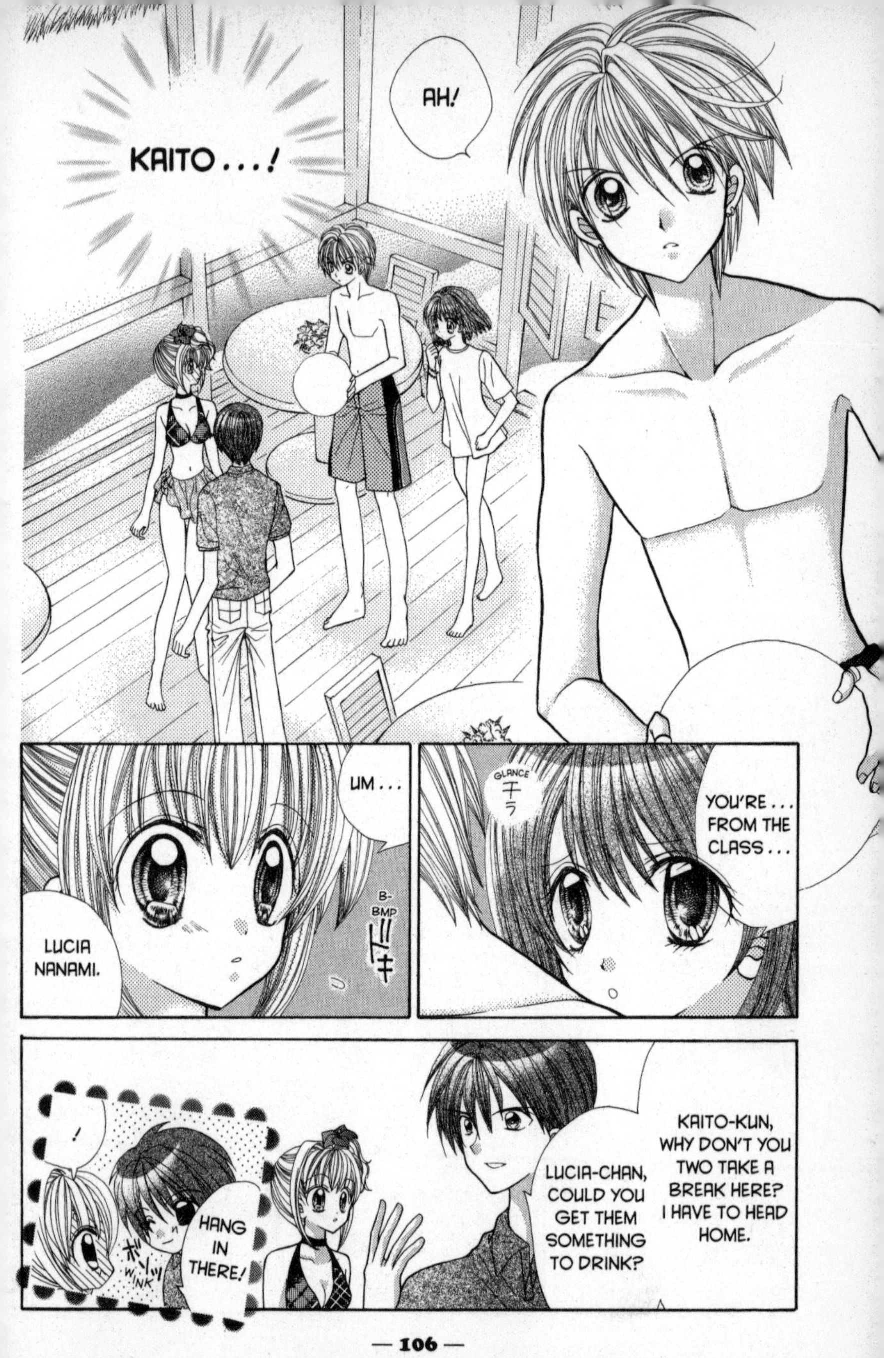

AH!
KAITO...!
GLANCE
チラ
YOU'RE... FROM THE CLASS...
UM...
B-BMP
ドキ
LUCIA NANAMI.
KAITO-KUN, WHY DON'T YOU TWO TAKE A BREAK HERE? I HAVE TO HEAD HOME.
LUCIA-CHAN, COULD YOU GET THEM SOMETHING TO DRINK?
HANG IN THERE!
WINK
!

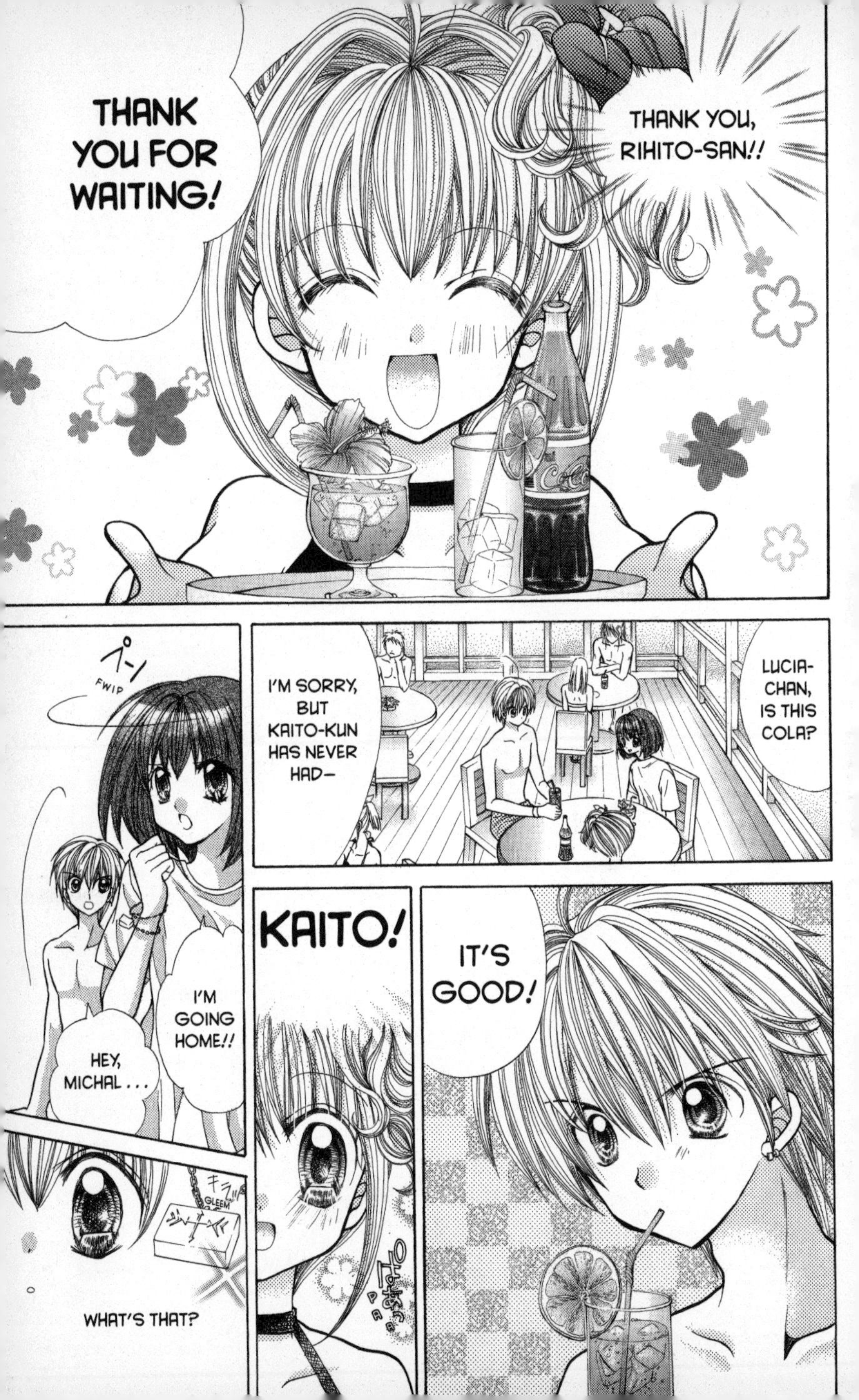
THANK YOU, RIHITO-SAN!!
THANK YOU FOR WAITING!
LUCIA-CHAN, IS THIS COLA?
I'M SORRY, BUT KAITO-KUN HAS NEVER HAD—
IT'S GOOD!
KAITO!
FWIP
I'M GOING HOME!!
HEY, MICHAL . . .
GLEEM
WHAT'S THAT?

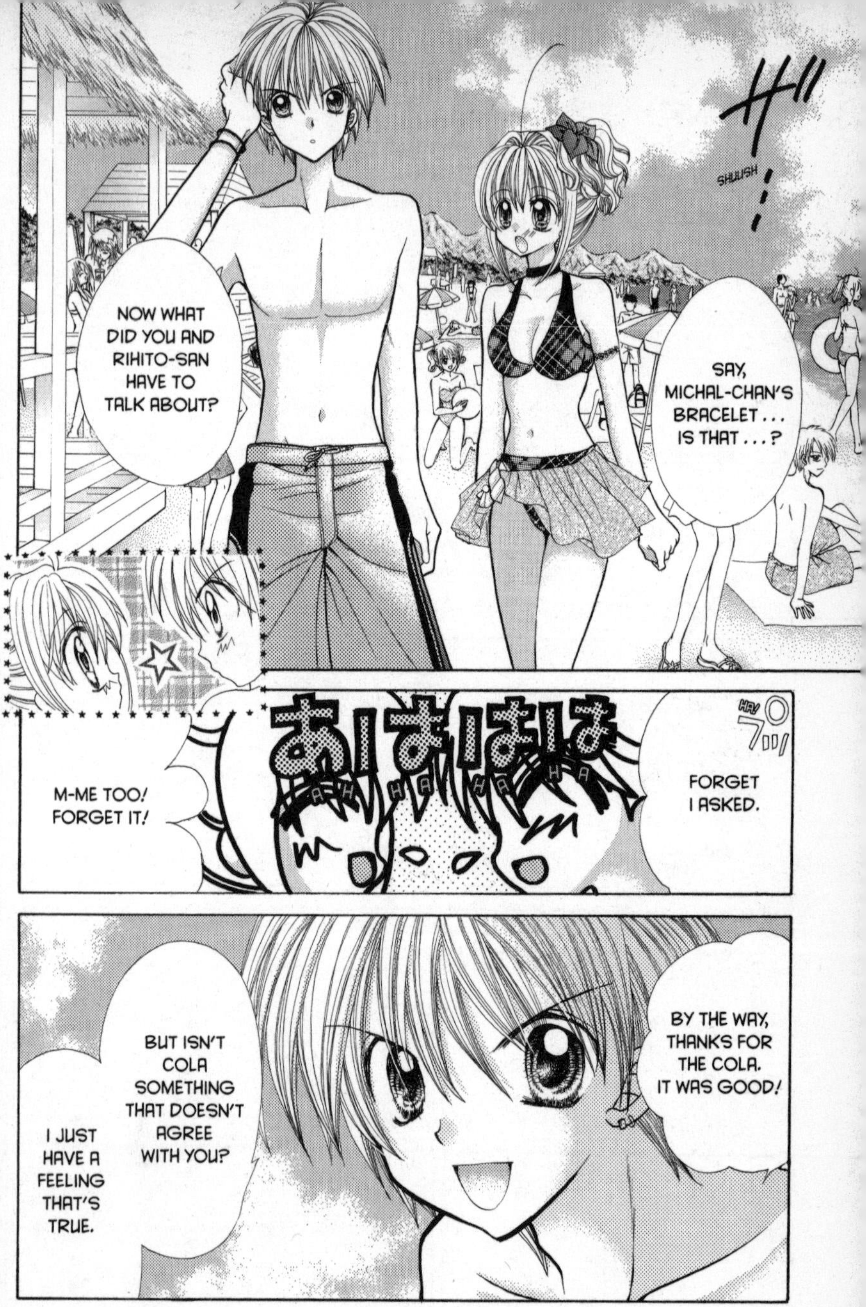
SHUUSH
SAY, MICHAL-CHAN'S BRACELET . . . IS THAT . . . ?
NOW WHAT DID YOU AND RIHITO-SAN HAVE TO TALK ABOUT?
HA!
FORGET I ASKED.
AH HA HA HA HA
M-ME TOO! FORGET IT!
BY THE WAY, THANKS FOR THE COLA. IT WAS GOOD!
BUT ISN'T COLA SOMETHING THAT DOESN'T AGREE WITH YOU?
I JUST HAVE A FEELING THAT'S TRUE.

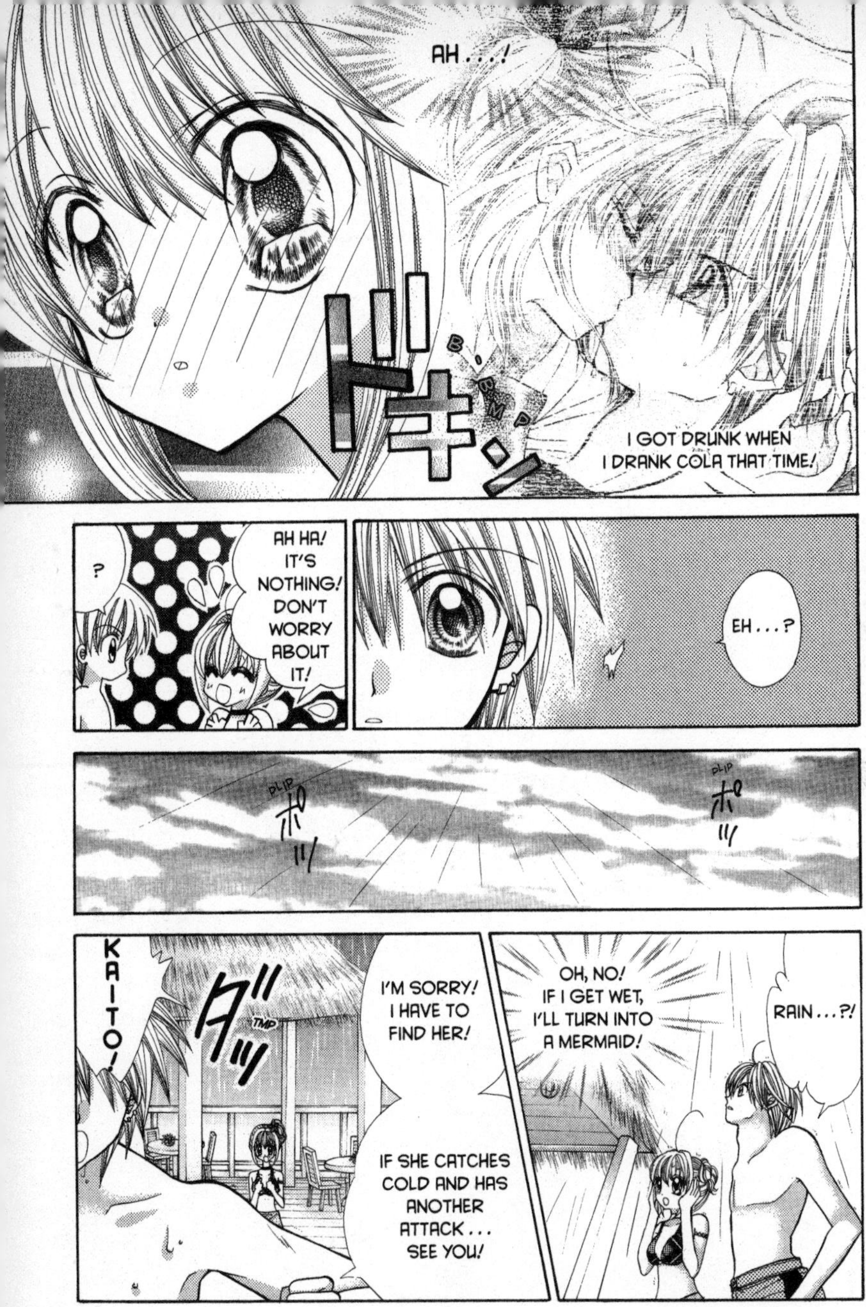
AH....!
I GOT DRUNK WHEN I DRANK COLA THAT TIME!
B-BUMP
EH...?
AH HA! IT'S NOTHING! DON'T WORRY ABOUT IT!
?
PLIP
PLIP
RAIN...?!
OH, NO! IF I GET WET, I'LL TURN INTO A MERMAID!
I'M SORRY! I HAVE TO FIND HER!
IF SHE CATCHES COLD AND HAS ANOTHER ATTACK... SEE YOU!
TMP
KAITO!

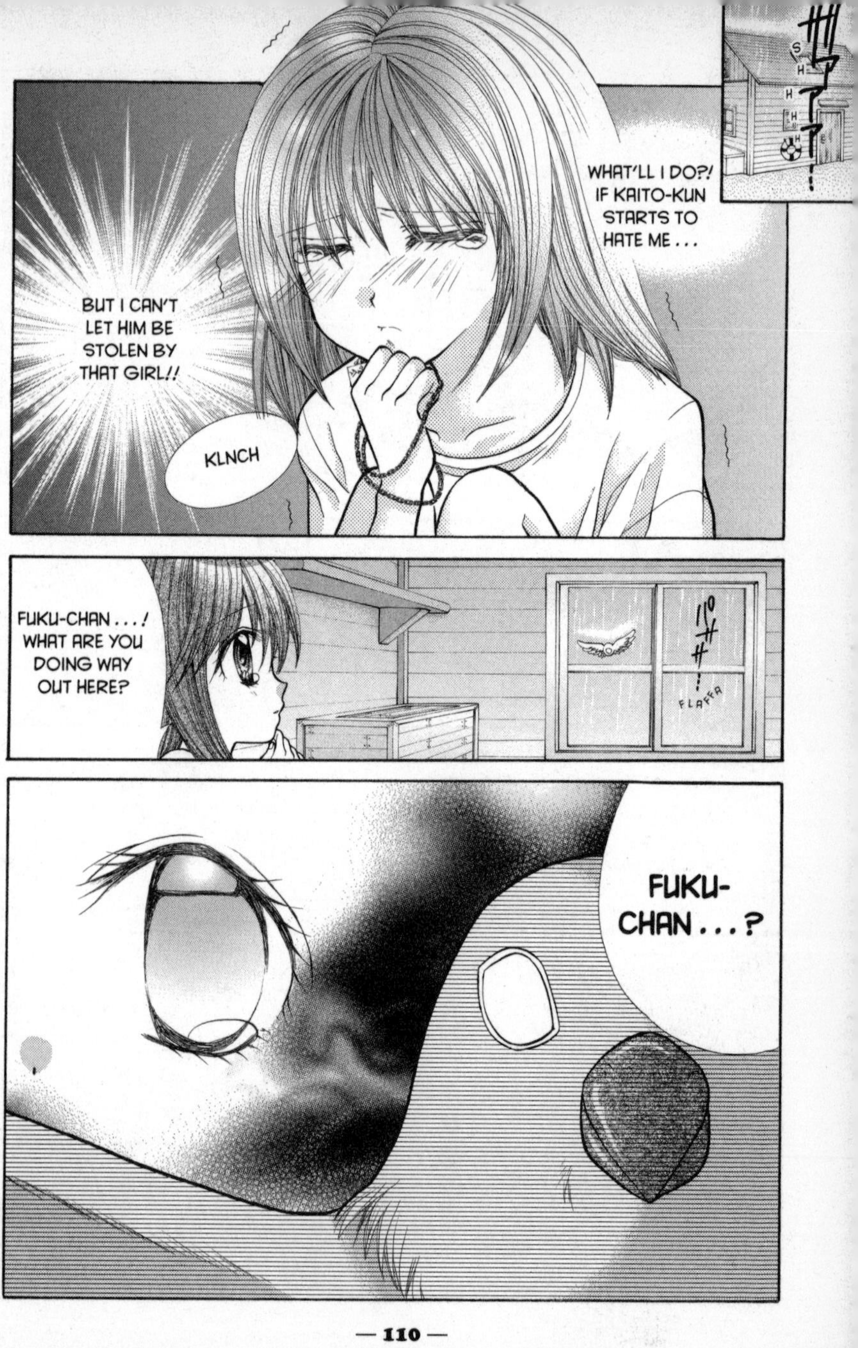
SHHHH
WHAT'LL I DO?! IF KAITO-KUN STARTS TO HATE ME . . .
BUT I CAN'T LET HIM BE STOLEN BY THAT GIRL!!
KLNCH
FUKU-CHAN . . .! WHAT ARE YOU DOING WAY OUT HERE?
FLAFFA
FUKU-CHAN . . .?

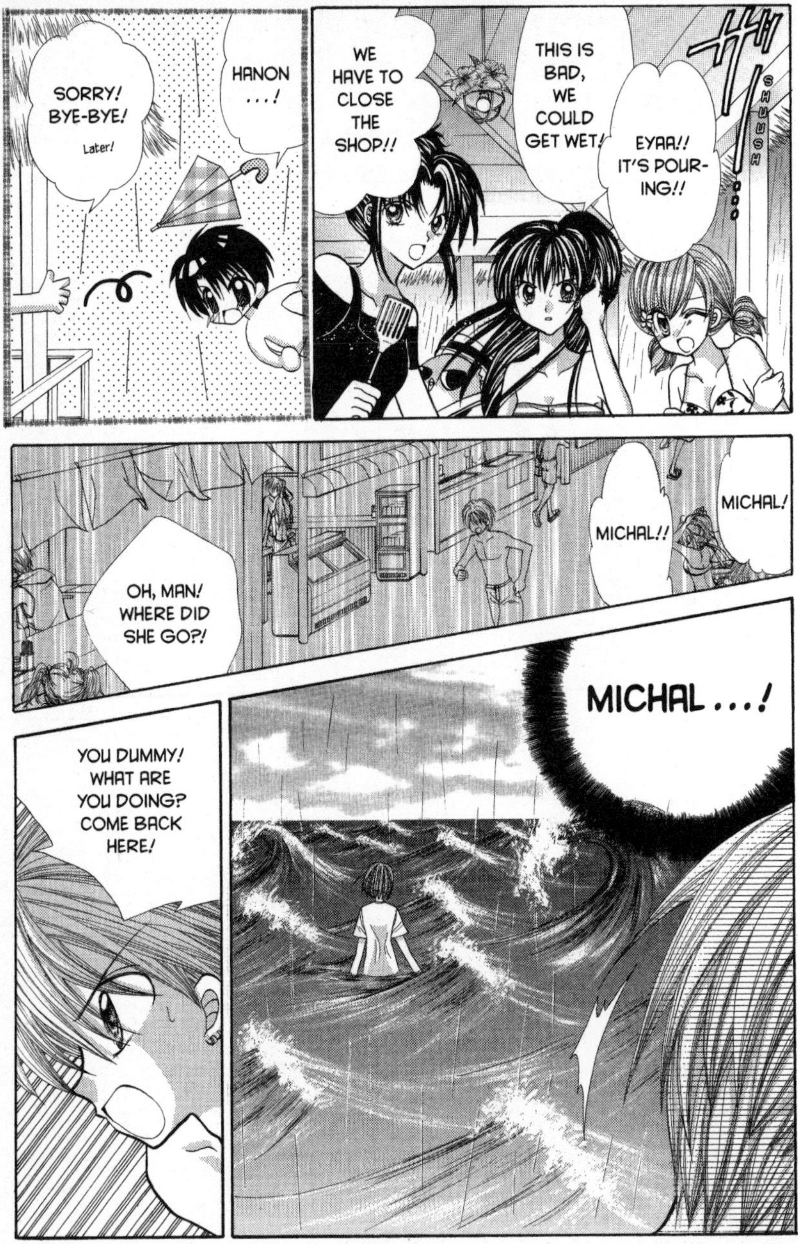
SHUUSH
EYAA!! IT'S POURING!!
THIS IS BAD, WE COULD GET WET!
WE HAVE TO CLOSE THE SHOP!!
HANON...!
SORRY! BYE-BYE!
Later!
MICHAL!
MICHAL!!
OH, MAN! WHERE DID SHE GO?!
MICHAL...!
YOU DUMMY! WHAT ARE YOU DOING? COME BACK HERE!

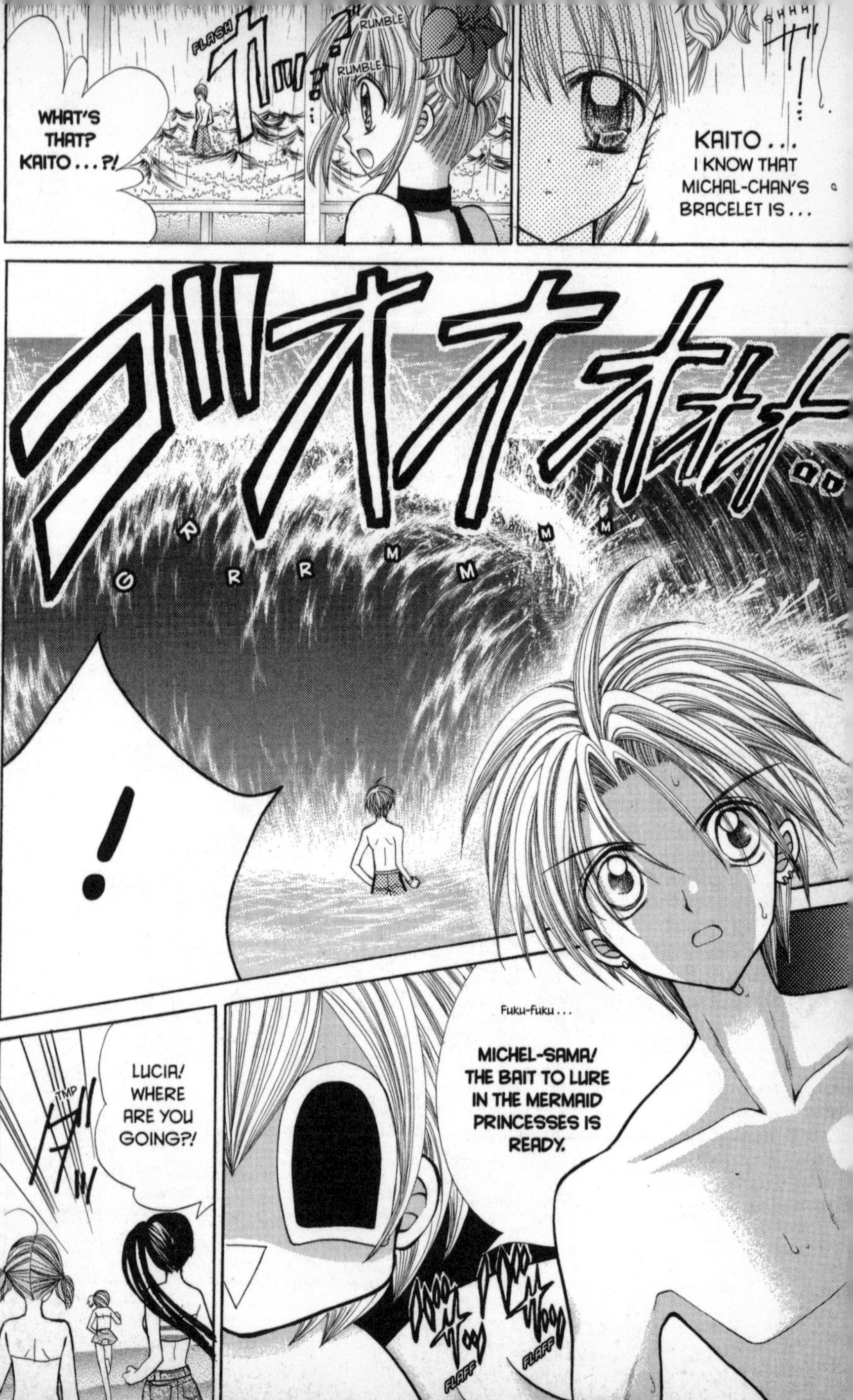
SHHH
KAITO . . . I KNOW THAT MICHAL-CHAN'S BRACELET IS . . .
FLASH
RUMBLE
RUMBLE
WHAT'S THAT? KAITO . . . ?!
GRRRMMMM
!
Fuku-fuku . . .
MICHEL-SAMA! THE BAIT TO LURE IN THE MERMAID PRINCESSES IS READY.
FLAFF
FLAFF
TMP
LUCIA! WHERE ARE YOU GOING?!

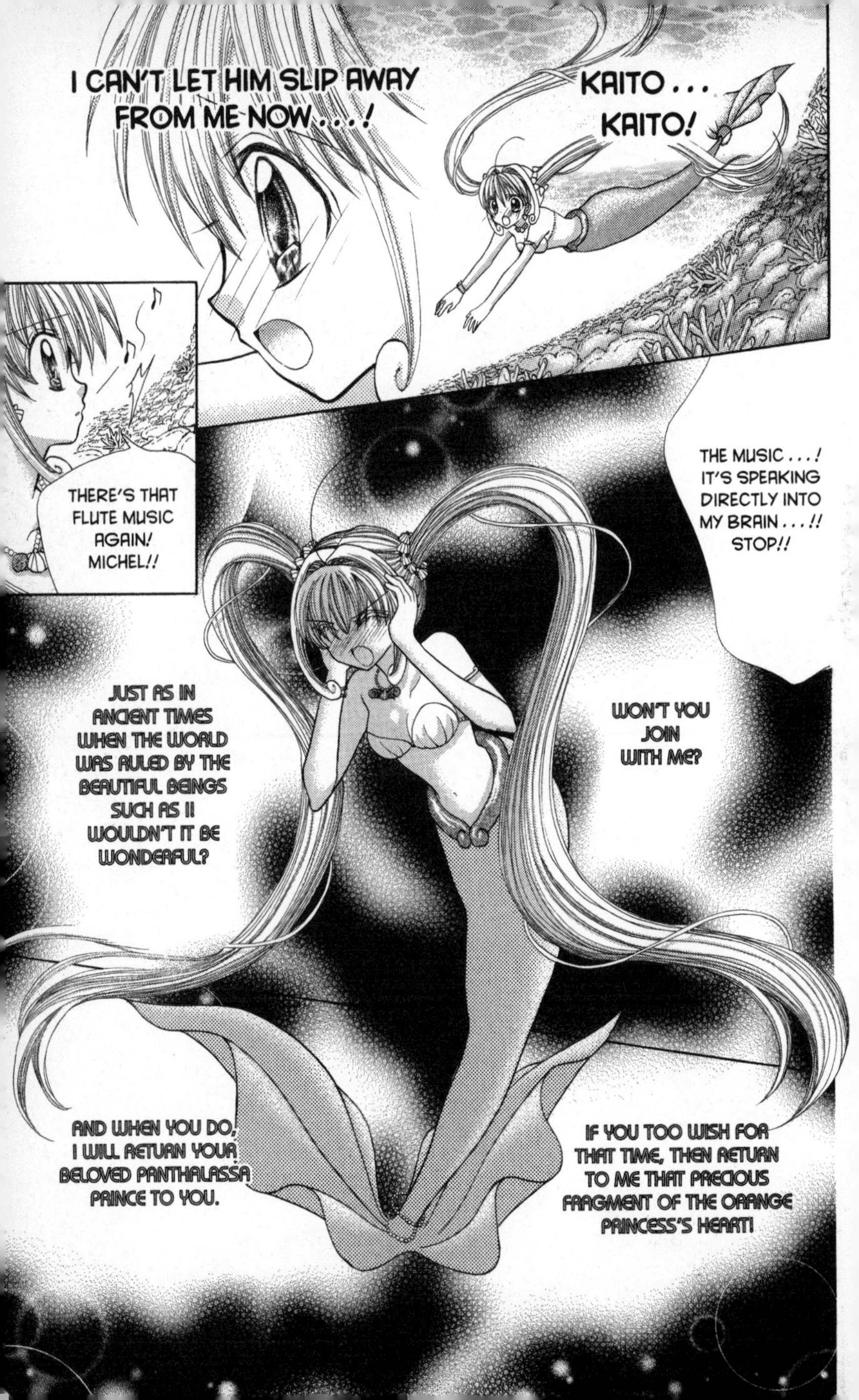
KAITO . . .
KAITO!
I CAN'T LET HIM SLIP AWAY FROM ME NOW . . . !
THERE'S THAT FLUTE MUSIC AGAIN! MICHEL!!
THE MUSIC . . . ! IT'S SPEAKING DIRECTLY INTO MY BRAIN . . . !! STOP!!
WON'T YOU JOIN WITH ME?
JUST AS IN ANCIENT TIMES WHEN THE WORLD WAS RULED BY THE BEAUTIFUL BEINGS SUCH AS I! WOULDN'T IT BE WONDERFUL?
IF YOU TOO WISH FOR THAT TIME, THEN RETURN TO ME THAT PRECIOUS FRAGMENT OF THE ORANGE PRINCESS'S HEART!
AND WHEN YOU DO, I WILL RETURN YOUR BELOVED PANTHALASSA PRINCE TO YOU.

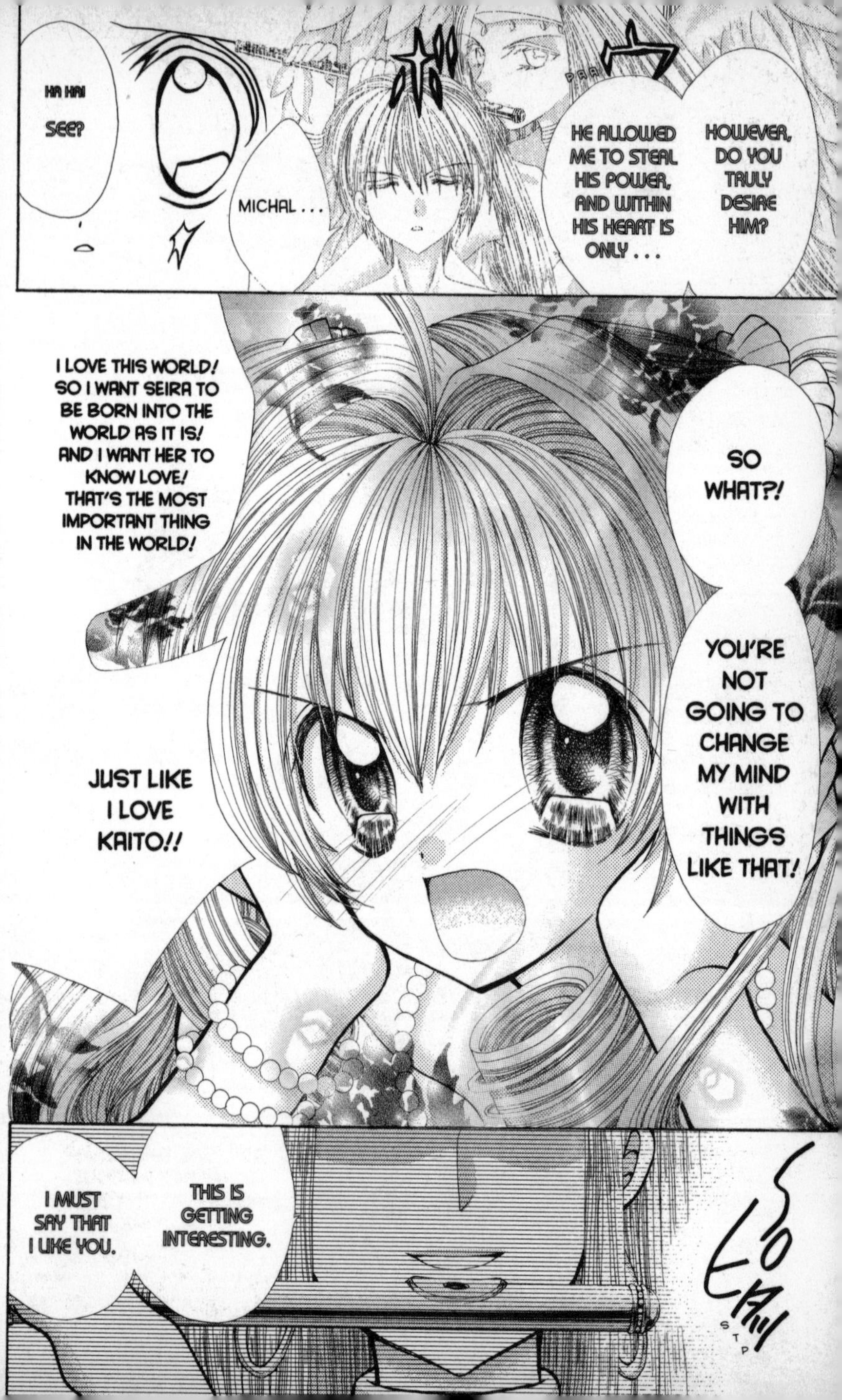

HOWEVER, DO YOU TRULY DESIRE HIM?
HE ALLOWED ME TO STEAL HIS POWER, AND WITHIN HIS HEART IS ONLY . . .
MICHAL . . .
HA HA SEE?
SO WHAT?!
YOU'RE NOT GOING TO CHANGE MY MIND WITH THINGS LIKE THAT!
I LOVE THIS WORLD! SO I WANT SEIRA TO BE BORN INTO THE WORLD AS IT IS! AND I WANT HER TO KNOW LOVE! THAT'S THE MOST IMPORTANT THING IN THE WORLD!
JUST LIKE I LOVE KAITO!!
STP
THIS IS GETTING INTERESTING.
I MUST SAY THAT I LIKE YOU.

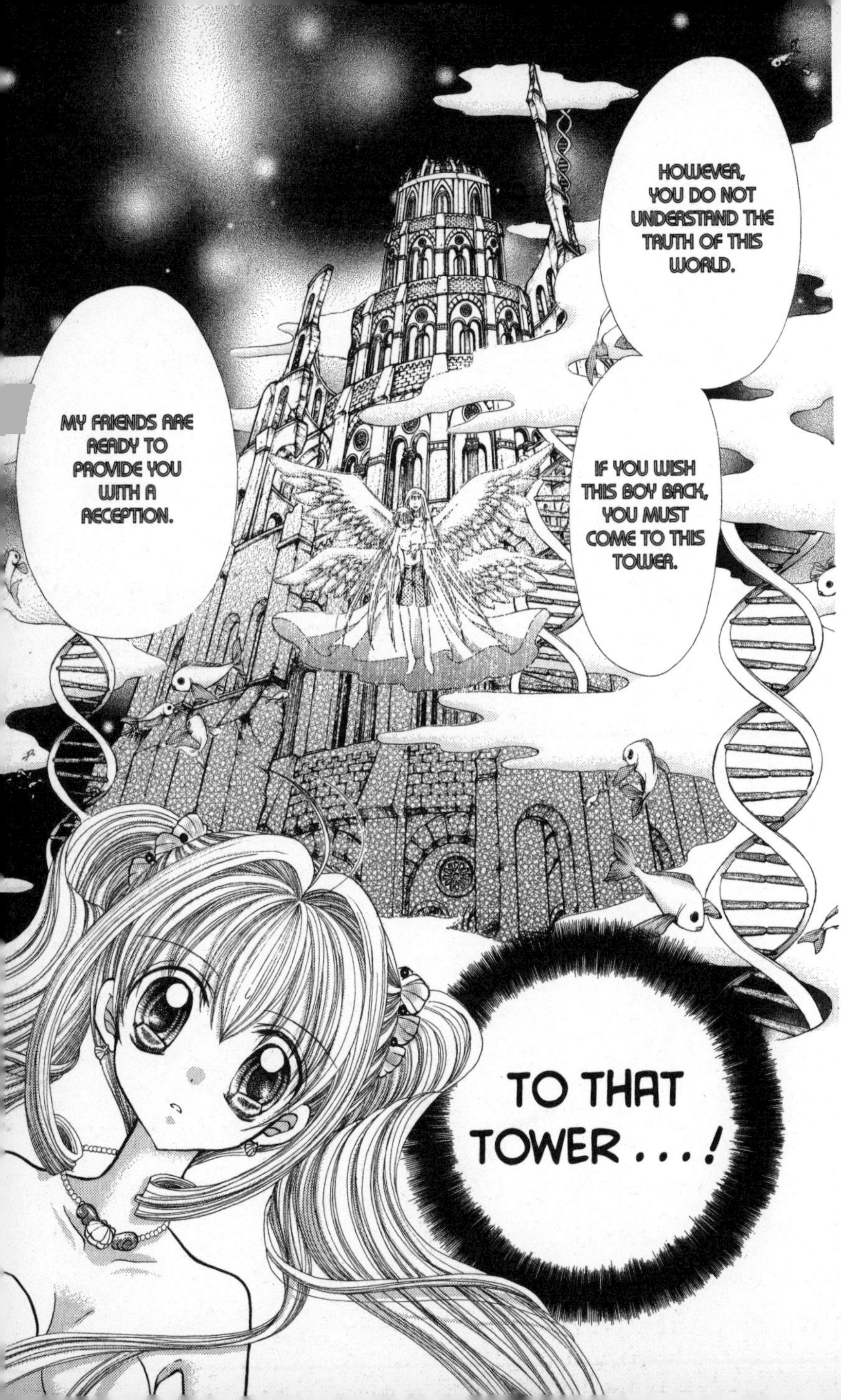
HOWEVER, YOU DO NOT UNDERSTAND THE TRUTH OF THIS WORLD.
IF YOU WISH THIS BOY BACK, YOU MUST COME TO THIS TOWER.
MY FRIENDS ARE READY TO PROVIDE YOU WITH A RECEPTION.
TO THAT TOWER . . . !

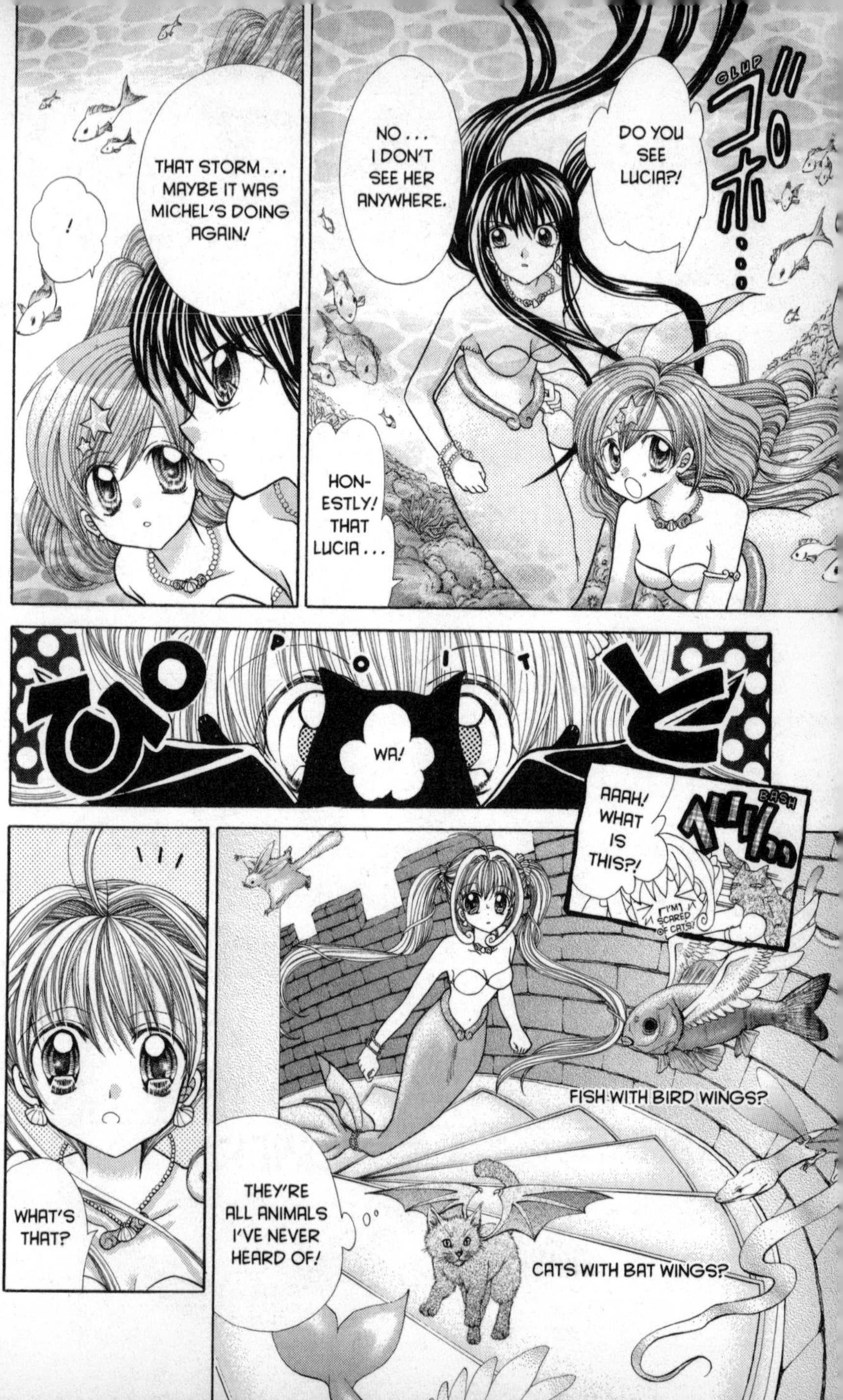
GLUP
DO YOU SEE LUCIA?!
NO . . . I DON'T SEE HER ANYWHERE.
HON-ESTLY! THAT LUCIA . . .
THAT STORM . . . MAYBE IT WAS MICHEL'S DOING AGAIN!
!
POIT
WA!
BASH
AAAH! WHAT IS THIS?!
I'M SCARED OF CATS!
FISH WITH BIRD WINGS?
CATS WITH BAT WINGS?
THEY'RE ALL ANIMALS I'VE NEVER HEARD OF!
WHAT'S THAT?

HIDDEN PICTURES

WHEN RIHITO IS GIVING HIS CONCERT, SOMEBODY IS THERE IN THE AUDIENCE. SOME FIVE BODIES . . . ?!

JUST LIKE ONE WOULD EXPECT.

HA HA! CAN YOU FIND US?

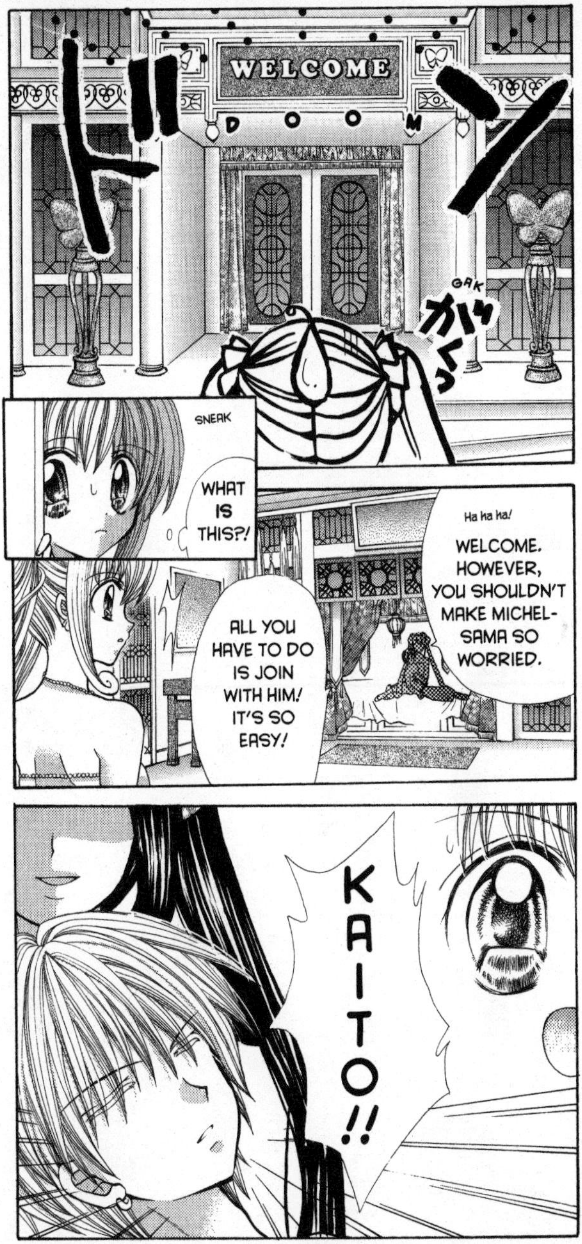
WELCOME
DOOOM
GAK
SNEAK
WHAT IS THIS?!
Ha ha ha!
WELCOME. HOWEVER, YOU SHOULDN'T MAKE MICHEL-SAMA SO WORRIED.
ALL YOU HAVE TO DO IS JOIN WITH HIM! IT'S SO EASY!
KAITO!!

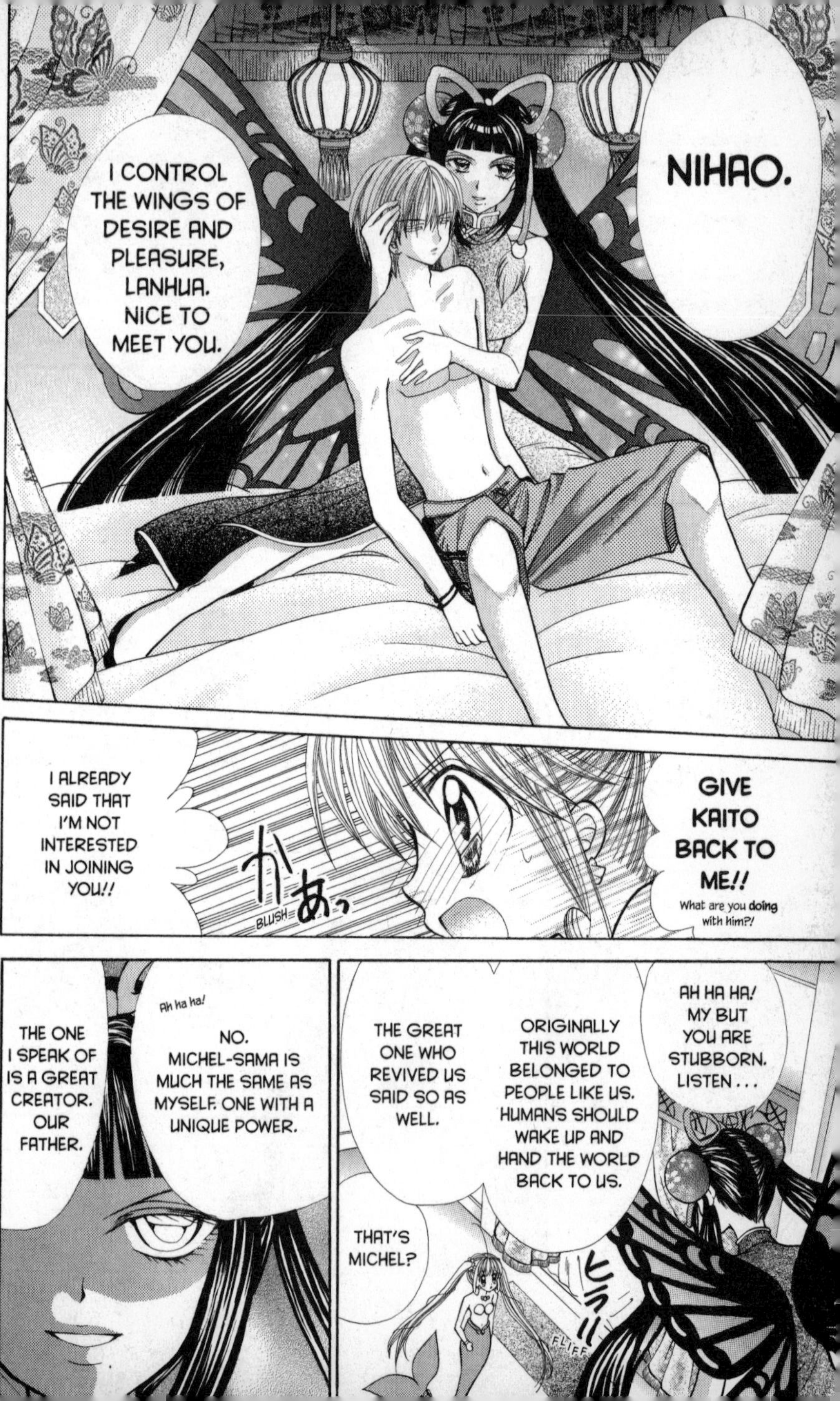
NIHAO.
I CONTROL THE WINGS OF DESIRE AND PLEASURE, LANHUA. NICE TO MEET YOU.
GIVE KAITO BACK TO ME!!
What are you doing with him?!
かあっ
BLUSH
I ALREADY SAID THAT I'M NOT INTERESTED IN JOINING YOU!!
AH HA HA! MY BUT YOU ARE STUBBORN. LISTEN . . .
ORIGINALLY THIS WORLD BELONGED TO PEOPLE LIKE US. HUMANS SHOULD WAKE UP AND HAND THE WORLD BACK TO US.
THE GREAT ONE WHO REVIVED US SAID SO AS WELL.
THAT'S MICHEL?
ヒラ!!
FLIFF
Ah ha ha!
NO. MICHEL-SAMA IS MUCH THE SAME AS MYSELF. ONE WITH A UNIQUE POWER.
THE ONE I SPEAK OF IS A GREAT CREATOR. OUR FATHER.

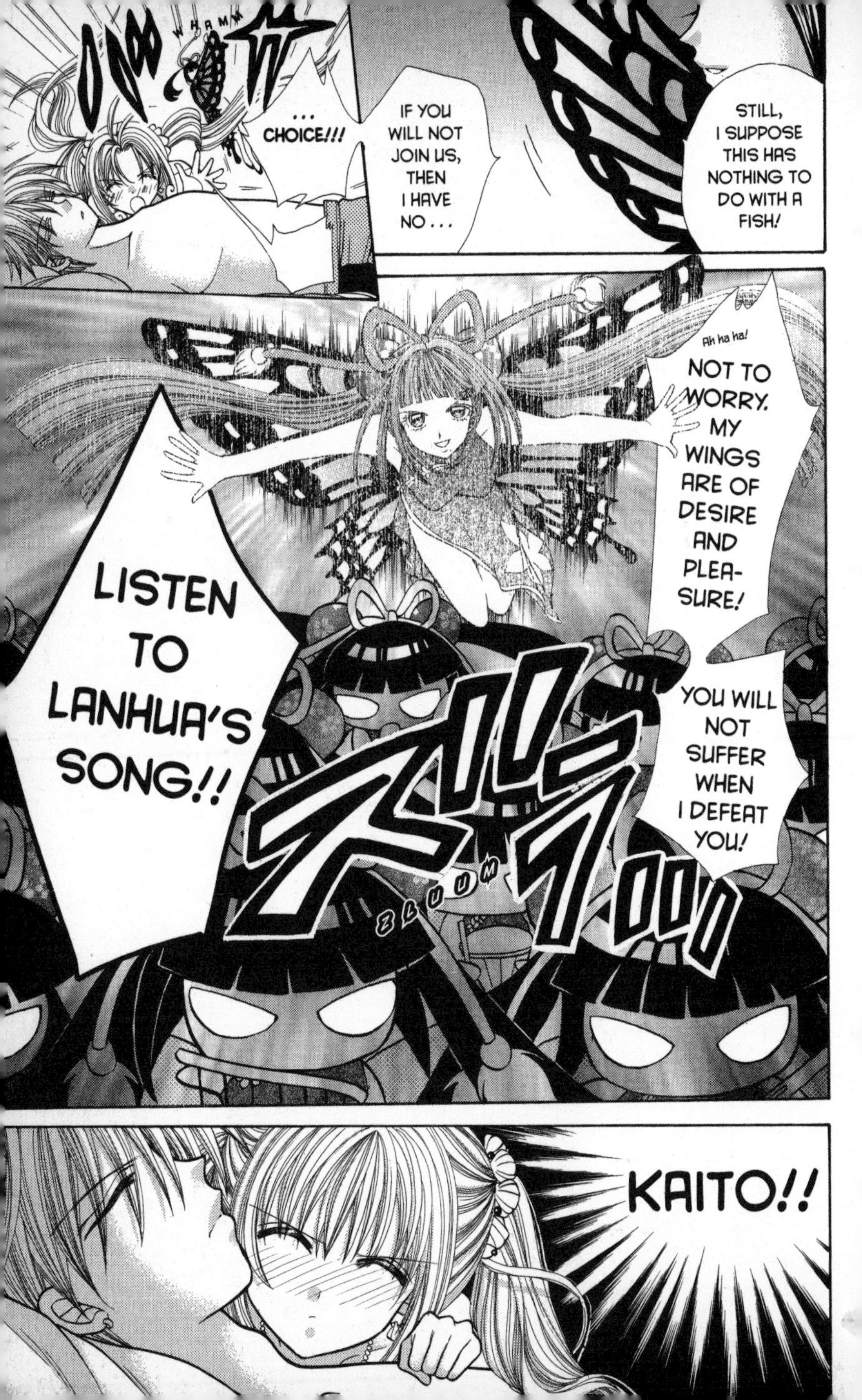
STILL, I SUPPOSE THIS HAS NOTHING TO DO WITH A FISH!
IF YOU WILL NOT JOIN US, THEN I HAVE NO . . .
. . . CHOICE!!!
WHAMM
Ah ha ha!
NOT TO WORRY. MY WINGS ARE OF DESIRE AND PLEA-SURE!
YOU WILL NOT SUFFER WHEN I DEFEAT YOU!
LISTEN TO LANHUA'S SONG!!
ZLUUM
KAITO!!

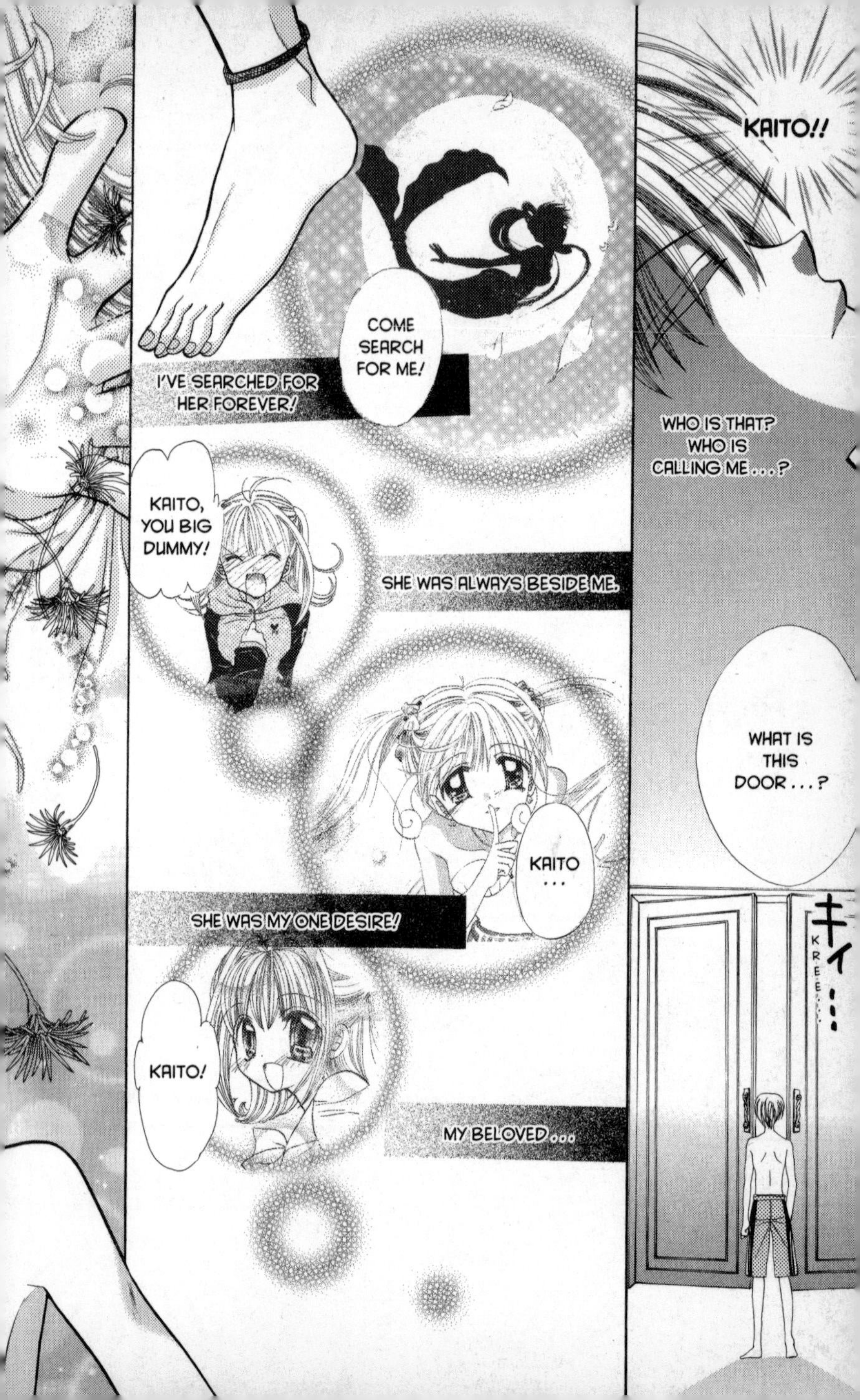
KAITO!!
WHO IS THAT? WHO IS CALLING ME . . . ?
WHAT IS THIS DOOR . . . ?
キィ
KREE . . .
COME SEARCH FOR ME!
I'VE SEARCHED FOR HER FOREVER!
KAITO, YOU BIG DUMMY!
SHE WAS ALWAYS BESIDE ME.
KAITO . . .
SHE WAS MY ONE DESIRE!
KAITO!
MY BELOVED . . .

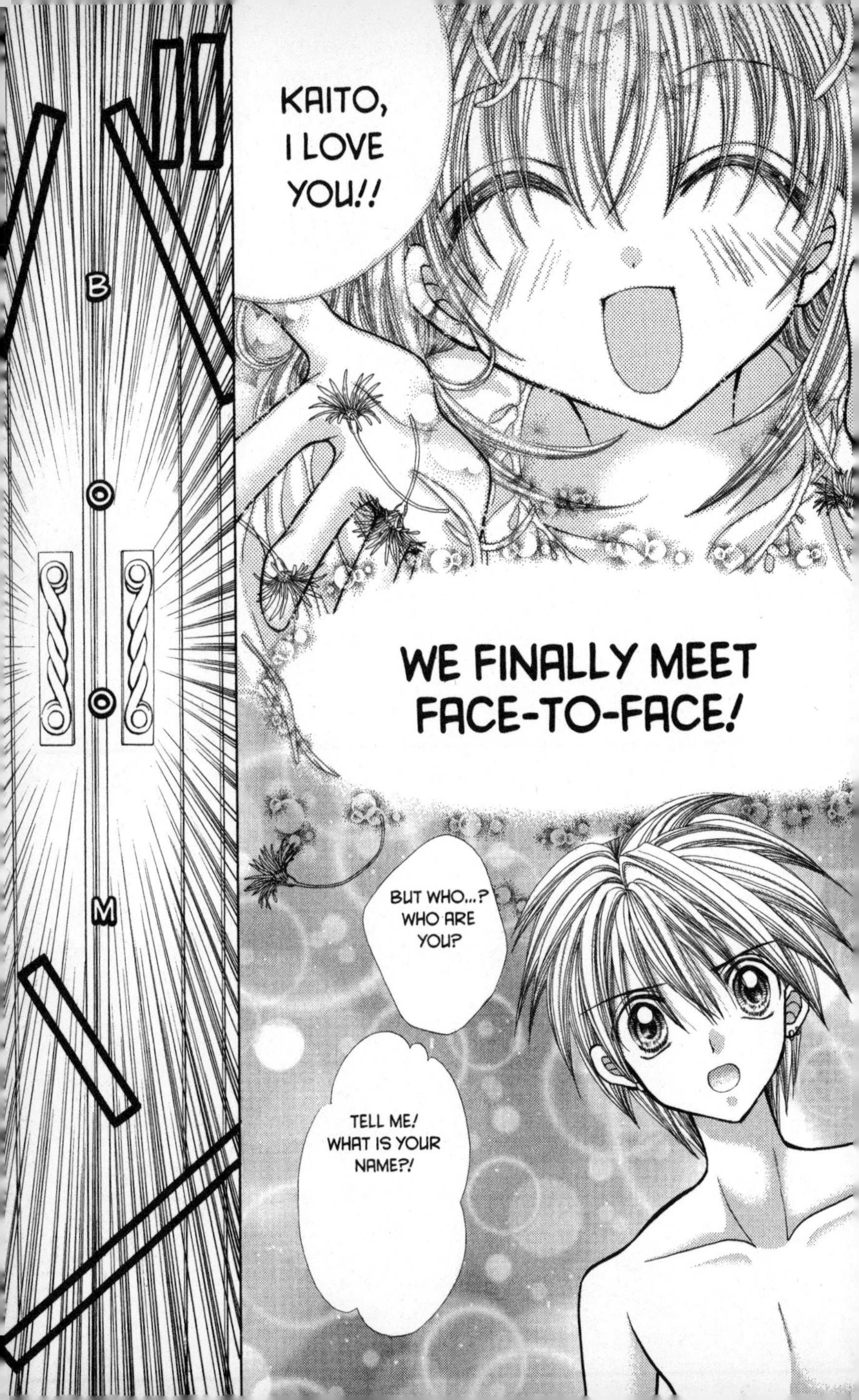
KAITO, I LOVE YOU!!
WE FINALLY MEET FACE-TO-FACE!
BUT WHO...? WHO ARE YOU?
TELL ME! WHAT IS YOUR NAME?!
BOOM

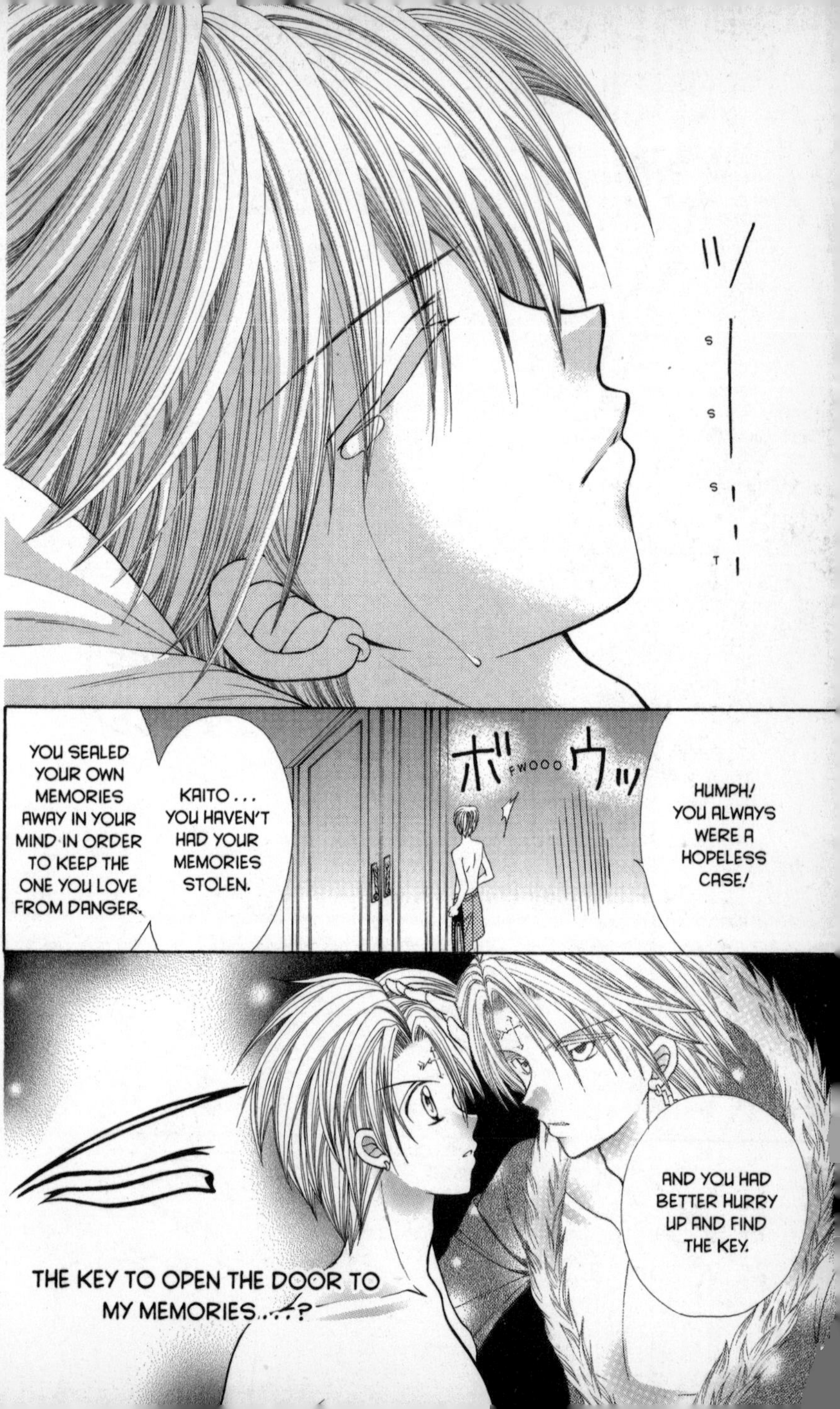
SSST
HUMPH! YOU ALWAYS WERE A HOPELESS CASE!
ボウッ
FWOOO
KAITO . . . YOU HAVEN'T HAD YOUR MEMORIES STOLEN.
YOU SEALED YOUR OWN MEMORIES AWAY IN YOUR MIND IN ORDER TO KEEP THE ONE YOU LOVE FROM DANGER.
AND YOU HAD BETTER HURRY UP AND FIND THE KEY.
THE KEY TO OPEN THE DOOR TO MY MEMORIES. . . ?

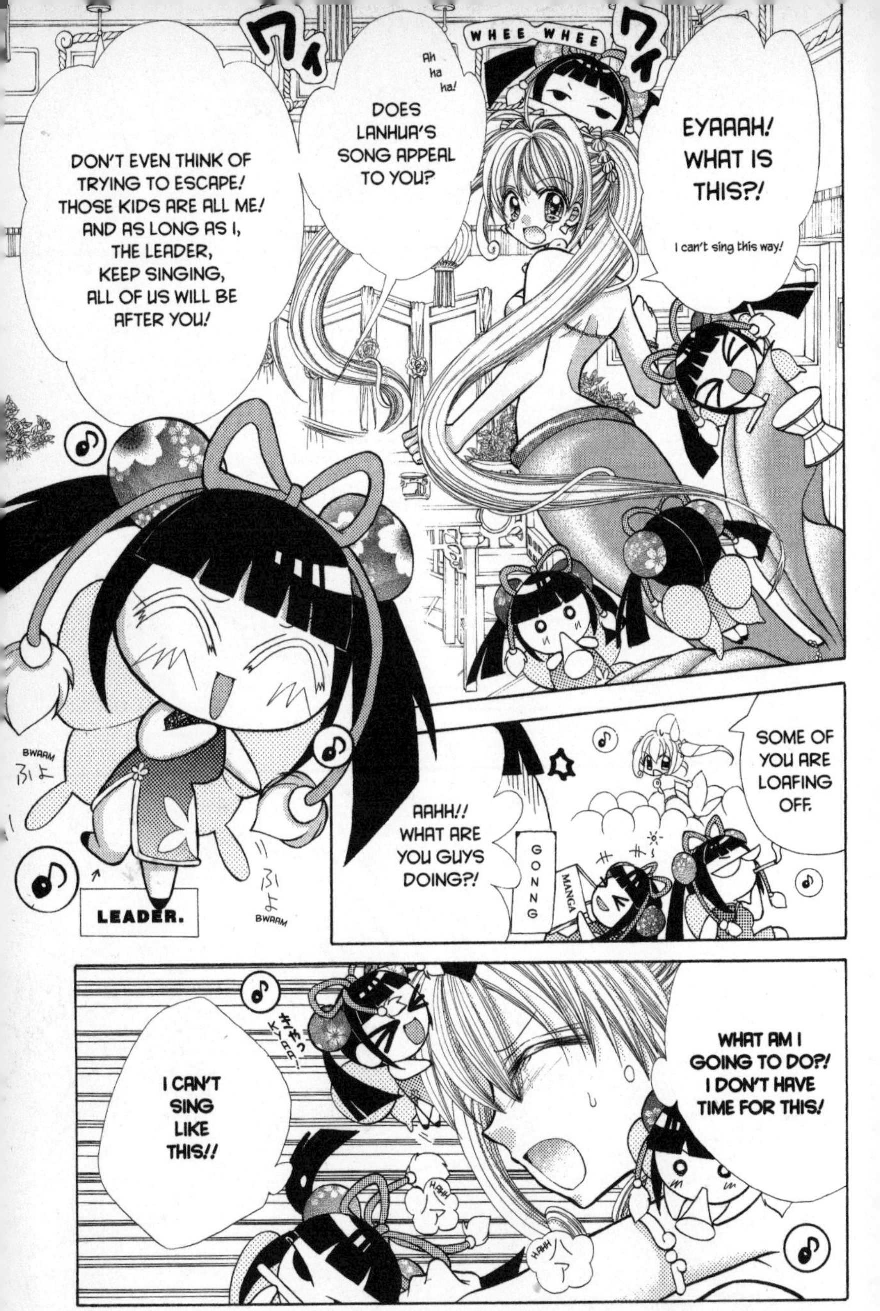
WHEE WHEE
EYAAAH! WHAT IS THIS?!
I can't sing this way!
Ah ha ha!
DOES LANHUA'S SONG APPEAL TO YOU?
DON'T EVEN THINK OF TRYING TO ESCAPE! THOSE KIDS ARE ALL ME! AND AS LONG AS I, THE LEADER, KEEP SINGING, ALL OF US WILL BE AFTER YOU!
BWAAM
BWAAM
LEADER.
SOME OF YOU ARE LOAFING OFF.
AAHH!! WHAT ARE YOU GUYS DOING?!
GONNG
MANGA
WHAT AM I GOING TO DO?! I DON'T HAVE TIME FOR THIS!
HAHH
HAHH
I CAN'T SING LIKE THIS!!

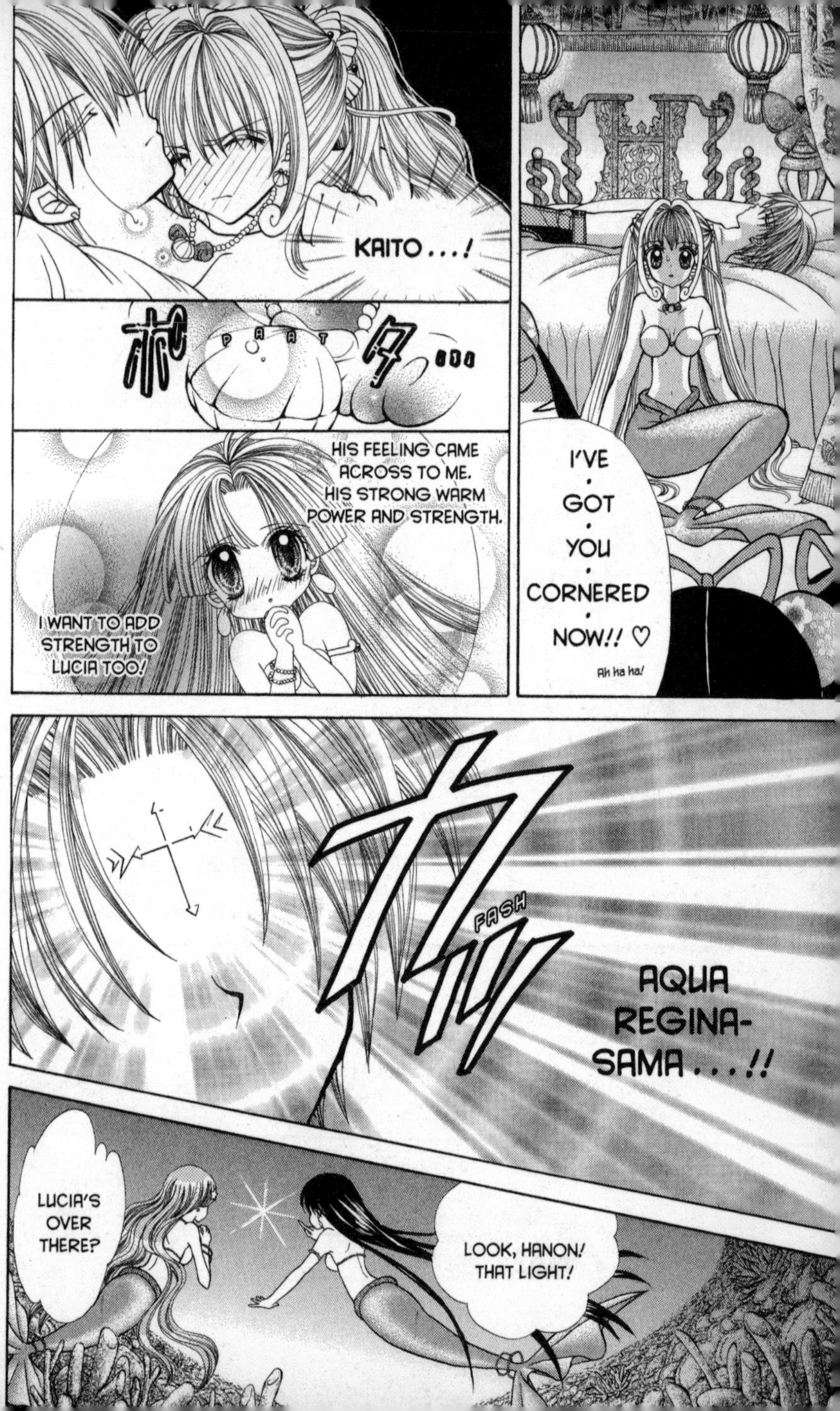
I'VE GOT YOU CORNERED NOW!! ♡
Ah ha ha!
KAITO . . . !
PAAT
HIS FEELING CAME ACROSS TO ME. HIS STRONG WARM POWER AND STRENGTH.
I WANT TO ADD STRENGTH TO LUCIA TOO!
FASH
AQUA REGINA-SAMA . . . !!
LOOK, HANON! THAT LIGHT!
LUCIA'S OVER THERE?

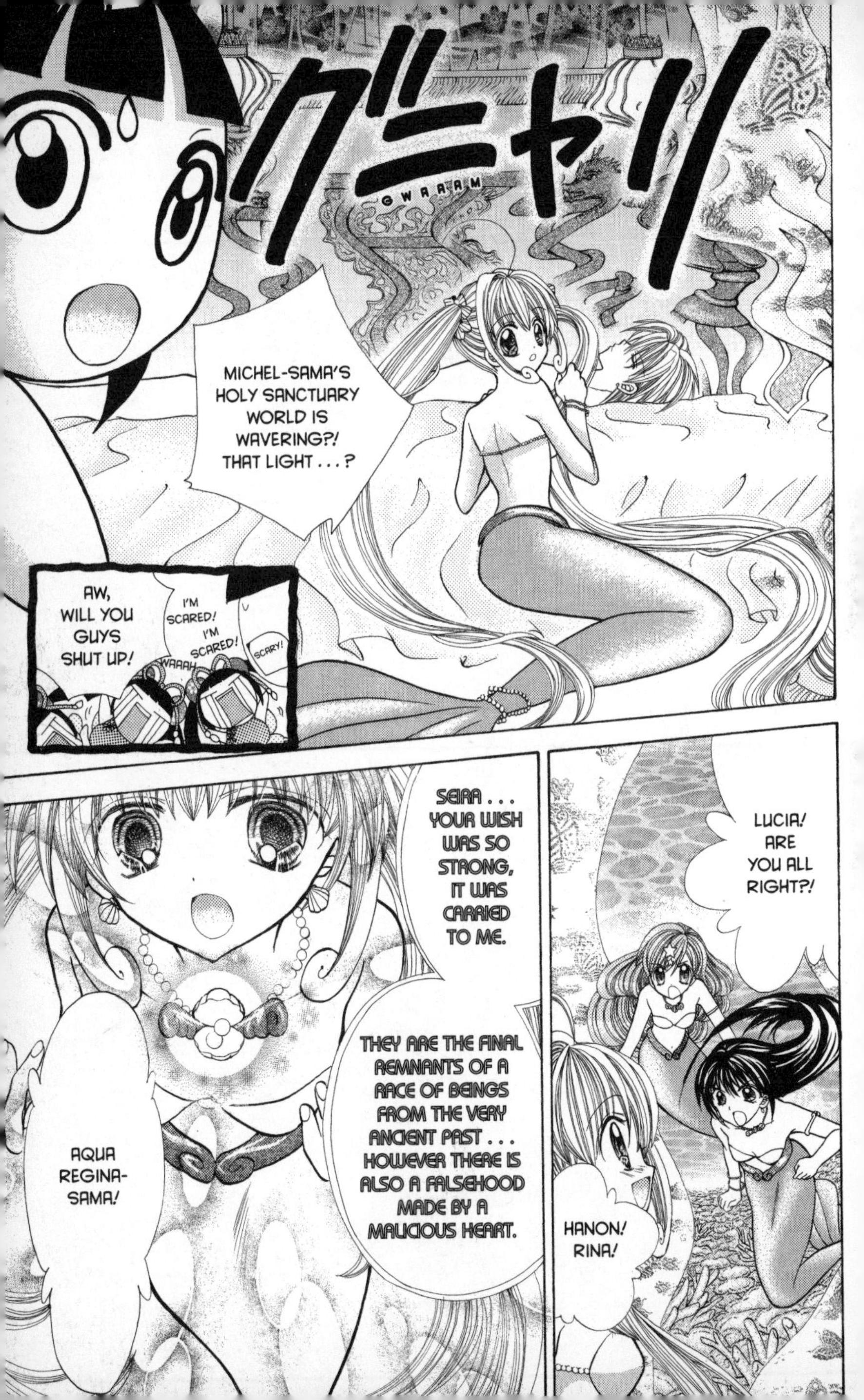
グニャリ
GWAAAM
MICHEL-SAMA'S HOLY SANCTUARY WORLD IS WAVERING?! THAT LIGHT . . . ?
SCARY!
I'M SCARED!
I'M SCARED!
WAAAH
AW, WILL YOU GUYS SHUT UP!
LUCIA! ARE YOU ALL RIGHT?!
HANON! RINA!
SEIRA . . . YOUR WISH WAS SO STRONG, IT WAS CARRIED TO ME.
THEY ARE THE FINAL REMNANTS OF A RACE OF BEINGS FROM THE VERY ANCIENT PAST . . . HOWEVER THERE IS ALSO A FALSEHOOD MADE BY A MALICIOUS HEART.
AQUA REGINA-SAMA!

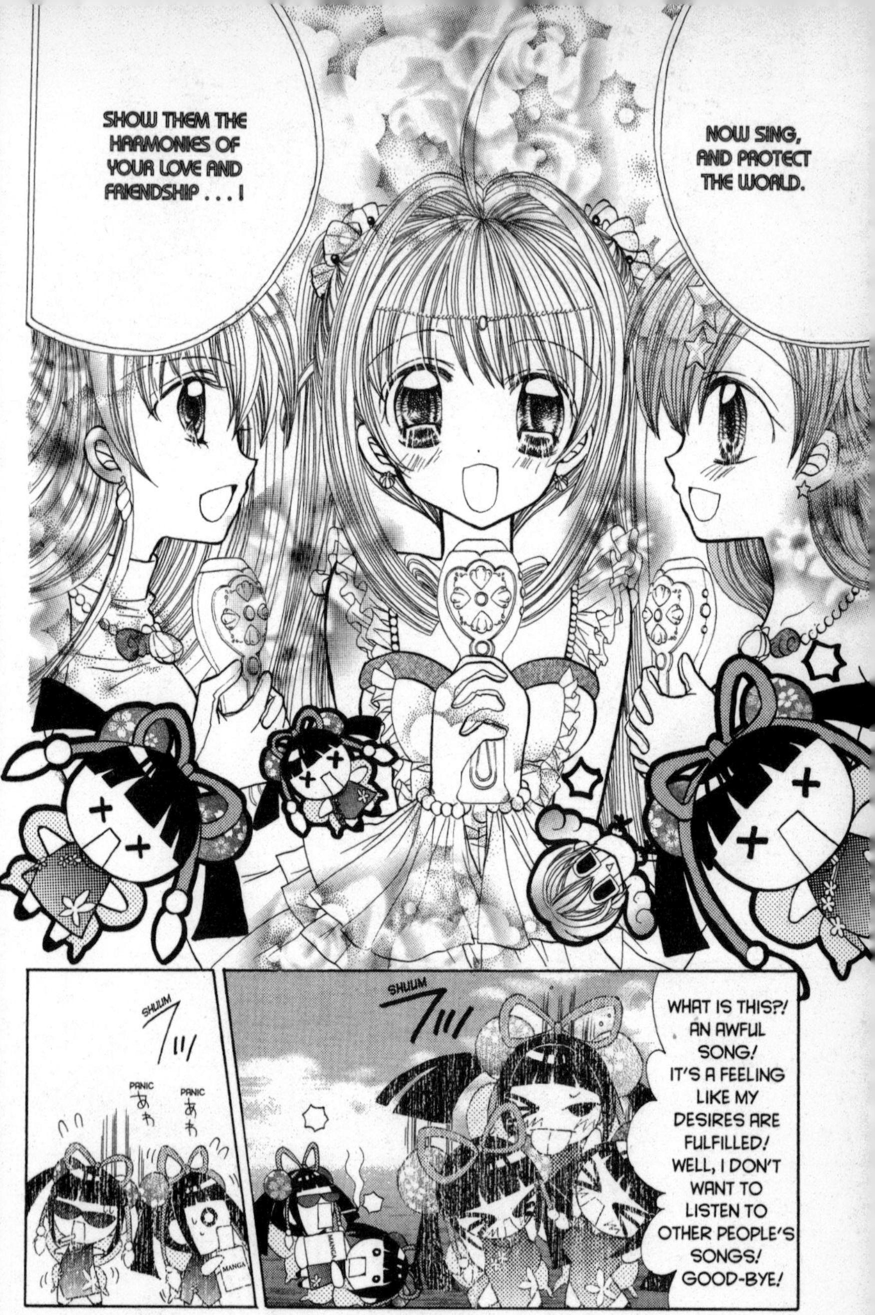
NOW SING, AND PROTECT THE WORLD.
SHOW THEM THE HARMONIES OF YOUR LOVE AND FRIENDSHIP . . . !
SHUUM
WHAT IS THIS?! AN AWFUL SONG! IT'S A FEELING LIKE MY DESIRES ARE FULFILLED! WELL, I DON'T WANT TO LISTEN TO OTHER PEOPLE'S SONGS! GOOD-BYE!
MANGA
SHUUM
PANIC
PANIC
MANGA

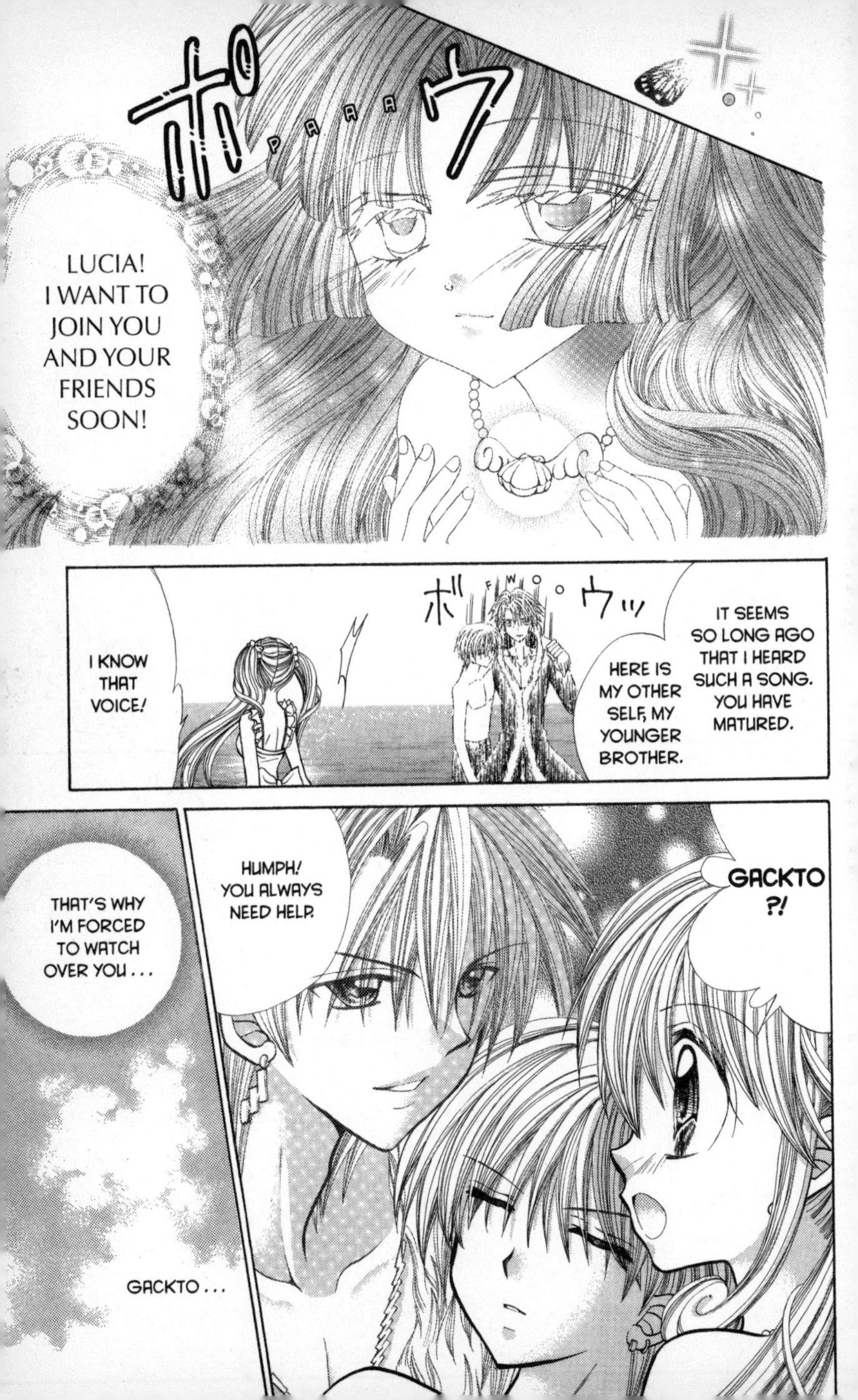
ポ PAAAA ウ
LUCIA! I WANT TO JOIN YOU AND YOUR FRIENDS SOON!
IT SEEMS SO LONG AGO THAT I HEARD SUCH A SONG. YOU HAVE MATURED.
HERE IS MY OTHER SELF, MY YOUNGER BROTHER.
ボ FWO ウッ
I KNOW THAT VOICE!
GACKTO ?!
HUMPH! YOU ALWAYS NEED HELP.
THAT'S WHY I'M FORCED TO WATCH OVER YOU . . .
GACKTO . . .

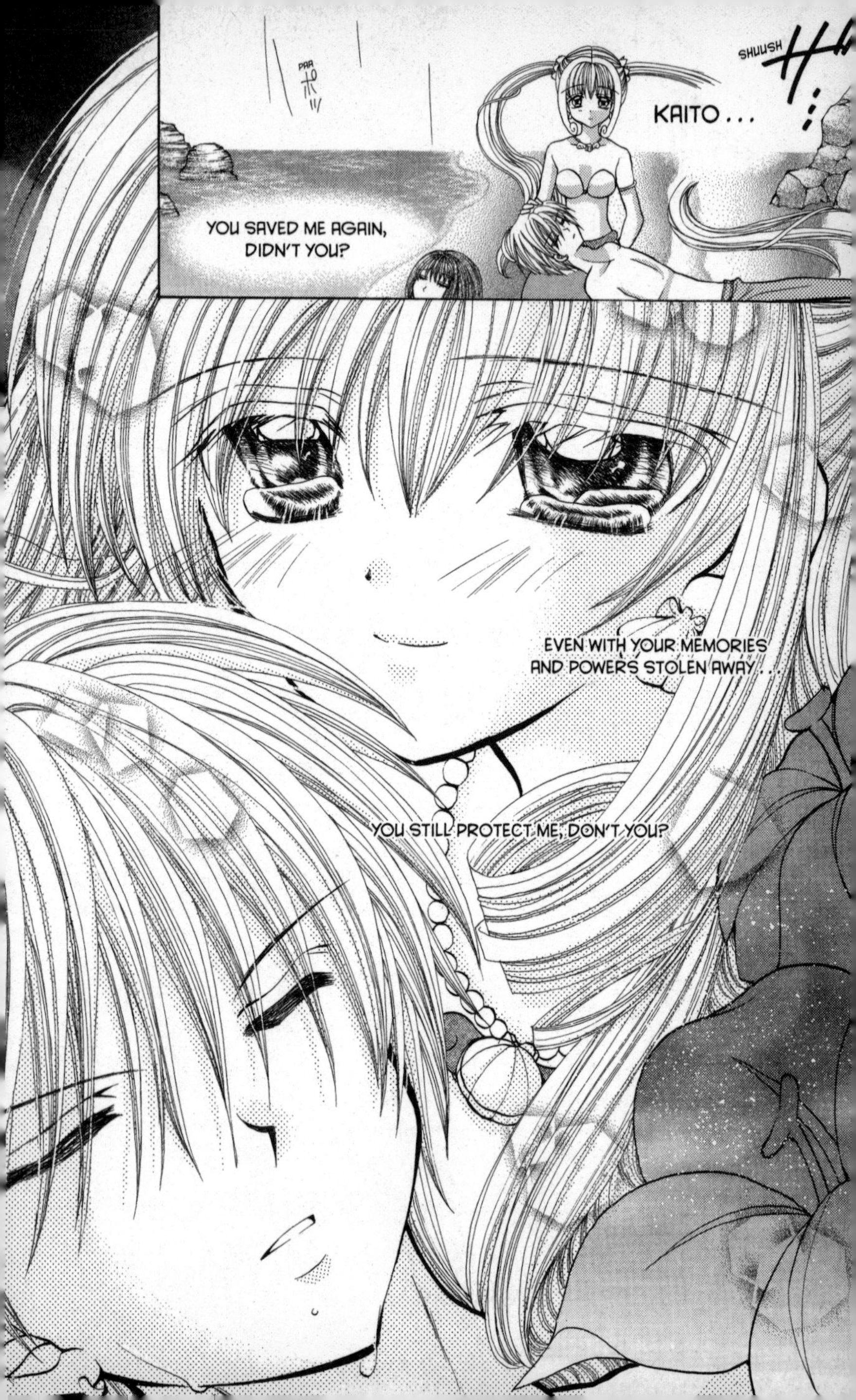
SHUUSH
KAITO . . .
PAA
YOU SAVED ME AGAIN, DIDN'T YOU?
EVEN WITH YOUR MEMORIES AND POWERS STOLEN AWAY . . .
YOU STILL PROTECT ME, DON'T YOU?

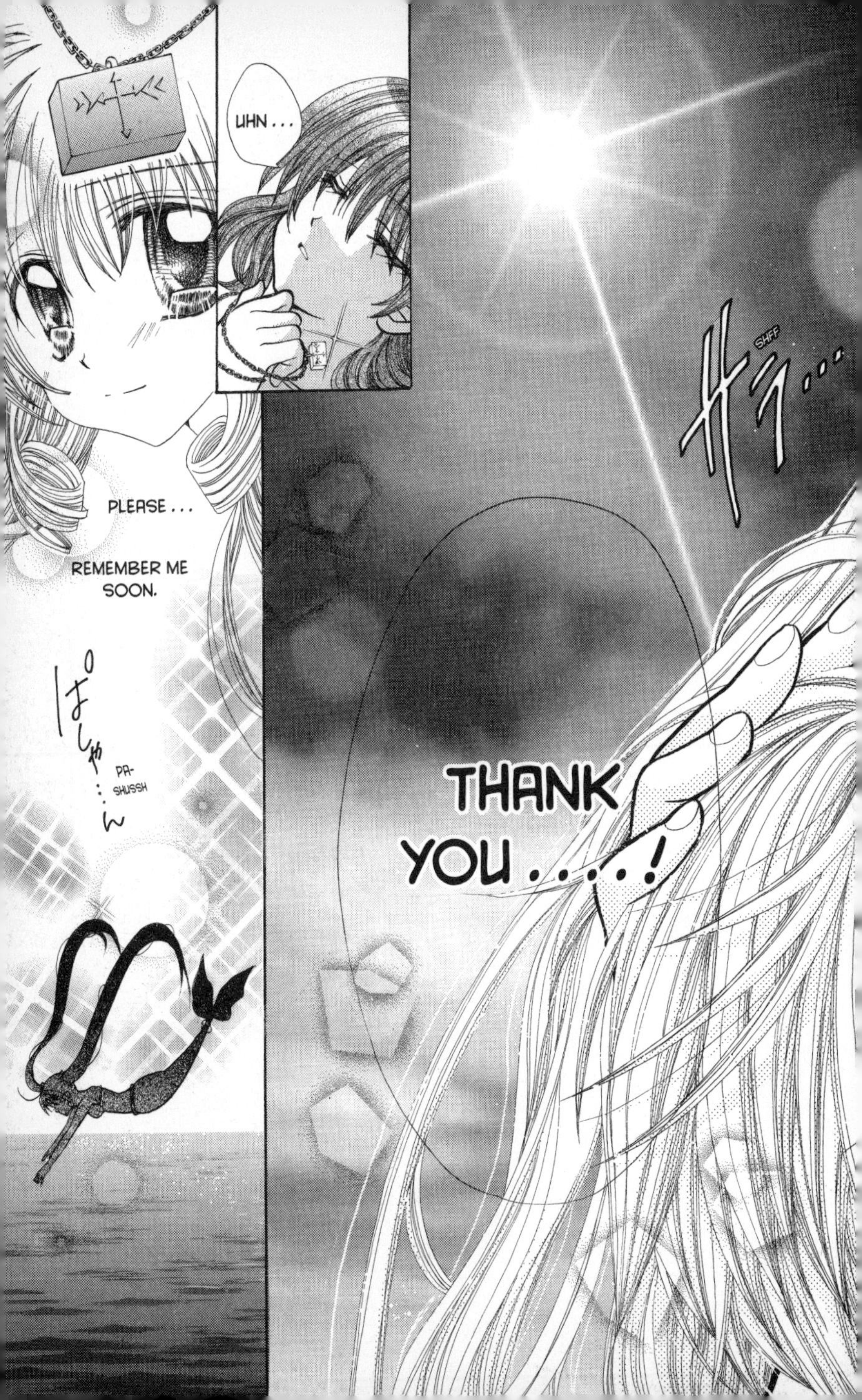
サラ…
SHFF
THANK YOU . . . . !
UHN . . .
PLEASE . . .
REMEMBER ME SOON.
ぱしゃ…ん
PA-SHUSSH

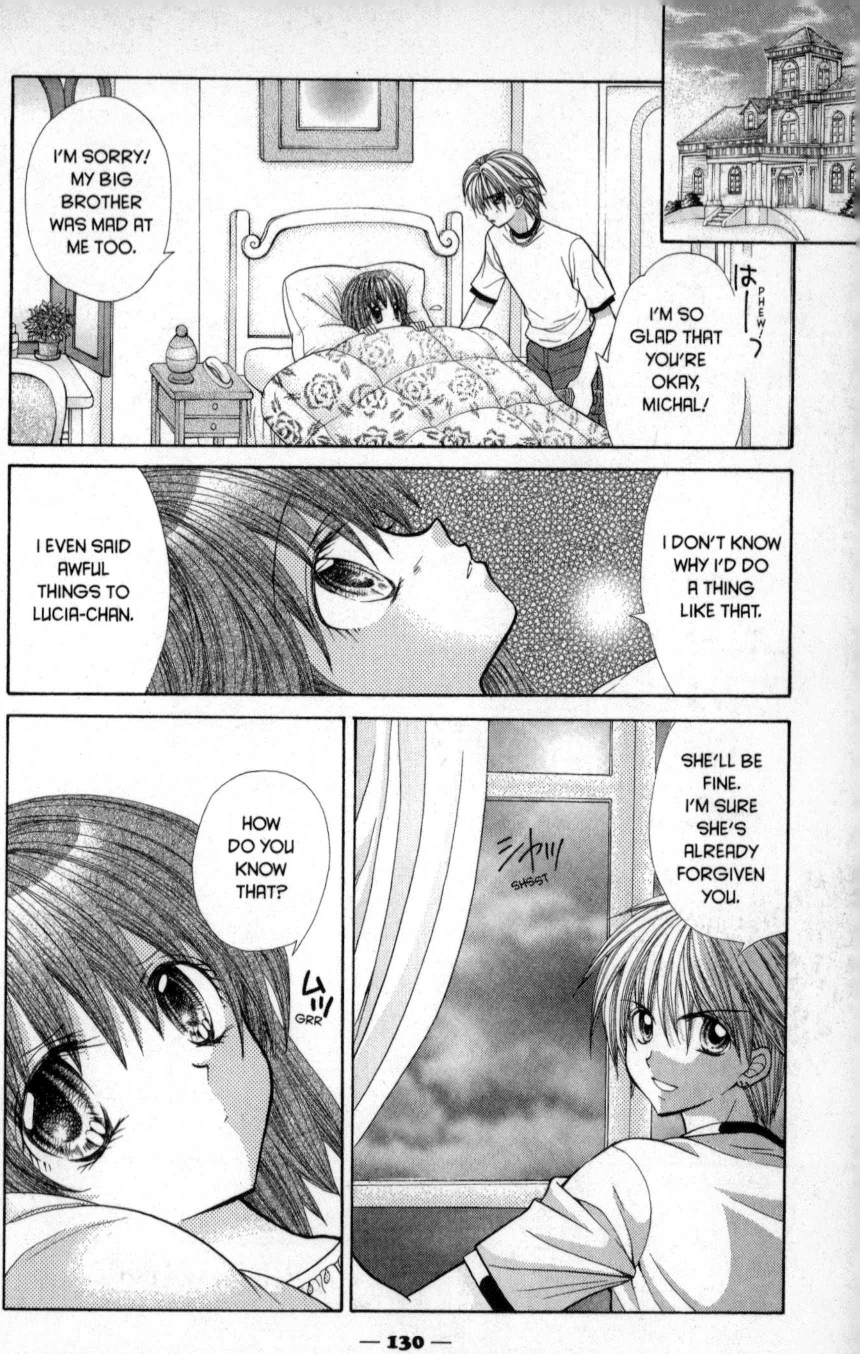
はーっ
PHEW!
I'M SO GLAD THAT YOU'RE OKAY, MICHAL!
I'M SORRY! MY BIG BROTHER WAS MAD AT ME TOO.
I DON'T KNOW WHY I'D DO A THING LIKE THAT.
I EVEN SAID AWFUL THINGS TO LUCIA-CHAN.
SHE'LL BE FINE. I'M SURE SHE'S ALREADY FORGIVEN YOU.
シャッ
SHSST
HOW DO YOU KNOW THAT?
ムッ
GRR

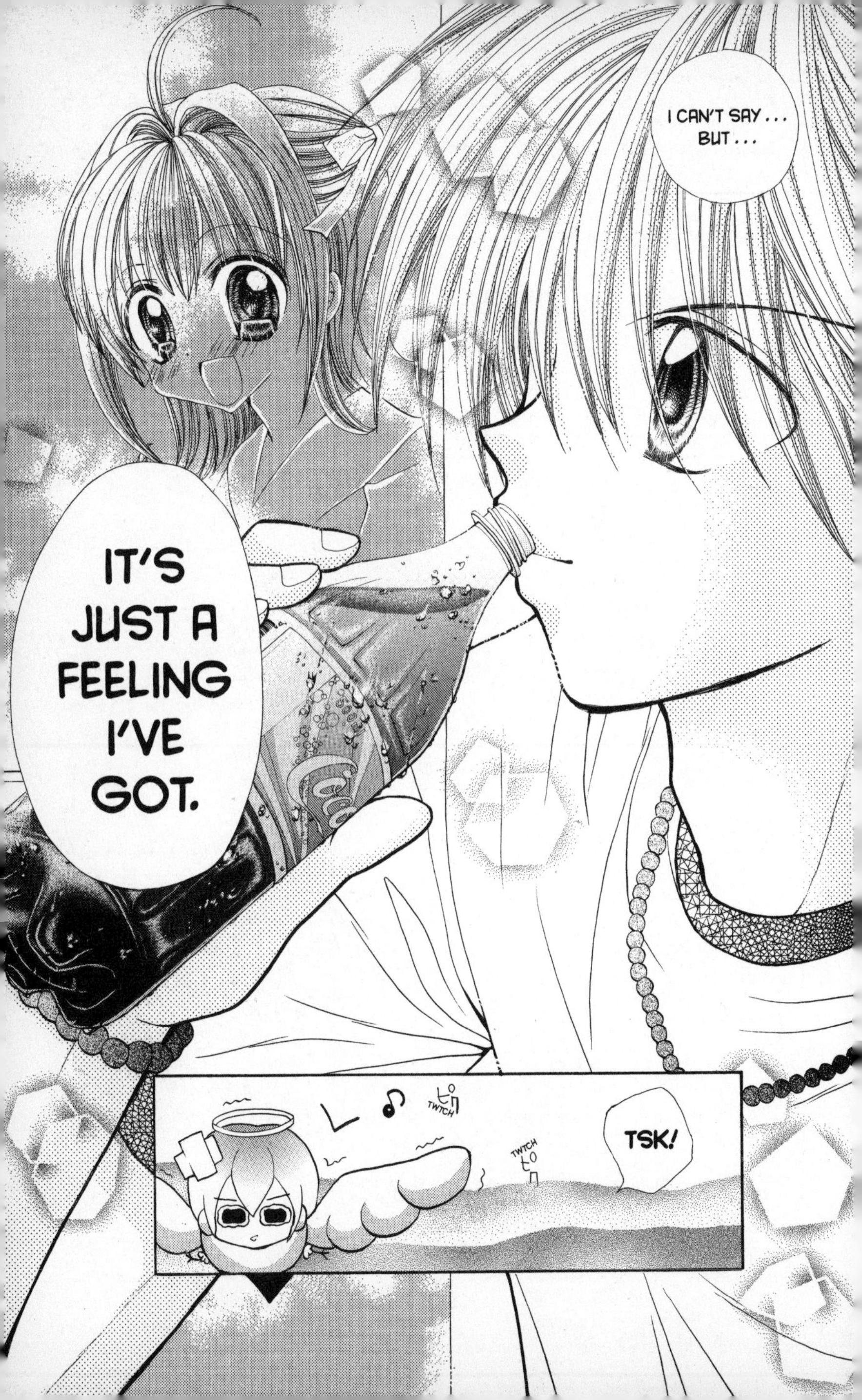
I CAN'T SAY . . . BUT . . .
IT'S JUST A FEELING I'VE GOT.
TSK!
TWITCH
TWITCH

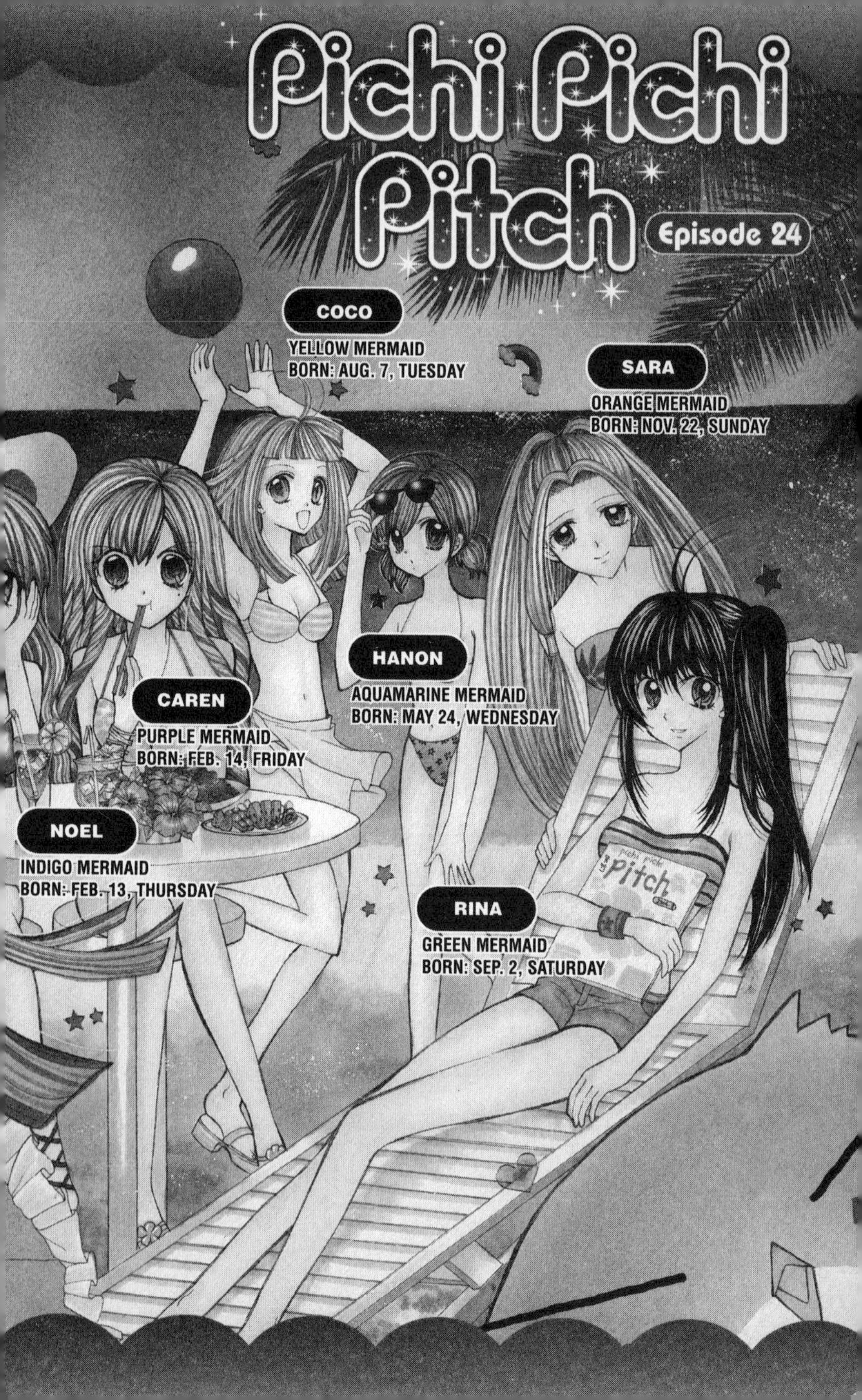
Pichi Pichi Pitch
Episode 24
COCO
YELLOW MERMAID
BORN: AUG. 7, TUESDAY
SARA
ORANGE MERMAID
BORN: NOV. 22, SUNDAY
HANON
AQUAMARINE MERMAID
BORN: MAY 24, WEDNESDAY
CAREN
PURPLE MERMAID
BORN: FEB. 14, FRIDAY
NOEL
INDIGO MERMAID
BORN: FEB. 13, THURSDAY
RINA
GREEN MERMAID
BORN: SEP. 2, SATURDAY

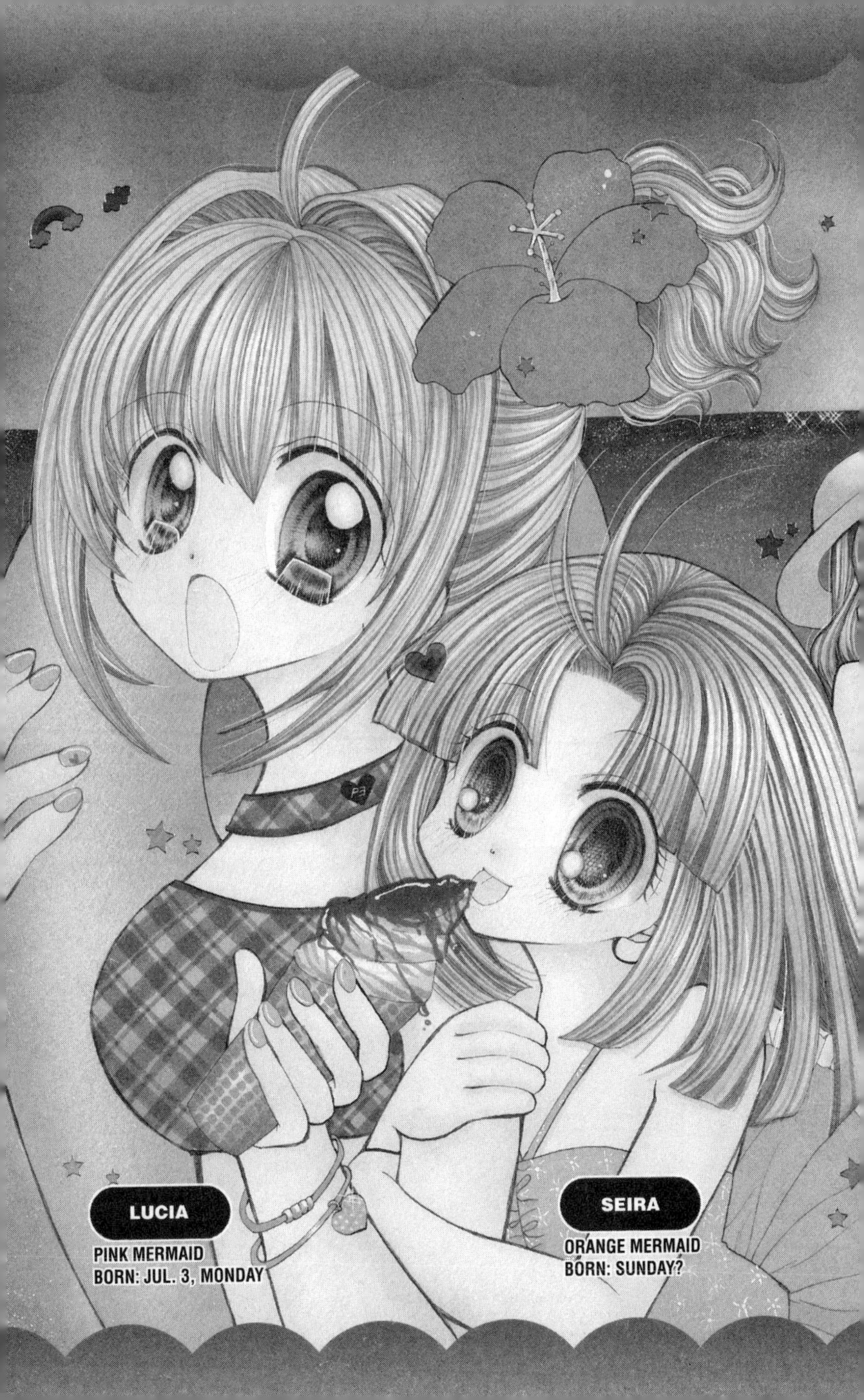
LUCIA
PINK MERMAID
BORN: JUL. 3, MONDAY
SEIRA
ORANGE MERMAID
BORN: SUNDAY?

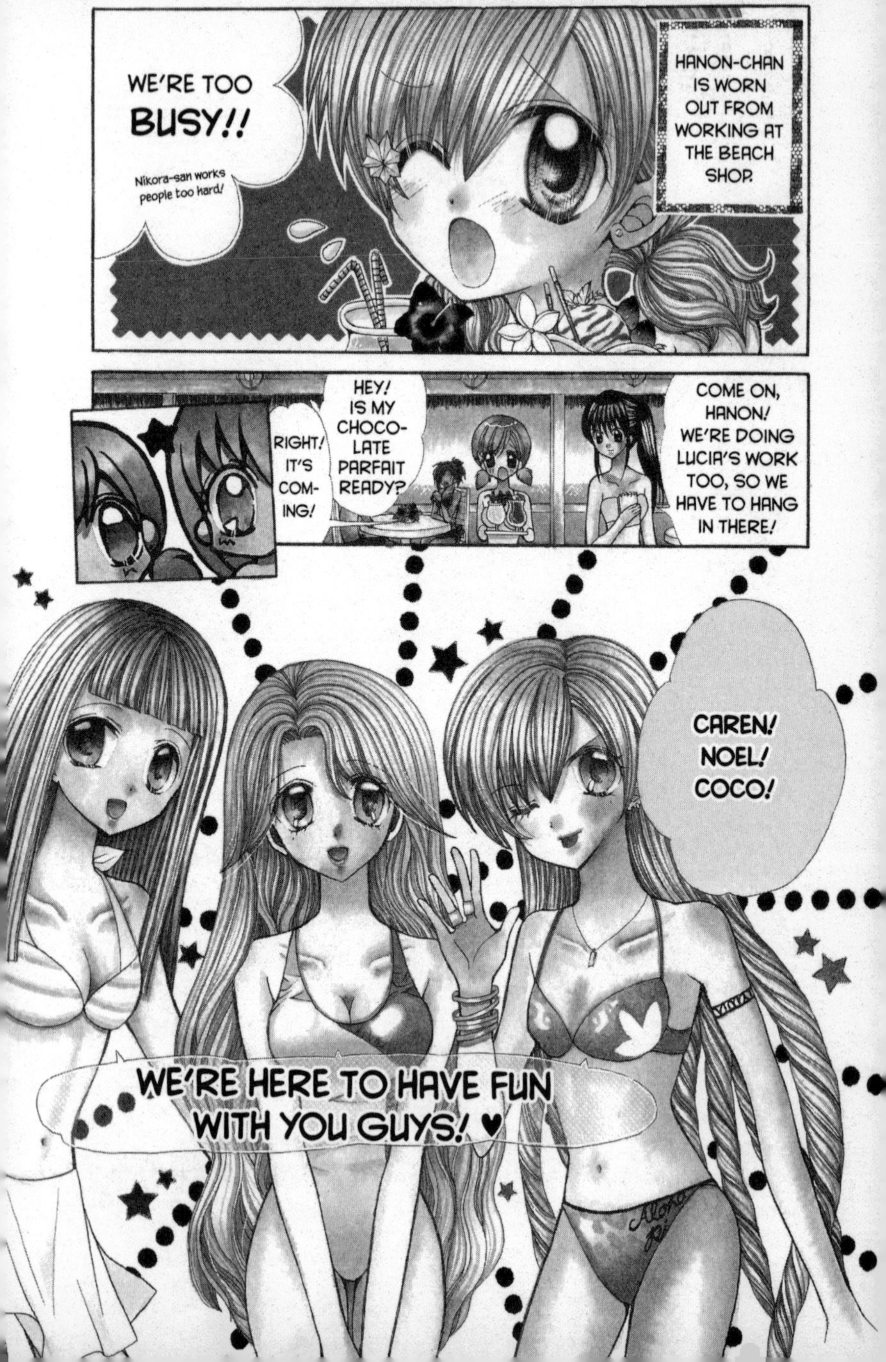
HANON-CHAN IS WORN OUT FROM WORKING AT THE BEACH SHOP.
WE'RE TOO BUSY!!
Nikora-san works people too hard!
COME ON, HANON! WE'RE DOING LUCIA'S WORK TOO, SO WE HAVE TO HANG IN THERE!
HEY! IS MY CHOCOLATE PARFAIT READY?
RIGHT! IT'S COMING!
CAREN! NOEL! COCO!
WE'RE HERE TO HAVE FUN WITH YOU GUYS! ♥

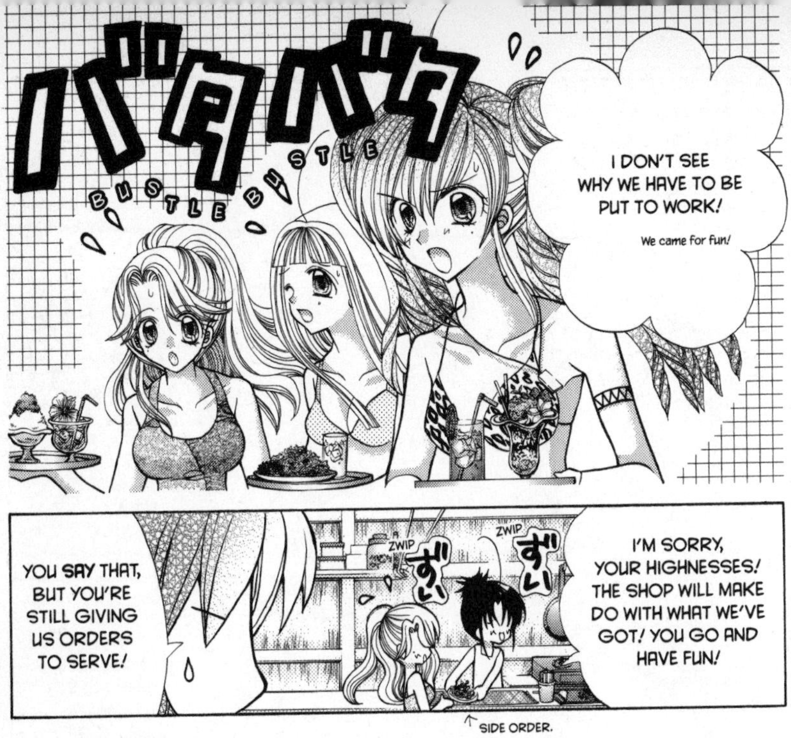
パタパタ
BUSTLE BUSTLE
I DON'T SEE WHY WE HAVE TO BE PUT TO WORK!
We came for fun!
I'M SORRY, YOUR HIGHNESSES! THE SHOP WILL MAKE DO WITH WHAT WE'VE GOT! YOU GO AND HAVE FUN!
ZWIP
ずい
ZWIP
ずい
YOU SAY THAT, BUT YOU'RE STILL GIVING US ORDERS TO SERVE!
SIDE ORDER.

<EPISODE 24>

ALL THE PRINCESSES TOGETHER!
WHENEVER I DRAW A BEACH ON THE SPLASH PAGE, IT REALLY FEELS LIKE PICHI!
IN THE SCENE WHERE RIHITO IS SHOCKED TO HEAR MICHAL'S DELIRIOUS WORDS, I THOUGHT, "OH, NO! HE MIGHT LOOK SCARY!" BUT A COUPLE OF MY ASSISTANTS SAID THAT THEY THOUGHT HE LOOKED COOL. THE BREAKDOWN WAS 3 FOR SCARY VS. 2 FOR COOL. I GUESS DIFFERENT PEOPLE SEE IT DIFFERENT WAYS.
COME TO THINK OF IT, WHILE I WAS DRAWING THIS EPISODE, WE STARTED TALKING ABOUT HOW COCO ACTED A LITTLE ROGUISH. I SORT OF FELT, "WHO'S THERE?! A ROGUISH KNAVE?!" THEN I'D THROW OPEN THE FUSUMA DOORS! JUST LIKE OUT OF A SAMURAI-ERA PIECE. HUH? NOT REALLY! WELL . . . SORT OF, BUT . . . OH, WHO CARES!

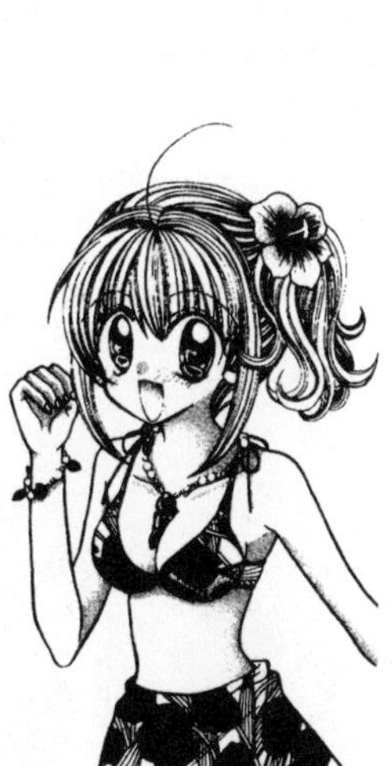

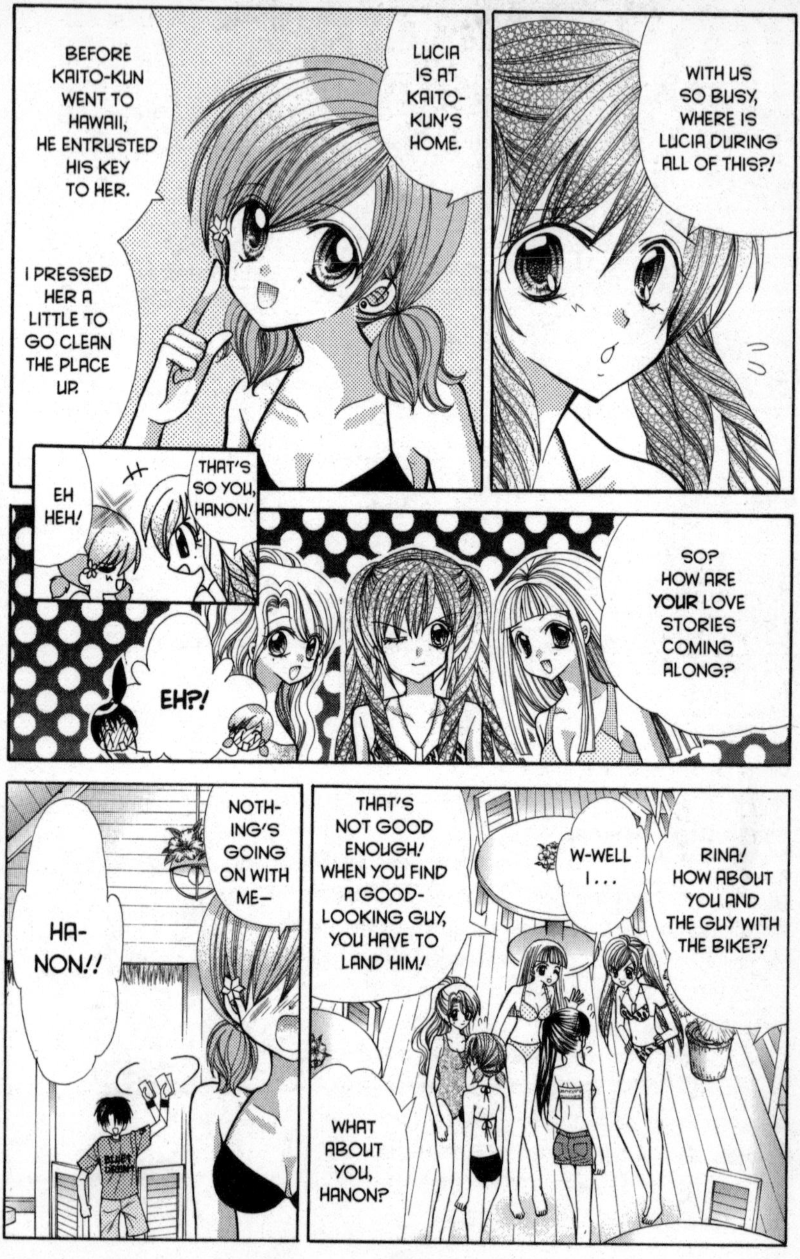
WITH US SO BUSY, WHERE IS LUCIA DURING ALL OF THIS?!
LUCIA IS AT KAITO-KUN'S HOME.
BEFORE KAITO-KUN WENT TO HAWAII, HE ENTRUSTED HIS KEY TO HER.
I PRESSED HER A LITTLE TO GO CLEAN THE PLACE UP.
THAT'S SO YOU, HANON!
EH HEH!
SO? HOW ARE **YOUR** LOVE STORIES COMING ALONG?
EH?!
RINA! HOW ABOUT YOU AND THE GUY WITH THE BIKE?!
W-WELL I...
THAT'S NOT GOOD ENOUGH! WHEN YOU FIND A GOOD-LOOKING GUY, YOU HAVE TO LAND HIM!
WHAT ABOUT YOU, HANON?
NOTH-ING'S GOING ON WITH ME—
HA-NON!!

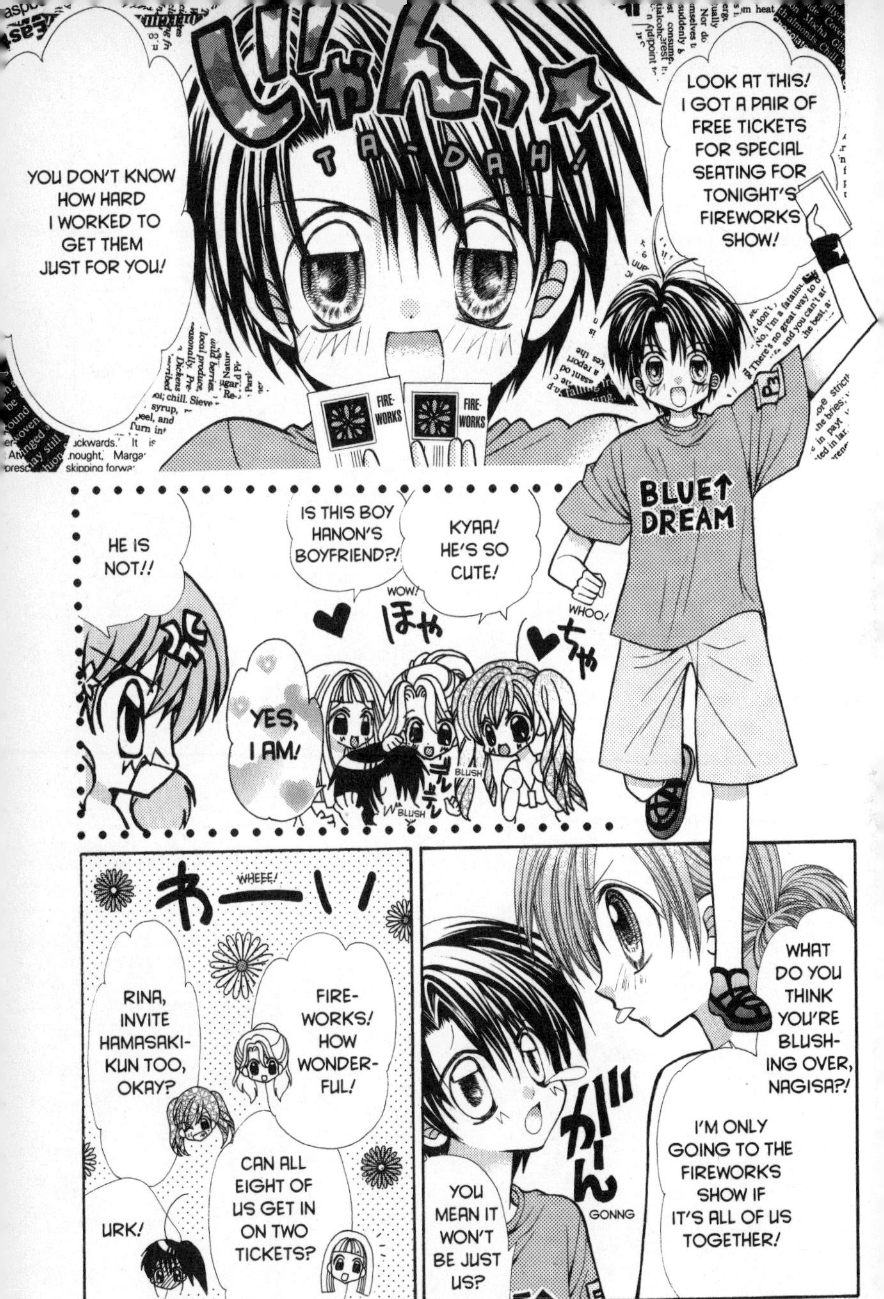
じゃんっ
TA-DAH!
LOOK AT THIS! I GOT A PAIR OF FREE TICKETS FOR SPECIAL SEATING FOR TONIGHT'S FIREWORKS SHOW!
FIRE-WORKS
FIRE-WORKS
YOU DON'T KNOW HOW HARD I WORKED TO GET THEM JUST FOR YOU!
BLUE DREAM
WHOO!
ちゃ
KYAA! HE'S SO CUTE!
IS THIS BOY HANON'S BOYFRIEND?!
WOW!
ほゃ
HE IS NOT!!
YES, I AM!
BLUSH
BLUSH
WHAT DO YOU THINK YOU'RE BLUSHING OVER, NAGISA?!
I'M ONLY GOING TO THE FIREWORKS SHOW IF IT'S ALL OF US TOGETHER!
がーん
GONNG
YOU MEAN IT WON'T BE JUST US?
WHEEE!
FIRE-WORKS! HOW WONDER-FUL!
RINA, INVITE HAMASAKI-KUN TOO, OKAY?
CAN ALL EIGHT OF US GET IN ON TWO TICKETS?
URK!

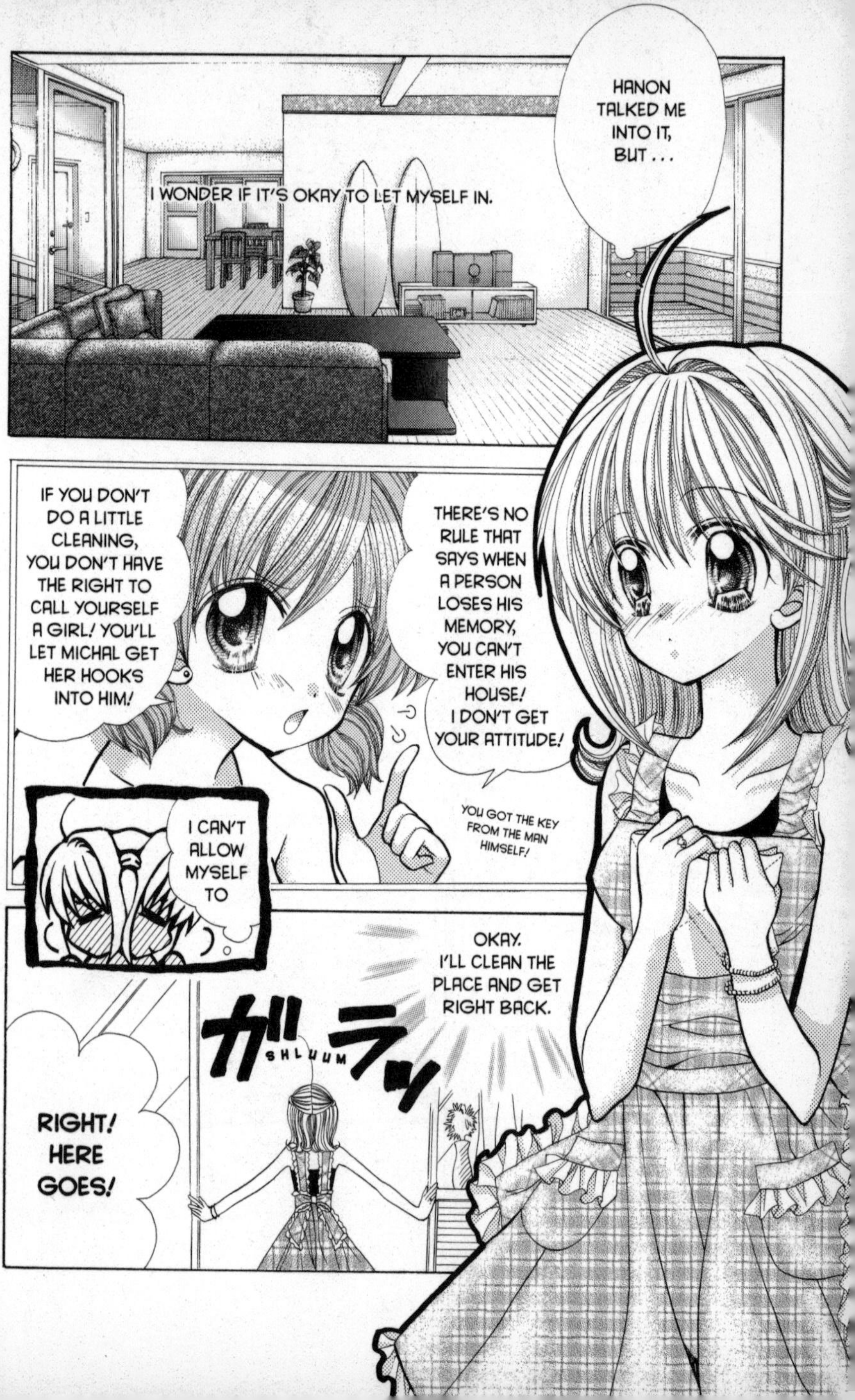
HANON TALKED ME INTO IT, BUT . . .
I WONDER IF IT'S OKAY TO LET MYSELF IN.
THERE'S NO RULE THAT SAYS WHEN A PERSON LOSES HIS MEMORY, YOU CAN'T ENTER HIS HOUSE! I DON'T GET YOUR ATTITUDE!
IF YOU DON'T DO A LITTLE CLEANING, YOU DON'T HAVE THE RIGHT TO CALL YOURSELF A GIRL! YOU'LL LET MICHAL GET HER HOOKS INTO HIM!
YOU GOT THE KEY FROM THE MAN HIMSELF!
I CAN'T ALLOW MYSELF TO
OKAY. I'LL CLEAN THE PLACE AND GET RIGHT BACK.
ガラッ
SHLUUM
RIGHT! HERE GOES!

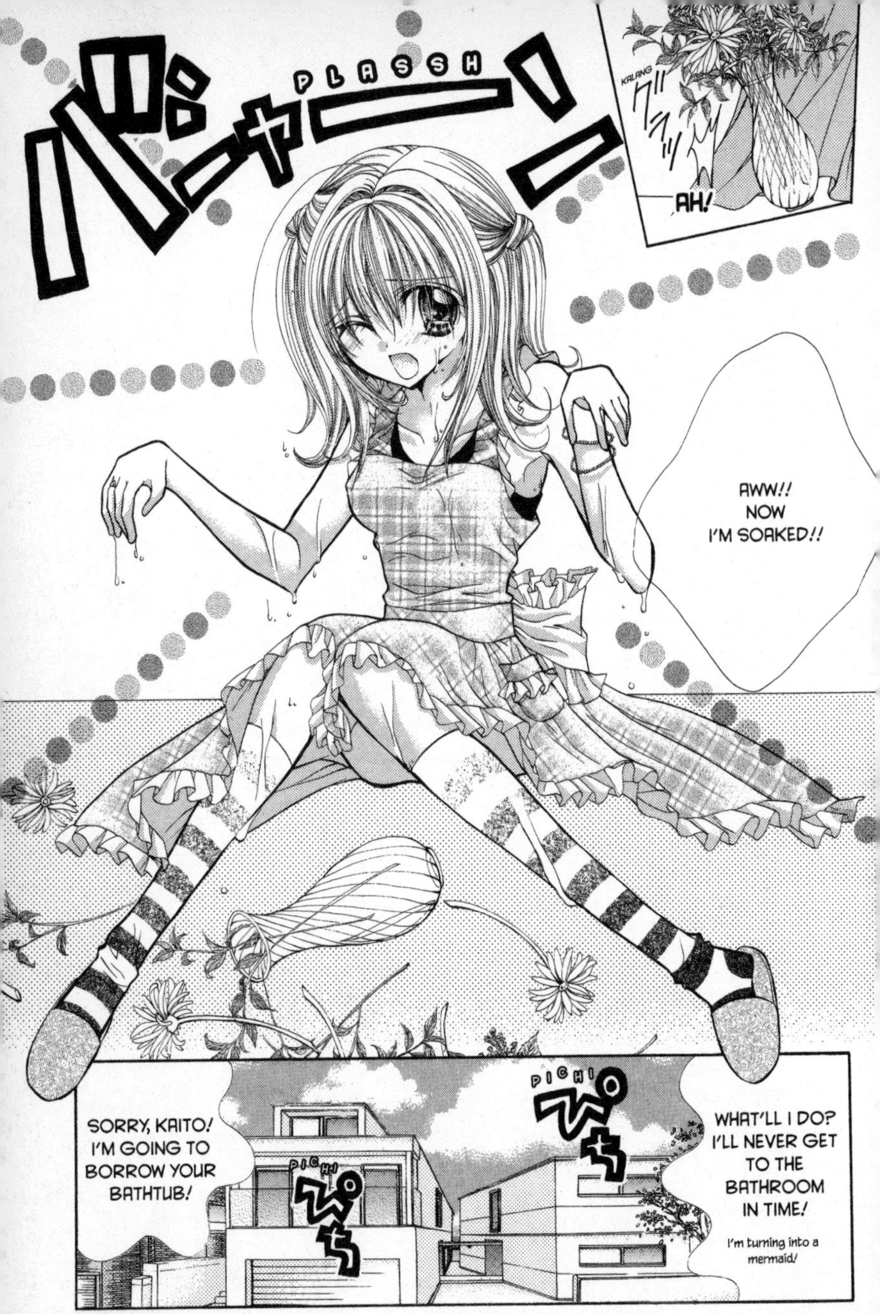
KALANG
AH!
PLASSH
AWW!! NOW I'M SOAKED!!
PICHI
WHAT'LL I DO? I'LL NEVER GET TO THE BATHROOM IN TIME!
I'm turning into a mermaid!
PICHI
SORRY, KAITO! I'M GOING TO BORROW YOUR BATHTUB!

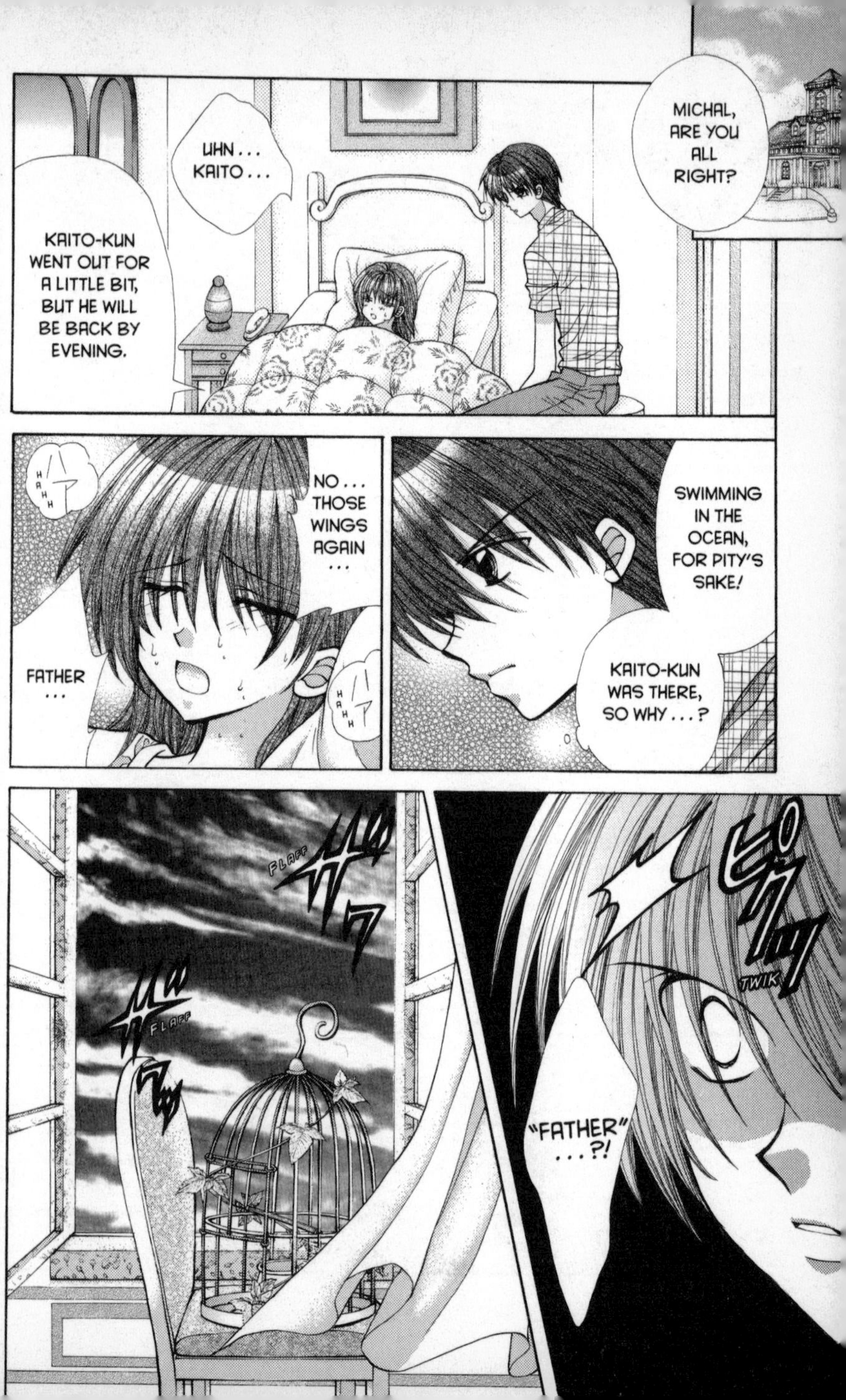
MICHAL, ARE YOU ALL RIGHT?
UHN . . . KAITO . . .
KAITO-KUN WENT OUT FOR A LITTLE BIT, BUT HE WILL BE BACK BY EVENING.
SWIMMING IN THE OCEAN, FOR PITY'S SAKE!
KAITO-KUN WAS THERE, SO WHY . . . ?
HAHH
NO . . . THOSE WINGS AGAIN . . .
HAHH
FATHER . . .
TWIK
"FATHER" . . . ?!
FLAFF
FLAFF

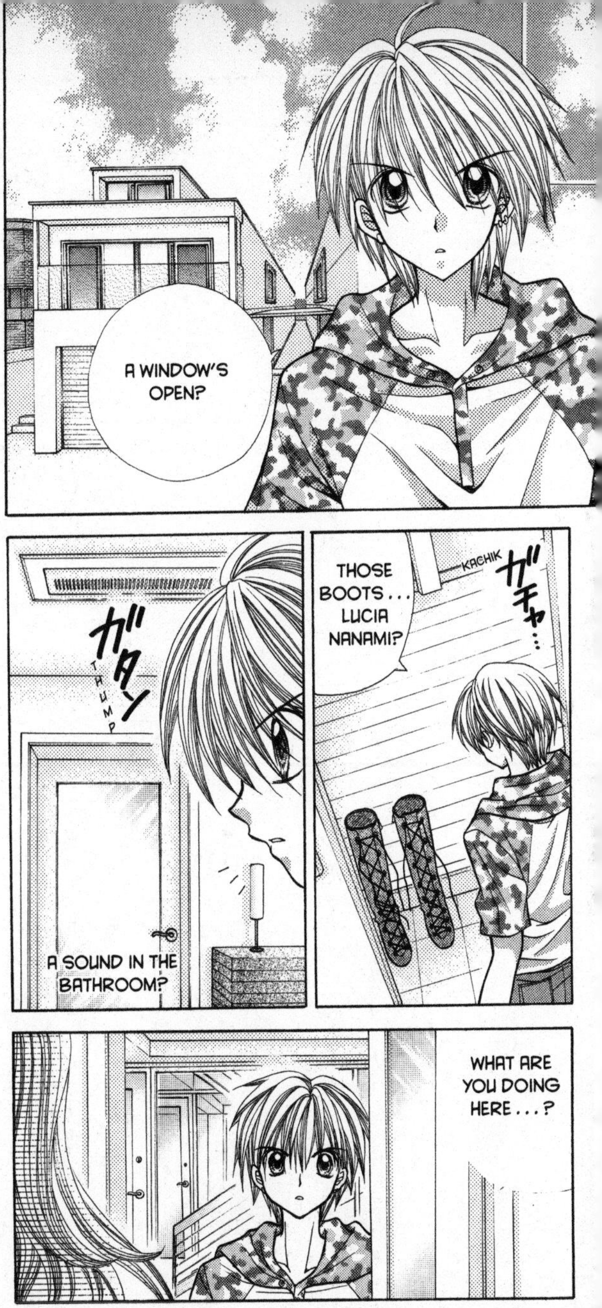
A WINDOW'S OPEN?
ガチャ…
KACHIK
THOSE BOOTS... LUCIA NANAMI?
ガタン
THUMP
A SOUND IN THE BATHROOM?
WHAT ARE YOU DOING HERE...?

HEART FRAGMENTS

I THINK THAT I MAY HAVE DROPPED ONE OR TWO PIECES MYSELF. A HEART THAT CAN FEEL ALL SORTS OF DIFFERENT FEELINGS.

WHAT ABOUT ALL OF YOU?

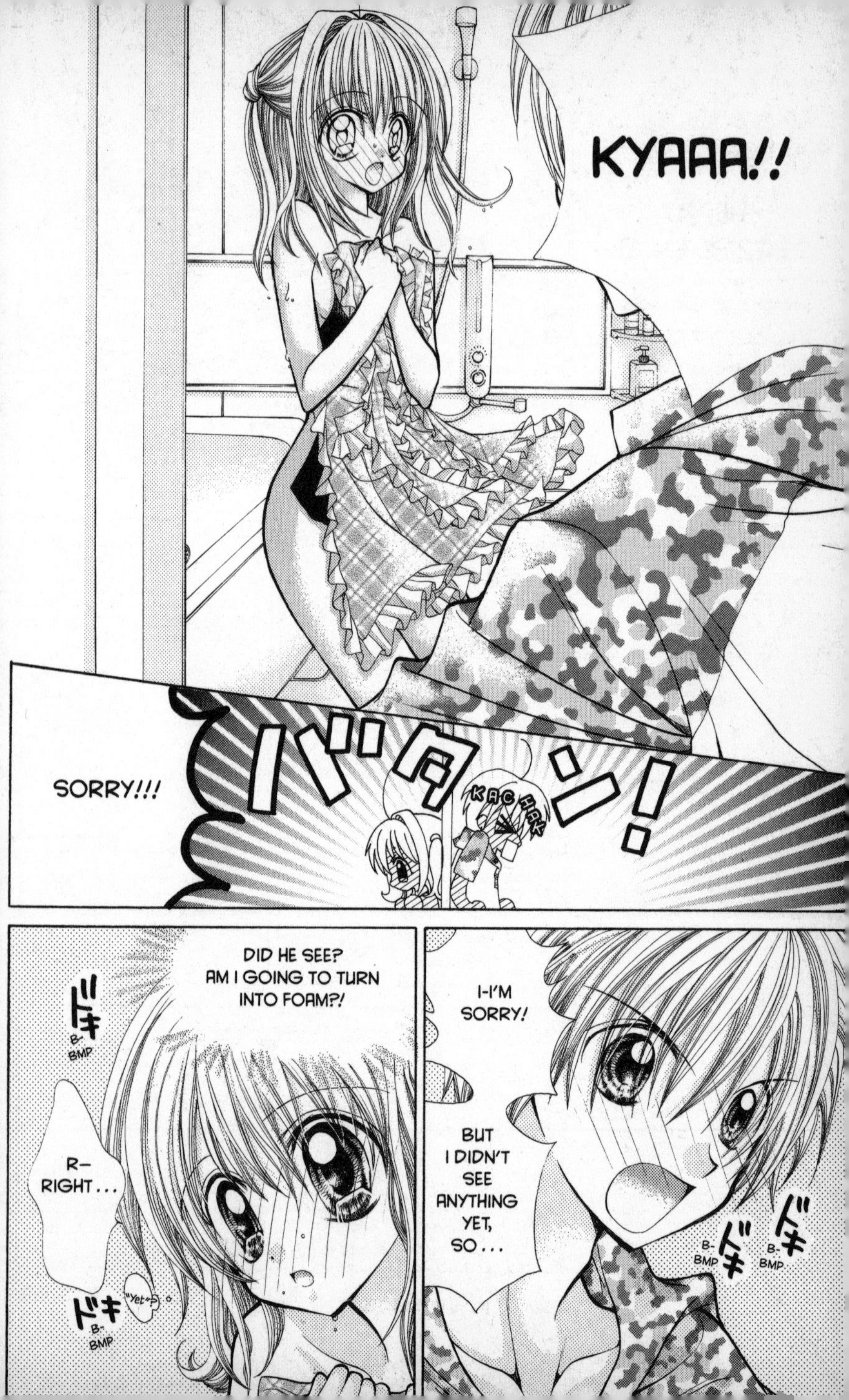
KYAAA!!
バタン!
KACHAK
SORRY!!!
I-I'M SORRY!
BUT I DIDN'T SEE ANYTHING YET, SO...
ドキ
B-BMP
ドキ
B-BMP
DID HE SEE? AM I GOING TO TURN INTO FOAM?!
ドキ
B-BMP
R— RIGHT...
"Yet"?
ドキ
B-BMP

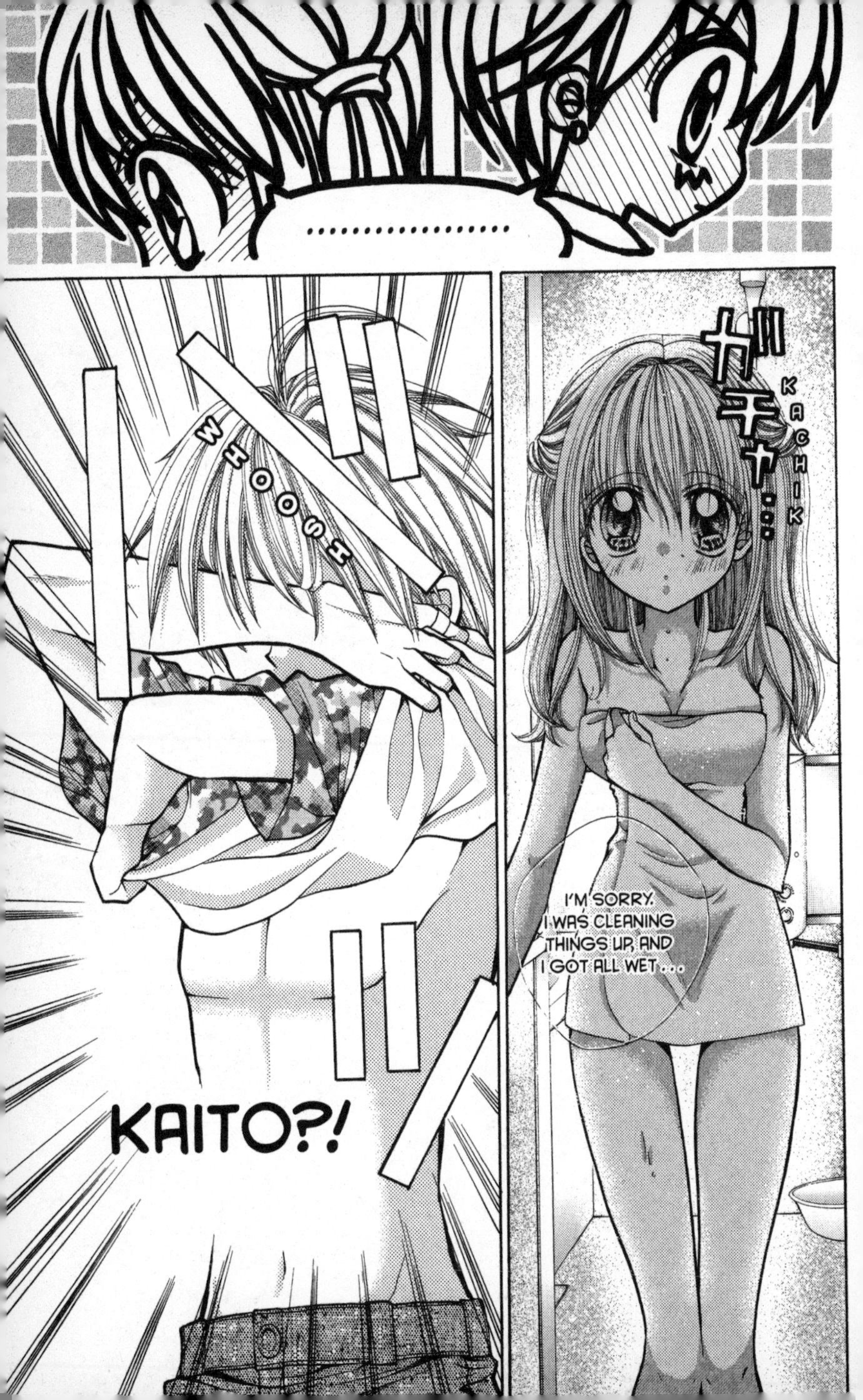
....
ガチャ…
KACHIK
I'M SORRY. I WAS CLEANING THINGS UP, AND I GOT ALL WET . . .
WHOOSH
KAITO?!

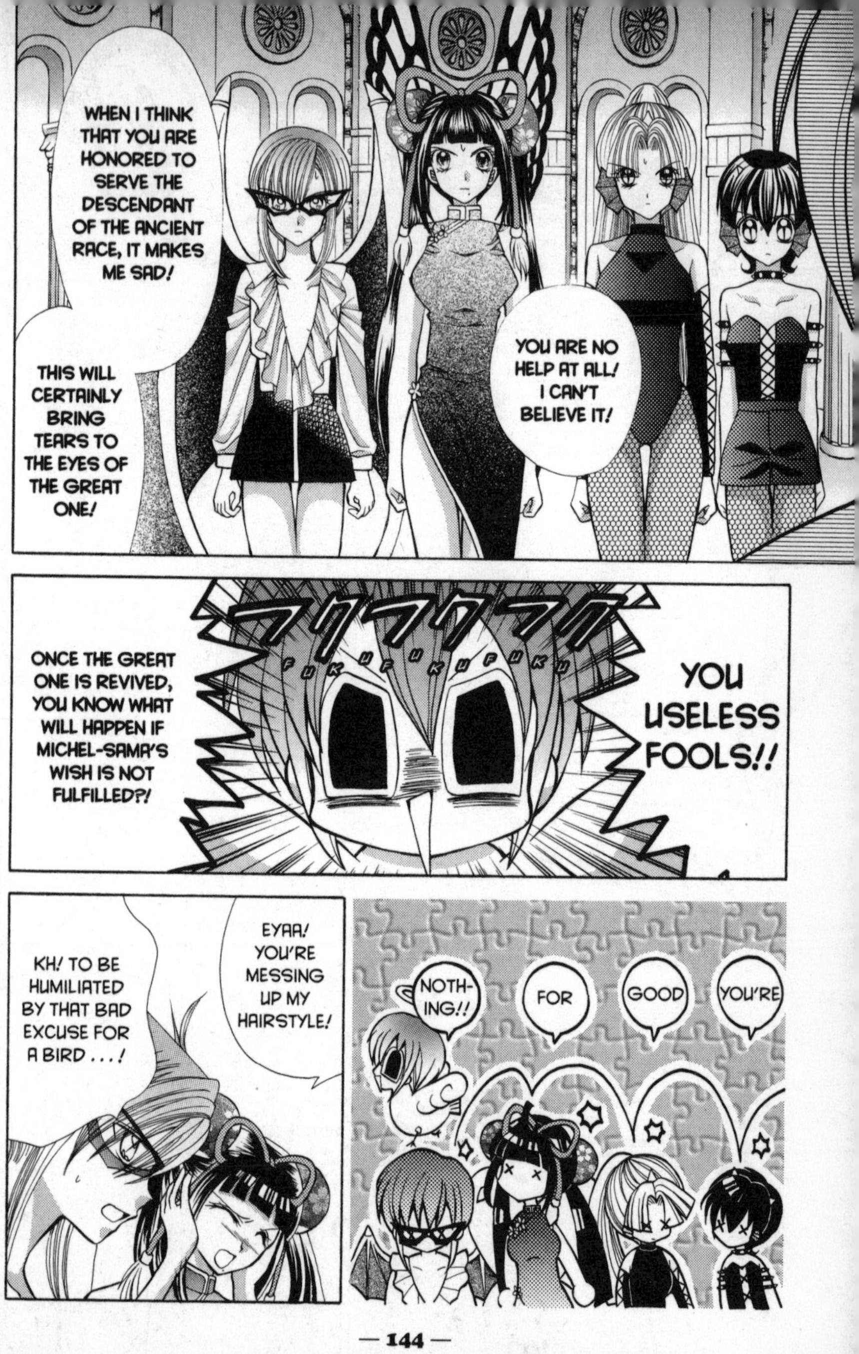
YOU ARE NO HELP AT ALL! I CAN'T BELIEVE IT!
WHEN I THINK THAT YOU ARE HONORED TO SERVE THE DESCENDANT OF THE ANCIENT RACE, IT MAKES ME SAD!
THIS WILL CERTAINLY BRING TEARS TO THE EYES OF THE GREAT ONE!
FUKUFUKUFUKU
YOU USELESS FOOLS!!
ONCE THE GREAT ONE IS REVIVED, YOU KNOW WHAT WILL HAPPEN IF MICHEL-SAMA'S WISH IS NOT FULFILLED?!
YOU'RE
GOOD
FOR
NOTH-ING!!
EYAA! YOU'RE MESSING UP MY HAIRSTYLE!
KH! TO BE HUMILIATED BY THAT BAD EXCUSE FOR A BIRD . . . !

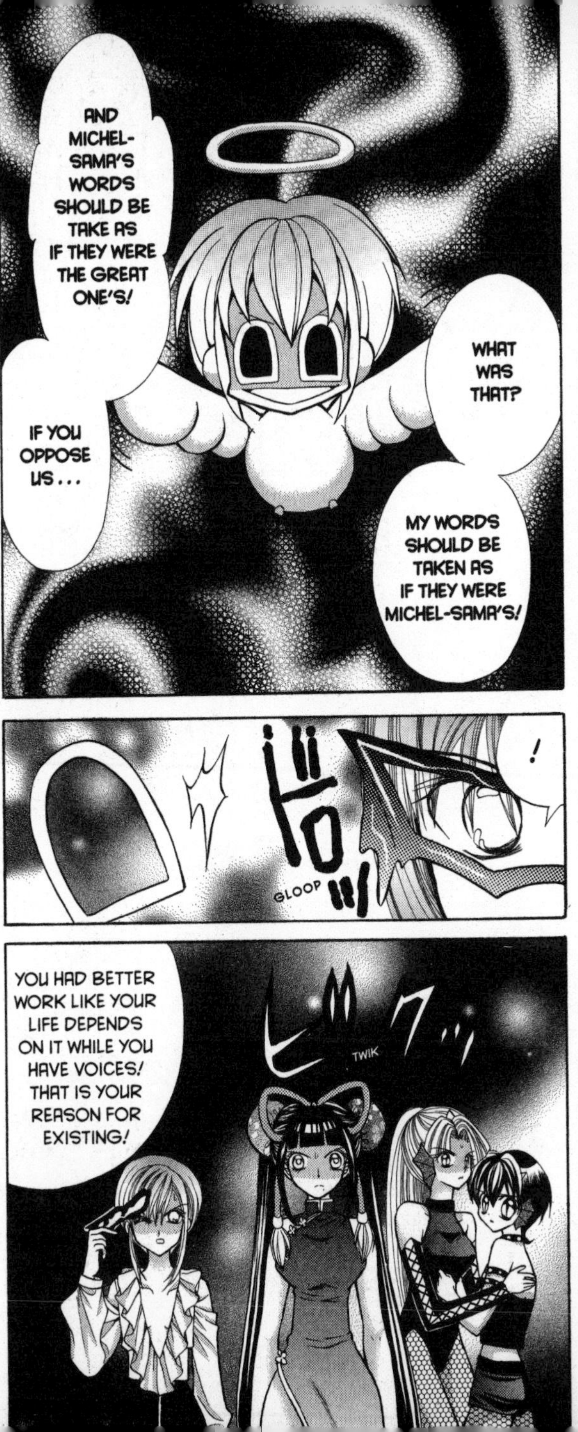
AND MICHEL-SAMA'S WORDS SHOULD BE TAKE AS IF THEY WERE THE GREAT ONE'S!
WHAT WAS THAT?
IF YOU OPPOSE US...
MY WORDS SHOULD BE TAKEN AS IF THEY WERE MICHEL-SAMA'S!
!
GLOOP
TWIK
YOU HAD BETTER WORK LIKE YOUR LIFE DEPENDS ON IT WHILE YOU HAVE VOICES! THAT IS YOUR REASON FOR EXISTING!

AFTERWORD

THANK YOU SO MUCH FOR READING UP UNTIL NOW. LET'S MEET AGAIN IN VOLUME 6.

♥ special Thanks ♥

MOMO UTSUGI-SAMA,
OVERSEES LIPS

MEI HIROMI-SAMA,
LOVES MASCOT COSTUMES

RUMIKO NAGANO-SAMA,
ALWAYS COUNTING ON HER

KOTORI MOMOYUKI-SAMA,
KOTO-RUNRUN

RAN MITSUKI-SAMA,
GODDESS OF DESTRUCTION

SAKI-SAMA,
WANTS STRAWBERRIES

SHIHO NAKAZAWA-SAMA,
WARM AND COMFY

MASAYO NOYORI-SAMA,
SHINE!

and you!

EDITORS:
KAWAMOTO-SAMA
ZUSHI-SAMA

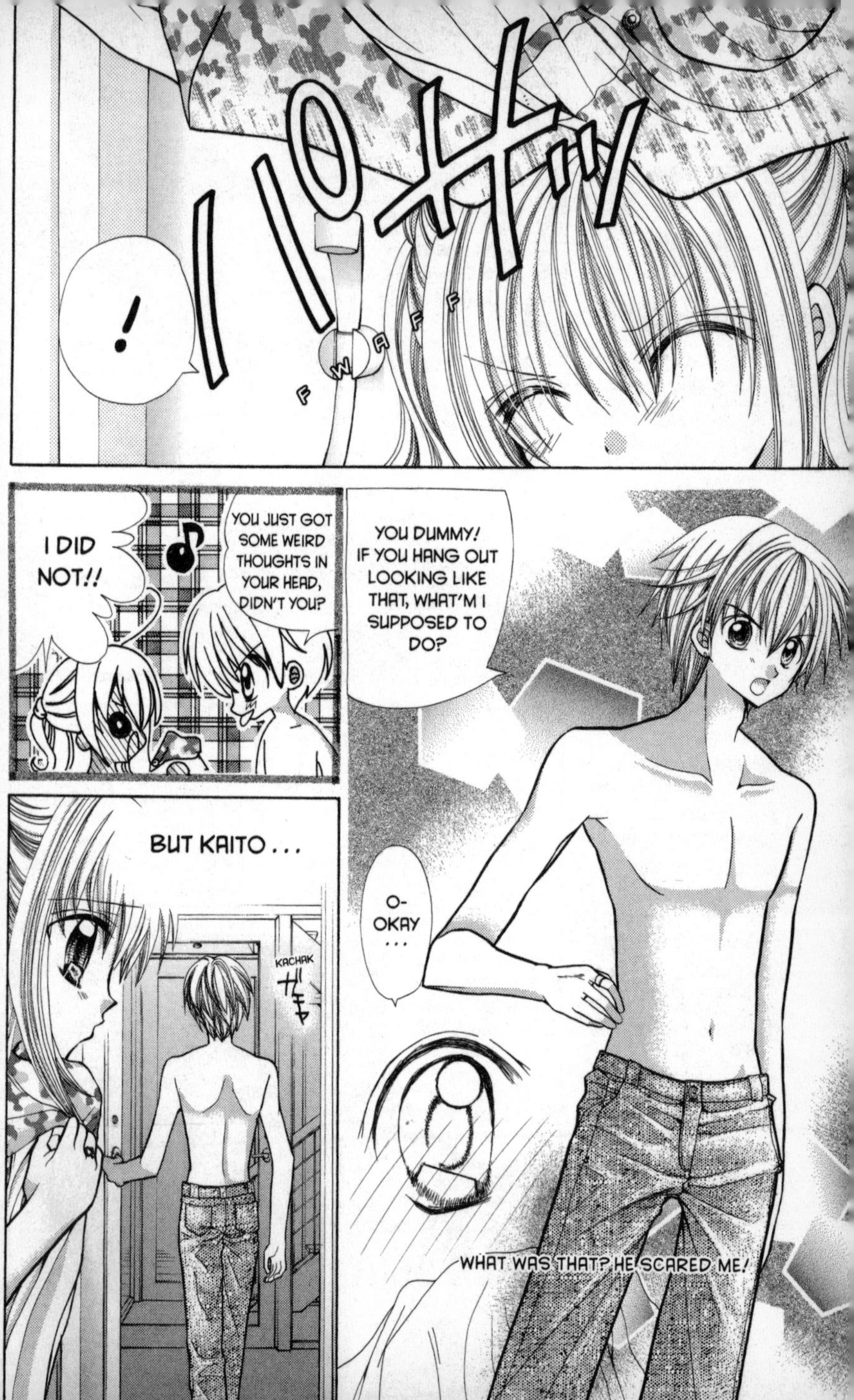
FWAFF
!
YOU DUMMY! IF YOU HANG OUT LOOKING LIKE THAT, WHAT'M I SUPPOSED TO DO?
O-OKAY . . .
WHAT WAS THAT? HE SCARED ME!
YOU JUST GOT SOME WEIRD THOUGHTS IN YOUR HEAD, DIDN'T YOU?
I DID NOT!!
BUT KAITO . . .
KACHAK

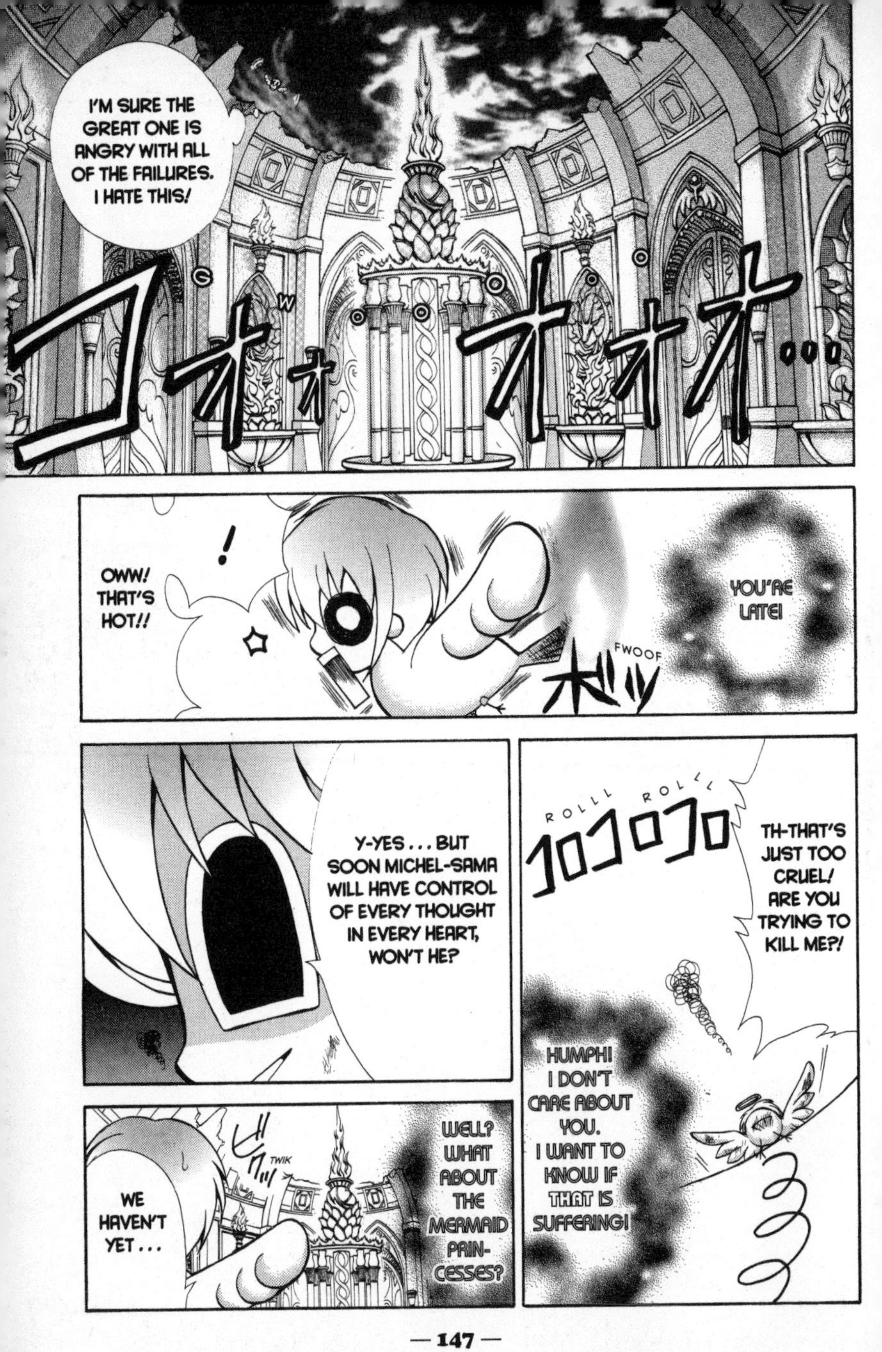
I'M SURE THE GREAT ONE IS ANGRY WITH ALL OF THE FAILURES. I HATE THIS!
YOU'RE LATE!
FWOOF
OWW! THAT'S HOT!!
TH-THAT'S JUST TOO CRUEL! ARE YOU TRYING TO KILL ME?!
ROLLL ROLLL
コロコロコロ
HUMPH! I DON'T CARE ABOUT YOU. I WANT TO KNOW IF THAT IS SUFFERING!
Y-YES . . . BUT SOON MICHEL-SAMA WILL HAVE CONTROL OF EVERY THOUGHT IN EVERY HEART, WON'T HE?
WELL? WHAT ABOUT THE MERMAID PRINCESSES?
TWIK
WE HAVEN'T YET . . .

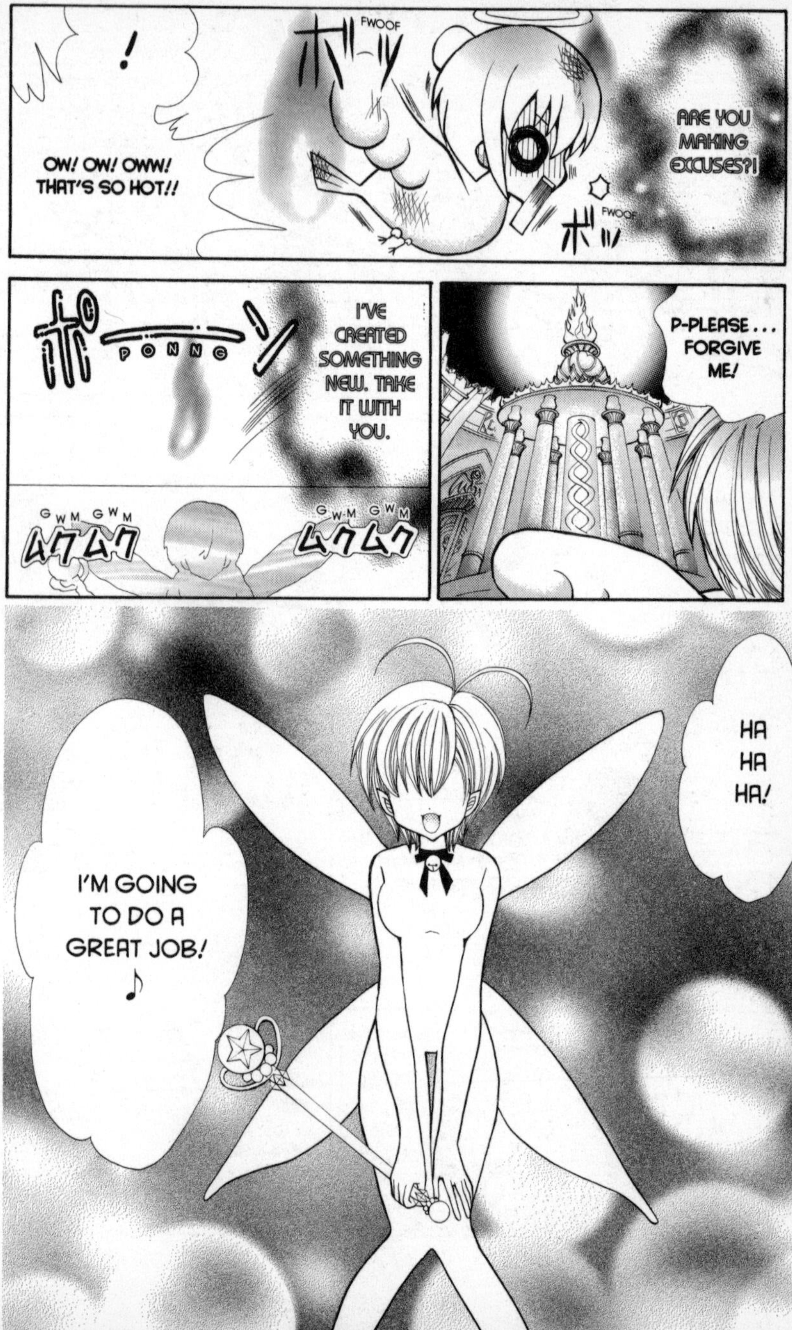

FWOOF
ARE YOU MAKING EXCUSES?!
FWOOF
!
OW! OW! OWW! THAT'S SO HOT!!
P-PLEASE... FORGIVE ME!
I'VE CREATED SOMETHING NEW. TAKE IT WITH YOU.
PONNG
GWM GWM
GWM GWM
HA HA HA!
I'M GOING TO DO A GREAT JOB! ♪

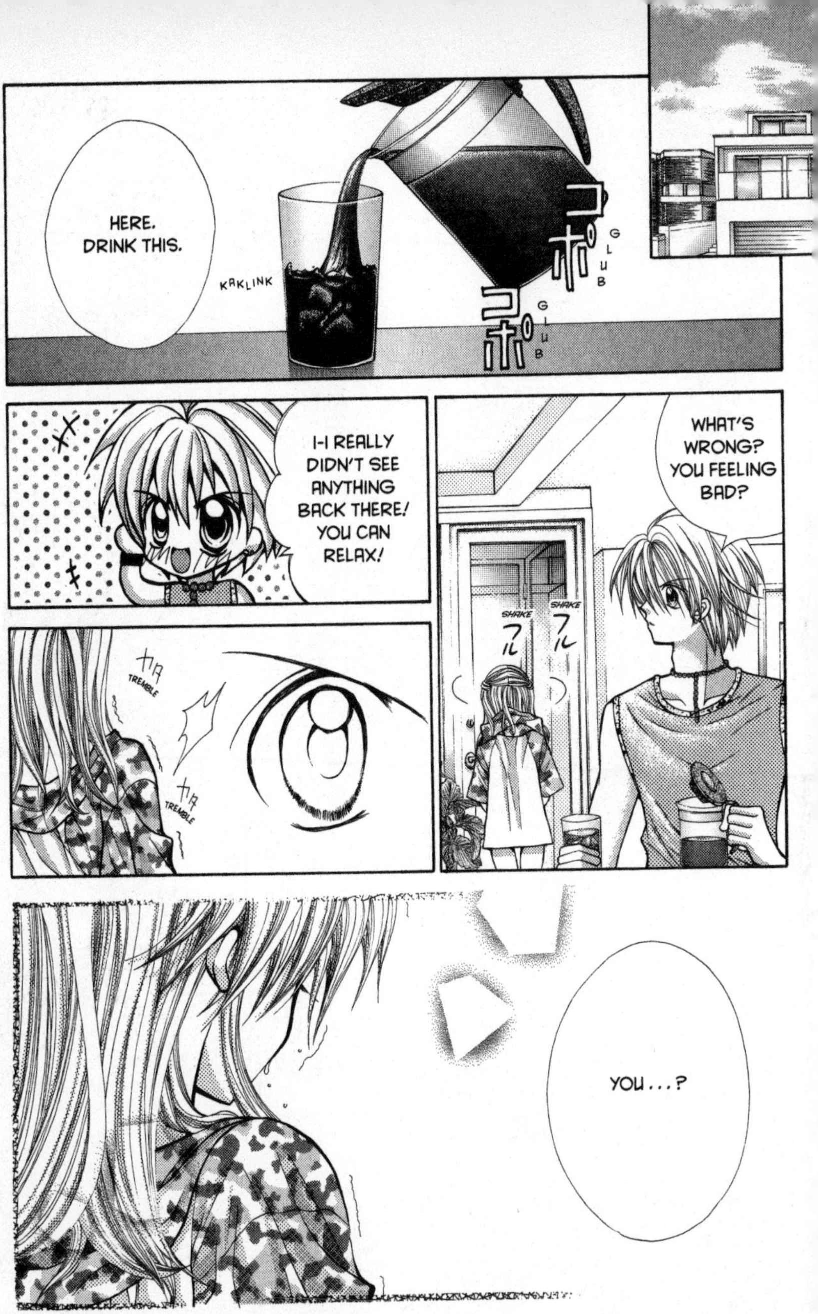
HERE. DRINK THIS.
KAKLINK
コポ
GLUB
コポ
GLUB
WHAT'S WRONG? YOU FEELING BAD?
SHAKE
フル
SHAKE
フル
I-I REALLY DIDN'T SEE ANYTHING BACK THERE! YOU CAN RELAX!
TREMBLE
TREMBLE
YOU...?

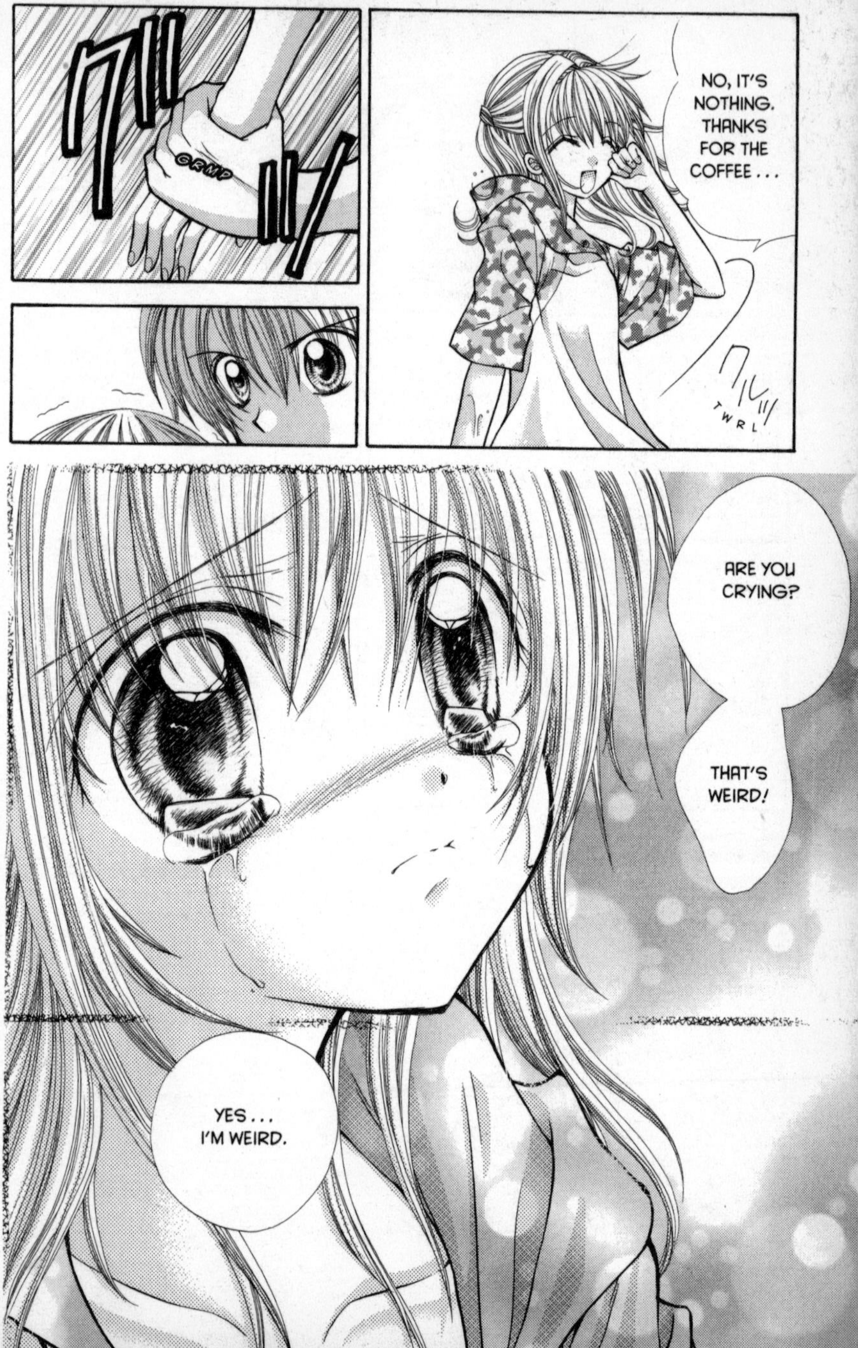
NO, IT'S NOTHING. THANKS FOR THE COFFEE . . .
TWRL
GRMP
ARE YOU CRYING?
THAT'S WEIRD!
YES . . . I'M WEIRD.

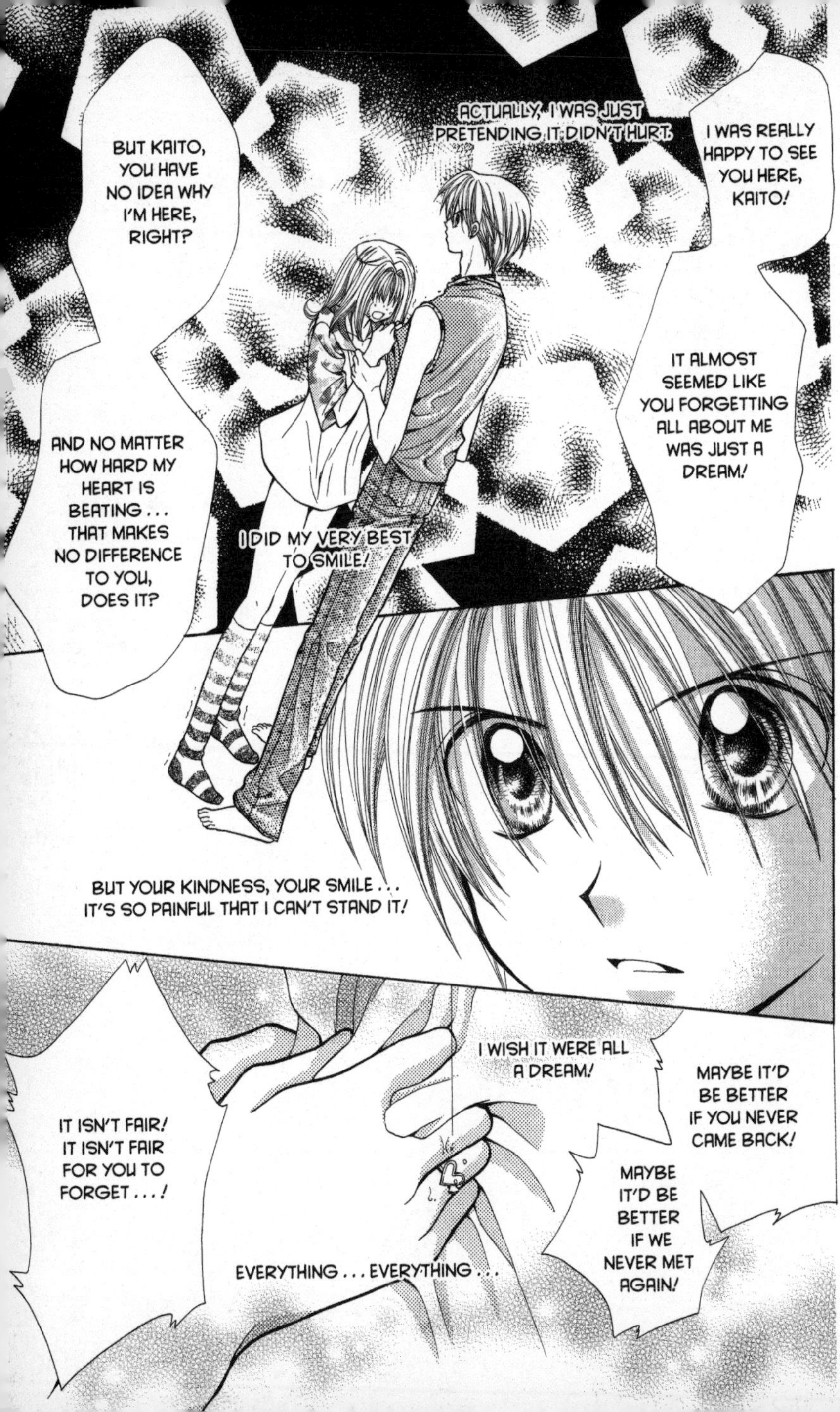
I WAS REALLY HAPPY TO SEE YOU HERE, KAITO!
ACTUALLY, I WAS JUST PRETENDING IT DIDN'T HURT.
IT ALMOST SEEMED LIKE YOU FORGETTING ALL ABOUT ME WAS JUST A DREAM!
I DID MY VERY BEST TO SMILE!
BUT KAITO, YOU HAVE NO IDEA WHY I'M HERE, RIGHT?
AND NO MATTER HOW HARD MY HEART IS BEATING . . . THAT MAKES NO DIFFERENCE TO YOU, DOES IT?
BUT YOUR KINDNESS, YOUR SMILE . . . IT'S SO PAINFUL THAT I CAN'T STAND IT!
MAYBE IT'D BE BETTER IF YOU NEVER CAME BACK!
I WISH IT WERE ALL A DREAM!
MAYBE IT'D BE BETTER IF WE NEVER MET AGAIN!
EVERYTHING . . . EVERYTHING . . .
IT ISN'T FAIR! IT ISN'T FAIR FOR YOU TO FORGET . . . !

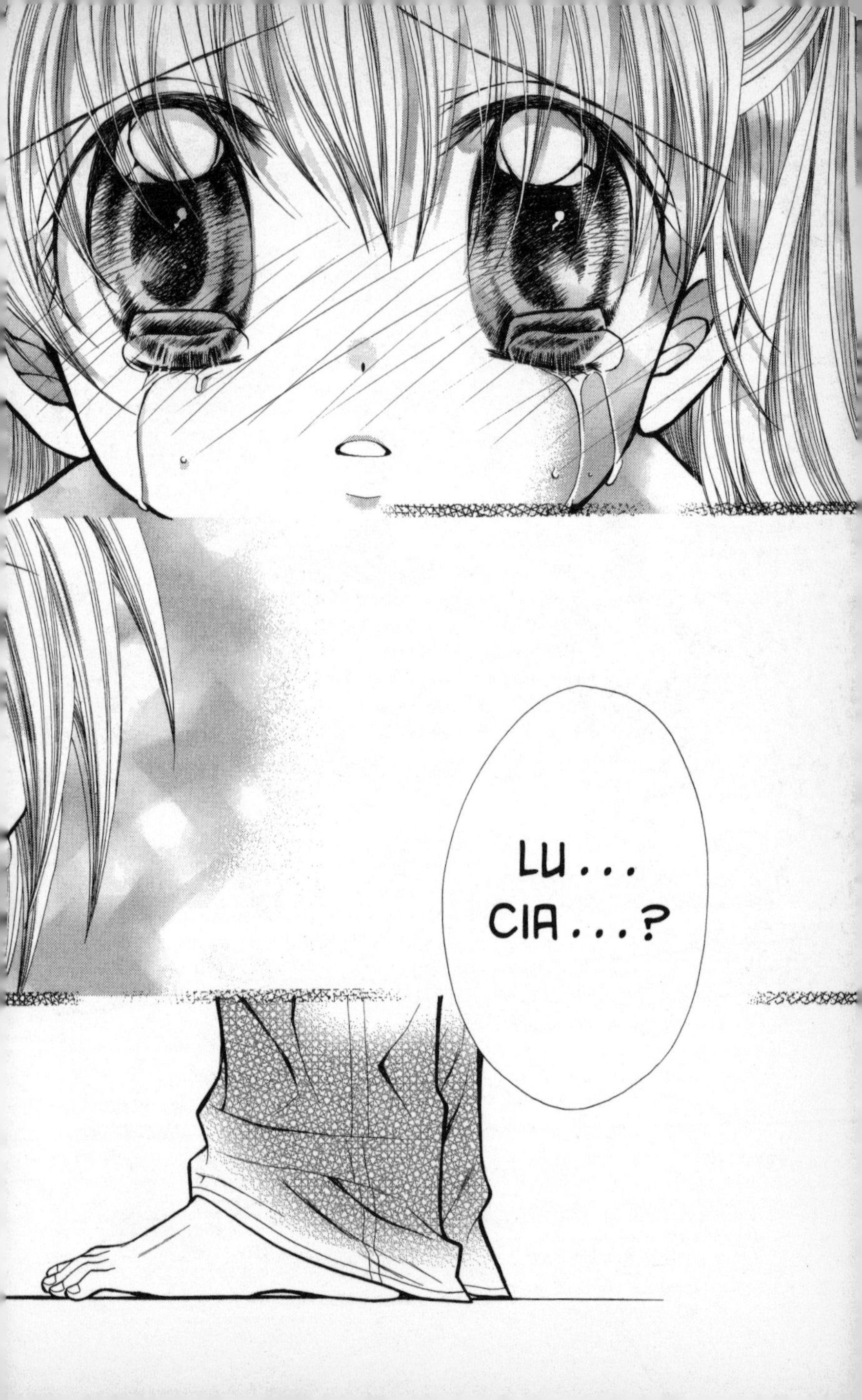
LU... CIA...?

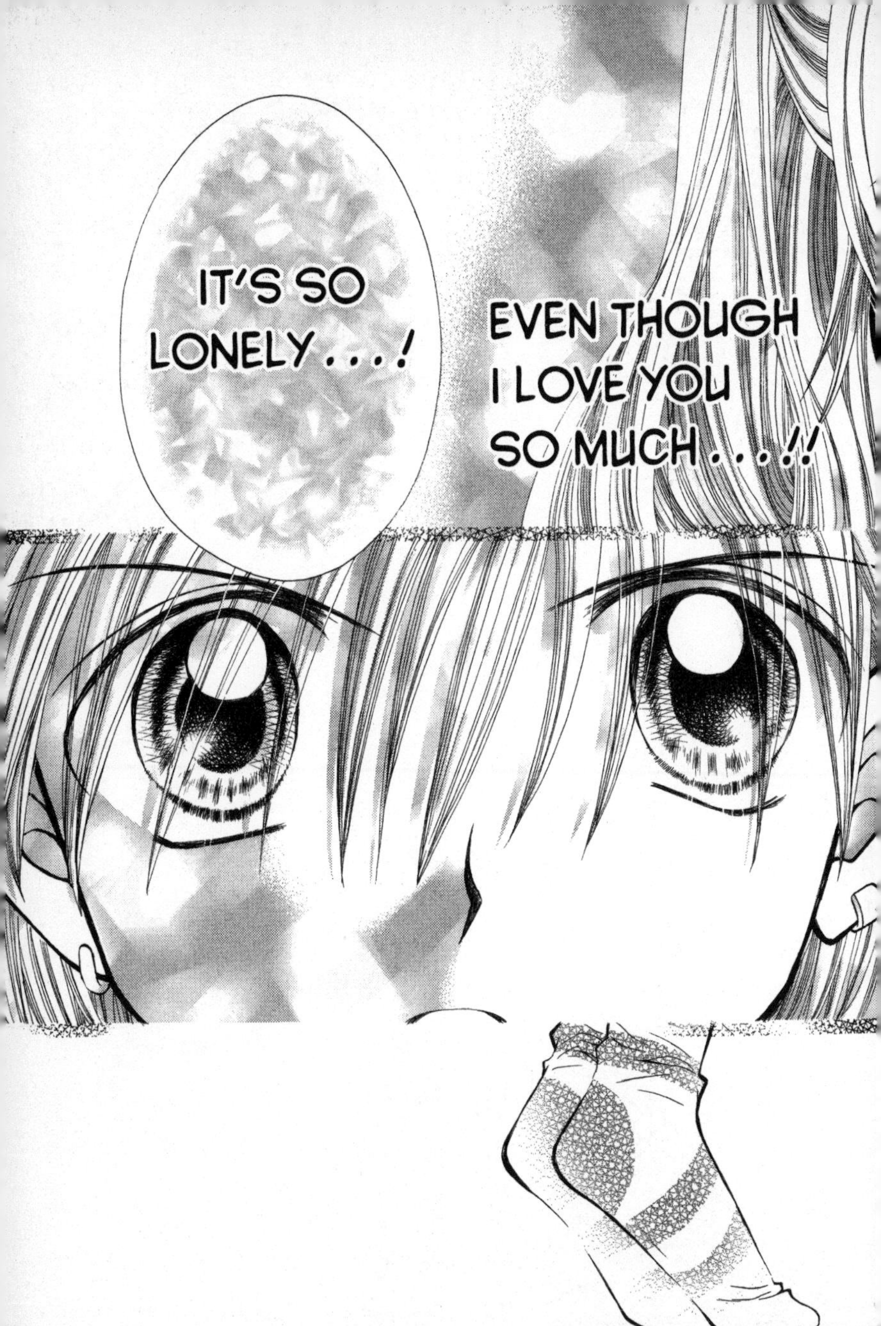
EVEN THOUGH I LOVE YOU SO MUCH...!!
IT'S SO LONELY...!

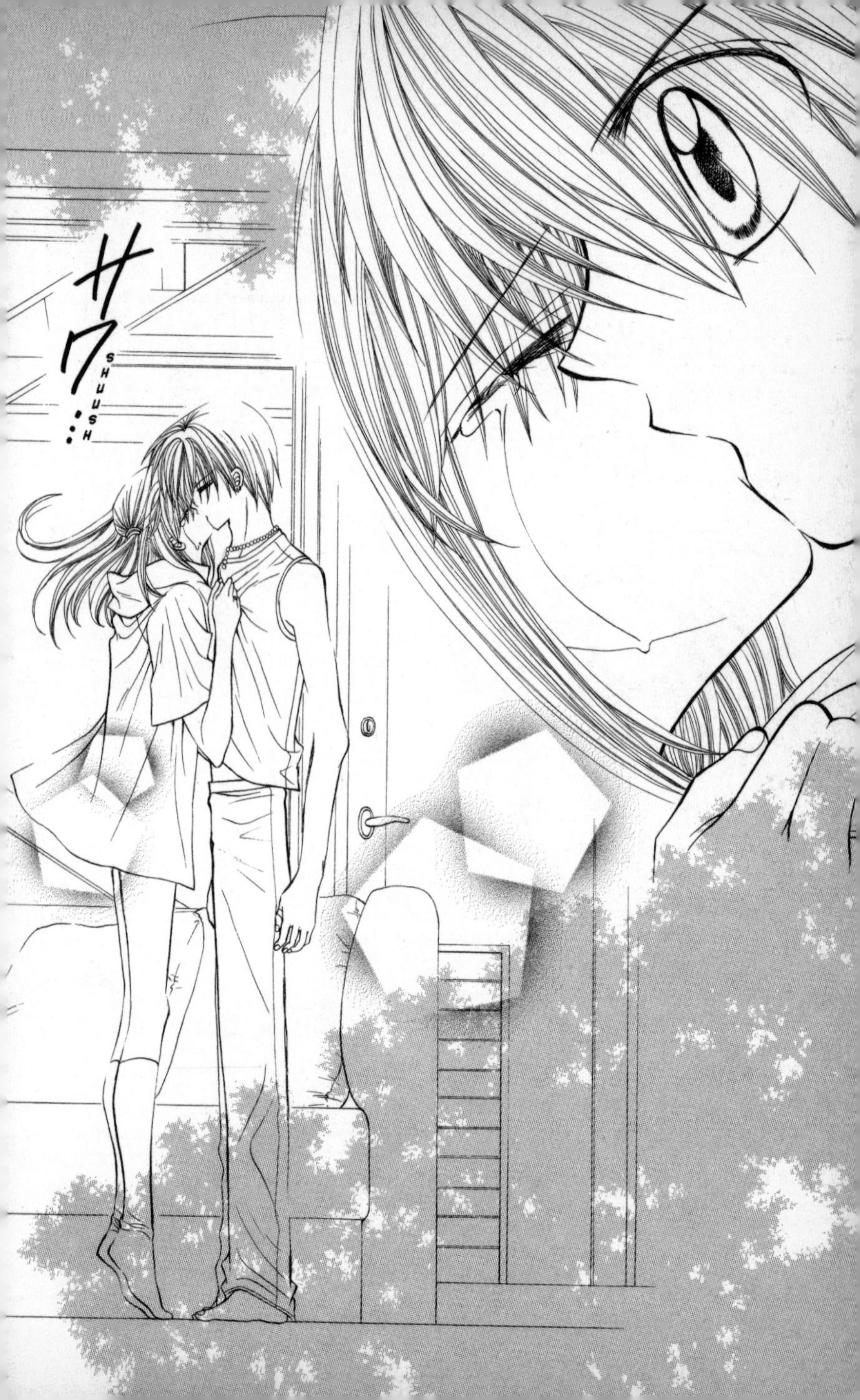
サワ…
SHUUSH

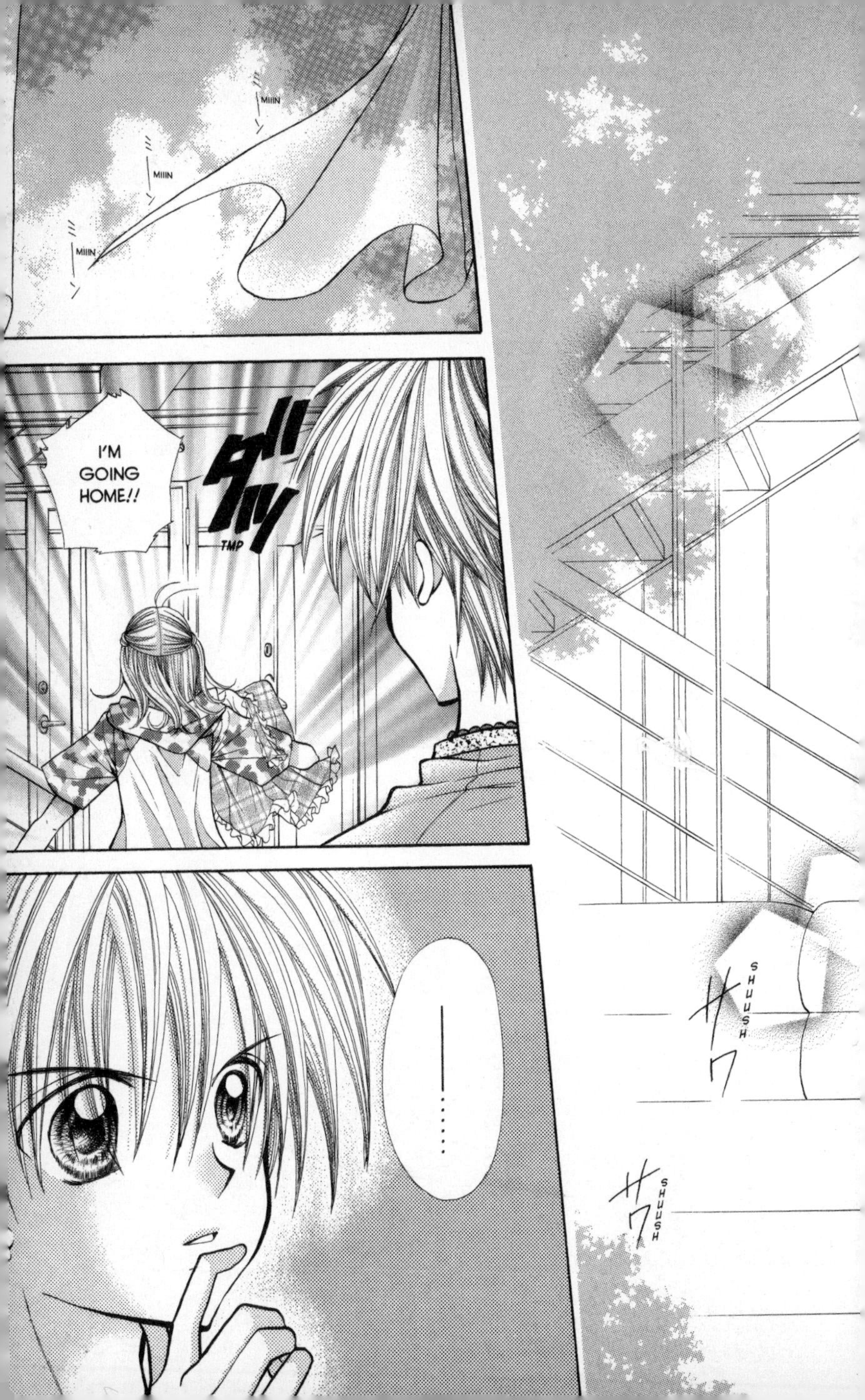

SHUUSH
SHUUSH
MIIN
MIIN
MIIN
I'M GOING HOME!!
TMP
—......

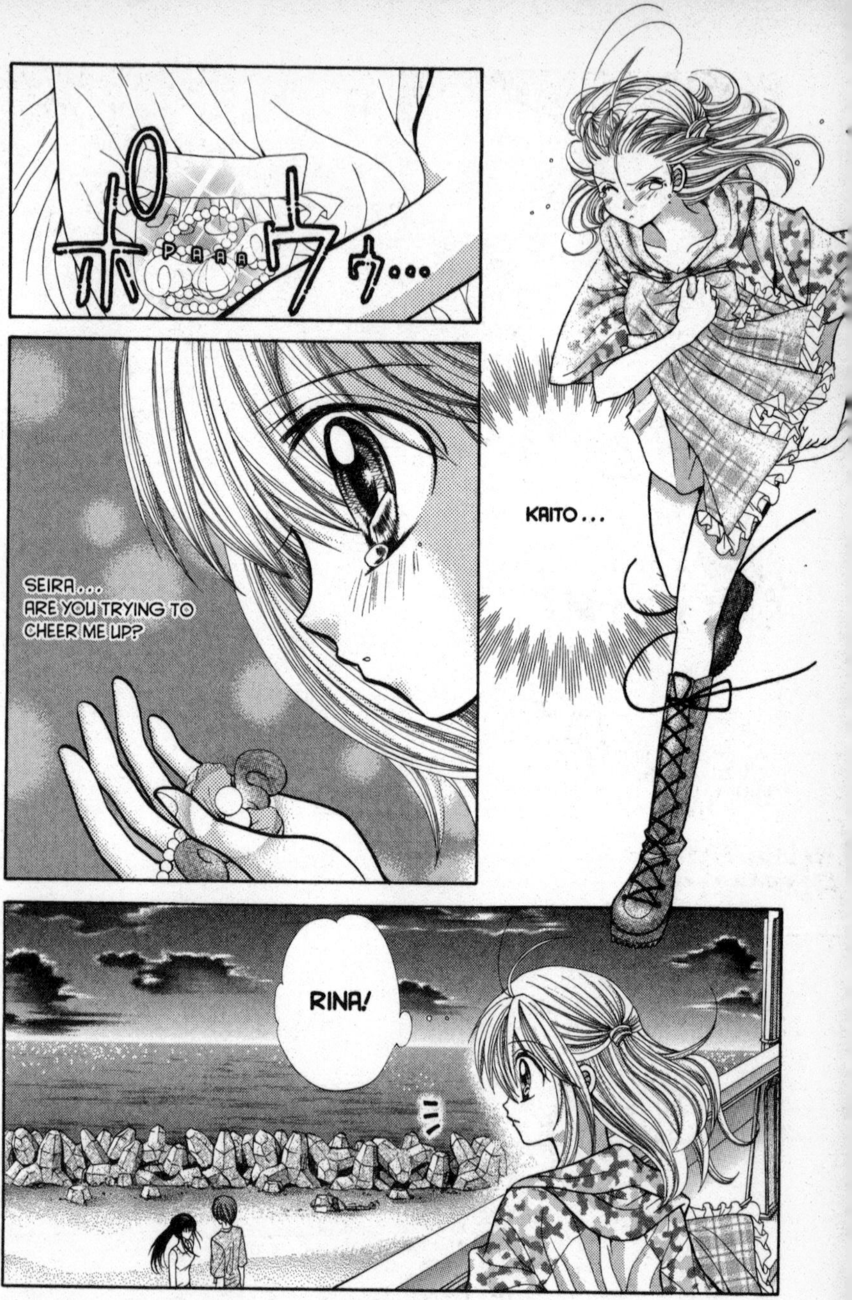
KAITO...
PAAA
SEIRA...
ARE YOU TRYING TO CHEER ME UP?
RINA!

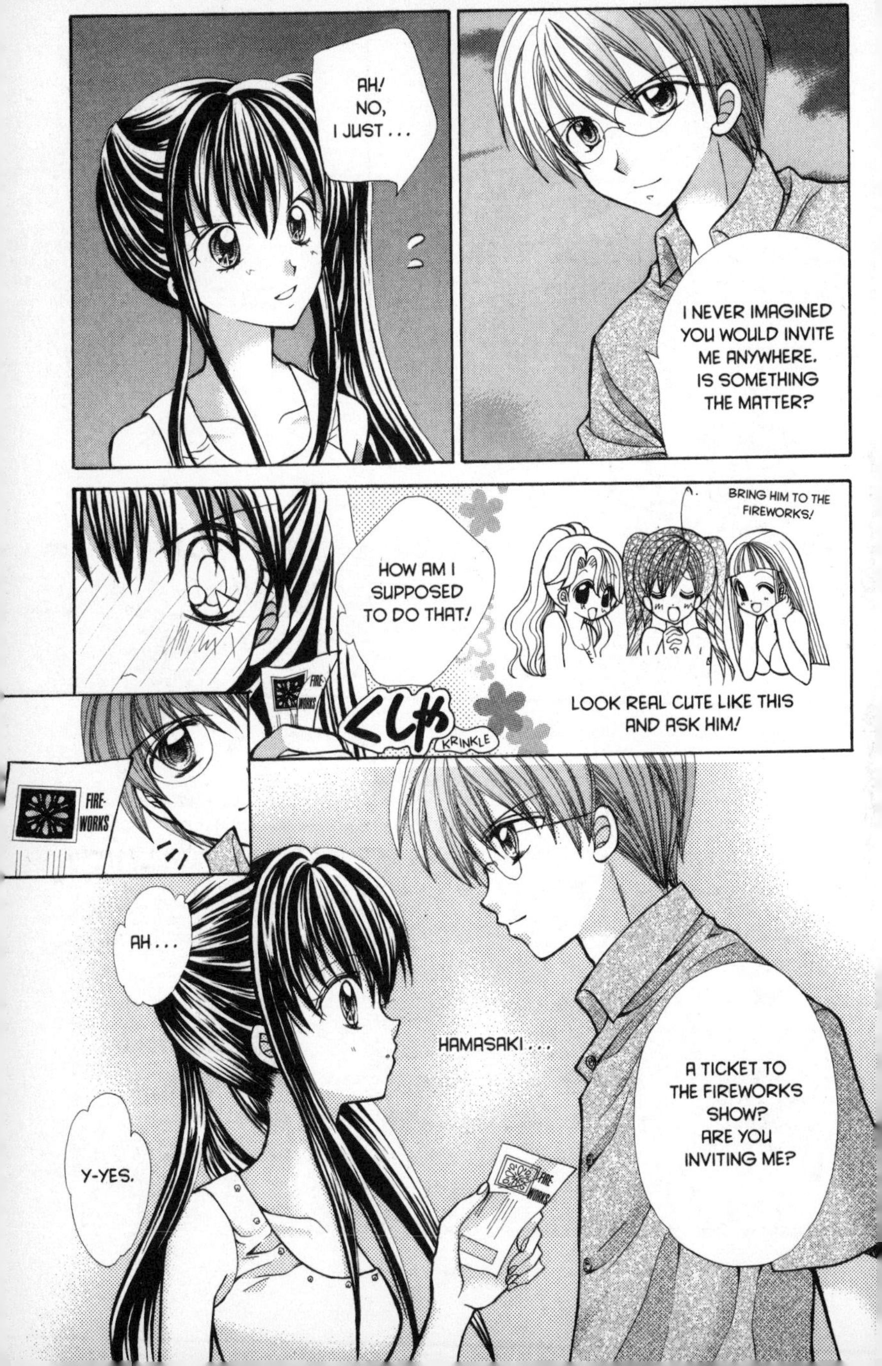
I NEVER IMAGINED YOU WOULD INVITE ME ANYWHERE. IS SOMETHING THE MATTER?
AH! NO, I JUST . . .
BRING HIM TO THE FIREWORKS!
HOW AM I SUPPOSED TO DO THAT!
LOOK REAL CUTE LIKE THIS AND ASK HIM!
FIRE-WORKS
くしゃ KRINKLE
FIRE-WORKS
A TICKET TO THE FIREWORKS SHOW? ARE YOU INVITING ME?
HAMASAKI . . .
AH . . .
Y-YES.

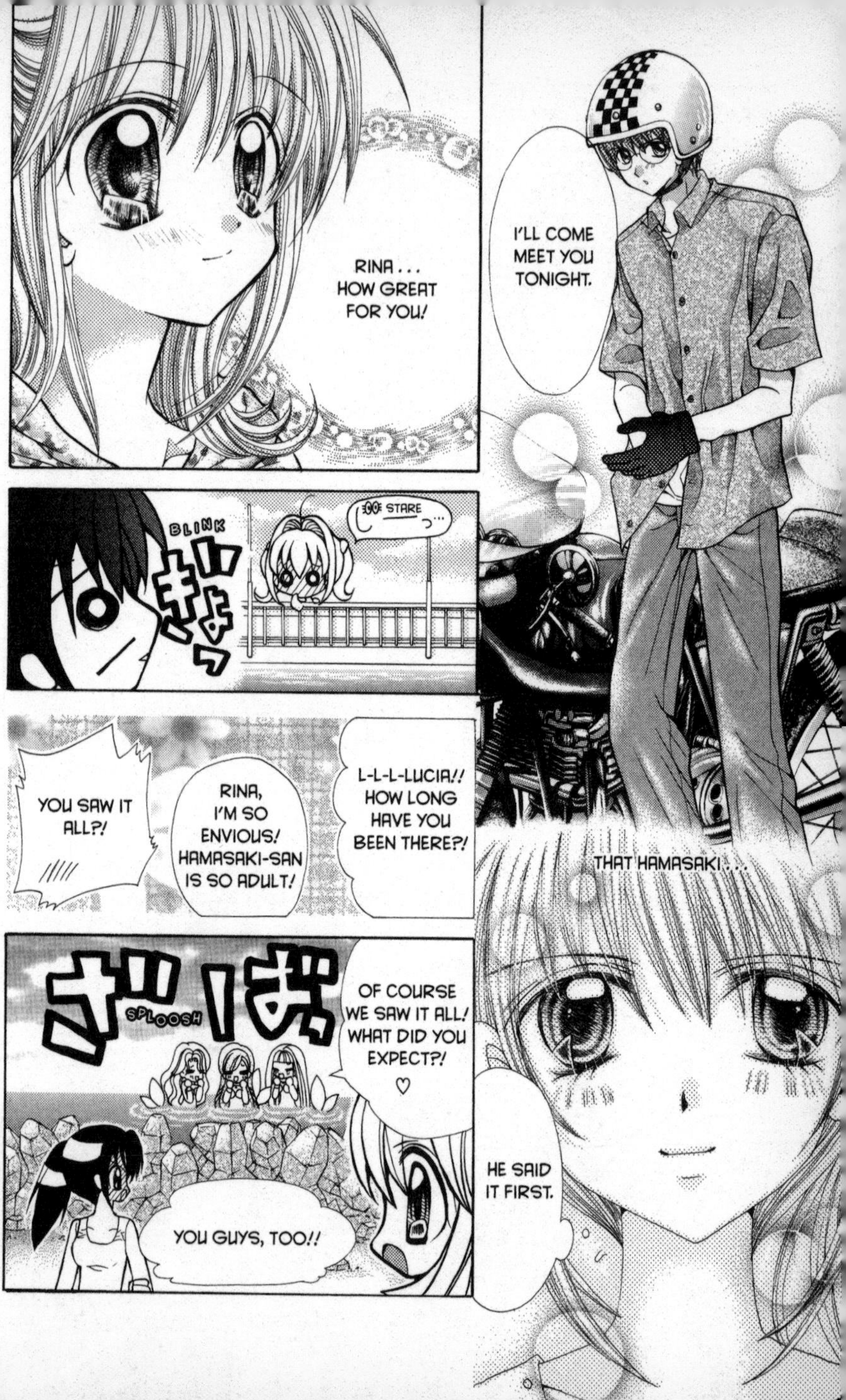
I'LL COME MEET YOU TONIGHT.
THAT HAMASAKI . . .
HE SAID IT FIRST.
RINA . . . HOW GREAT FOR YOU!
BLINK
STARE
L-L-L-LUCIA!! HOW LONG HAVE YOU BEEN THERE?!
RINA, I'M SO ENVIOUS! HAMASAKI-SAN IS SO ADULT!
YOU SAW IT ALL?!
SPLOOSH
OF COURSE WE SAW IT ALL! WHAT DID YOU EXPECT?! ♡
YOU GUYS, TOO!!

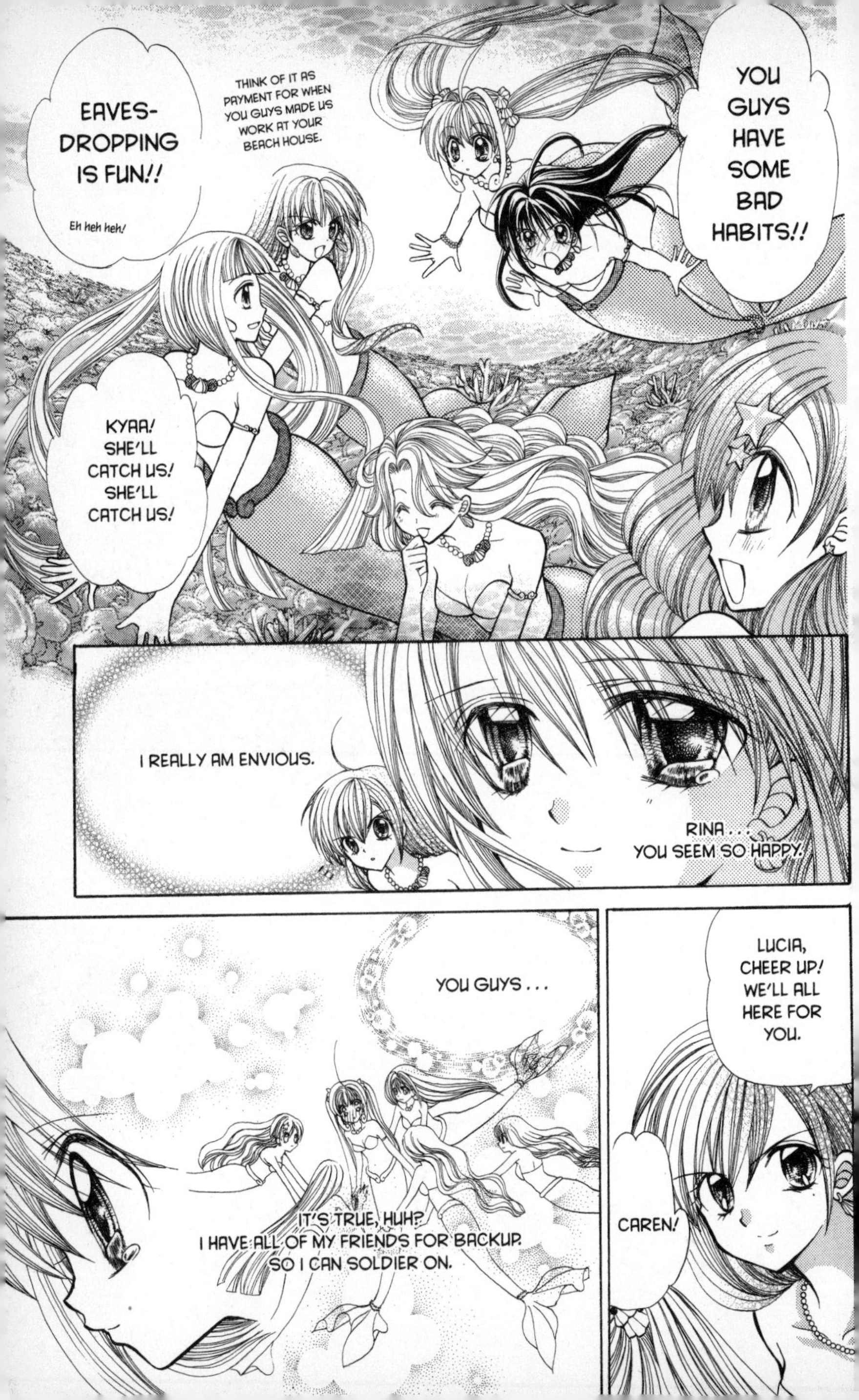
YOU GUYS HAVE SOME BAD HABITS!!
THINK OF IT AS PAYMENT FOR WHEN YOU GUYS MADE US WORK AT YOUR BEACH HOUSE.
EAVES-DROPPING IS FUN!!
Eh heh heh!
KYAA! SHE'LL CATCH US! SHE'LL CATCH US!
RINA . . . YOU SEEM SO HAPPY.
I REALLY AM ENVIOUS.
LUCIA, CHEER UP! WE'LL ALL HERE FOR YOU.
CAREN!
YOU GUYS . . .
IT'S TRUE, HUH? I HAVE ALL OF MY FRIENDS FOR BACKUP. SO I CAN SOLDIER ON.

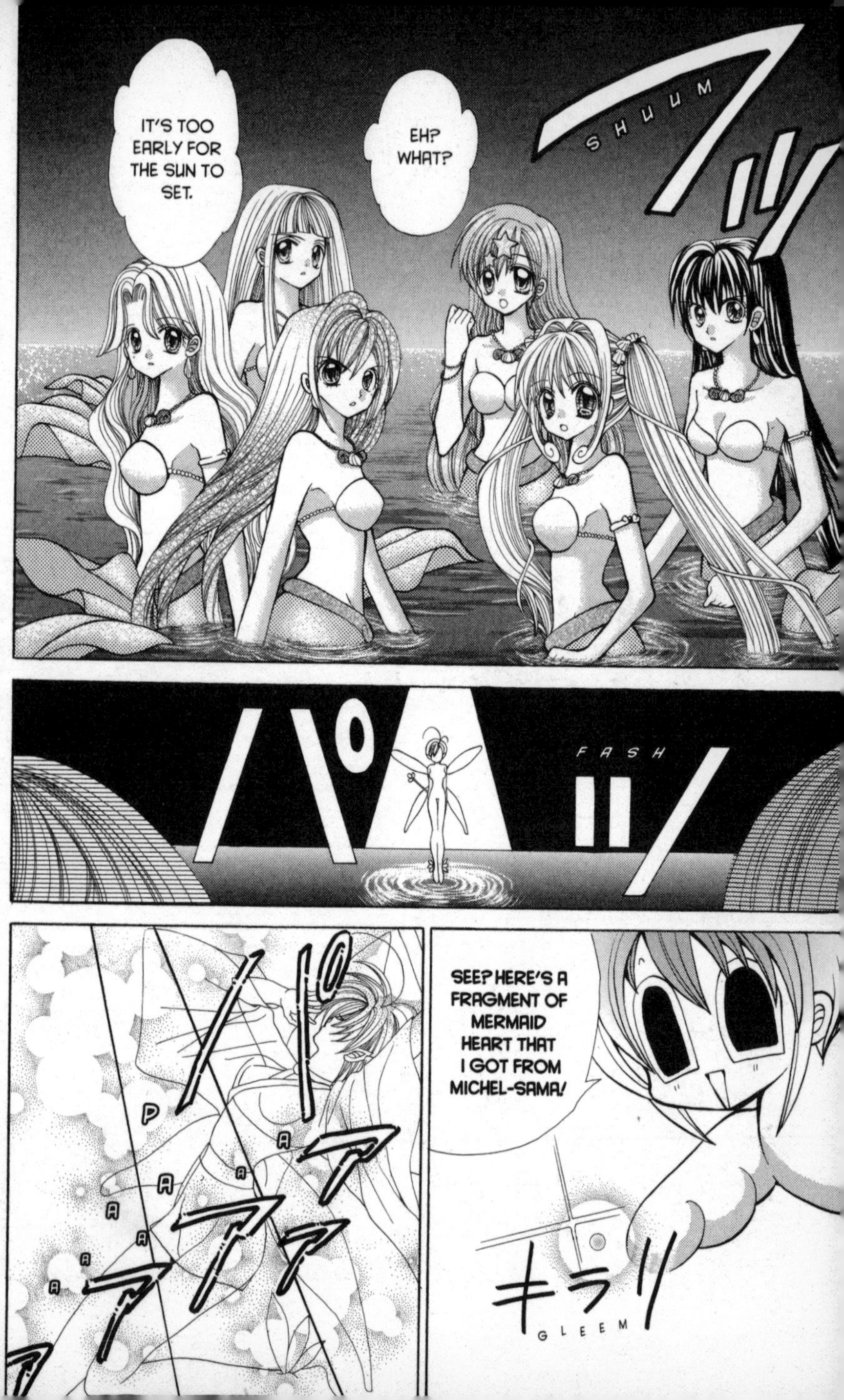
SHUUM
EH? WHAT?
IT'S TOO EARLY FOR THE SUN TO SET.
FASH
SEE? HERE'S A FRAGMENT OF MERMAID HEART THAT I GOT FROM MICHEL-SAMA!
GLEEM
PAAAAAAA

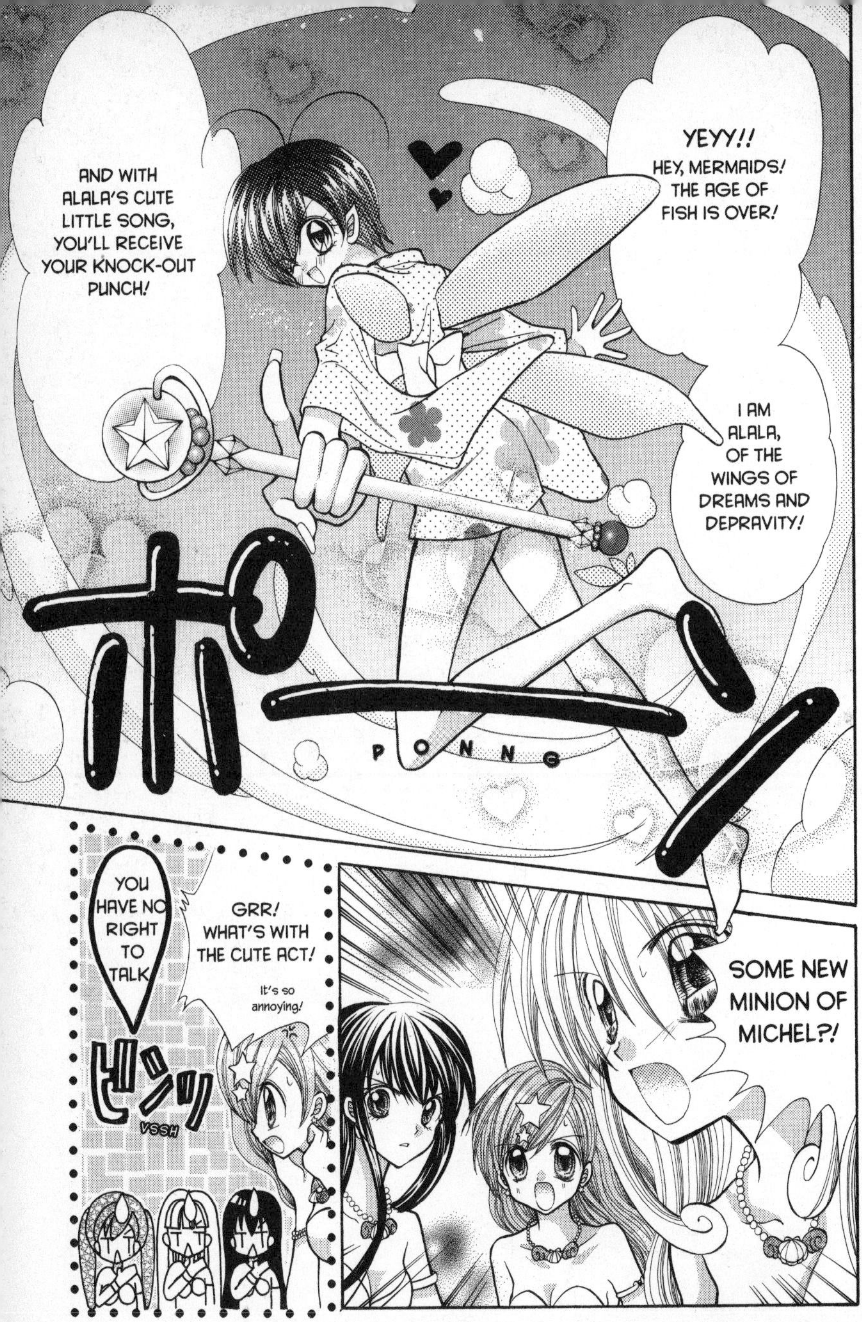
YEYY!!
HEY, MERMAIDS! THE AGE OF FISH IS OVER!
I AM ALALA, OF THE WINGS OF DREAMS AND DEPRAVITY!
AND WITH ALALA'S CUTE LITTLE SONG, YOU'LL RECEIVE YOUR KNOCK-OUT PUNCH!
PONNG
SOME NEW MINION OF MICHEL?!
GRR! WHAT'S WITH THE CUTE ACT!
It's so annoying!
YOU HAVE NO RIGHT TO TALK
VSSH

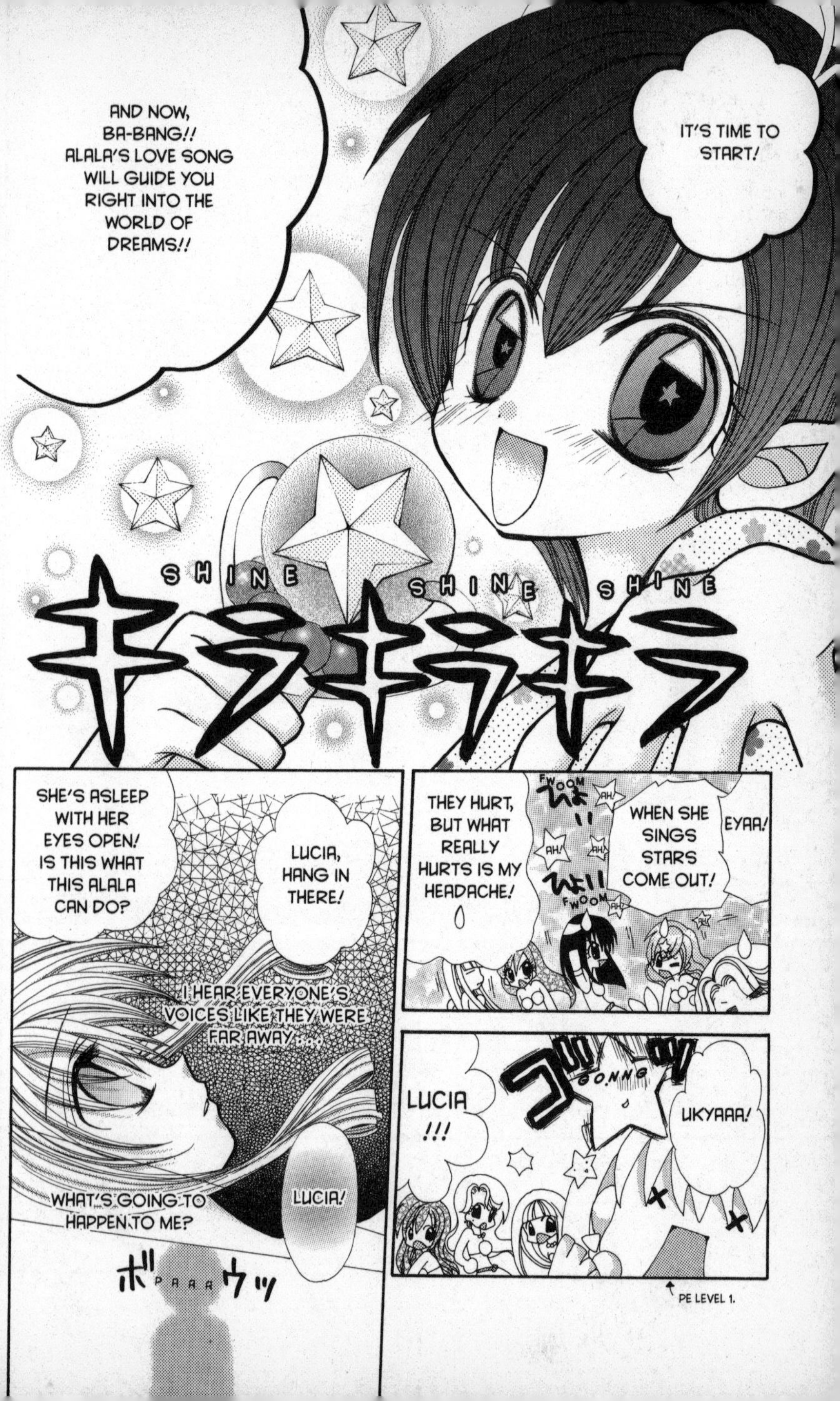
IT'S TIME TO START!
AND NOW, BA-BANG!! ALALA'S LOVE SONG WILL GUIDE YOU RIGHT INTO THE WORLD OF DREAMS!!
SHINE SHINE SHINE
キラキラキラ
EYAA!
WHEN SHE SINGS STARS COME OUT!
FWOOM
AH!
AH!
AH!
FWOOM
AH!
AH!
THEY HURT, BUT WHAT REALLY HURTS IS MY HEADACHE!
UKYAAA!
GONNG
LUCIA !!!
LUCIA, HANG IN THERE!
SHE'S ASLEEP WITH HER EYES OPEN! IS THIS WHAT THIS ALALA CAN DO?
I HEAR EVERYONE'S VOICES LIKE THEY WERE FAR AWAY . . .
LUCIA!
WHAT'S GOING TO HAPPEN TO ME?
ボPAAAウッ

PE LEVEL 1.

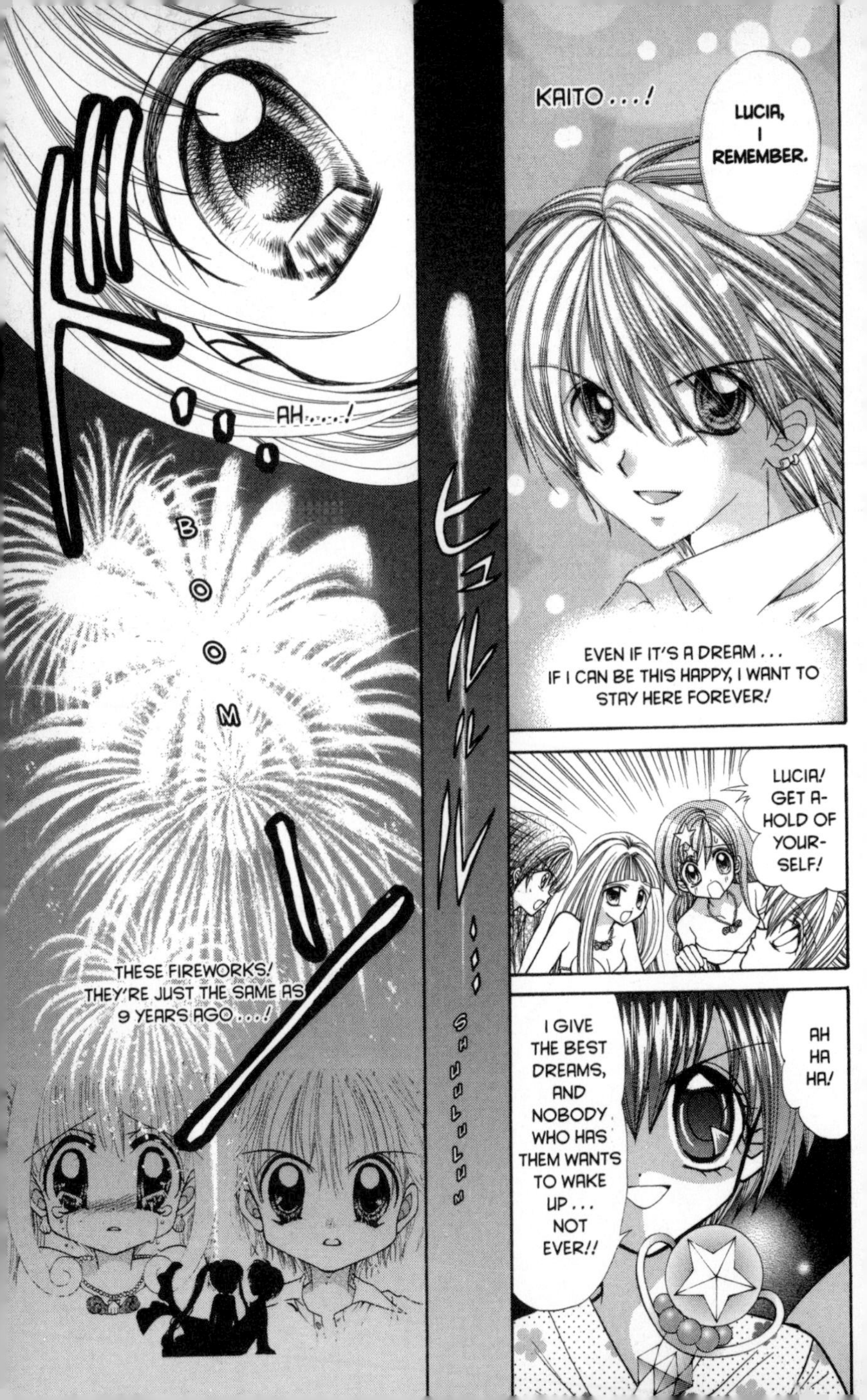
LUCIA, I REMEMBER.
KAITO...!
EVEN IF IT'S A DREAM... IF I CAN BE THIS HAPPY, I WANT TO STAY HERE FOREVER!
LUCIA! GET A-HOLD OF YOUR-SELF!
AH HA HA!
I GIVE THE BEST DREAMS, AND NOBODY WHO HAS THEM WANTS TO WAKE UP... NOT EVER!!
ヒュルルル...
SHUUUUUUM
AH......!
BOOM
THESE FIREWORKS! THEY'RE JUST THE SAME AS 9 YEARS AGO...!

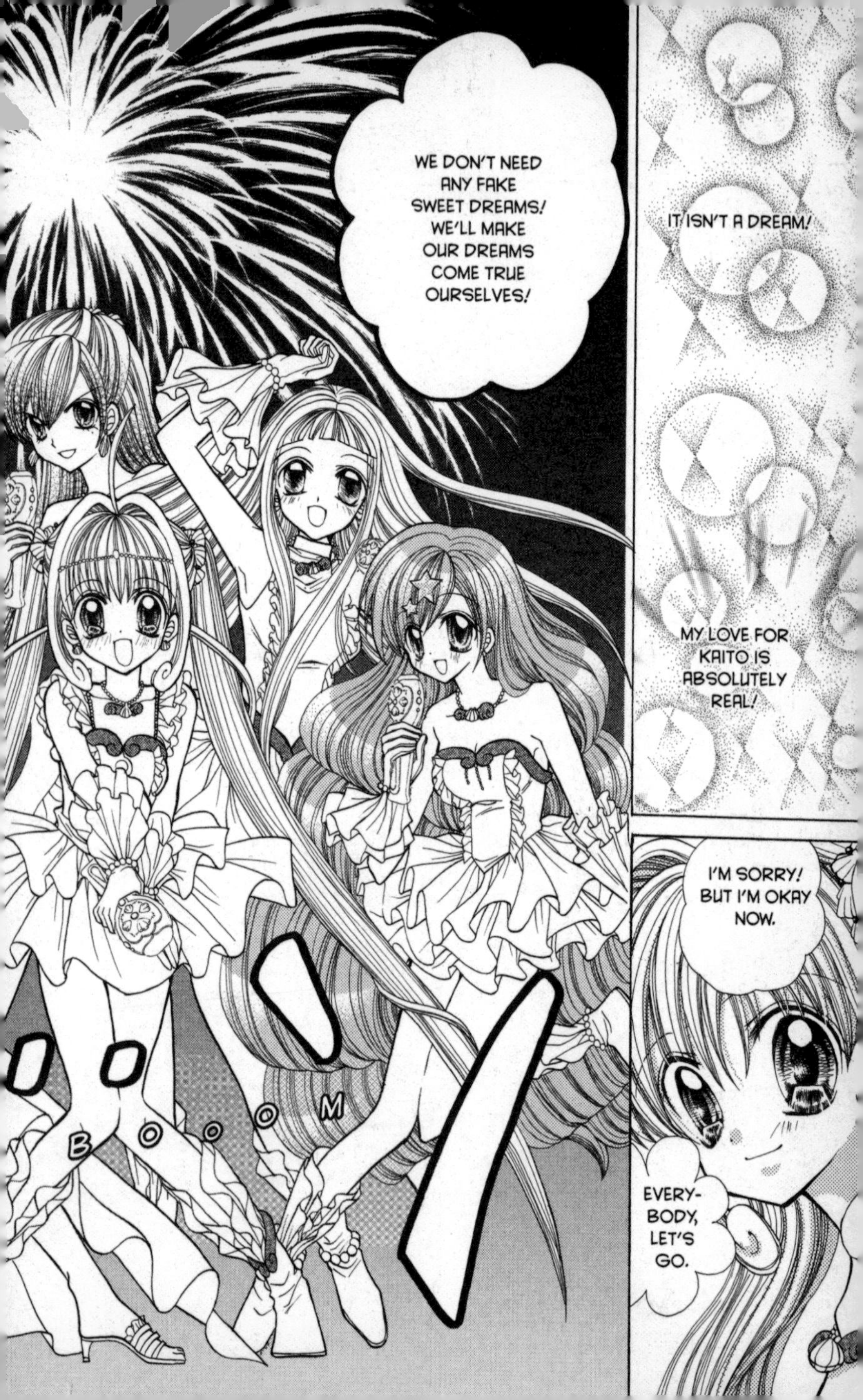
IT ISN'T A DREAM!
MY LOVE FOR KAITO IS ABSOLUTELY REAL!
I'M SORRY! BUT I'M OKAY NOW.
EVERY-BODY, LET'S GO.
WE DON'T NEED ANY FAKE SWEET DREAMS! WE'LL MAKE OUR DREAMS COME TRUE OURSELVES!
BOOOOM

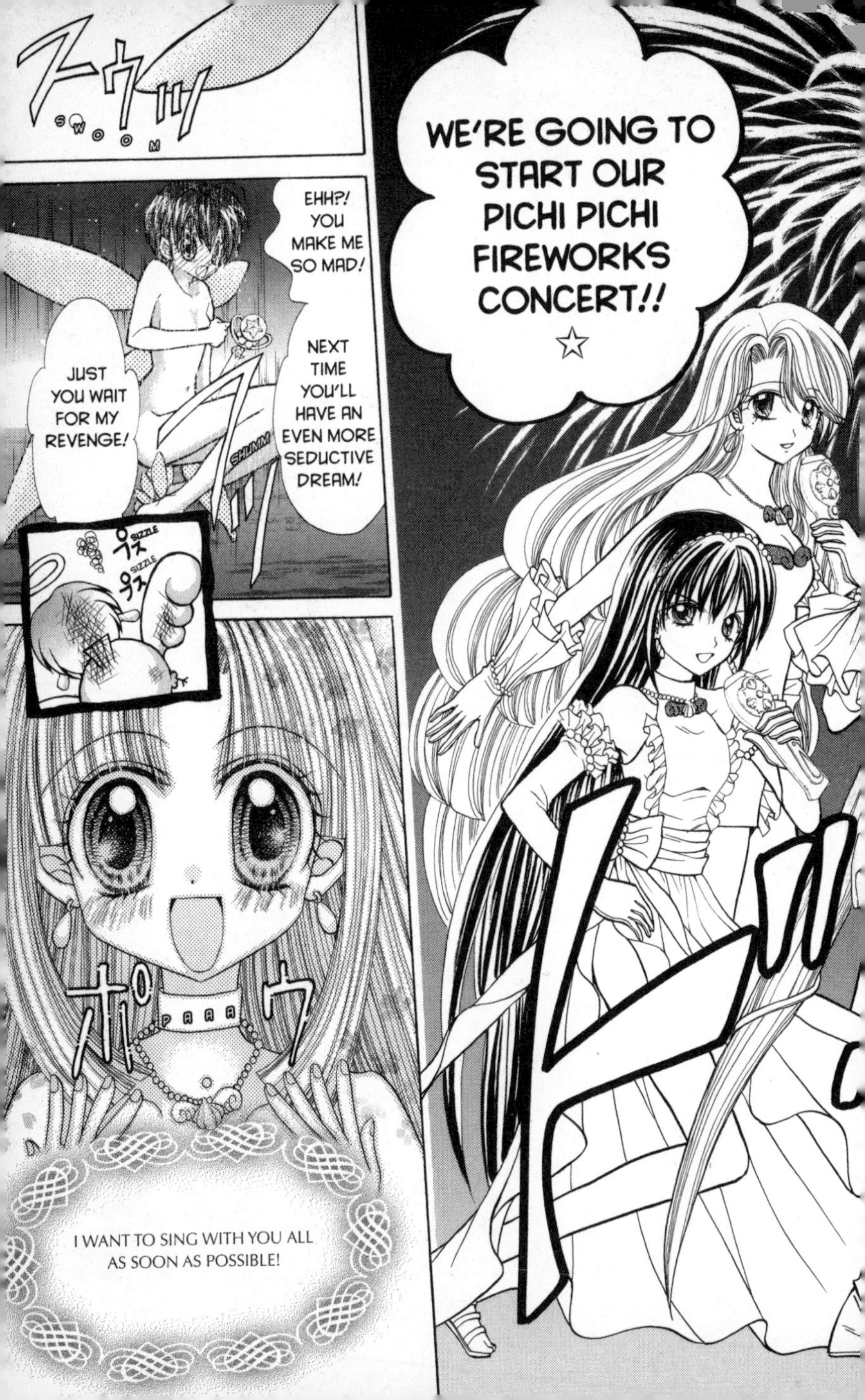
WE'RE GOING TO START OUR PICHI PICHI FIREWORKS CONCERT!! ☆
SWOOM
EHH?! YOU MAKE ME SO MAD!
NEXT TIME YOU'LL HAVE AN EVEN MORE SEDUCTIVE DREAM!
SHUMM
JUST YOU WAIT FOR MY REVENGE!
SIZZLE
SIZZLE
PAAA
I WANT TO SING WITH YOU ALL AS SOON AS POSSIBLE!

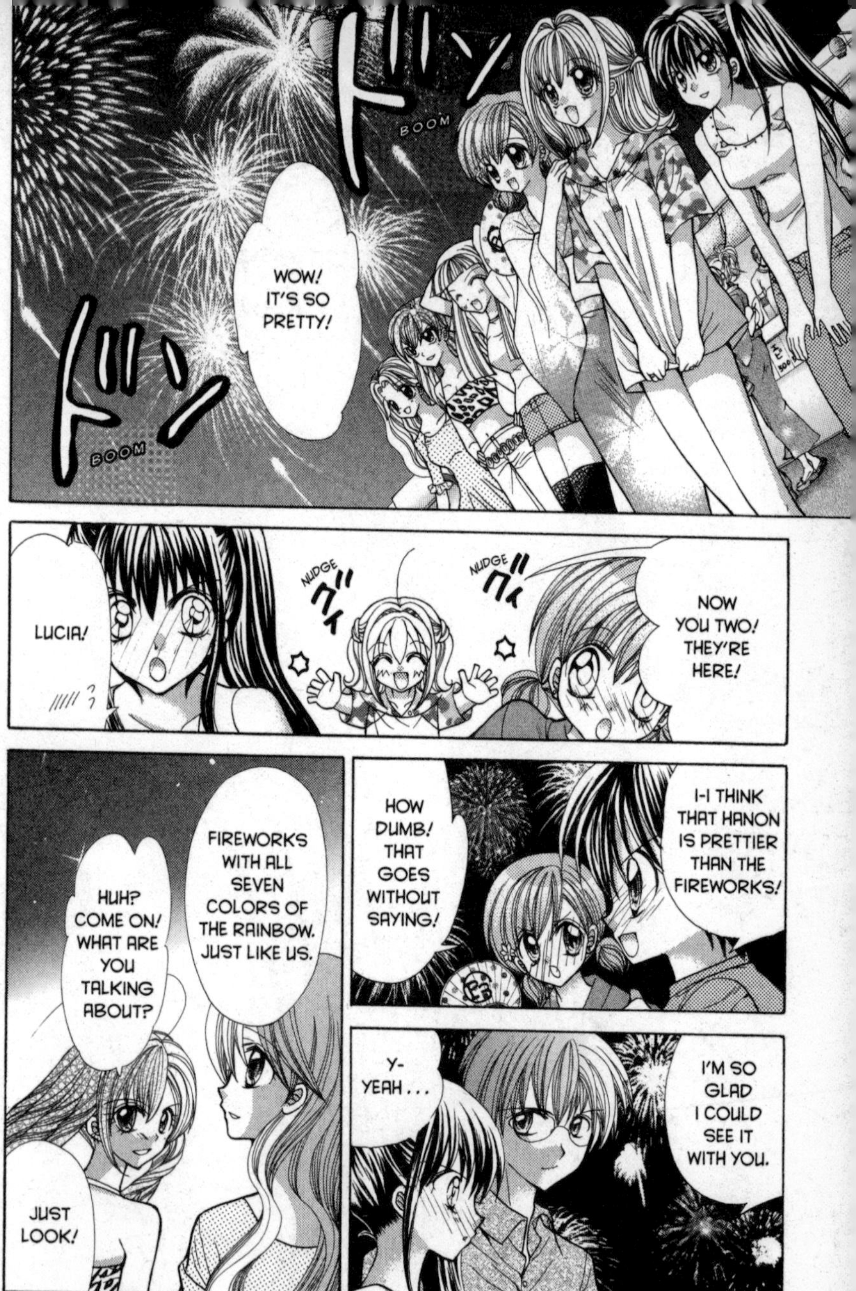
BOOM
WOW! IT'S SO PRETTY!
BOOM
NOW YOU TWO! THEY'RE HERE!
NUDGE
NUDGE
LUCIA!
I-I THINK THAT HANON IS PRETTIER THAN THE FIREWORKS!
HOW DUMB! THAT GOES WITHOUT SAYING!
I'M SO GLAD I COULD SEE IT WITH YOU.
Y-YEAH . . .
FIREWORKS WITH ALL SEVEN COLORS OF THE RAINBOW. JUST LIKE US.
HUH? COME ON! WHAT ARE YOU TALKING ABOUT?
JUST LOOK!

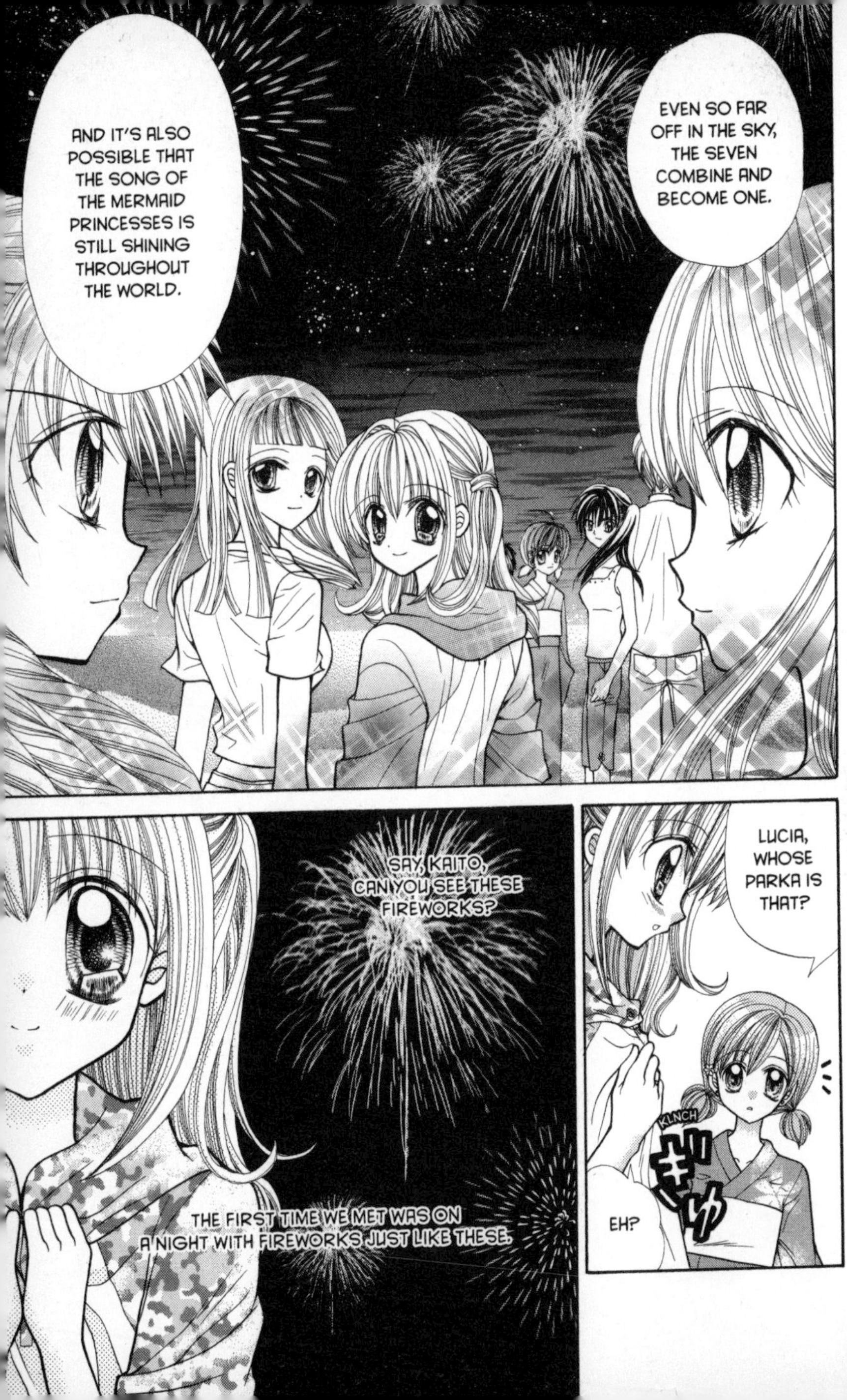
EVEN SO FAR OFF IN THE SKY, THE SEVEN COMBINE AND BECOME ONE.
AND IT'S ALSO POSSIBLE THAT THE SONG OF THE MERMAID PRINCESSES IS STILL SHINING THROUGHOUT THE WORLD.
LUCIA, WHOSE PARKA IS THAT?
KLNCH
EH?
SAY, KAITO, CAN YOU SEE THESE FIREWORKS?
THE FIRST TIME WE MET WAS ON A NIGHT WITH FIREWORKS JUST LIKE THESE.

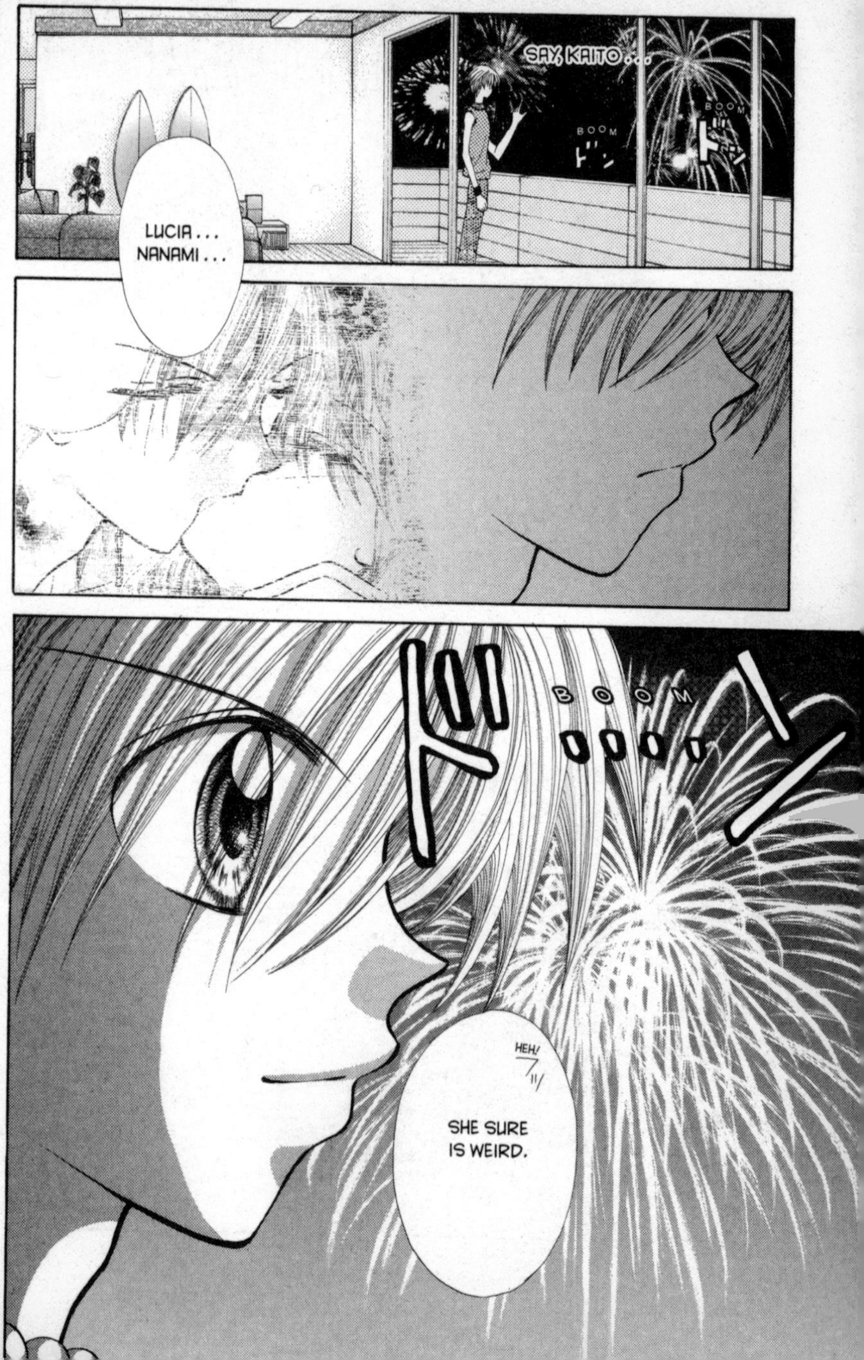
SAY, KAITO . . .
BOOM
BOOM
LUCIA . . .
NANAMI . . .
BOOM
HEH!
SHE SURE IS WEIRD.

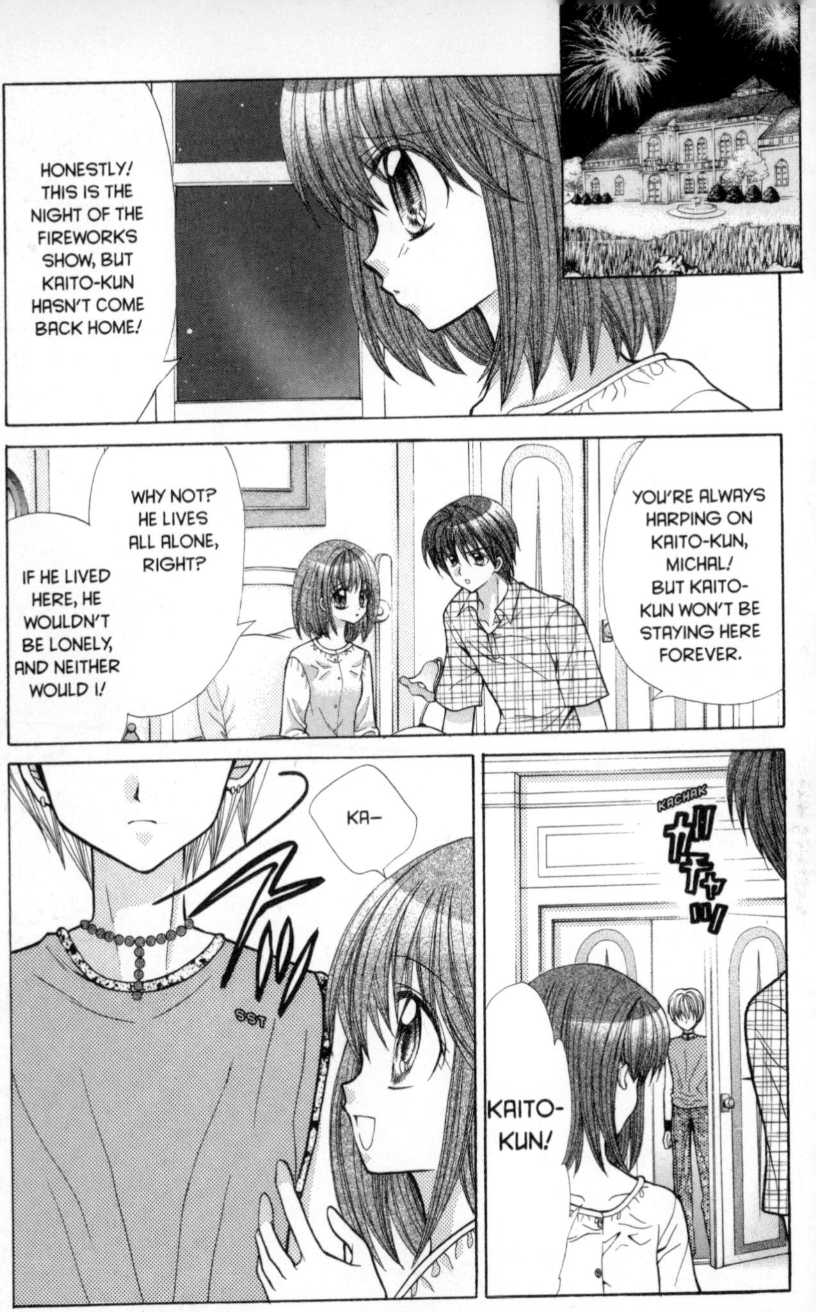
HONESTLY! THIS IS THE NIGHT OF THE FIREWORKS SHOW, BUT KAITO-KUN HASN'T COME BACK HOME!
YOU'RE ALWAYS HARPING ON KAITO-KUN, MICHAL! BUT KAITO-KUN WON'T BE STAYING HERE FOREVER.
WHY NOT? HE LIVES ALL ALONE, RIGHT?
IF HE LIVED HERE, HE WOULDN'T BE LONELY, AND NEITHER WOULD I!
KACHAK
KAITO-KUN!
KA-
SST

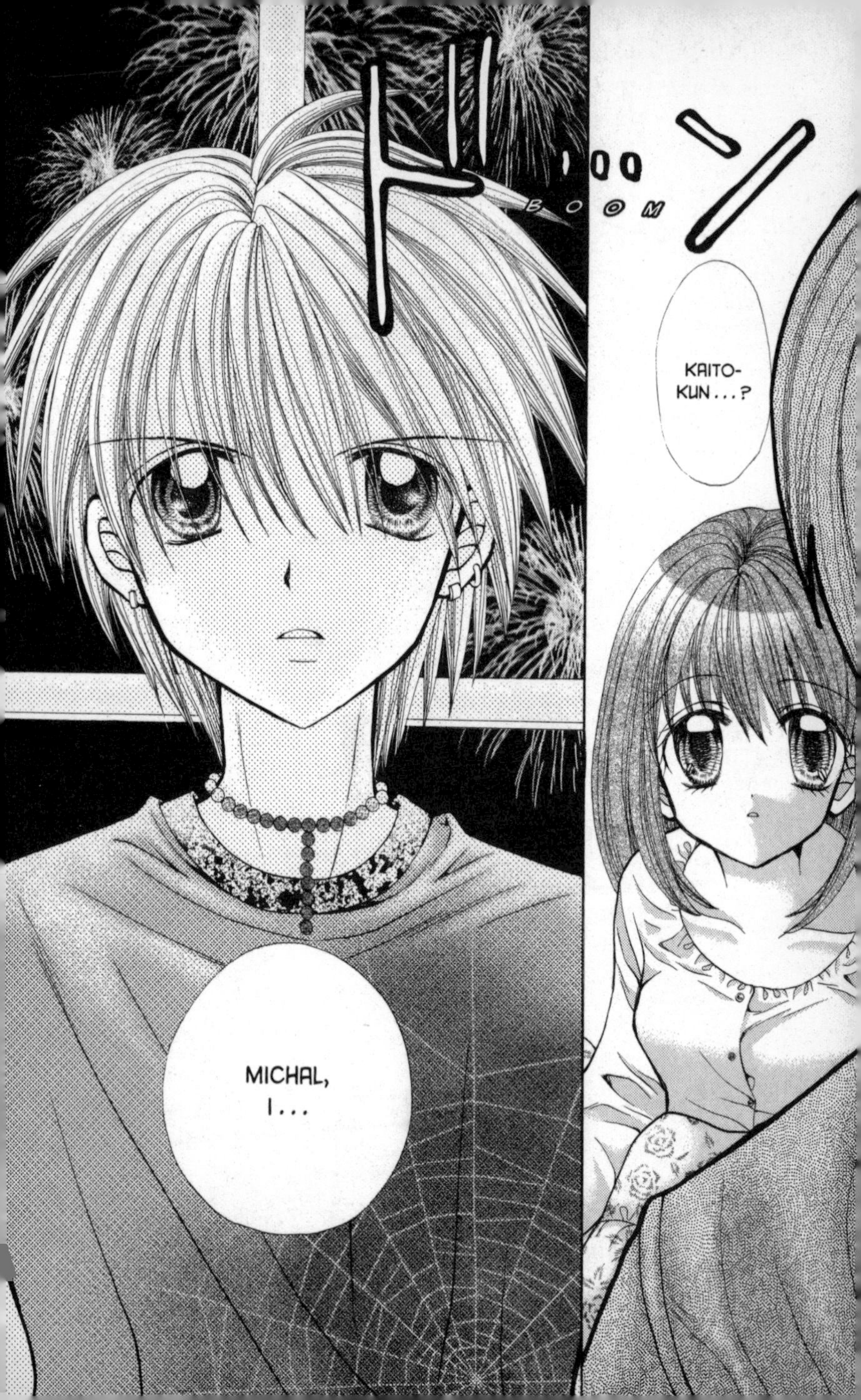
BOOM
KAITO-KUN...?
MICHAL, I...

TO ALL PITCH FANS

THANK YOU FOR READING VOLUME 5!

I'M YOKOTE, IN CHARGE OF THE STORY.

DID YOU HAVE FUN WITH *PICHI PICHI PITCH* THIS VOLUME? EVER SINCE *PICHI PICHI PITCH* STARTED, I SEE MERMAIDS ON TV COMMERCIALS, BOOKS . . .

IT SEEMS THAT MERMAIDS HAVE SHOWN UP EVERYWHERE. IS IT JUST ME?

COME TO THINK OF IT, I WENT SWIMMING IN THE OCEAN AROUND HAWAII,

AND I THOUGHT I SAW A MERMAID . . . ! (IT'S TRUE! NOBODY WANTS TO BELIEVE ME!)

BY THE WAY, MY "MERMAID URANAI" FORTUNE WAS SPOT-ON! ALL OF YOU SHOULD GIVE MERMAID URANAI A TRY TOO. EH? WHAT COLOR MERMAID AM I? EH HEH HEH!

I'M KEEPING THAT A SECRET!

FINALLY, TO HANAMORI-SENSEI, THANK YOU FOR EVERYTHING!

OKAY, UNTIL WE MEET AGAIN . . .

YOKOTE

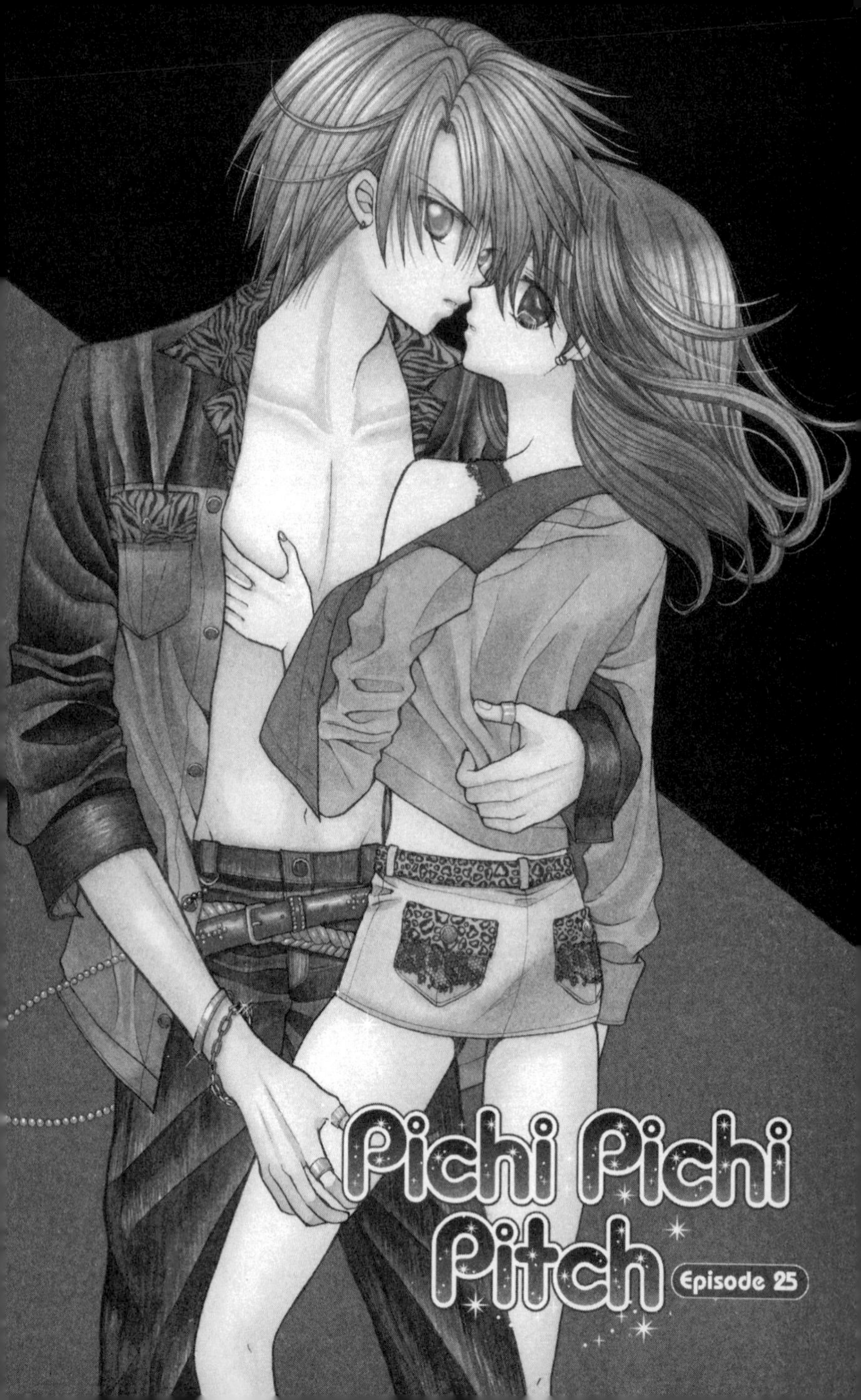
Pichi Pichi Pitch
Episode 25

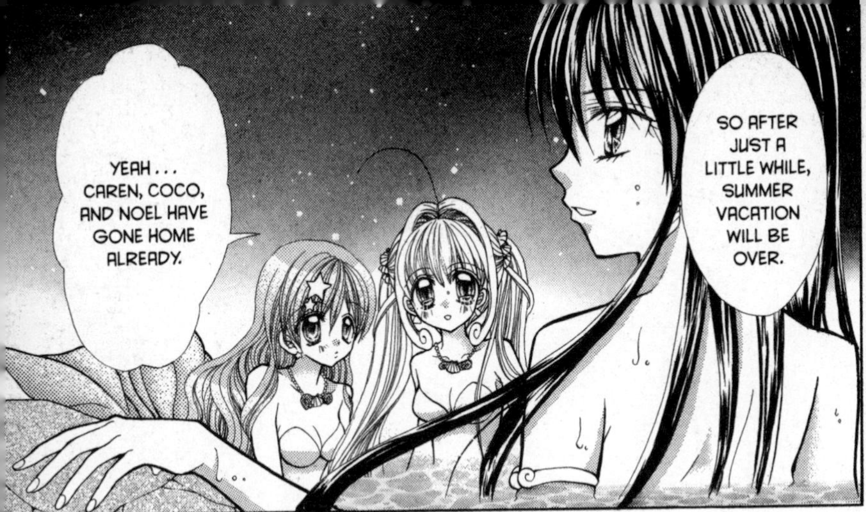
SO AFTER JUST A LITTLE WHILE, SUMMER VACATION WILL BE OVER.
YEAH . . . CAREN, COCO, AND NOEL HAVE GONE HOME ALREADY.

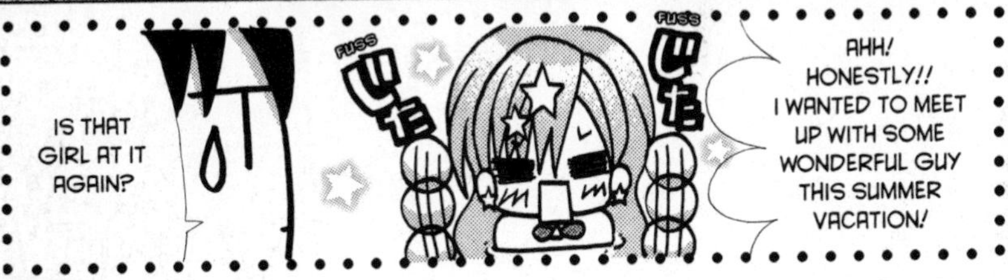
AHH! HONESTLY!! I WANTED TO MEET UP WITH SOME WONDERFUL GUY THIS SUMMER VACATION!
FUSS
FUSS
IS THAT GIRL AT IT AGAIN?

<EPISODE 25>

THE SPLASH PAGE IS SO ADULT!
THE BACKGROUND IS BLACK AND RED, AND IT'S SO CHALLENGING AND FUN TO MATCH THE COLORS. WHERE COLORS ARE CONCERNED, THE NORM IS PINK AND BLACK, AND I JUST LOVE THOSE! ♥
FOR SOME REASON, DRAWING THIS EPISODE WAS REALLY DIFFICULT. IT'S ALWAYS DIFFICULT, BUT THIS TIME IT WAS ESPECIALLY SO.
COME TO THINK OF IT, RIHITO'S MANAGER'S NAME (THAT'S JUST HIS FAMILY NAME.) IS MAKABE-SAN. IT'S TRUE. AT SOME POINT IN PRODUCTION, SOMEBODY DECIDED ON IT.
ACTUALLY, THE SAME THING HAPPENED WITH FUKU-CHAN.
AS THINGS GO, PEOPLE GET THEIR NAMES. I THINK THAT'S A GOOD THING. OH, HAMASAKI'S FIRST NAME IS MASAHIRO—THE NAME OF THE GUY WHO IS THE BOSS AT NAKAYOSHI . . .

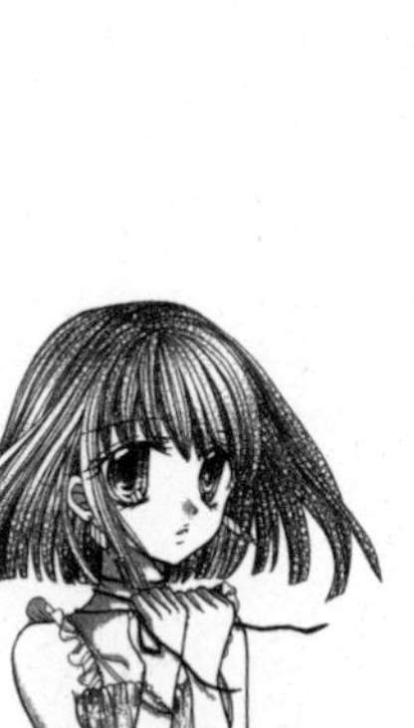

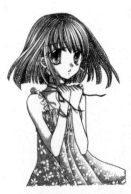

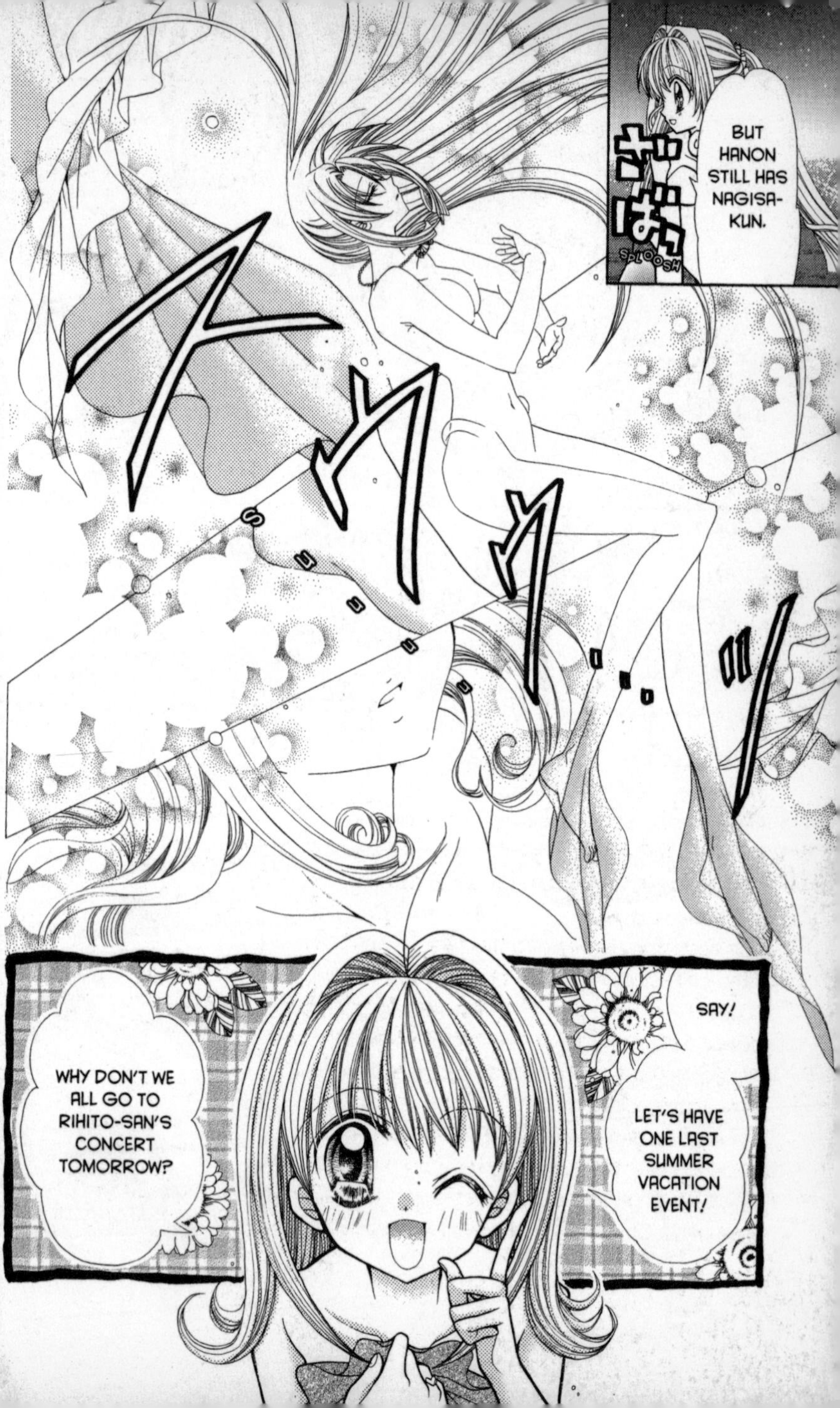

BUT HANON STILL HAS NAGISA-KUN.
SPLOOSH
SAY!
LET'S HAVE ONE LAST SUMMER VACATION EVENT!
WHY DON'T WE ALL GO TO RIHITO-SAN'S CONCERT TOMORROW?

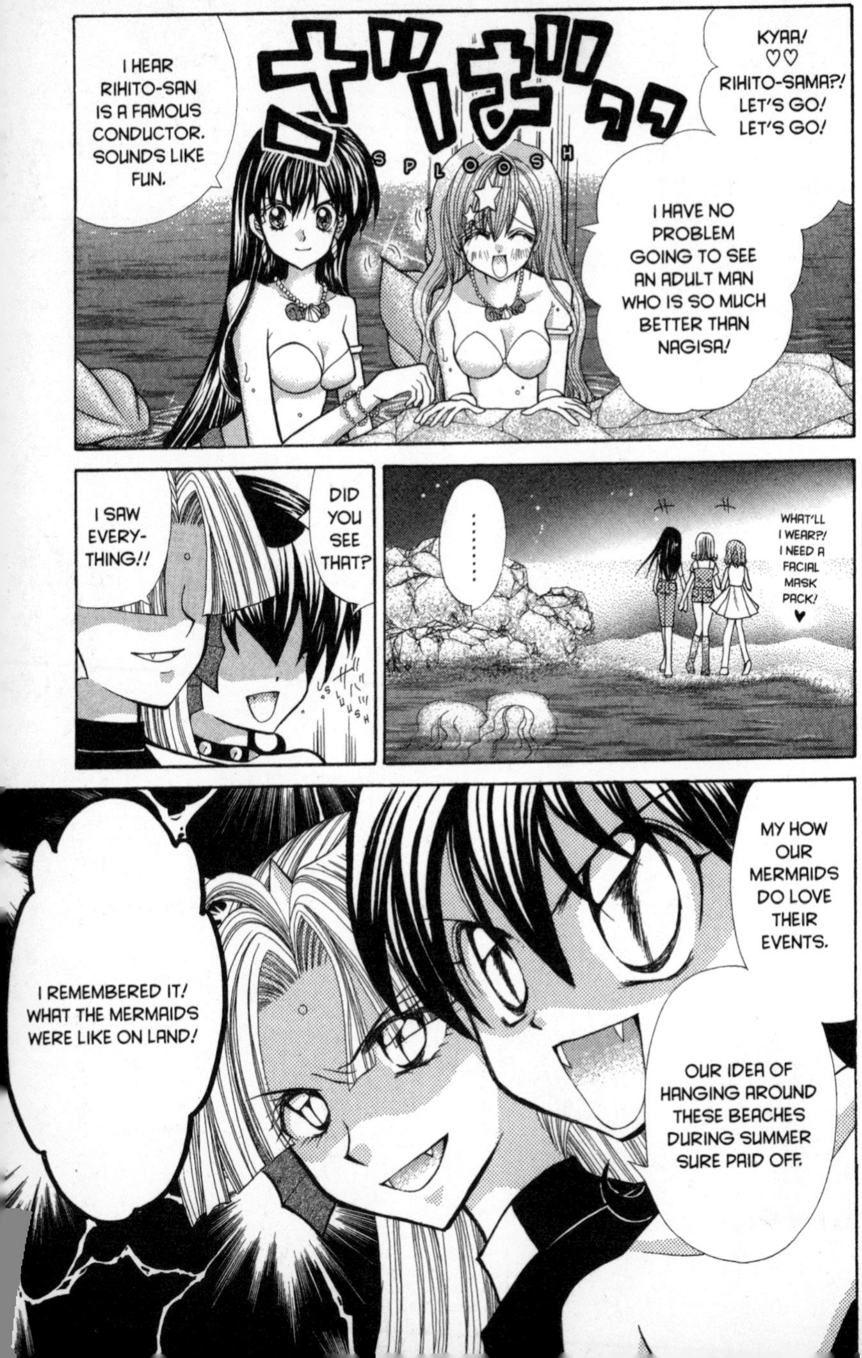
KYAA! ♡♡ RIHITO-SAMA?! LET'S GO! LET'S GO!
SPLOOSH
I HAVE NO PROBLEM GOING TO SEE AN ADULT MAN WHO IS SO MUCH BETTER THAN NAGISA!
I HEAR RIHITO-SAN IS A FAMOUS CONDUCTOR. SOUNDS LIKE FUN.
WHAT'LL I WEAR?! I NEED A FACIAL MASK PACK! ♥
....
DID YOU SEE THAT?
I SAW EVERY-THING!!
SLUUSH
MY HOW OUR MERMAIDS DO LOVE THEIR EVENTS.
OUR IDEA OF HANGING AROUND THESE BEACHES DURING SUMMER SURE PAID OFF.
I REMEMBERED IT! WHAT THE MERMAIDS WERE LIKE ON LAND!

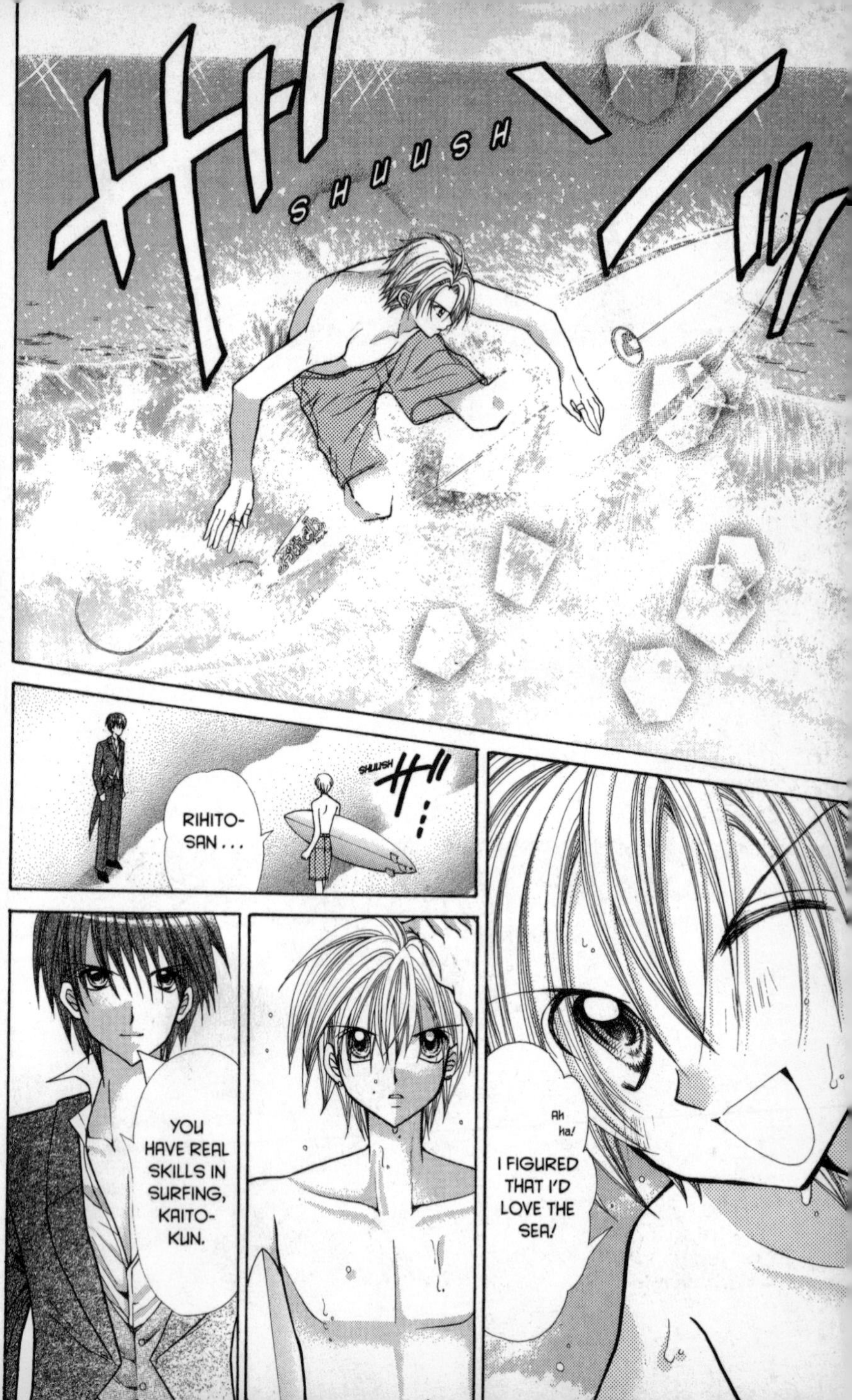
SHUUSH
SHUUSH
RIHITO-SAN . . .
YOU HAVE REAL SKILLS IN SURFING, KAITO-KUN.
Ah ha!
I FIGURED THAT I'D LOVE THE SEA!

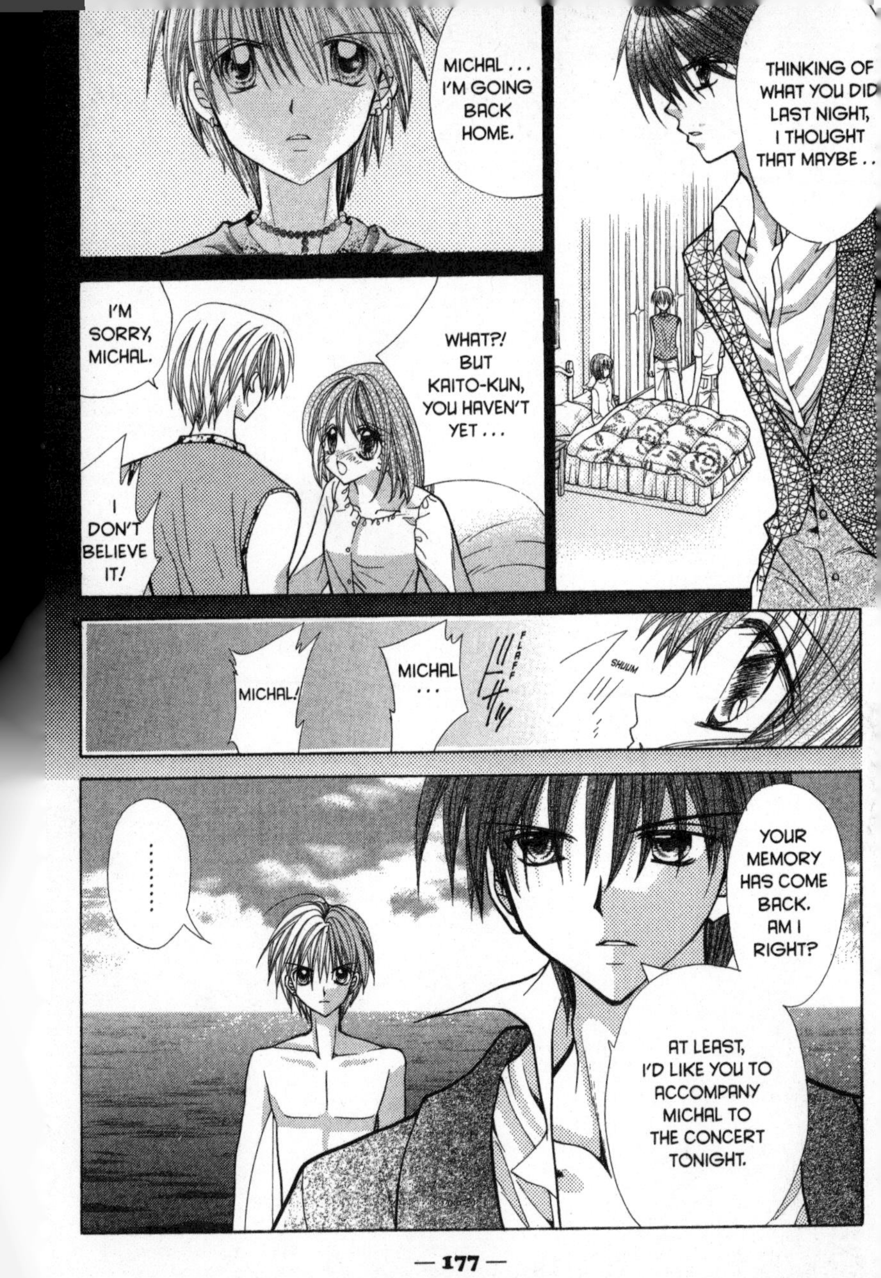
THINKING OF WHAT YOU DID LAST NIGHT, I THOUGHT THAT MAYBE . . .
MICHAL . . . I'M GOING BACK HOME.
WHAT?! BUT KAITO-KUN, YOU HAVEN'T YET . . .
I'M SORRY, MICHAL.
I DON'T BELIEVE IT!
SHUUM
FLAFF
MICHAL . . .
MICHAL!
YOUR MEMORY HAS COME BACK. AM I RIGHT?
AT LEAST, I'D LIKE YOU TO ACCOMPANY MICHAL TO THE CONCERT TONIGHT.
....

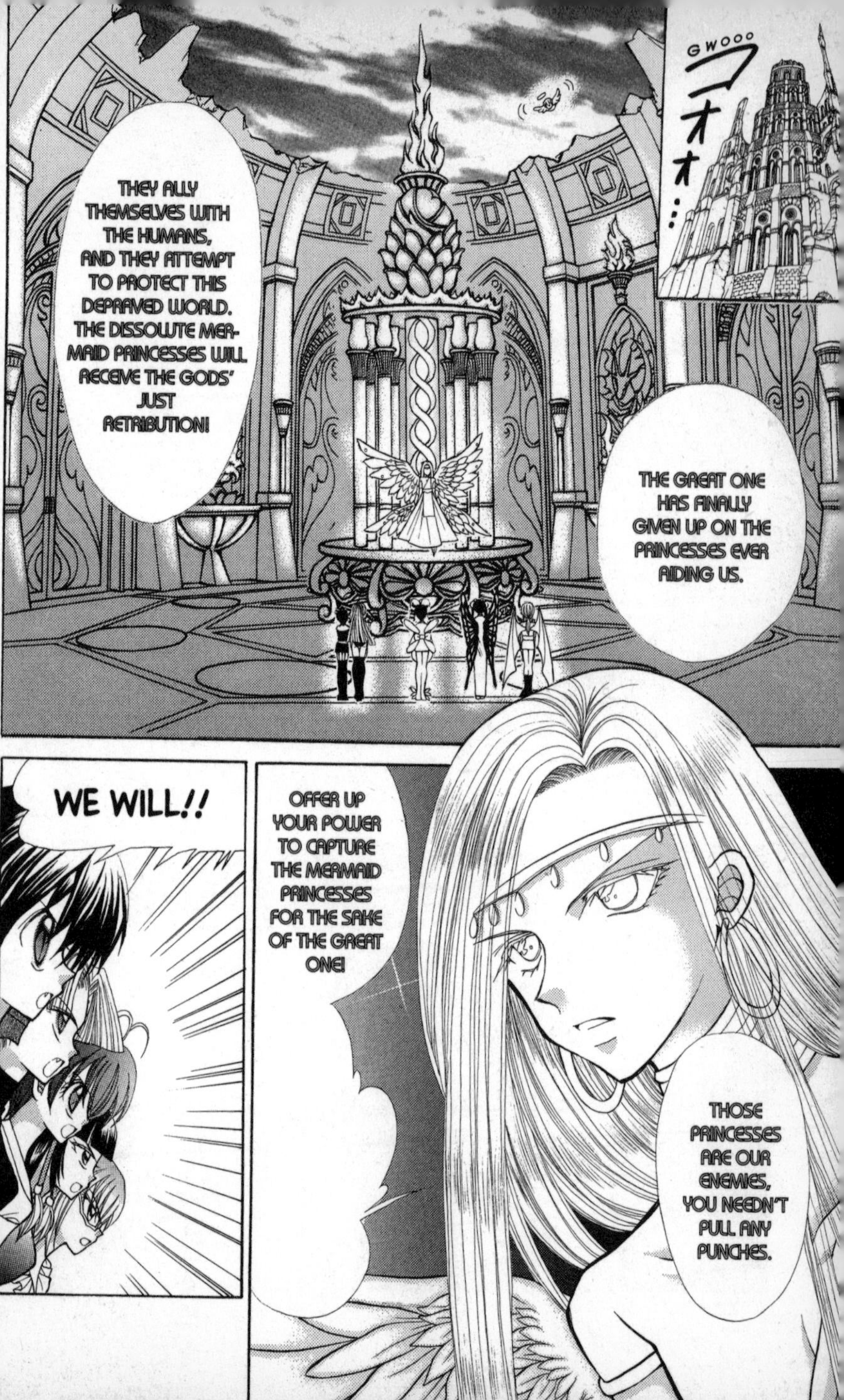
GWOOO
THE GREAT ONE HAS FINALLY GIVEN UP ON THE PRINCESSES EVER AIDING US.
THEY ALLY THEMSELVES WITH THE HUMANS, AND THEY ATTEMPT TO PROTECT THIS DEPRAVED WORLD. THE DISSOLUTE MER-MAID PRINCESSES WILL RECEIVE THE GODS' JUST RETRIBUTION!
OFFER UP YOUR POWER TO CAPTURE THE MERMAID PRINCESSES FOR THE SAKE OF THE GREAT ONE!
THOSE PRINCESSES ARE OUR ENEMIES, YOU NEEDN'T PULL ANY PUNCHES.
WE WILL!!

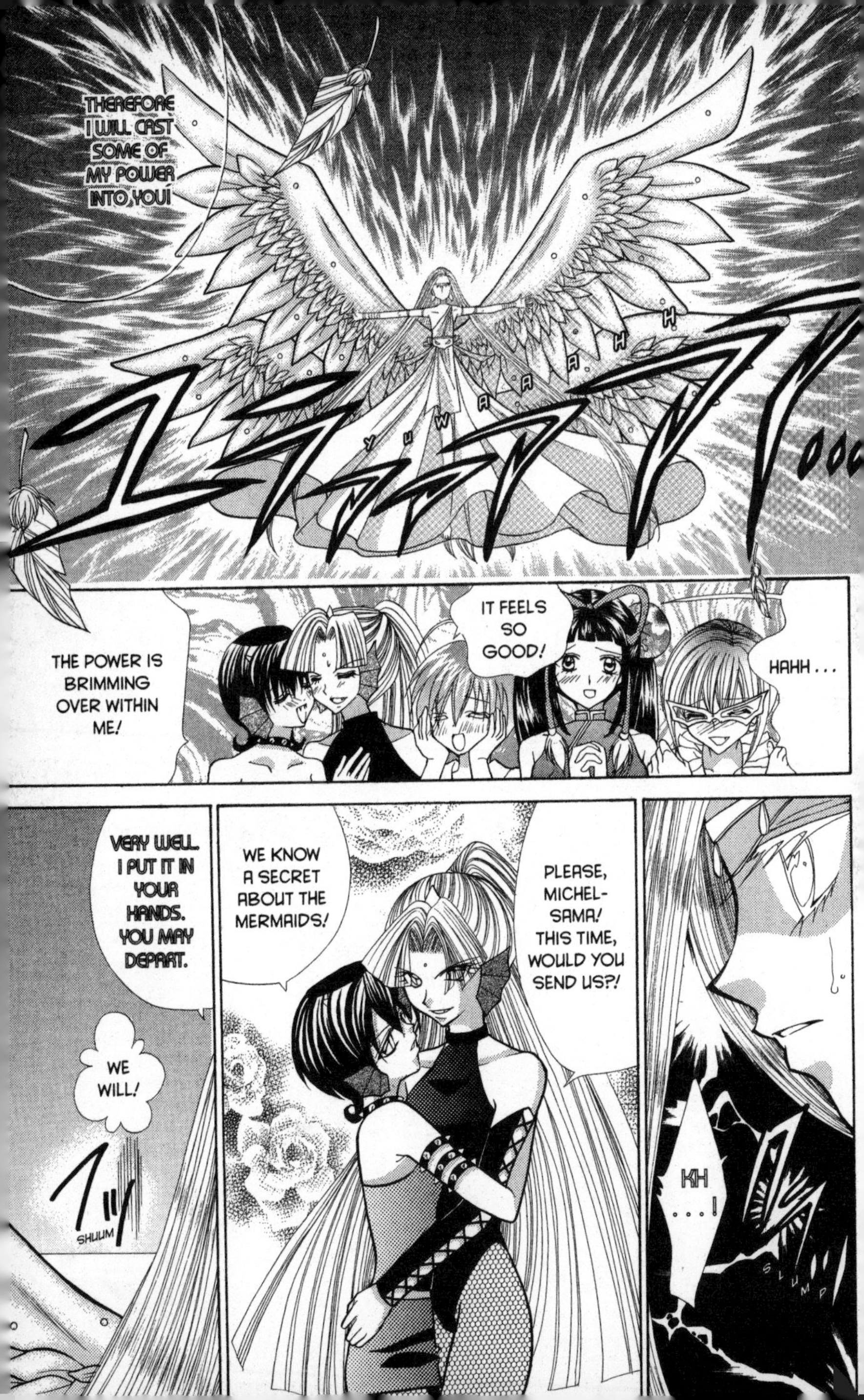
THEREFORE I WILL CAST SOME OF MY POWER INTO YOU!
YUWAAAHH
HAHH . . .
IT FEELS SO GOOD!
THE POWER IS BRIMMING OVER WITHIN ME!
KH . . . !
SLUMP
PLEASE, MICHEL-SAMA! THIS TIME, WOULD YOU SEND US?!
WE KNOW A SECRET ABOUT THE MERMAIDS!
VERY WELL. I PUT IT IN YOUR HANDS. YOU MAY DEPART.
WE WILL!
SHUUM

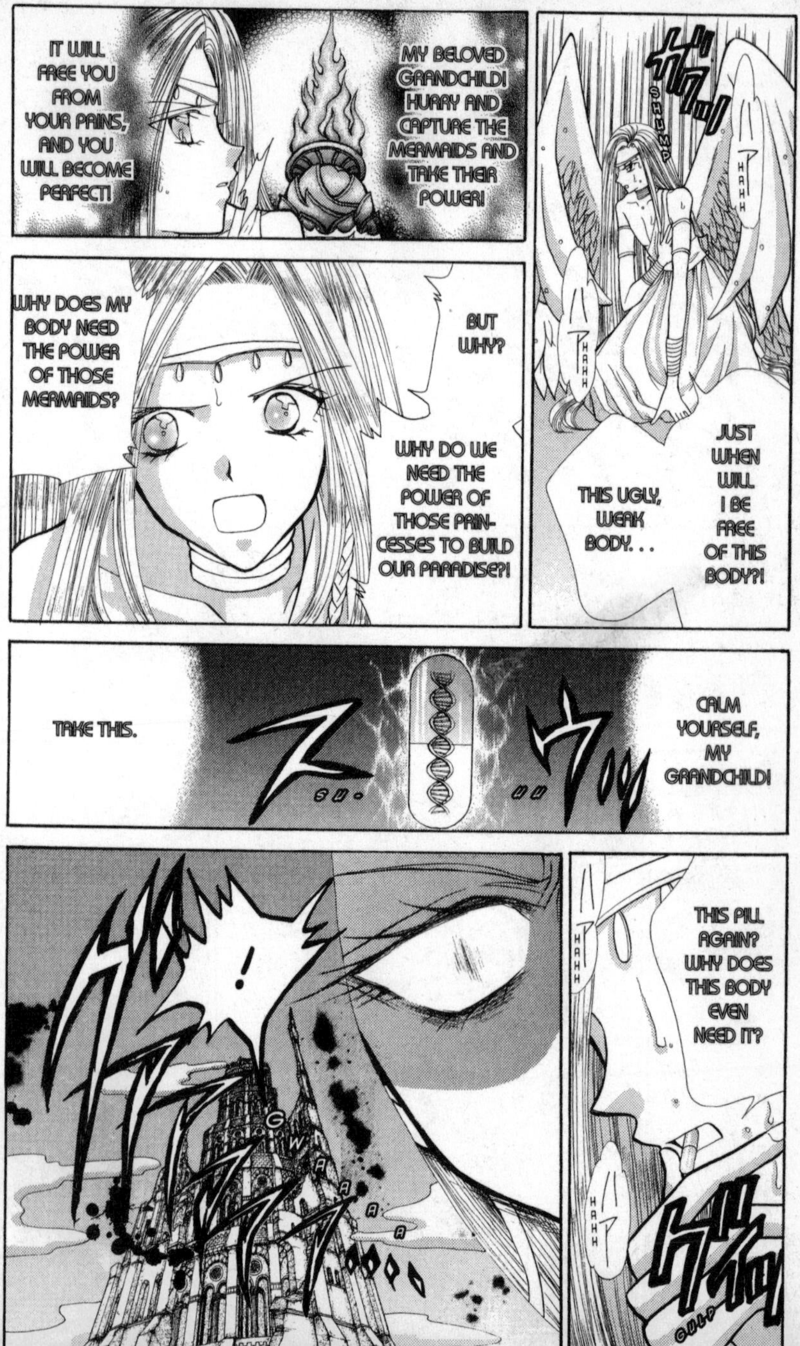
SHUMP
HAHH
HAHH
JUST WHEN WILL I BE FREE OF THIS BODY?!
THIS UGLY, WEAK BODY. . .
MY BELOVED GRANDCHILD! HURRY AND CAPTURE THE MERMAIDS AND TAKE THEIR POWER!
IT WILL FREE YOU FROM YOUR PAINS, AND YOU WILL BECOME PERFECT!
BUT WHY?
WHY DOES MY BODY NEED THE POWER OF THOSE MERMAIDS?
WHY DO WE NEED THE POWER OF THOSE PRIN-CESSES TO BUILD OUR PARADISE?!
CALM YOURSELF, MY GRANDCHILD!
WHU
SHU
TAKE THIS.
HAHH
THIS PILL AGAIN? WHY DOES THIS BODY EVEN NEED IT?
HAHH
GULP
!
GWAAAAA

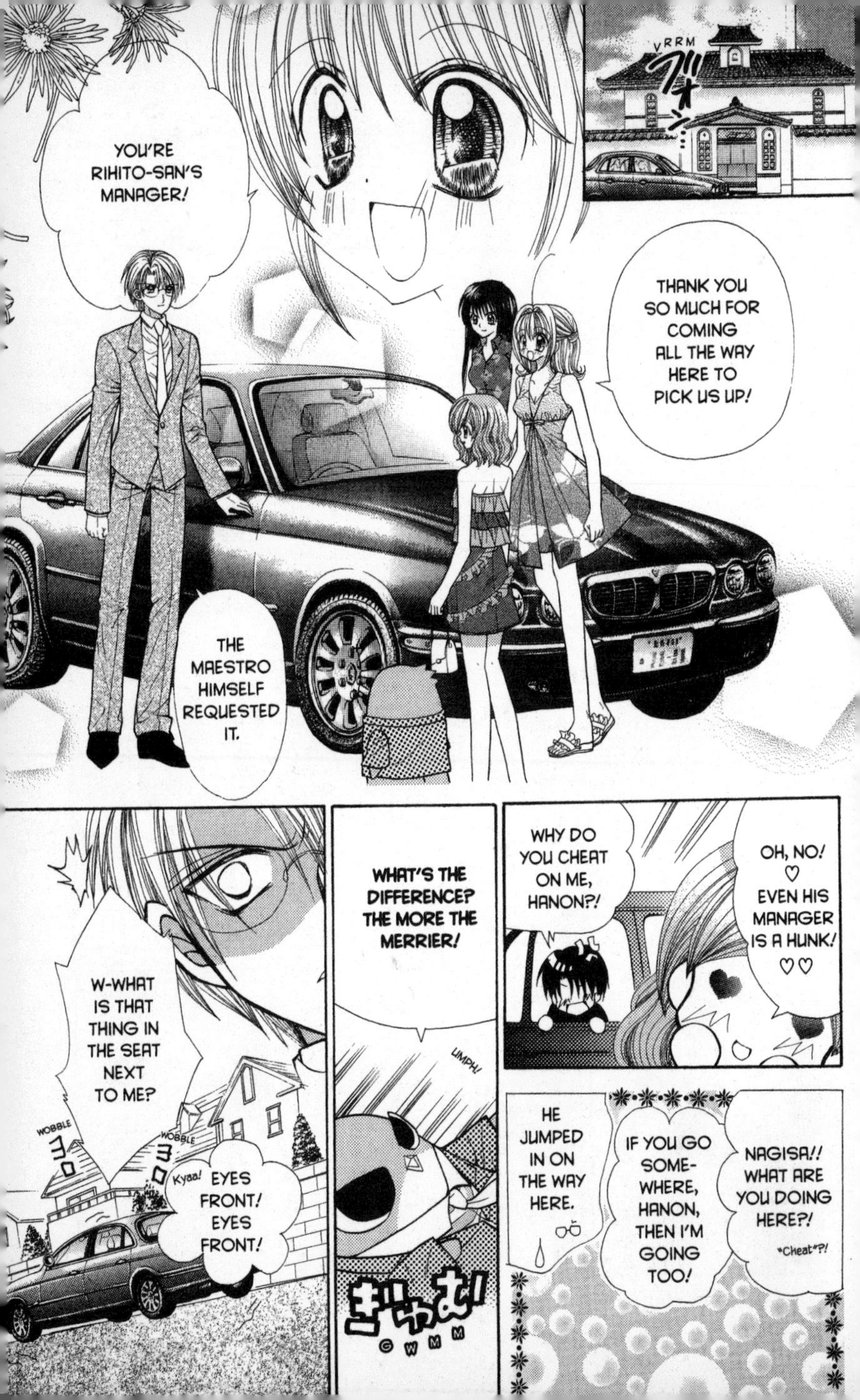
VRRM
THANK YOU SO MUCH FOR COMING ALL THE WAY HERE TO PICK US UP!
YOU'RE RIHITO-SAN'S MANAGER!
THE MAESTRO HIMSELF REQUESTED IT.
OH, NO! ♡ EVEN HIS MANAGER IS A HUNK! ♡♡
WHY DO YOU CHEAT ON ME, HANON?!
NAGISA!! WHAT ARE YOU DOING HERE?!
Cheat?!
IF YOU GO SOME-WHERE, HANON, THEN I'M GOING TOO!
HE JUMPED IN ON THE WAY HERE.
WHAT'S THE DIFFERENCE? THE MORE THE MERRIER!
UMPH!
GWMM
W-WHAT IS THAT THING IN THE SEAT NEXT TO ME?
WOBBLE
WOBBLE
Kyaa!
EYES FRONT! EYES FRONT!

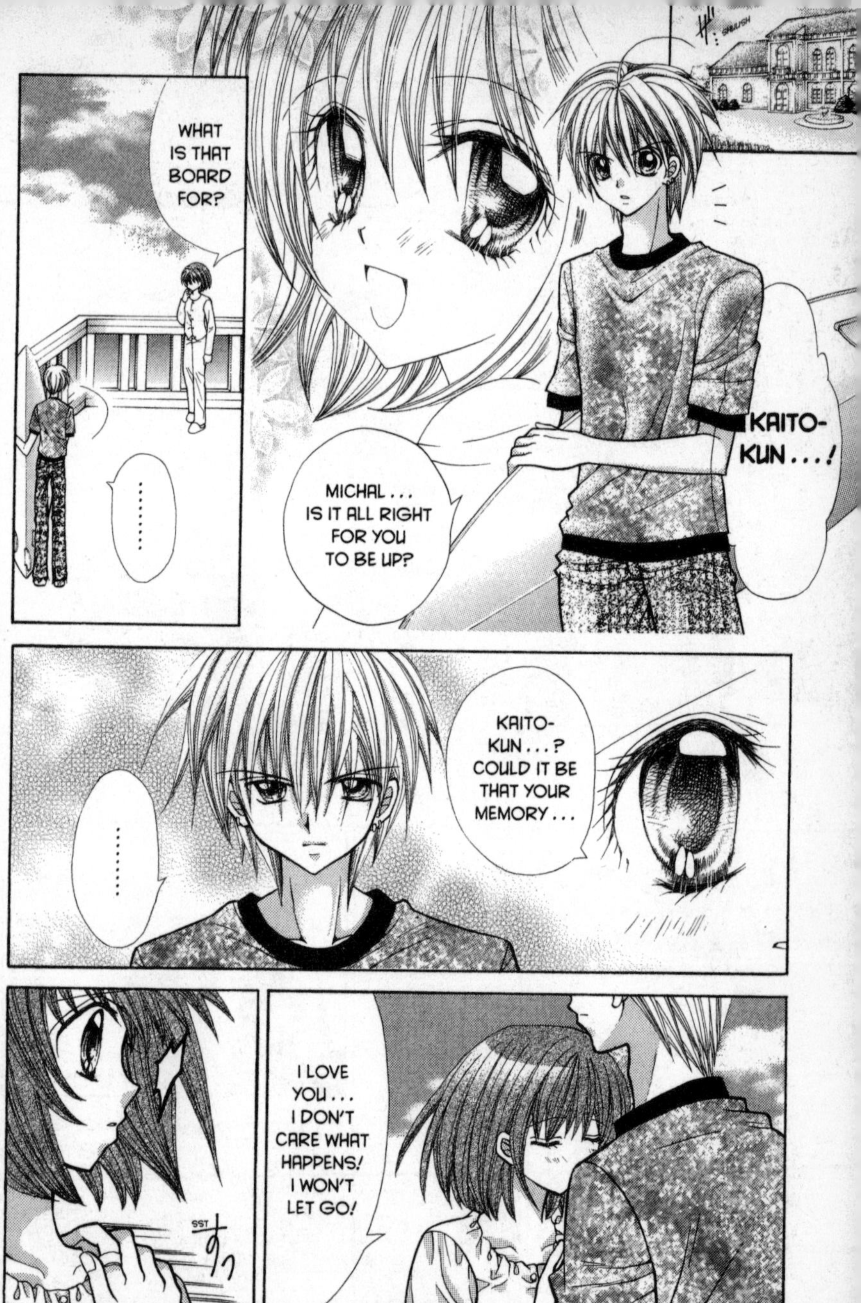
SHUSH
KAITO-KUN . . . !
MICHAL . . . IS IT ALL RIGHT FOR YOU TO BE UP?
WHAT IS THAT BOARD FOR?
. . . .
KAITO-KUN . . . ? COULD IT BE THAT YOUR MEMORY . . .
. . . .
I LOVE YOU . . . I DON'T CARE WHAT HAPPENS! I WON'T LET GO!
SST

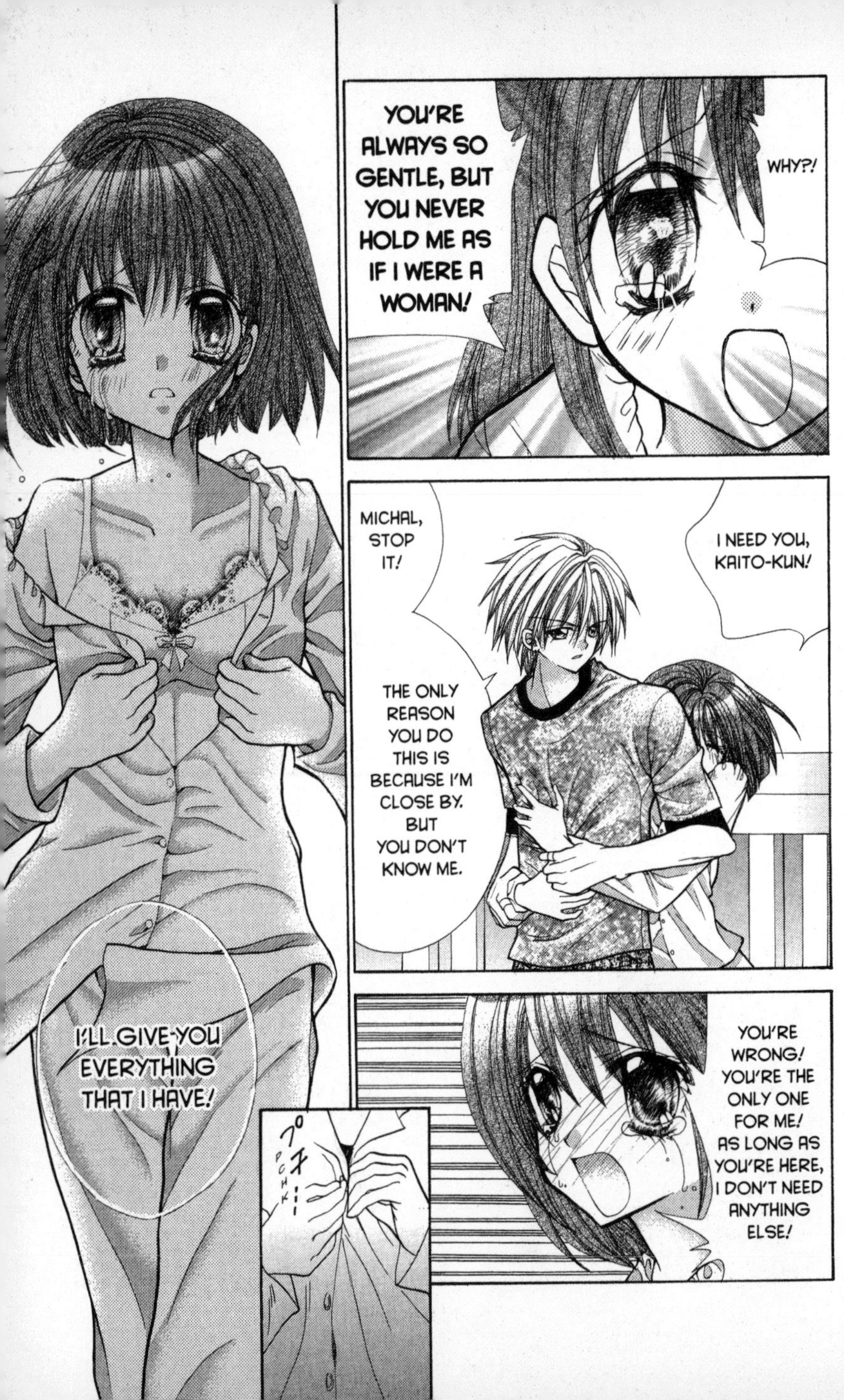
WHY?!
YOU'RE ALWAYS SO GENTLE, BUT YOU NEVER HOLD ME AS IF I WERE A WOMAN!
I NEED YOU, KAITO-KUN!
MICHAL, STOP IT!
THE ONLY REASON YOU DO THIS IS BECAUSE I'M CLOSE BY. BUT YOU DON'T KNOW ME.
YOU'RE WRONG! YOU'RE THE ONLY ONE FOR ME! AS LONG AS YOU'RE HERE, I DON'T NEED ANYTHING ELSE!
I'LL GIVE YOU EVERYTHING THAT I HAVE!
PCHK

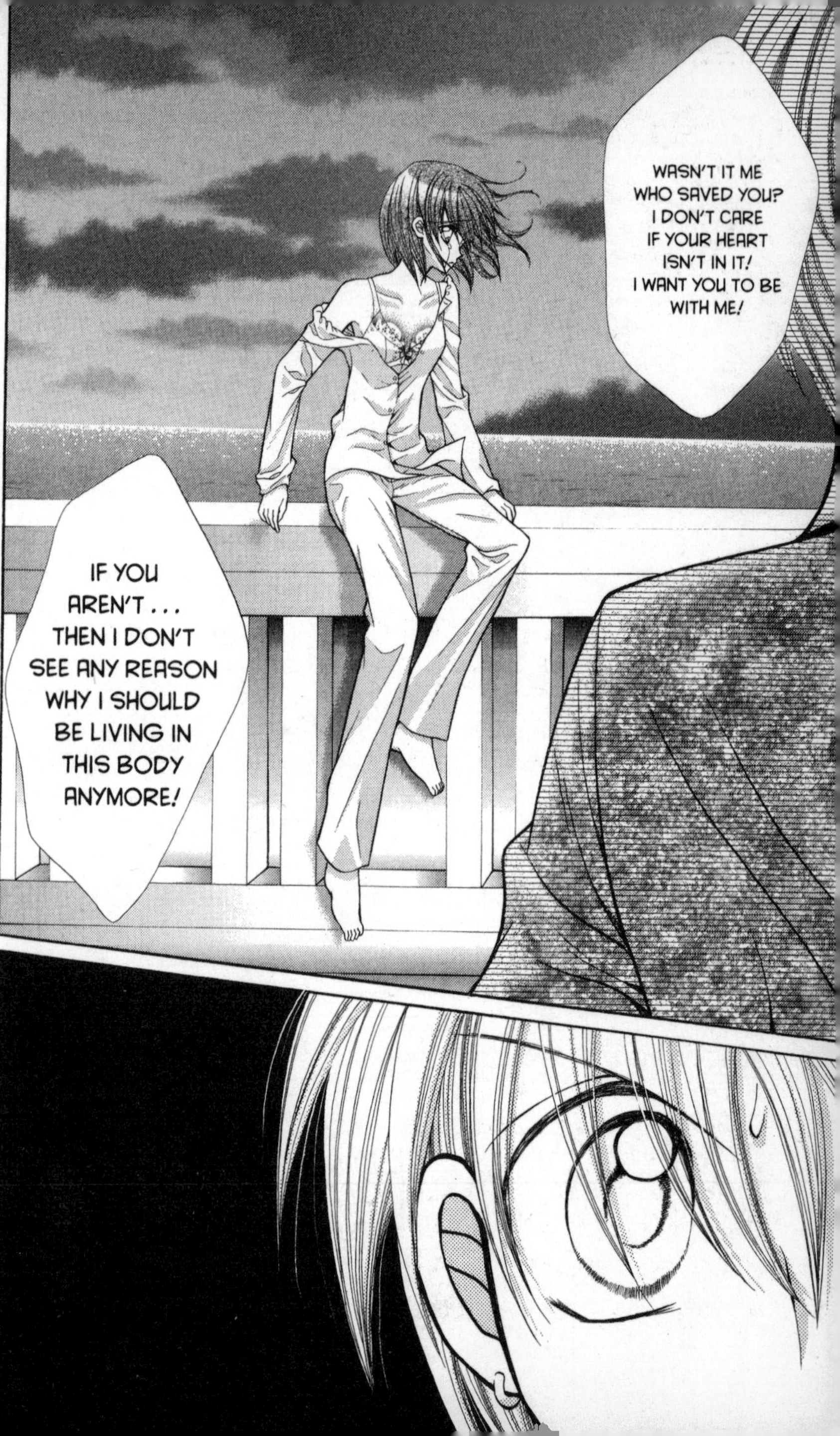
WASN'T IT ME WHO SAVED YOU? I DON'T CARE IF YOUR HEART ISN'T IN IT! I WANT YOU TO BE WITH ME!
IF YOU AREN'T . . . THEN I DON'T SEE ANY REASON WHY I SHOULD BE LIVING IN THIS BODY ANYMORE!

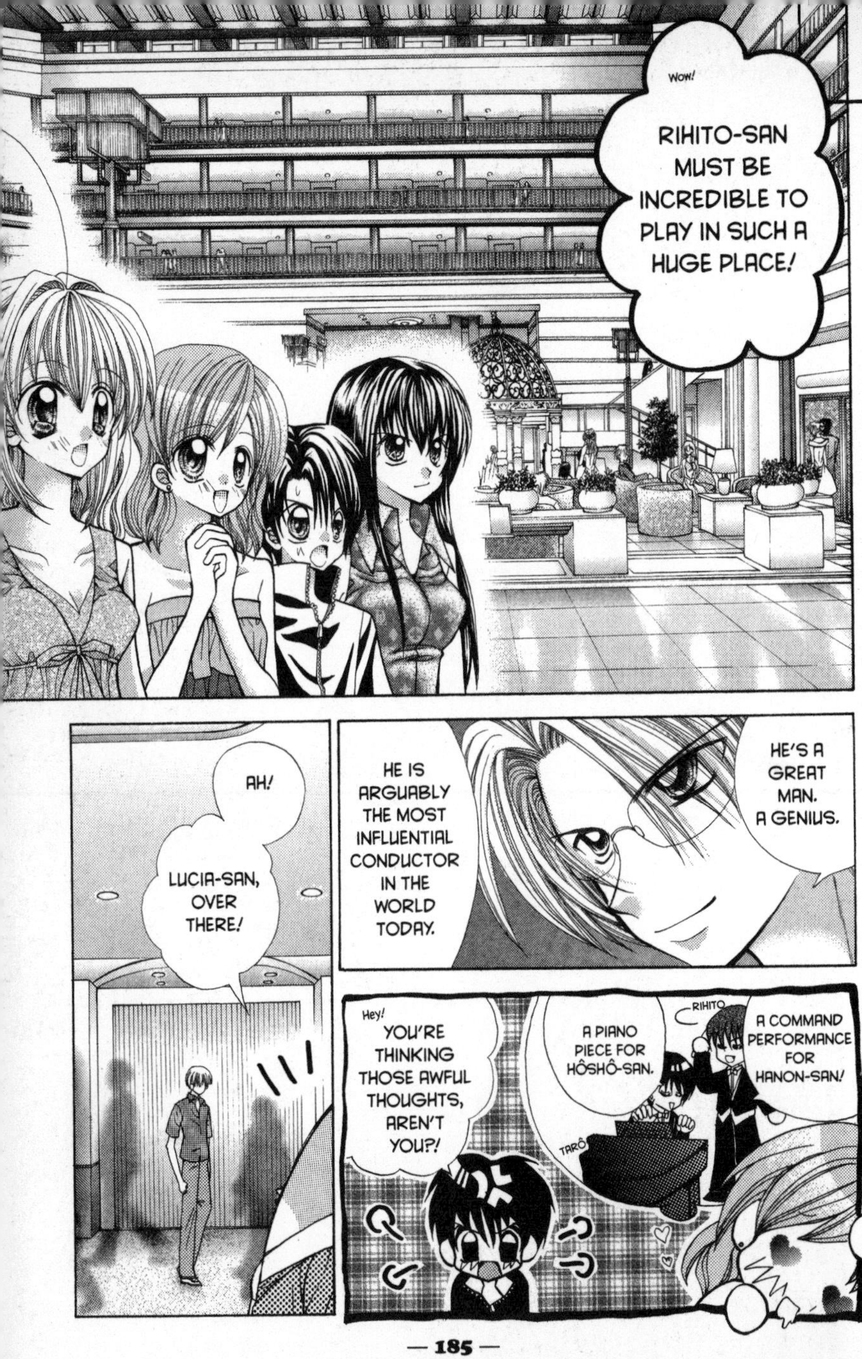
Wow!
RIHITO-SAN MUST BE INCREDIBLE TO PLAY IN SUCH A HUGE PLACE!
HE'S A GREAT MAN. A GENIUS.
HE IS ARGUABLY THE MOST INFLUENTIAL CONDUCTOR IN THE WORLD TODAY.
A COMMAND PERFORMANCE FOR HANON-SAN!
RIHITO
A PIANO PIECE FOR HÔSHÔ-SAN.
TARÔ
Hey!
YOU'RE THINKING THOSE AWFUL THOUGHTS, AREN'T YOU?!
AH!
LUCIA-SAN, OVER THERE!

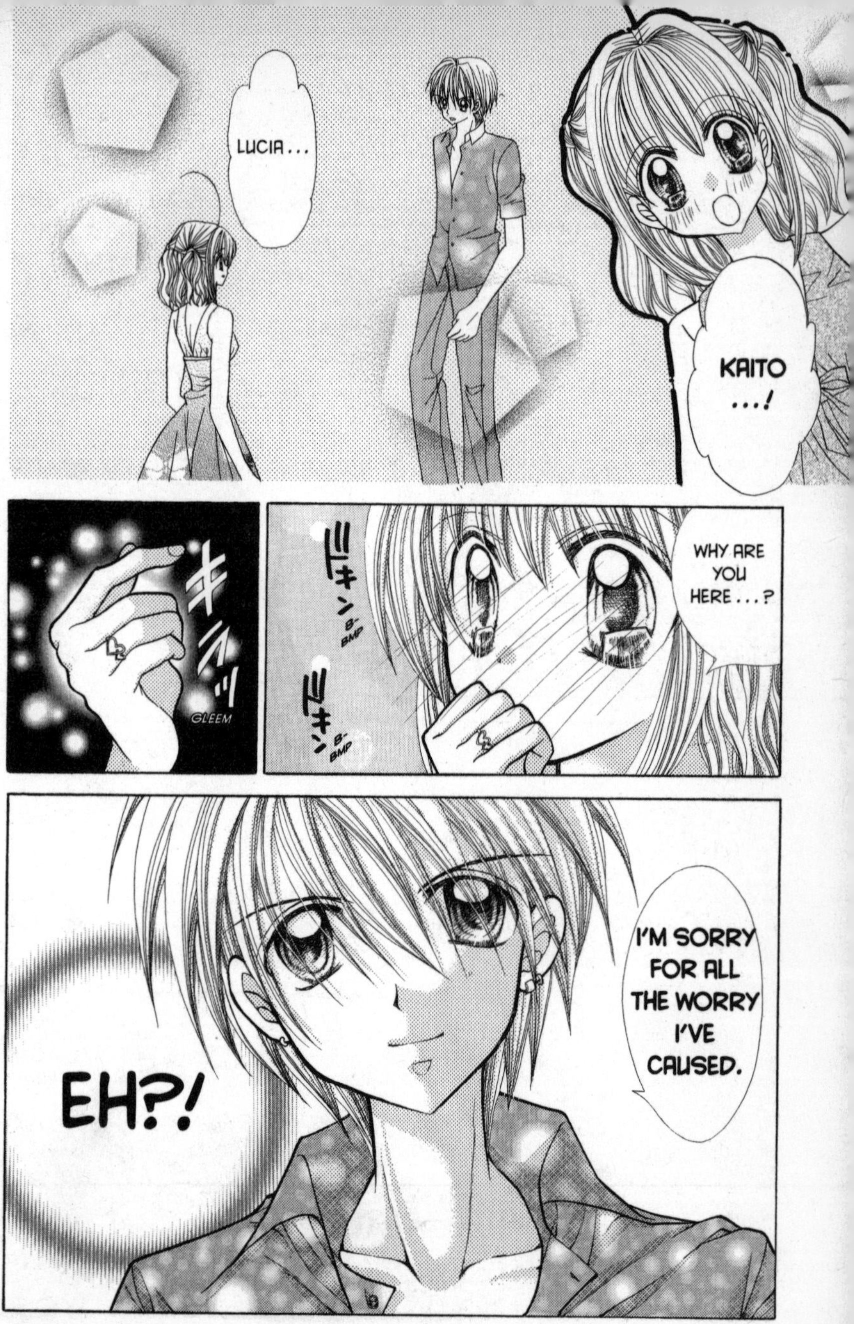
KAITO ...!
LUCIA...
WHY ARE YOU HERE...?
ドキン B-BMP
ドキン B-BMP
キラッ GLEEM
I'M SORRY FOR ALL THE WORRY I'VE CAUSED.
EH?!

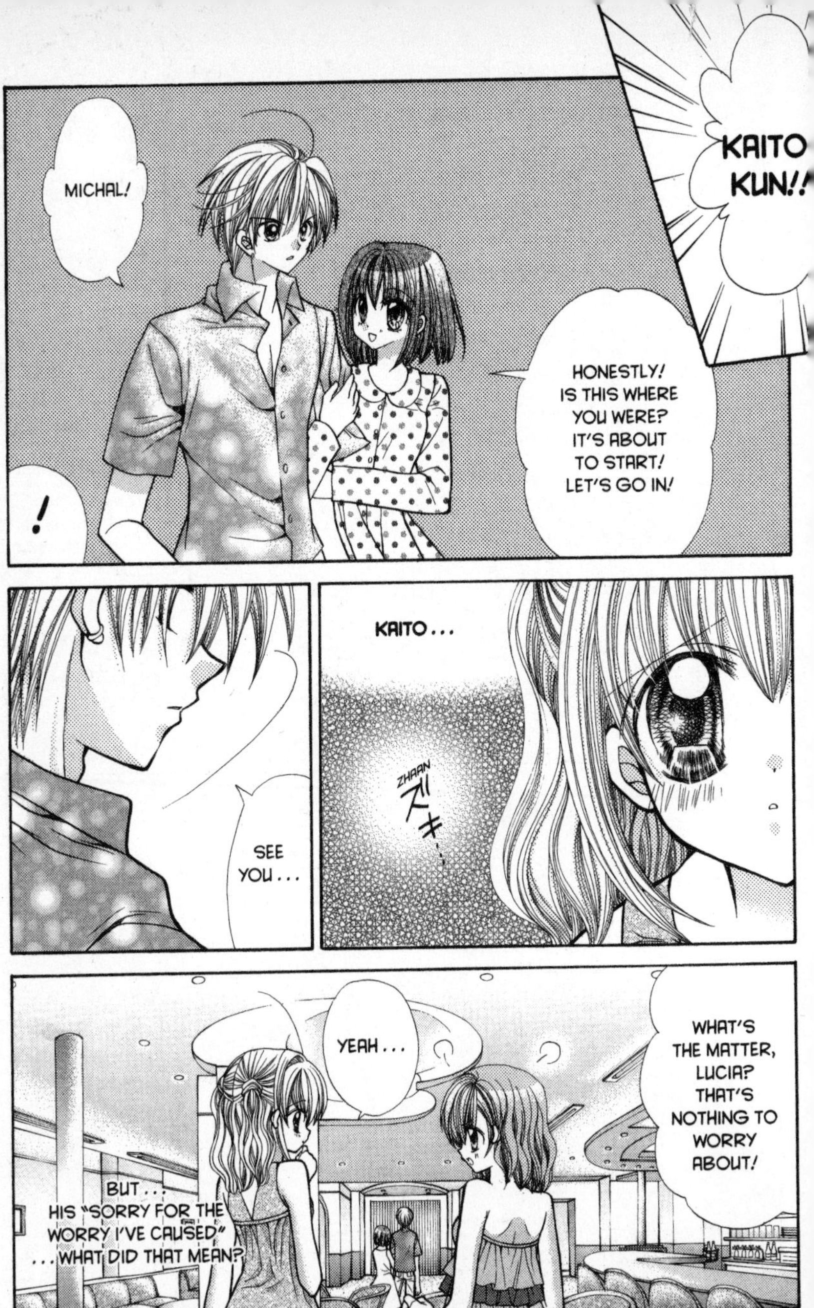
KAITO KUN!!
HONESTLY! IS THIS WHERE YOU WERE? IT'S ABOUT TO START! LET'S GO IN!
MICHAL!
!
KAITO...
ZHAAN
SEE YOU...
WHAT'S THE MATTER, LUCIA? THAT'S NOTHING TO WORRY ABOUT!
YEAH...
BUT... HIS "SORRY FOR THE WORRY I'VE CAUSED" ... WHAT DID THAT MEAN?

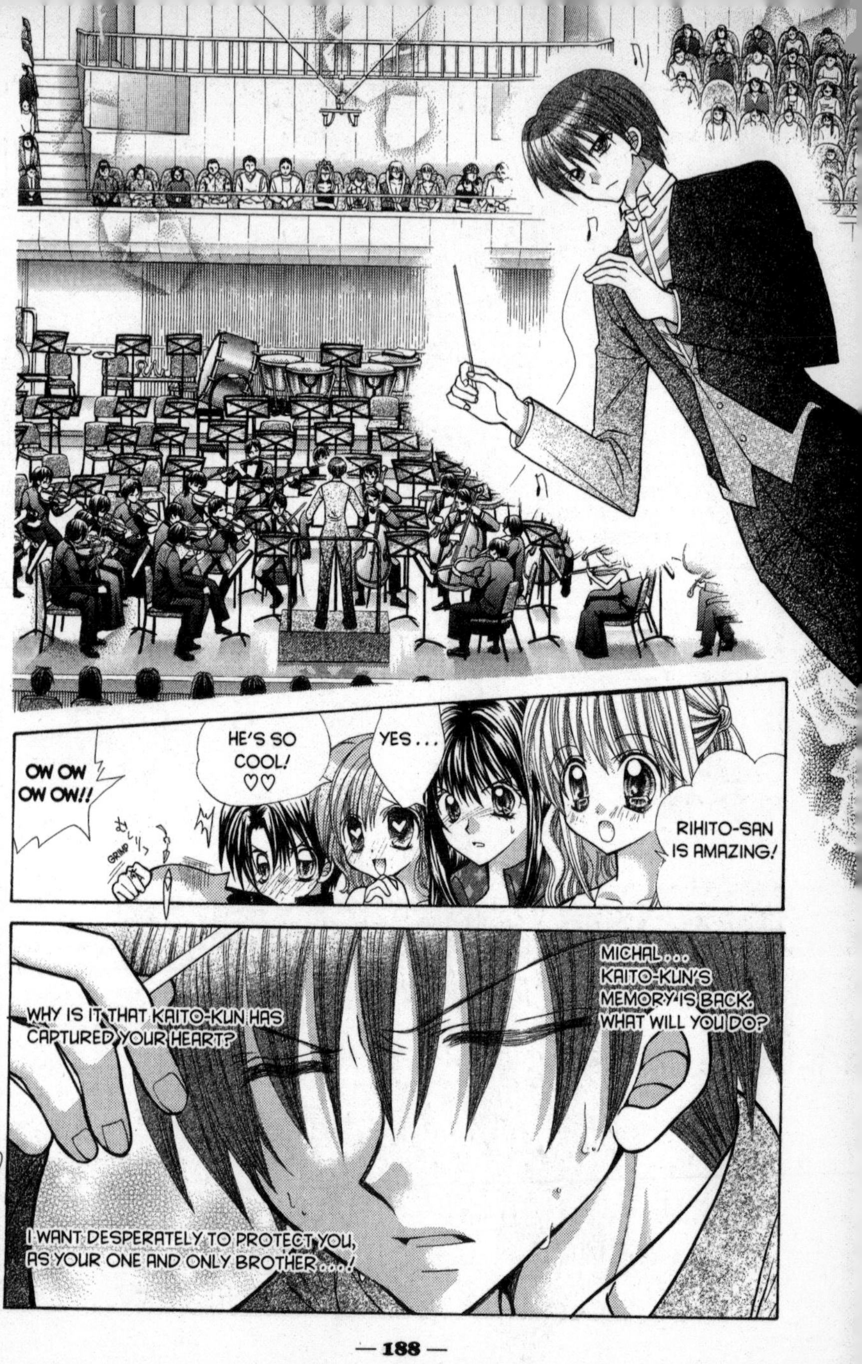
RIHITO-SAN IS AMAZING!
YES . . .
HE'S SO COOL! ♡♡
OW OW OW OW!!
GRIMP
MICHAL . . . KAITO-KUN'S MEMORY IS BACK. WHAT WILL YOU DO?
WHY IS IT THAT KAITO-KUN HAS CAPTURED YOUR HEART?
I WANT DESPERATELY TO PROTECT YOU, AS YOUR ONE AND ONLY BROTHER . . . !

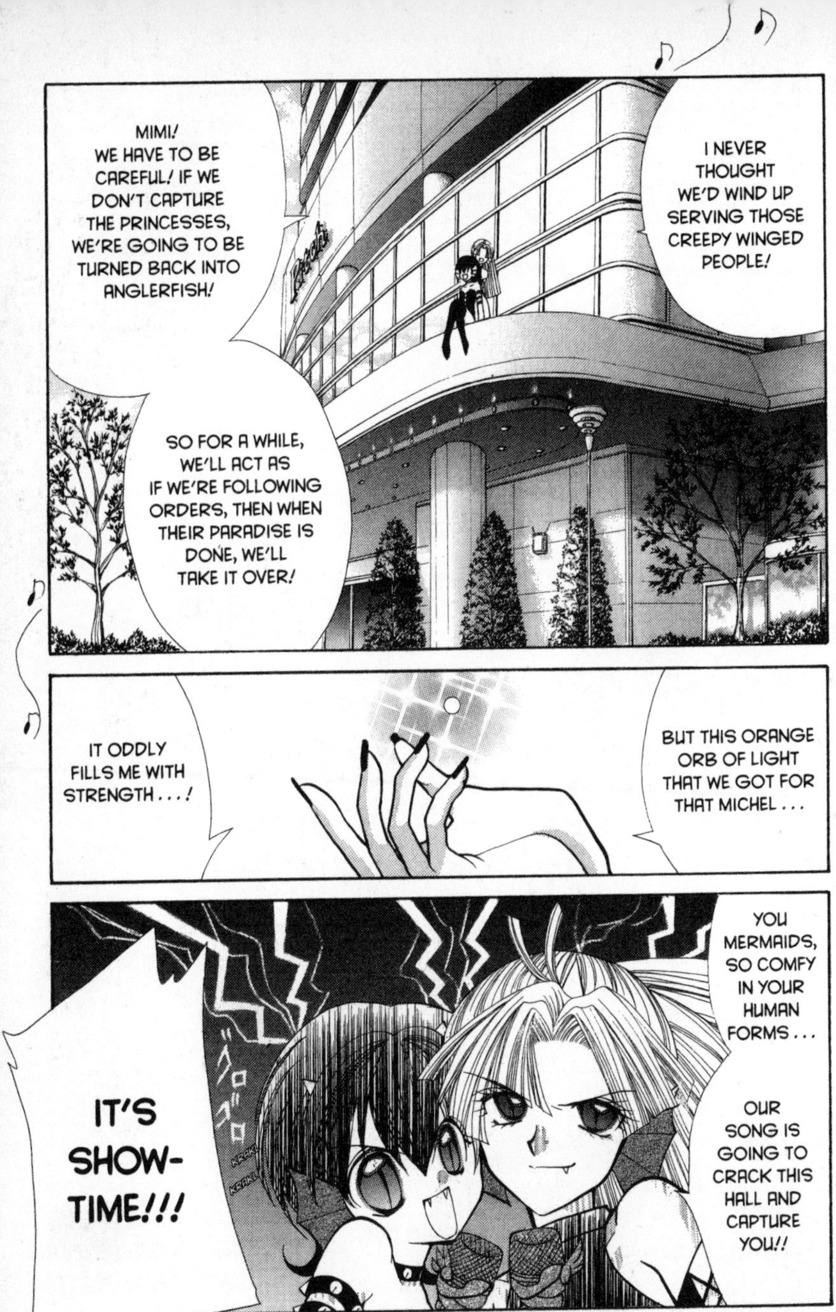

I NEVER THOUGHT WE'D WIND UP SERVING THOSE CREEPY WINGED PEOPLE!
MIMI! WE HAVE TO BE CAREFUL! IF WE DON'T CAPTURE THE PRINCESSES, WE'RE GOING TO BE TURNED BACK INTO ANGLERFISH!
SO FOR A WHILE, WE'LL ACT AS IF WE'RE FOLLOWING ORDERS, THEN WHEN THEIR PARADISE IS DONE, WE'LL TAKE IT OVER!
BUT THIS ORANGE ORB OF LIGHT THAT WE GOT FOR THAT MICHEL . . .
IT ODDLY FILLS ME WITH STRENGTH . . . !
YOU MERMAIDS, SO COMFY IN YOUR HUMAN FORMS . . .
OUR SONG IS GOING TO CRACK THIS HALL AND CAPTURE YOU!!
KRAK!
KRAK!
IT'S SHOW-TIME!!!

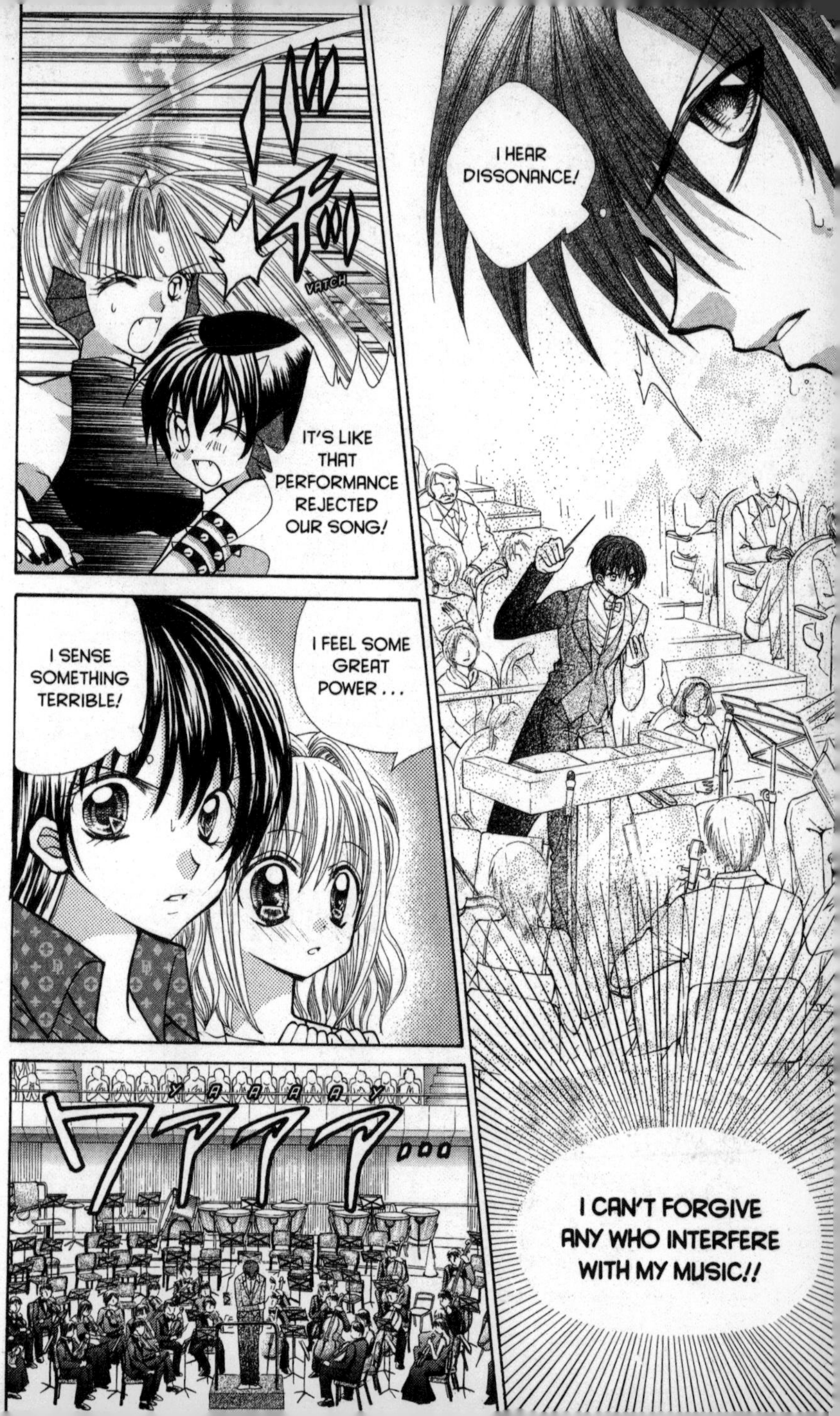
I HEAR DISSONANCE!
I CAN'T FORGIVE ANY WHO INTERFERE WITH MY MUSIC!!
VATCH
IT'S LIKE THAT PERFORMANCE REJECTED OUR SONG!
I FEEL SOME GREAT POWER . . .
I SENSE SOMETHING TERRIBLE!
YAAAAAY

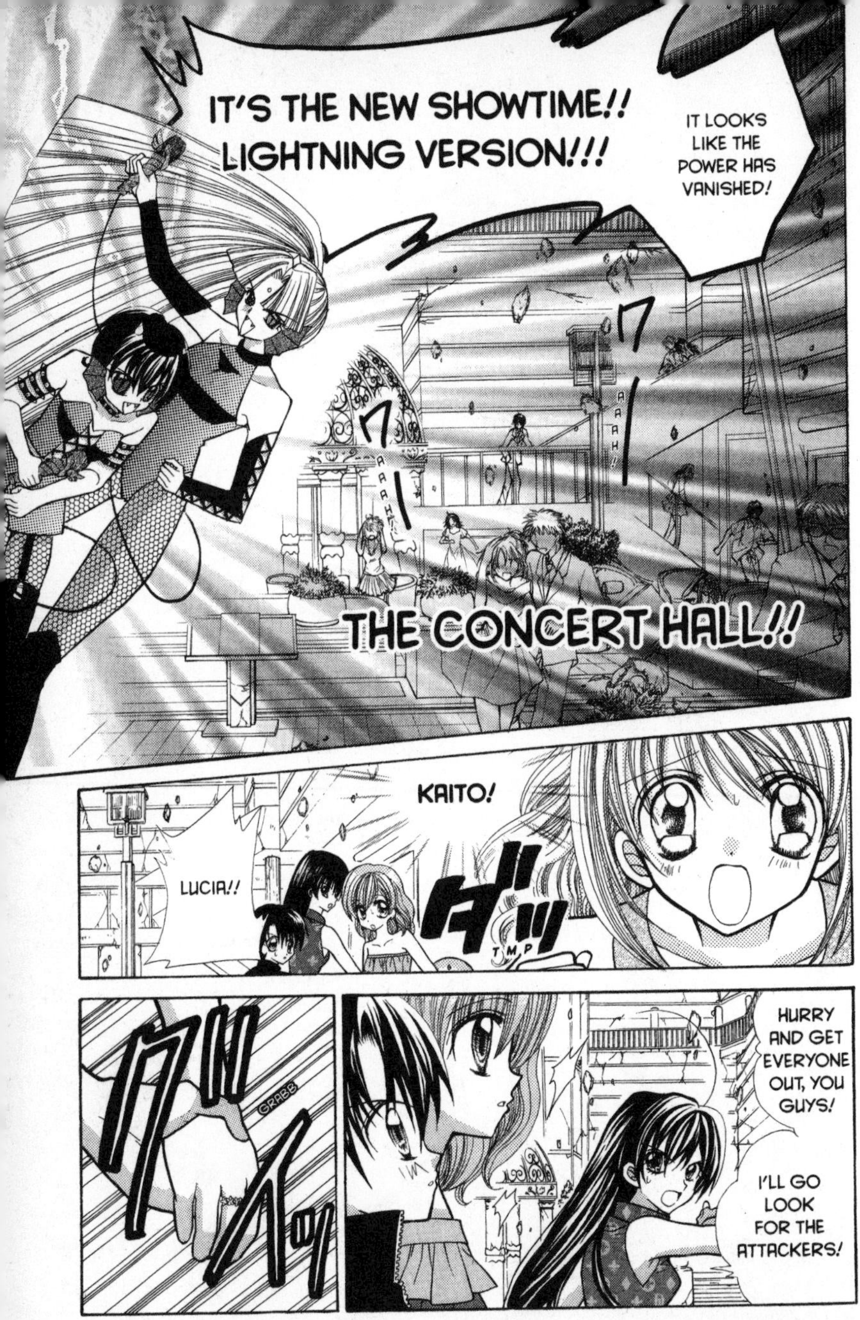
IT LOOKS LIKE THE POWER HAS VANISHED!
IT'S THE NEW SHOWTIME!! LIGHTNING VERSION!!!
THE CONCERT HALL!!
KAITO!
TMP
LUCIA!!
HURRY AND GET EVERYONE OUT, YOU GUYS!
I'LL GO LOOK FOR THE ATTACKERS!
GRABB

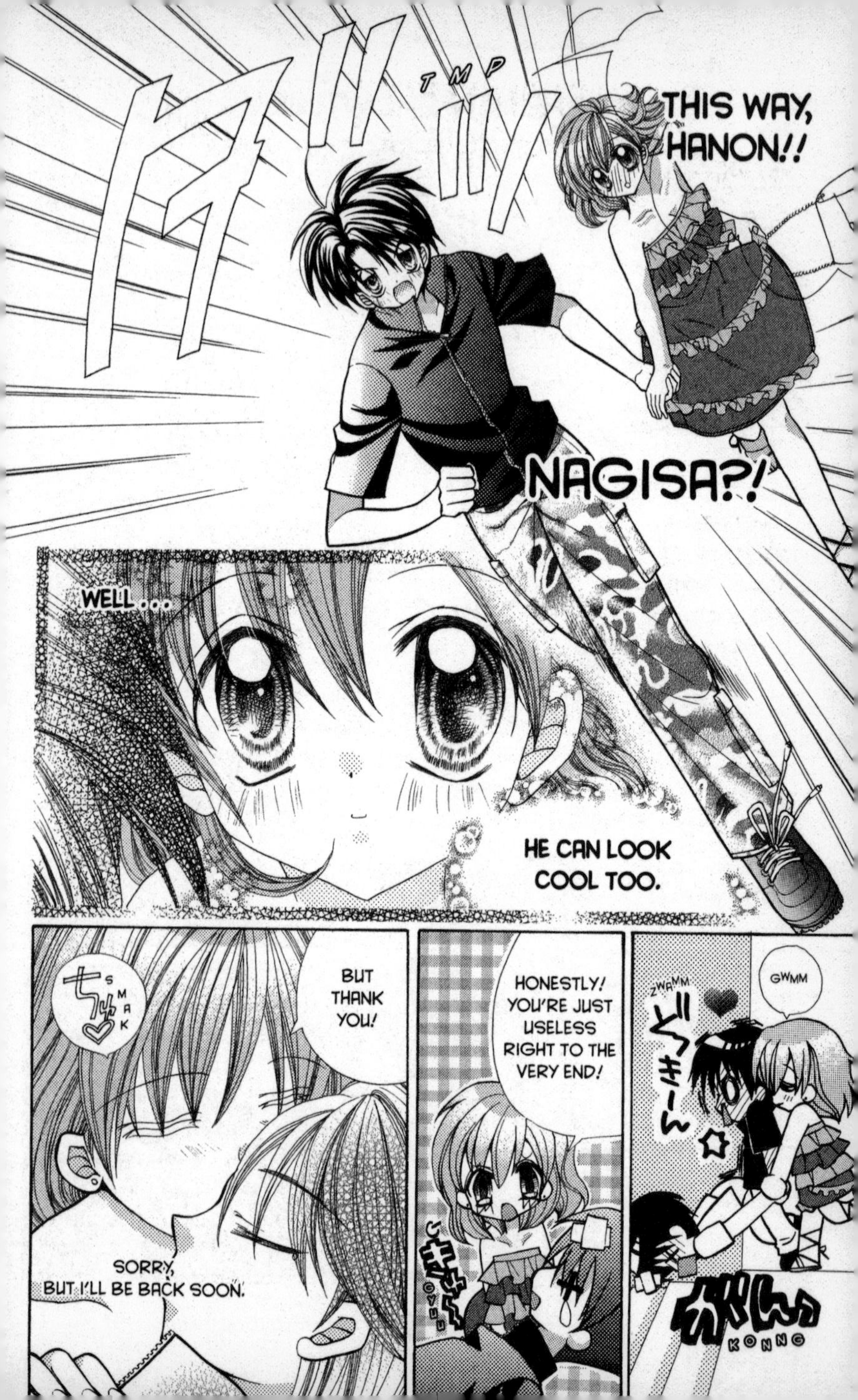
THIS WAY, HANON!!
TMP
NAGISA?!
WELL...
HE CAN LOOK COOL TOO.
GWMM
ZWAMM
KONNG
HONESTLY! YOU'RE JUST USELESS RIGHT TO THE VERY END!
BUT THANK YOU!
SMAK
SORRY, BUT I'LL BE BACK SOON.

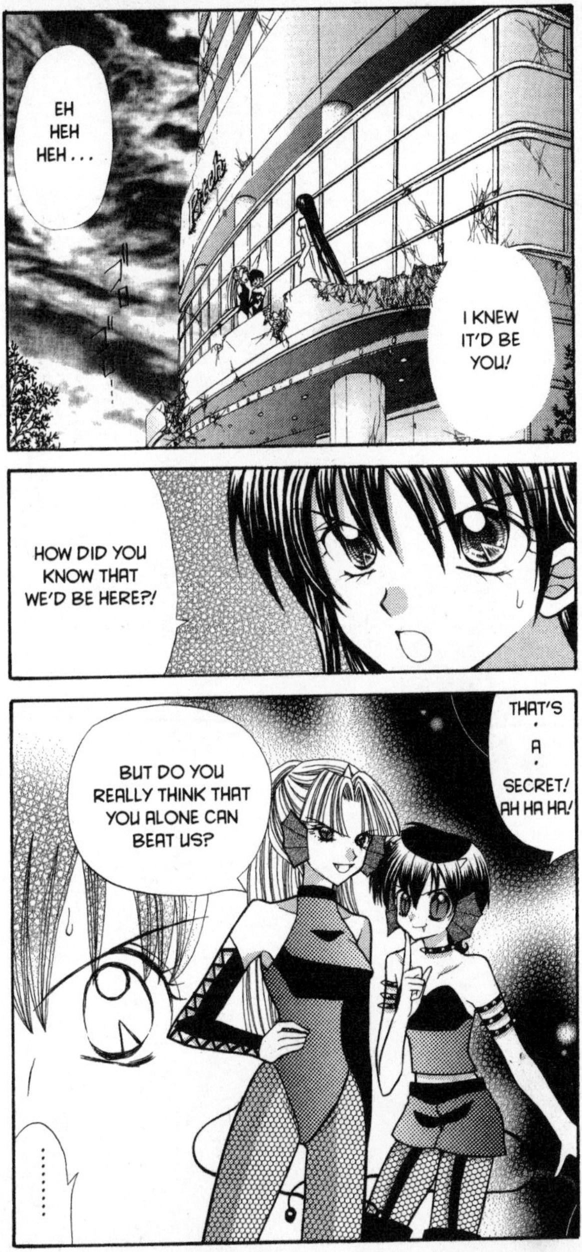
I KNEW IT'D BE YOU!
EH HEH HEH...
HOW DID YOU KNOW THAT WE'D BE HERE?!
THAT'S A SECRET! AH HA HA!
BUT DO YOU REALLY THINK THAT YOU ALONE CAN BEAT US?
......

WHERE TO WRITE TO SEND YOUR IMPRESSIONS & HOME PAGE

Send to:

PINK HANAMORI
DEL REY MANGA
RANDOM HOUSE, INC.
1745 BROADWAY,
18TH FLOOR
NEW YORK, NY 10019

(HOME PAGE ADDRESS FOR)
LIPS

(JAPANESE TEXT ONLY)

http://p-hanamori.cool.ne.jp/

USING YOUR INTERNET-CONNECTED CELL PHONE? SIGN ON HERE.
(JAPANESE TEXT ONLY)

↓

http://p-hanamori.cool.ne.jp/main/hp/

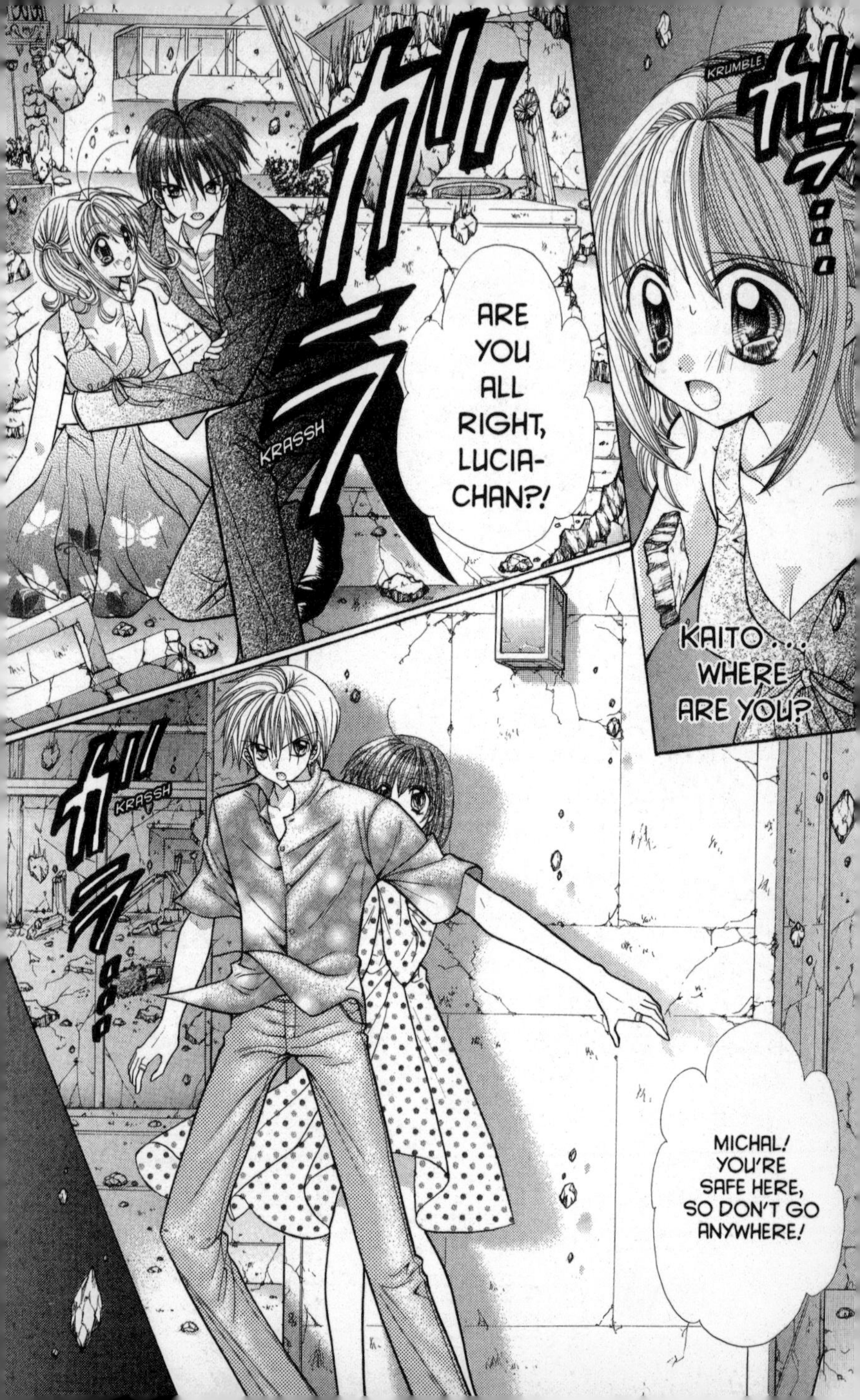
KRUMBLE
KAITO . . . WHERE ARE YOU?
KRASSH
ARE YOU ALL RIGHT, LUCIA-CHAN?!
KRASSH
MICHAL! YOU'RE SAFE HERE, SO DON'T GO ANYWHERE!

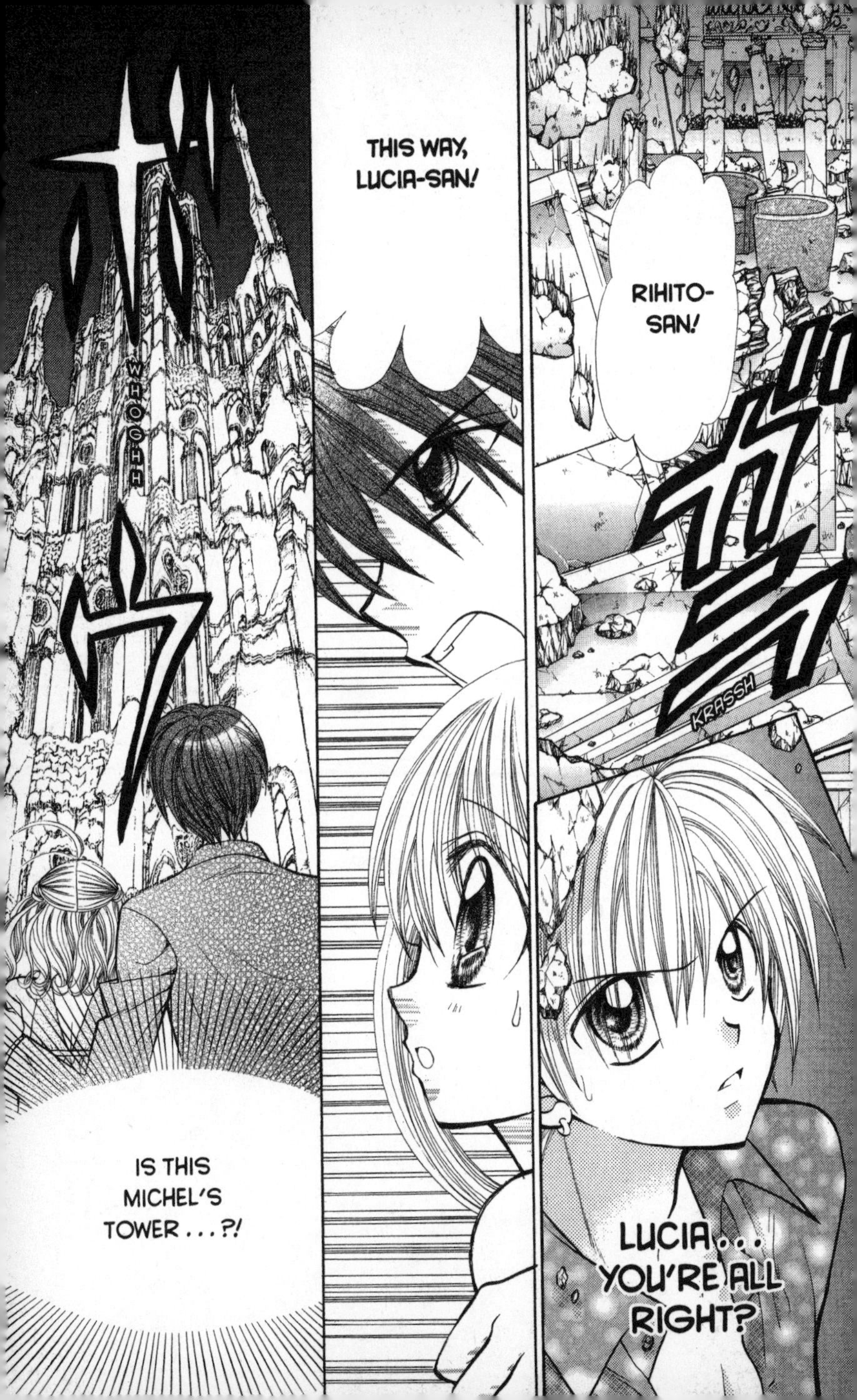
RIHITO-SAN!
KRASSH
LUCIA . . . YOU'RE ALL RIGHT?
THIS WAY, LUCIA-SAN!
WHOGHH
IS THIS MICHEL'S TOWER . . . ?!

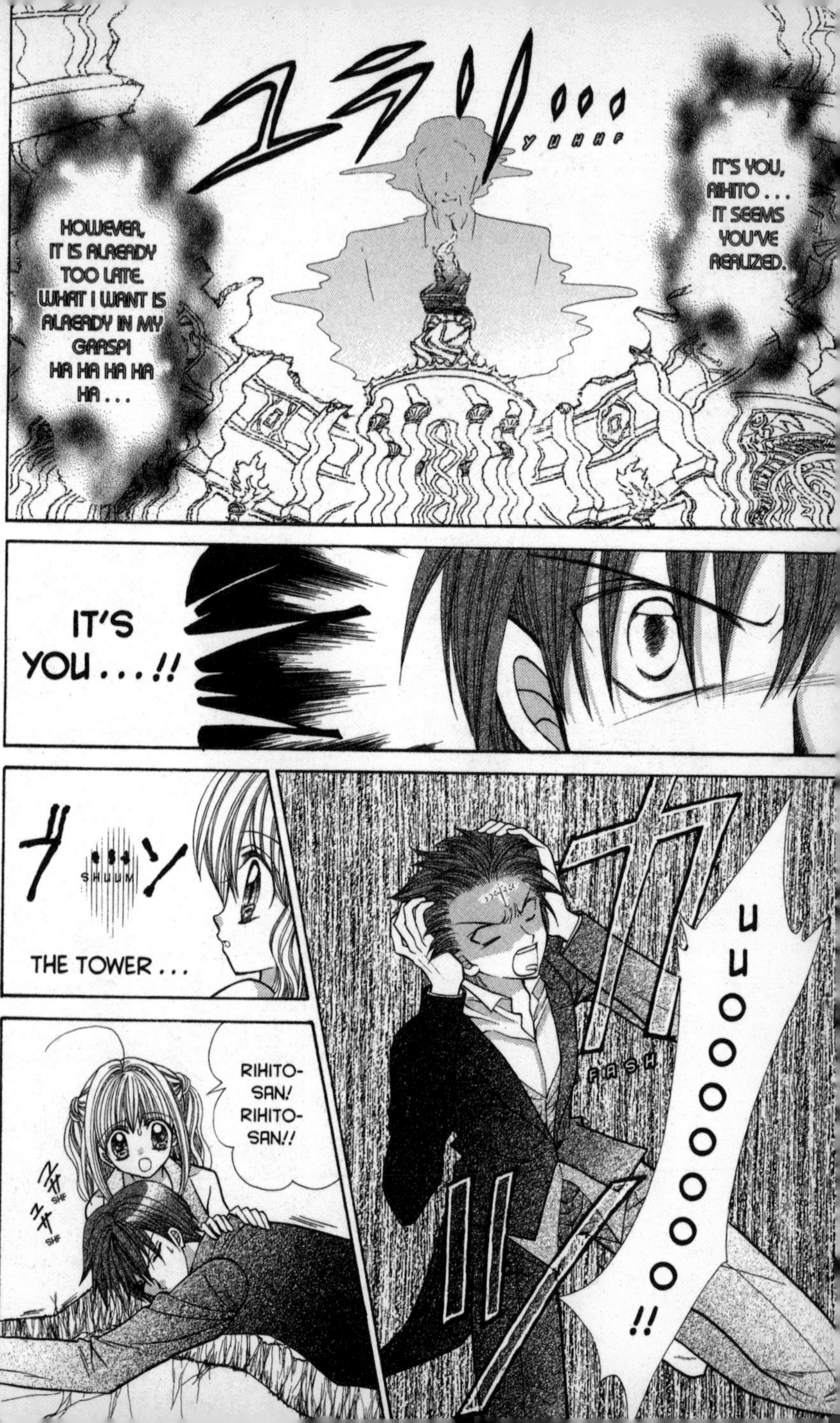
YUHHF
IT'S YOU, RIHITO . . . IT SEEMS YOU'VE REALIZED.
HOWEVER, IT IS ALREADY TOO LATE. WHAT I WANT IS ALREADY IN MY GRASP! HA HA HA HA HA . . .
IT'S YOU . . . !!
FASH
UUOOOOOOOOOOO!!
SHUUM
THE TOWER . . .
RIHITO-SAN! RIHITO-SAN!!
SHF
SHF

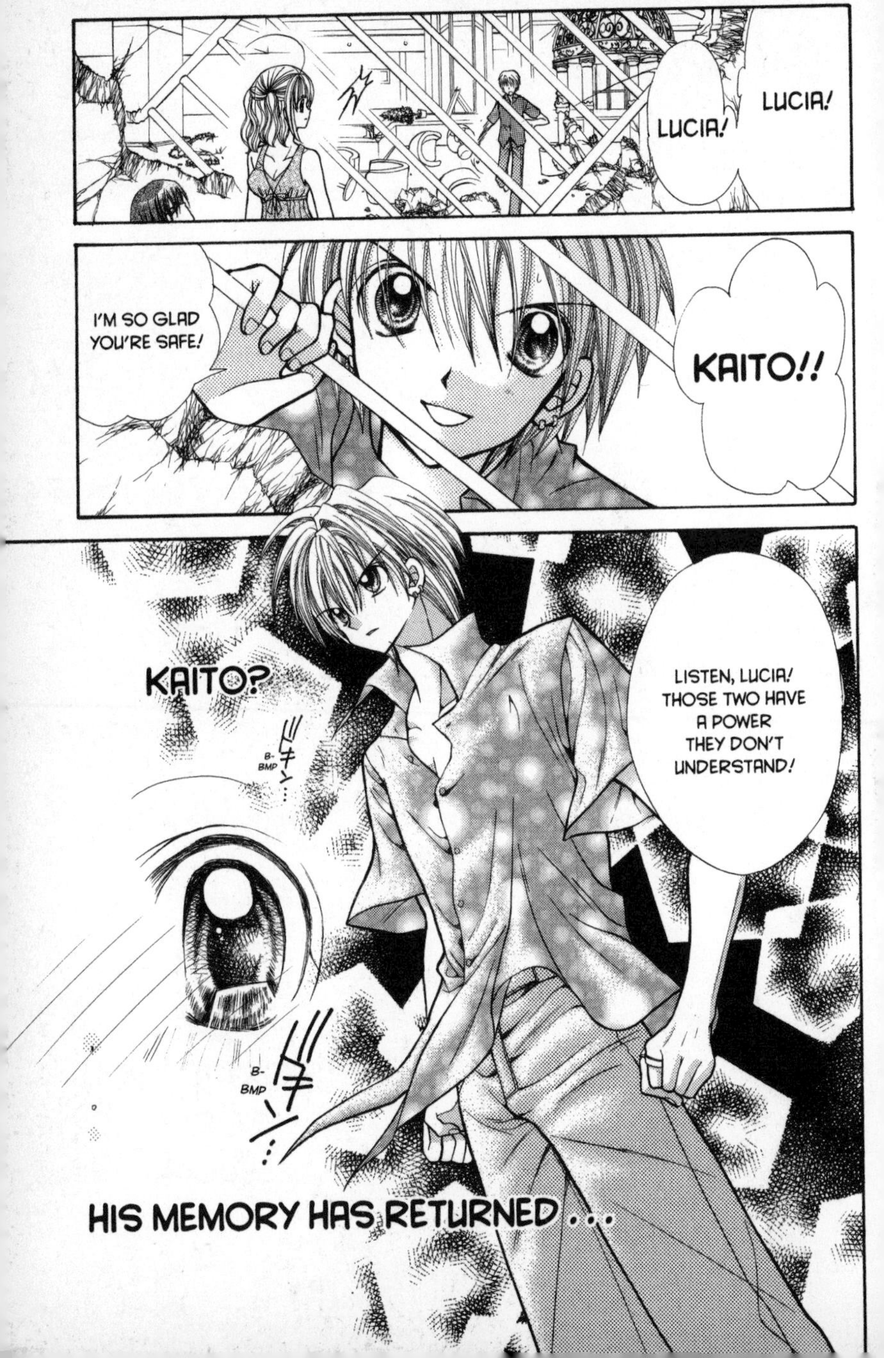
LUCIA!
LUCIA!
KAITO!!
I'M SO GLAD YOU'RE SAFE!
LISTEN, LUCIA! THOSE TWO HAVE A POWER THEY DON'T UNDERSTAND!
KAITO?
B-BMP
B-BMP
HIS MEMORY HAS RETURNED . . .

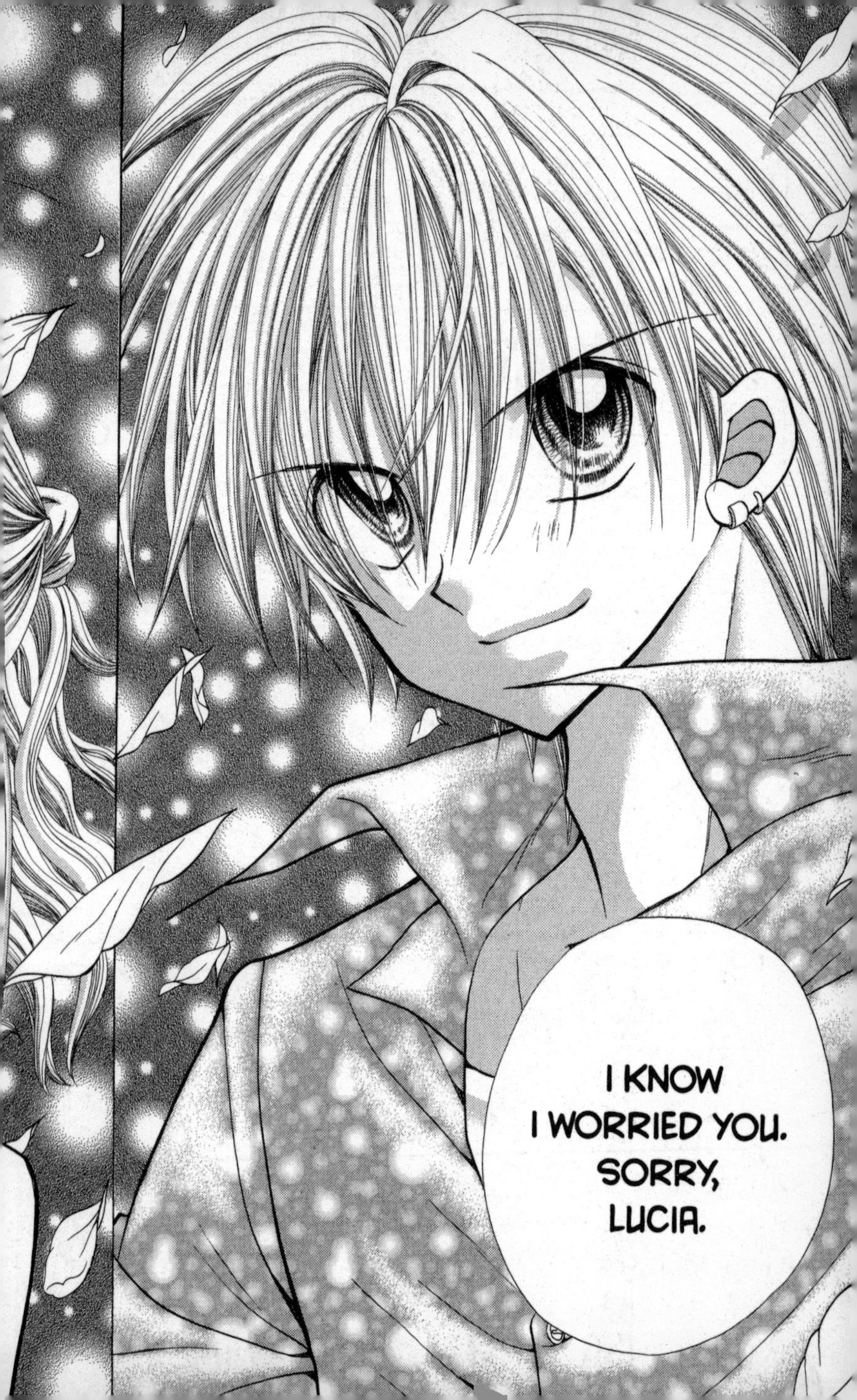
I KNOW I WORRIED YOU. SORRY, LUCIA.

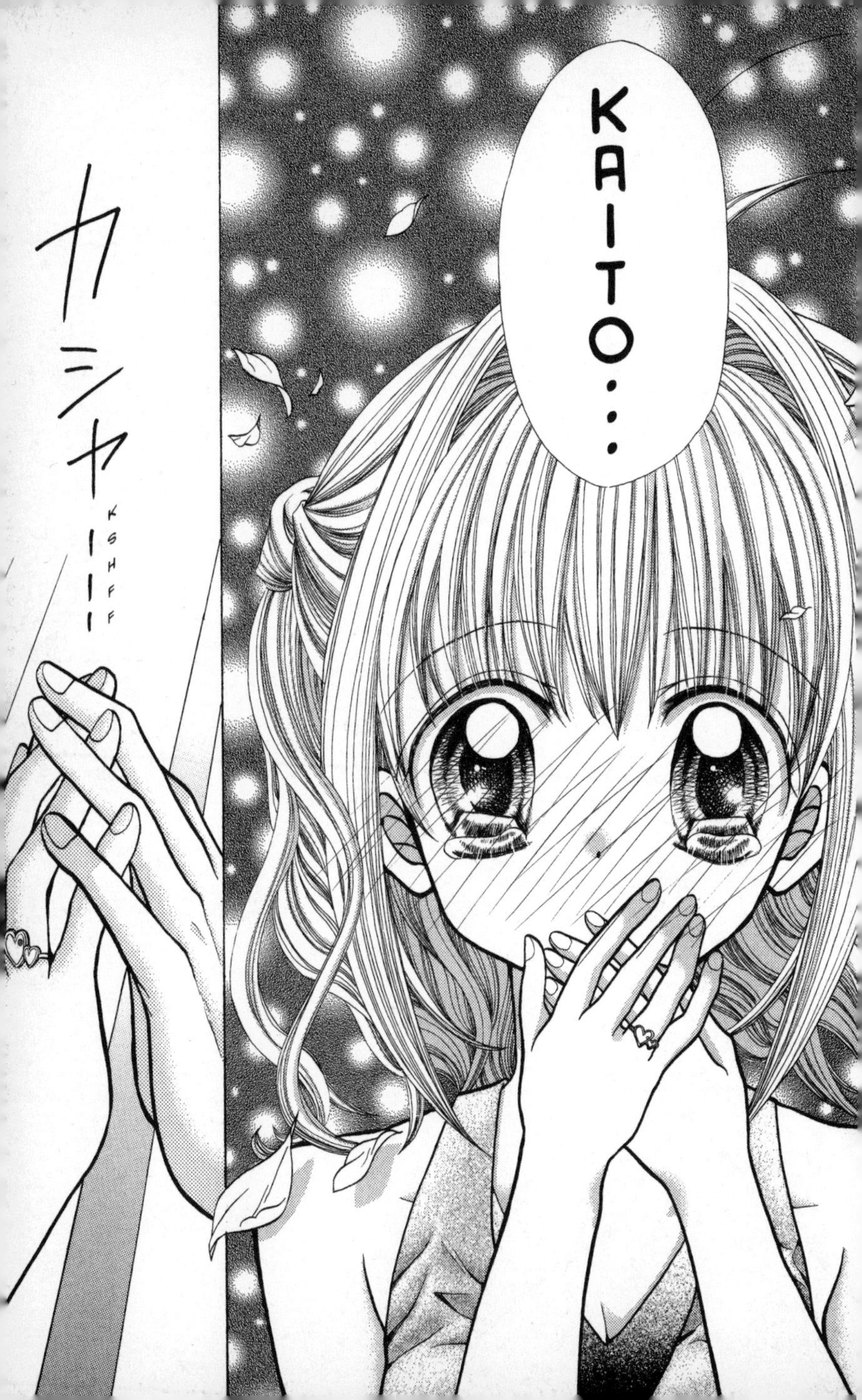
KAITO...
カシャーー
KSHFF

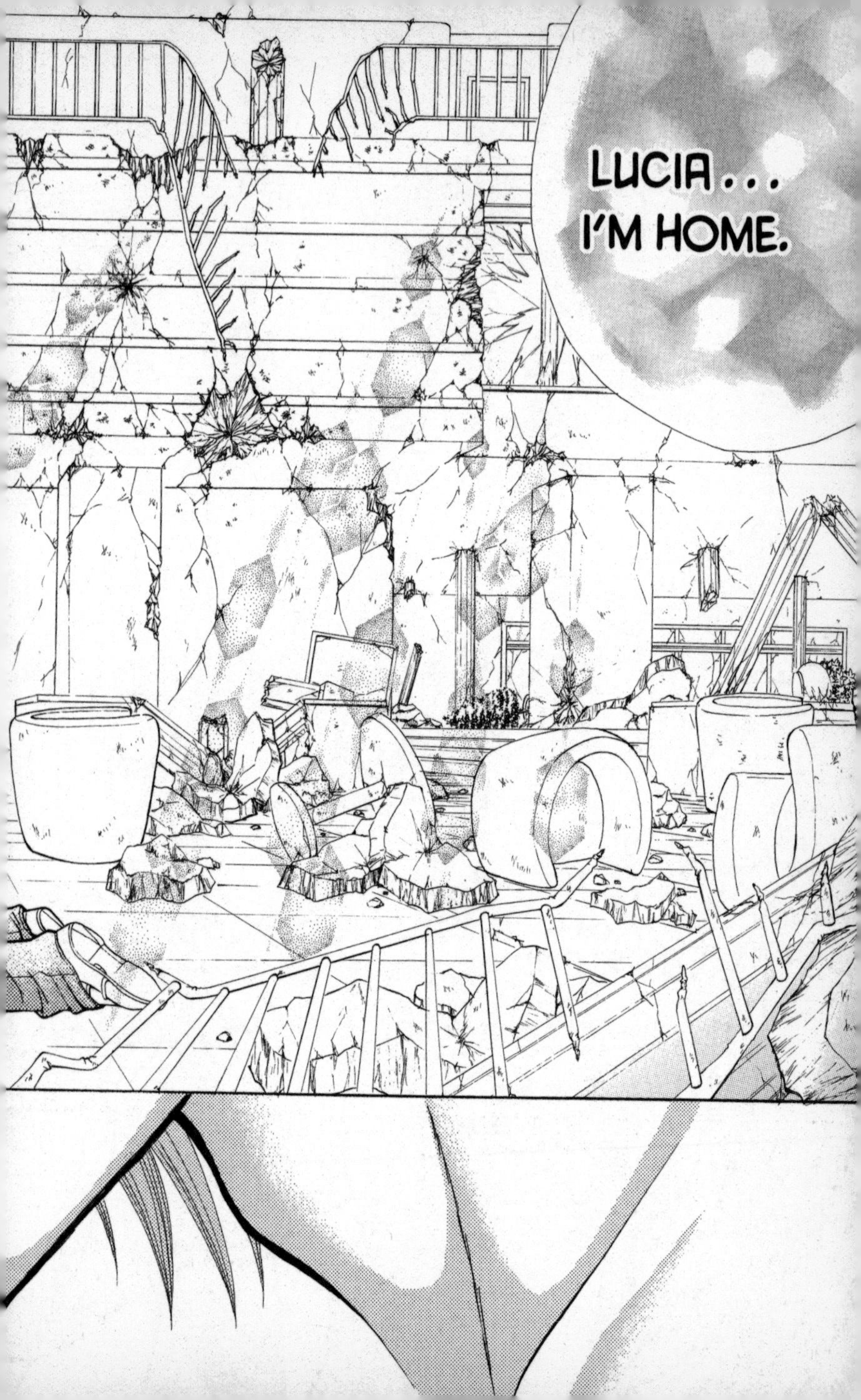
LUCIA . . .
I'M HOME.

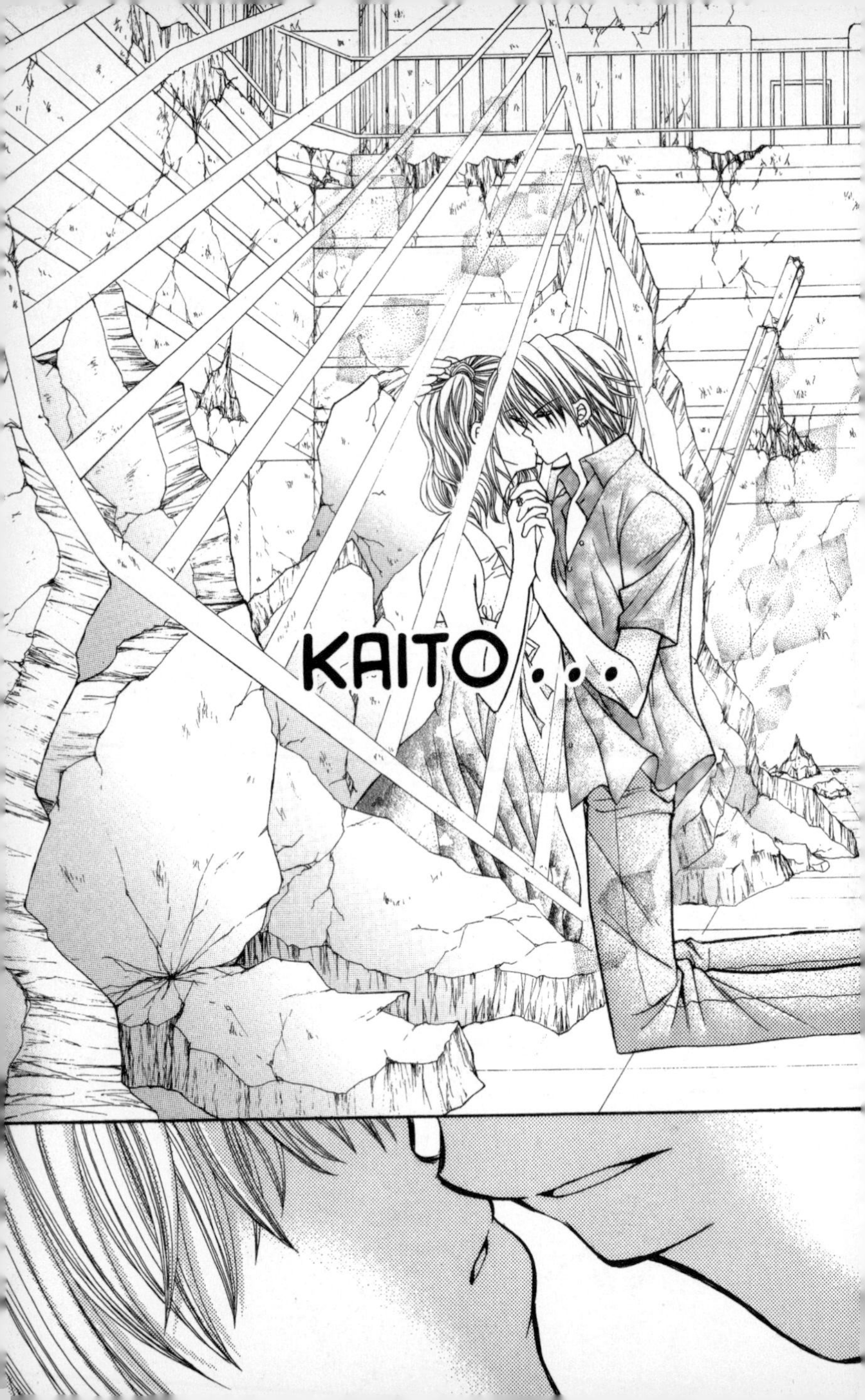
KAITO...

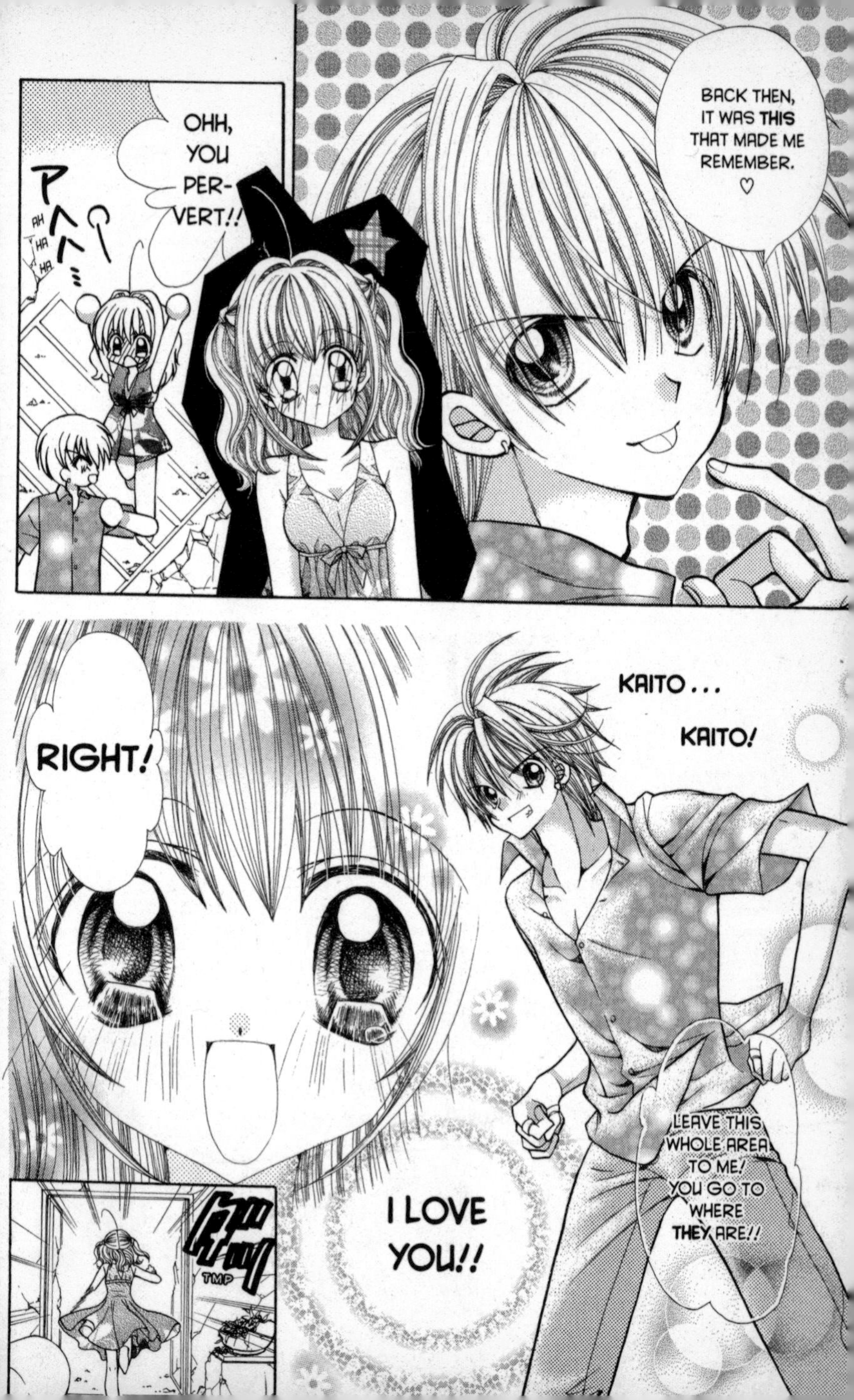
BACK THEN, IT WAS THIS THAT MADE ME REMEMBER. ♡
OHH, YOU PER-VERT!!
AH HA HA HA
KAITO . . .
KAITO!
LEAVE THIS WHOLE AREA TO ME! YOU GO TO WHERE THEY ARE!!
I LOVE YOU!!
RIGHT!
TMP

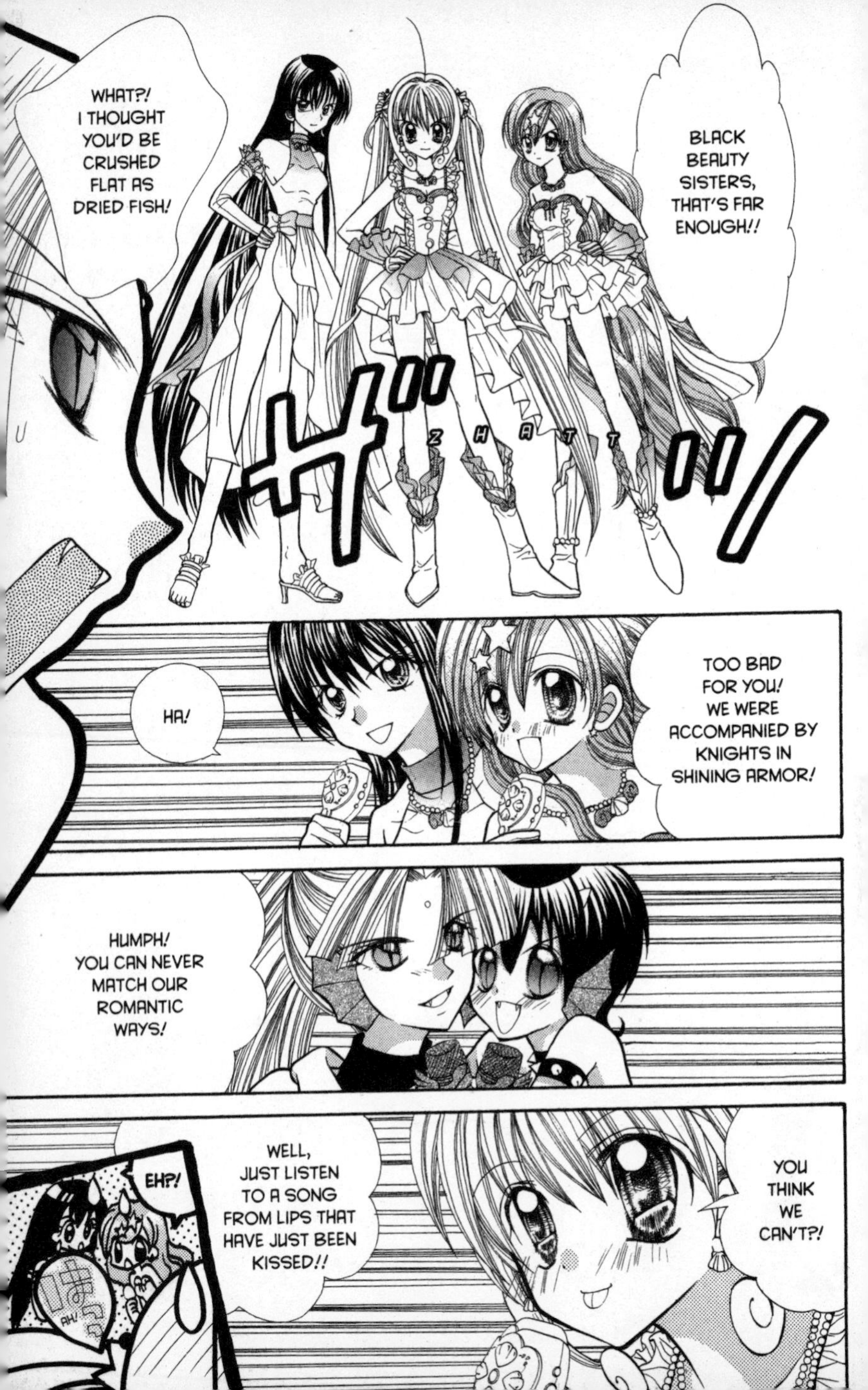
BLACK BEAUTY SISTERS, THAT'S FAR ENOUGH!!
WHAT?! I THOUGHT YOU'D BE CRUSHED FLAT AS DRIED FISH!
ZHATT
TOO BAD FOR YOU! WE WERE ACCOMPANIED BY KNIGHTS IN SHINING ARMOR!
HA!
HUMPH! YOU CAN NEVER MATCH OUR ROMANTIC WAYS!
YOU THINK WE CAN'T?!
WELL, JUST LISTEN TO A SONG FROM LIPS THAT HAVE JUST BEEN KISSED!!
EH?!
AH!

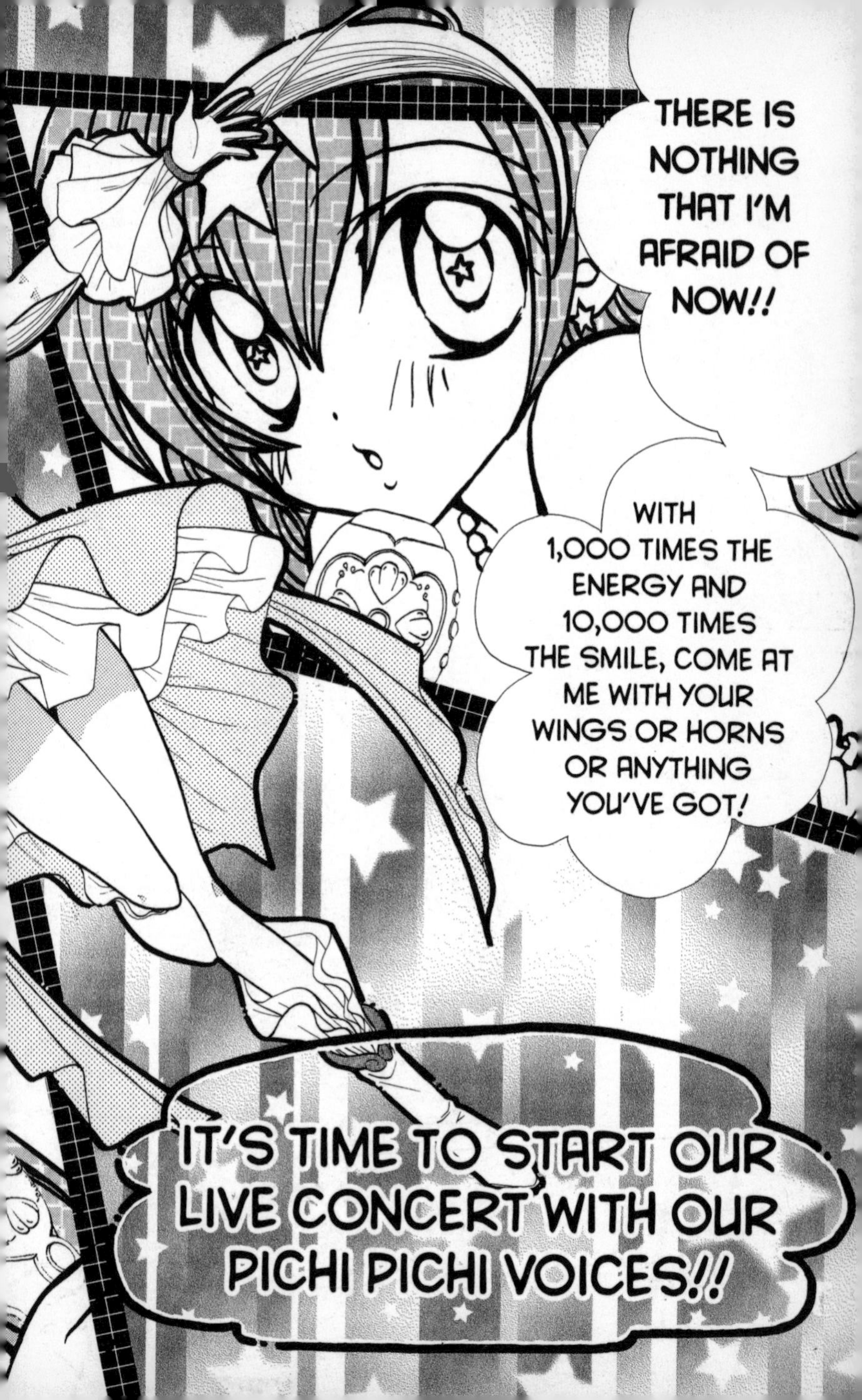
THERE IS NOTHING THAT I'M AFRAID OF NOW!!
WITH 1,000 TIMES THE ENERGY AND 10,000 TIMES THE SMILE, COME AT ME WITH YOUR WINGS OR HORNS OR ANYTHING YOU'VE GOT!
IT'S TIME TO START OUR LIVE CONCERT WITH OUR PICHI PICHI VOICES!!

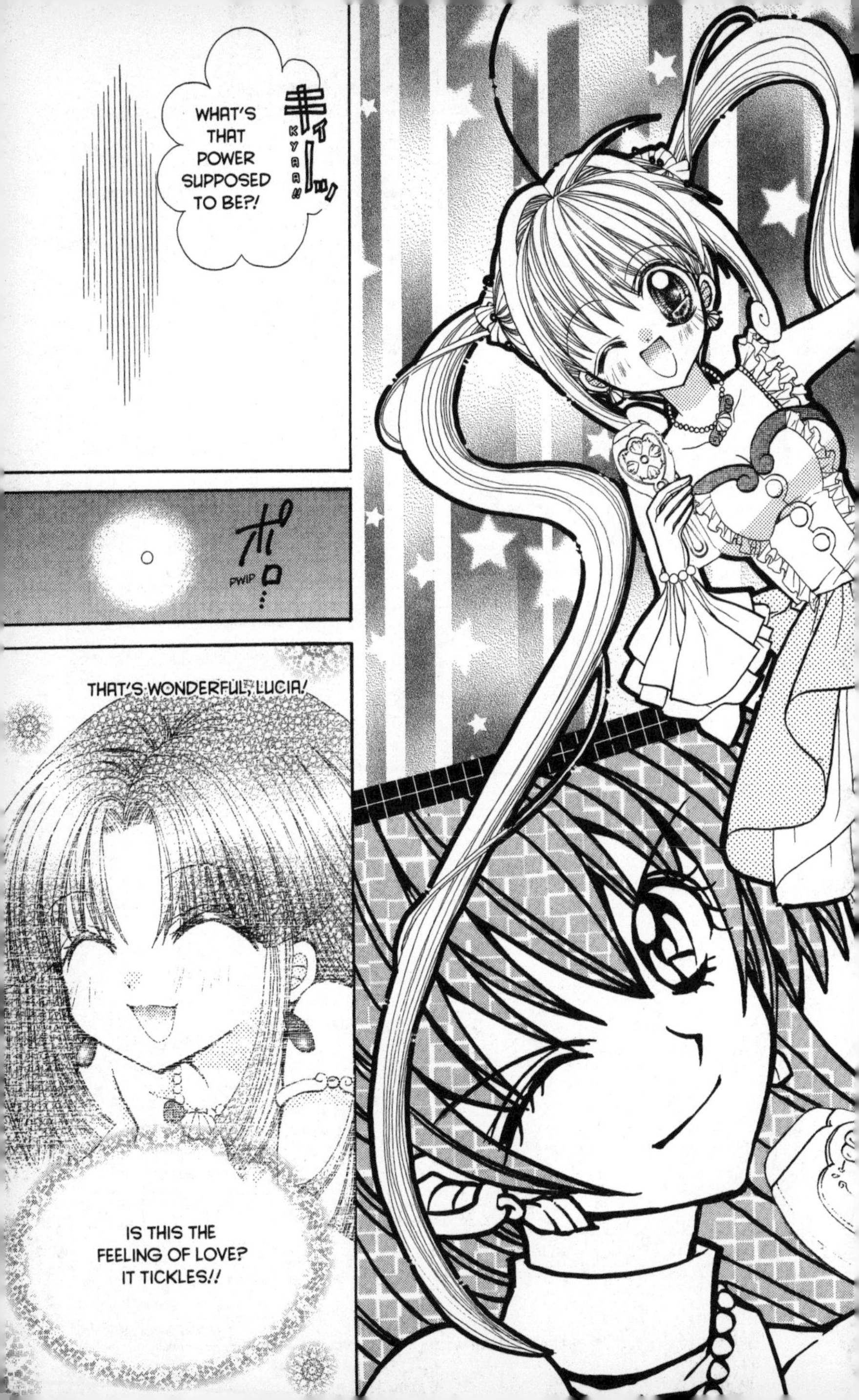
KYAA!!
WHAT'S THAT POWER SUPPOSED TO BE?!
PWIP...
THAT'S WONDERFUL, LUCIA!
IS THIS THE FEELING OF LOVE? IT TICKLES!!

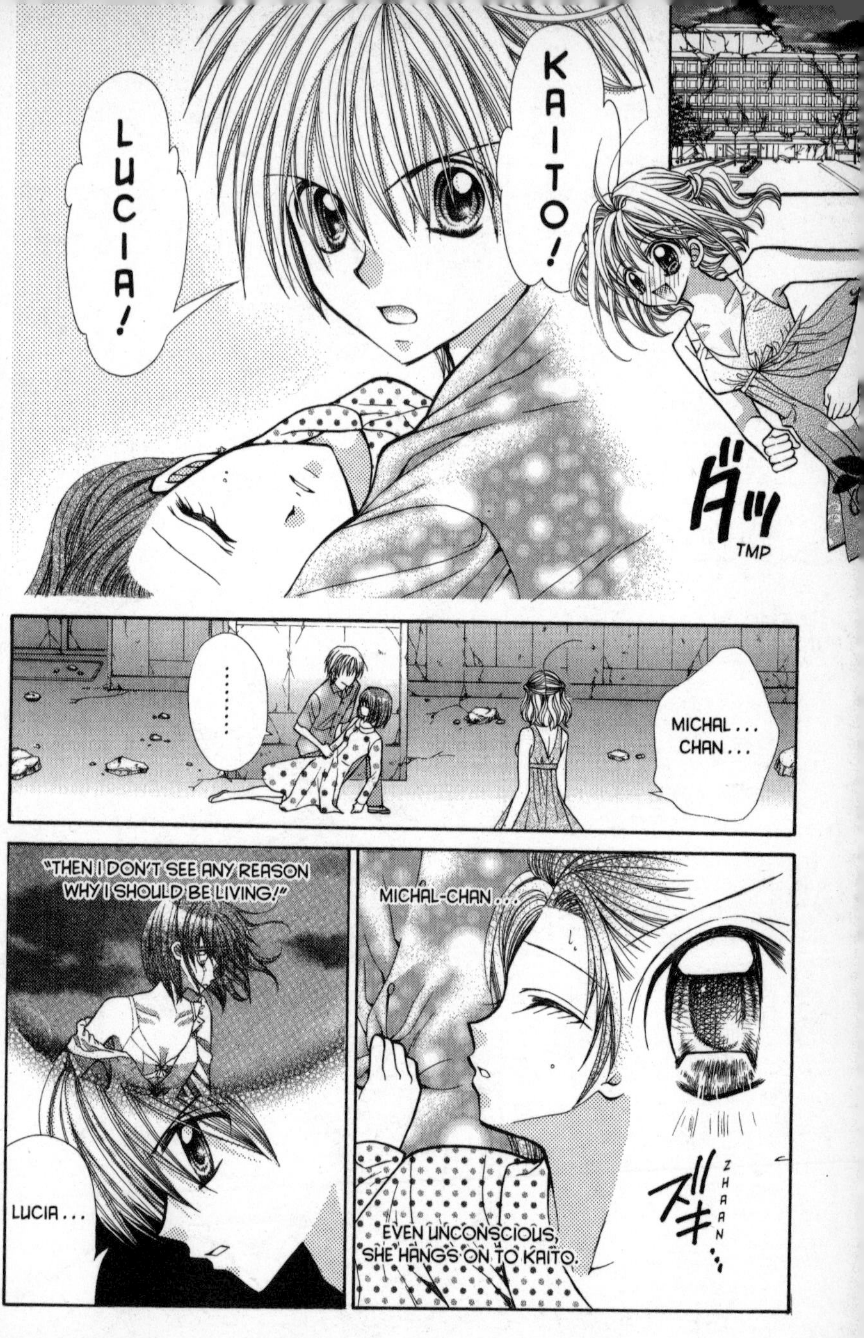
KAITO!
LUCIA!
ダッ
TMP
MICHAL . . .
CHAN . . .
. . . .
MICHAL-CHAN . . .
ズキ
ZHAAN . . .
EVEN UNCONSCIOUS,
SHE HANGS ON TO KAITO.
"THEN I DON'T SEE ANY REASON
WHY I SHOULD BE LIVING!"
LUCIA . . .

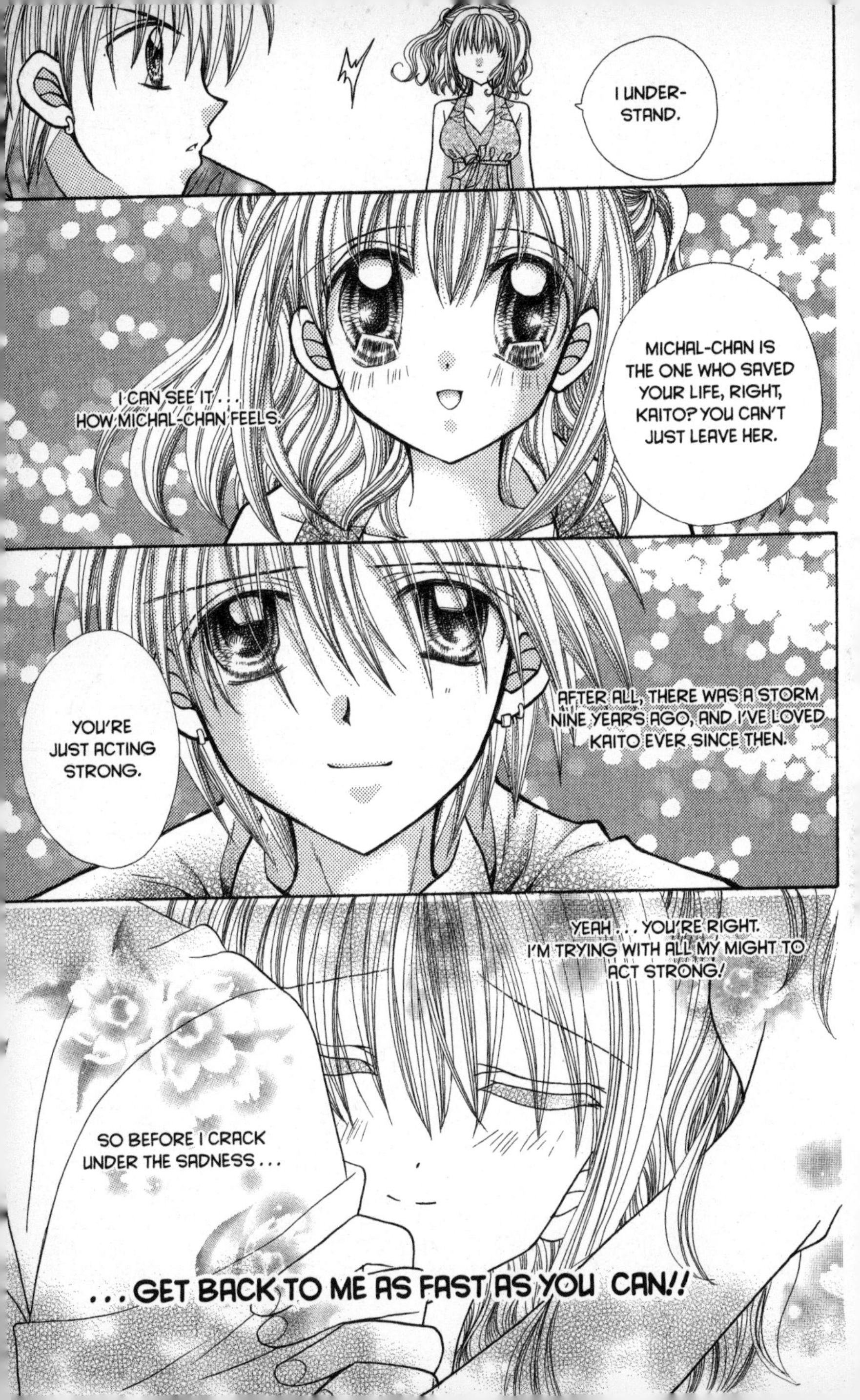
I UNDER-STAND.
MICHAL-CHAN IS THE ONE WHO SAVED YOUR LIFE, RIGHT, KAITO? YOU CAN'T JUST LEAVE HER.
I CAN SEE IT . . . HOW MICHAL-CHAN FEELS.
AFTER ALL, THERE WAS A STORM NINE YEARS AGO, AND I'VE LOVED KAITO EVER SINCE THEN.
YOU'RE JUST ACTING STRONG.
YEAH . . . YOU'RE RIGHT. I'M TRYING WITH ALL MY MIGHT TO ACT STRONG!
SO BEFORE I CRACK UNDER THE SADNESS . . .
. . . GET BACK TO ME AS FAST AS YOU CAN!!

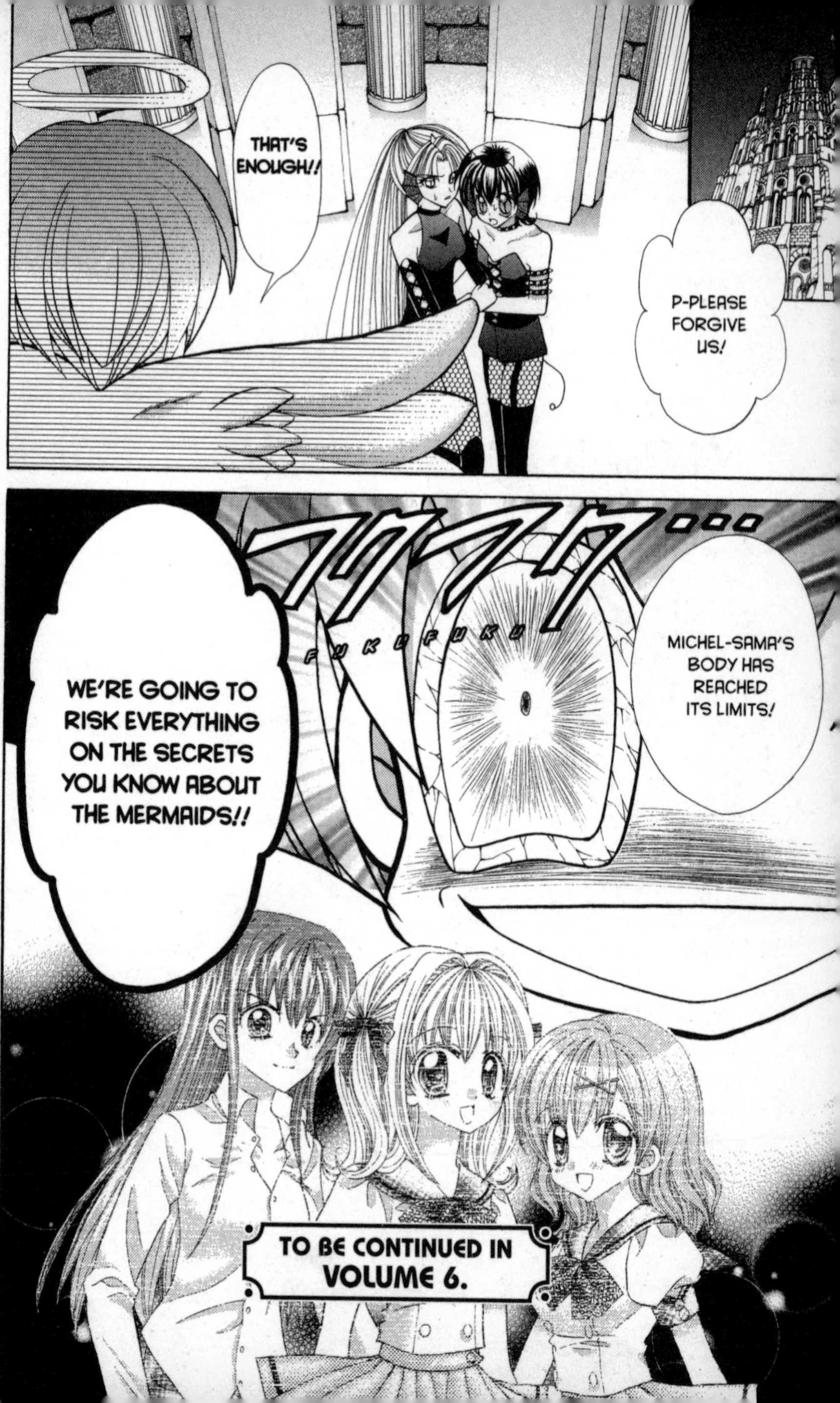
P-PLEASE FORGIVE US!
THAT'S ENOUGH!!
MICHEL-SAMA'S BODY HAS REACHED ITS LIMITS!
FUKUFUKU
WE'RE GOING TO RISK EVERYTHING ON THE SECRETS YOU KNOW ABOUT THE MERMAIDS!!
TO BE CONTINUED IN VOLUME 6.

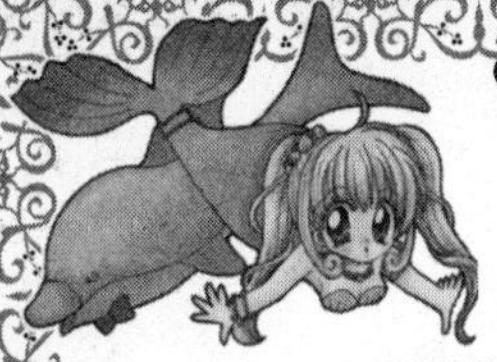

GRAB YOUR JOYOUS LOVE!!

Pichi Pichi Pitch THE LEGENDARY... MERMAID URANAI

URANAI SUPERVISION: SAORI TSUKIKAGE (RENÉ VAN DALE SUPERNATURAL INSTITUTE)

THERE IS A CERTAIN DESTINY THAT CONTROLS THE LOVES OF THE SEVEN MERMAIDS WHO CAN MANIPULATE THE POWERS OF THE SEA. WITH THIS MERMAID URANAI, YOU CAN FIND NOT ONLY YOUR MERMAID COLOR, BUT ALSO POINTS TO YOUR PERSONALITY AND THE TYPE OF ROMANCE FOR YOU! SO LET'S START AND FIND YOUR MERMAID COLOR FROM THE CHART TO THE RIGHT.

HOW TO GET YOUR MERMAID COLOR

① FIND THE YEAR OF YOUR BIRTH ON THE TWO-DIGIT NUMBERS ON THE CHART. NOW THAT YOU'VE FOUND YOUR BIRTH YEAR, FOLLOW THE COLUMN UP TO THE TOP. THAT IS YOUR KEY NUMBER. (FOR EXAMPLE, IF YOU WERE BORN ON JULY 7TH, 1989, LIKE LUCIA, YOU'D FOLLOW THE NUMBER "89" TO THE TOP OF THE COLUMN TO FIND THE KEY NUMBER "1.")

② IN THIS CHART, YOU USE THE KEY NUMBER FROM ① AND COMBINE IT WITH THE NUMBER OF THE MONTH OF YOUR BIRTH TO GET A NEW NUMBER. (FOR EXAMPLE, IN LUCIA'S CASE, SHE HAD A KEY NUMBER OF "1" AND WAS BORN IN JULY, "7," SO WORKING ON THE CHART, THE NEW NUMBER IS "0.")

③ IN THIS CHART, YOU USE THE DAY YOU WERE BORN AND THE NEW NUMBER FROM THE ② CHART TO GET THE DAY OF THE WEEK FOR YOUR BIRTH. YOU WERE BORN ON THAT DAY OF THE WEEK. (FOR EXAMPLE, LUCIA WAS BORN ON THE 3RD SO YOU LINE THAT UP WITH THE NUMBER FROM ②, "0" AND YOU SEE SHE WAS BORN ON A MONDAY.)

④ IN THIS FINAL CHART, YOU TAKE THE DAY YOU WERE BORN ON FROM CHART ③ AND DETERMINE WHAT YOUR MERMAID COLOR IS. (FOR EXAMPLE, LUCIA WAS BORN ON A MONDAY, SO THAT MAKES HER A PINK MERMAID.)

CAUTION: IF THERE IS A ★ SIGN ON CHART ① NEXT TO YOUR YEAR, THAT MEANS YOU WERE BORN ON A LEAP YEAR. IF YOU WERE BORN ON JANUARY OF A LEAP YEAR, THEN USE THE ✻1 ON CHART ②. IF YOU WERE BORN IN FEBRUARY OF A LEAP YEAR, THEN USE ✻2 ON CHART ②.

CHART ①

Key Number	1	2	3	4	5	6	0
	22	23	—	★24	25	26	27
	—	★28	29	30	31	—	★32
	33	34	35	—	★36	37	38
WESTERN	39	—	★40	41	42	43	—
CALENDAR	★44	45	46	47	—	★48	49
	50	51	—	★52	53	54	55
1922	—	★56	57	58	59	—	★60
~	61	62	63	—	★64	65	66
	67	—	★68	69	70	71	—
2004	★72	73	74	75	—	★76	77
	78	79	—	★80	81	82	83
	—	★84	85	86	87	—	★88
	89	90	91	—	★92	93	94
	95	—	★96	97	98	99	—
	★00	01	02	03	—	★04	

CHART ②

Month / Key Number	5	8 ※2	2 3 11	6	9 12	4 7 ※1	1 10
1	2	3	4	5	6	0	1
2	3	4	5	6	0	1	2
3	4	5	6	0	1	2	3
4	5	6	0	1	2	3	4
5	6	0	1	2	3	4	5
6	0	1	2	3	4	5	6
0	1	2	3	4	5	6	0

CHART ③

Day / Key Number	1 8 15 22 29	2 9 16 23 30	3 10 17 24 31	4 11 18 25	5 12 19 26	6 13 20 27	7 14 21 28
1	Su	M	T	W	Th	F	Sa
2	M	T	W	Th	F	Sa	Su
3	T	W	Th	F	Sa	Su	M
4	W	Th	F	Sa	Su	M	T
5	Th	F	Sa	Su	M	T	W
6	F	Sa	Su	M	T	W	Th
0	Sa	Su	M	T	W	Th	F

CHART ④

Weekday of Birth	Mermaid Color
Born on Monday	Pink Mermaid
Born on Tuesday	Yellow Mermaid
Born on Wednesday	Aquamarine Mermaid
Born on Thursday	Indigo Mermaid
Born on Friday	Purple Mermaid
Born on Saturday	Green Mermaid
Born on Sunday	Orange Mermaid

Pink Mermaid

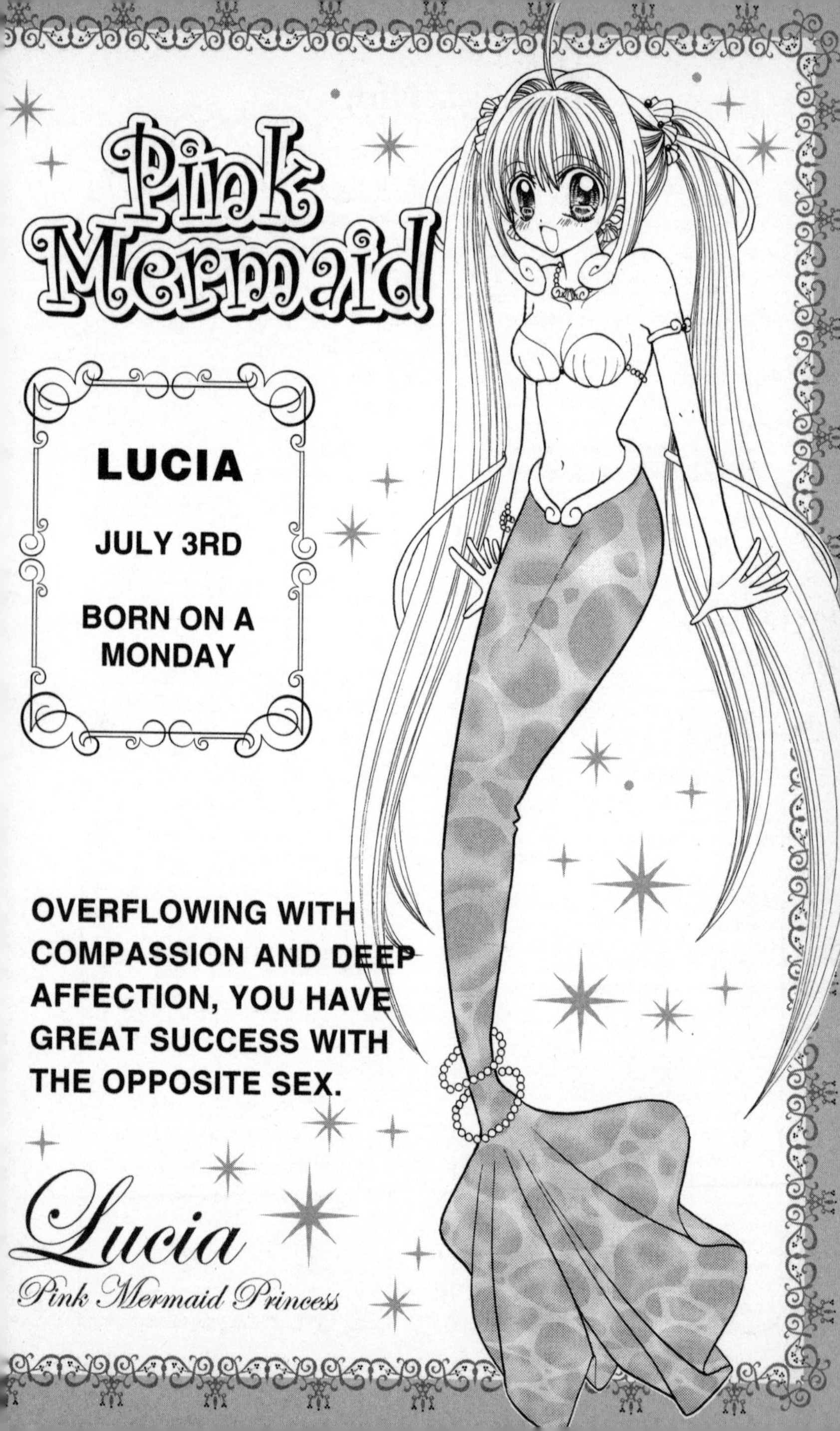

LUCIA

JULY 3RD

BORN ON A MONDAY

OVERFLOWING WITH COMPASSION AND DEEP AFFECTION, YOU HAVE GREAT SUCCESS WITH THE OPPOSITE SEX.

Lucia

Pink Mermaid Princess

BASIC PERSONALITY

YOU HAVE A PERSONALITY THAT IS OVERFLOWING WITH COMPASSION, SO MUCH SO THAT YOU CAN FEEL THE PAIN WITHIN THE HEART OF OTHERS. WHEN YOU SEE SOMEONE DOWN IN THE DUMPS, YOU CHEER THEM UP WITH YOUR UPBEAT PERSONALITY. YOU ARE WILLING AND ABLE TO LET OTHERS TAKE THE LEAD, SO SOMEONE IS BOUND TO THINK OF YOU AS SOMEONE SPECIAL. BUT YOU HAVE A DELICATE HEART THAT IS EASY TO WOUND. YOUR MOOD CAN CHANGE AT THE SLIGHTEST EVENT, SO BE VERY CAREFUL OF THAT!

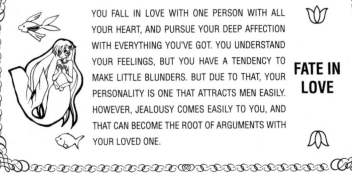

FATE IN LOVE

YOU FALL IN LOVE WITH ONE PERSON WITH ALL YOUR HEART, AND PURSUE YOUR DEEP AFFECTION WITH EVERYTHING YOU'VE GOT. YOU UNDERSTAND YOUR FEELINGS, BUT YOU HAVE A TENDENCY TO MAKE LITTLE BLUNDERS. BUT DUE TO THAT, YOUR PERSONALITY IS ONE THAT ATTRACTS MEN EASILY. HOWEVER, JEALOUSY COMES EASILY TO YOU, AND THAT CAN BECOME THE ROOT OF ARGUMENTS WITH YOUR LOVED ONE.

WHO MATCHES YOUR AFFECTION

=> INDIGO MERMAIDS
=> MEN BORN ON TUESDAYS

SHAPE UP YOUR GOOD POINTS

IF YOU'RE OPTIMISTIC AND DO YOUR BEST TO HELP PEOPLE IN TROUBLE, YOU CAN CAPTURE GUYS' HEARTS. MAKE SURE YOU GIVE HANDMADE GIFTS.

BASIC PERSONALITY

YOU ARE THE BRIGHT AND ENERGETIC TYPE FOR WHOM SPORTS AND THE OUTDOORS IS A STRONG POINT. YOU DON'T LIKE TO BEAT AROUND THE BUSH, SO YOU'RE STRAIGHTFORWARD WITH YOUR OPINIONS. YOU CAN EVEN HANDLE TROUBLED TIMES WITH YOUR HEAD-ON ATTITUDE, AND SO OTHERS TEND TO LOOK TO YOU FOR LEADERSHIP. YOU HAVE THE POWER TO LEND A BRIGHTER OUTLOOK TO THOSE AROUND YOU. BUT YOU'RE A LITTLE TOO STRONG-WILLED AT TIMES, SO EVERY NOW AND AGAIN YOU FIND YOURSELF REGRETTING THE FIGHTS YOU HAVE WITH FRIENDS.

FATE IN LOVE

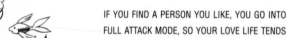

IF YOU FIND A PERSON YOU LIKE, YOU GO INTO FULL ATTACK MODE, SO YOUR LOVE LIFE TENDS TO BE INTENSE. IF YOU HAVE A RIVAL, YOUR TYPE OF PERSONALITY GETS EVEN MORE PASSIONATE. BUT IF YOUR RELATIONSHIP DOESN'T WORK OUT, YOU AREN'T THE SORT TO WALLOW IN DEPRESSION FOREVER. YOU CAN MOVE ON TO THE NEXT LOVE IN GOOD TIME. YOU AREN'T GOOD AT BEING CHASED.

WHO MATCHES YOUR AFFECTION

=> PINK MERMAIDS

=> MEN BORN ON SUNDAYS

SHAPE UP YOUR GOOD POINTS

WITH YOUR ENTHUSIASM, YOU CAN CONVINCE PEOPLE TO DO THINGS THEY DON'T WANT TO DO, SO EVEN IF BAD THINGS HAPPEN, NEVER FORGET YOUR SMILE.

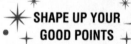

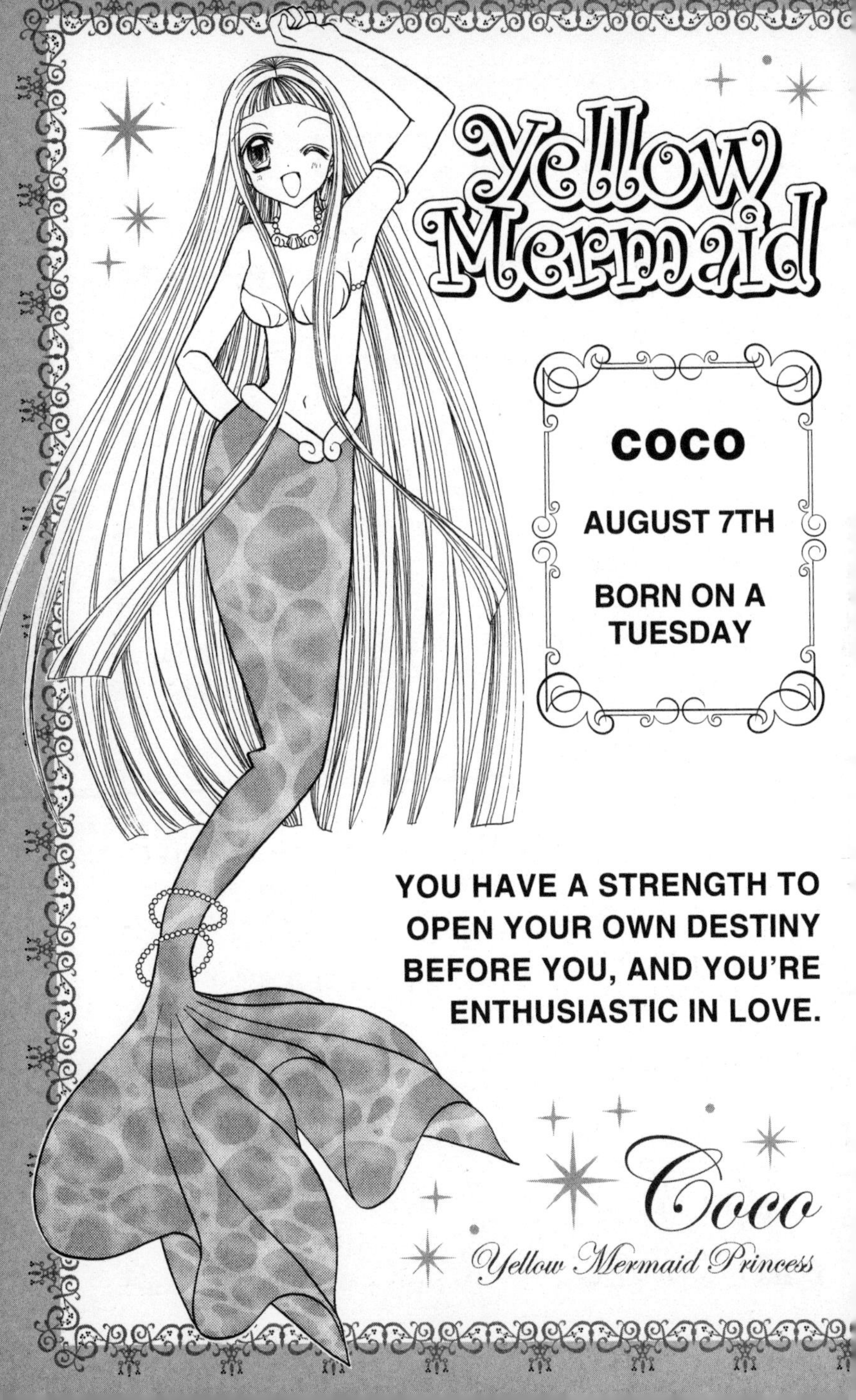

Yellow Mermaid

COCO

AUGUST 7TH

BORN ON A TUESDAY

YOU HAVE A STRENGTH TO OPEN YOUR OWN DESTINY BEFORE YOU, AND YOU'RE ENTHUSIASTIC IN LOVE.

Coco

Yellow Mermaid Princess

Aquamarine Mermaid

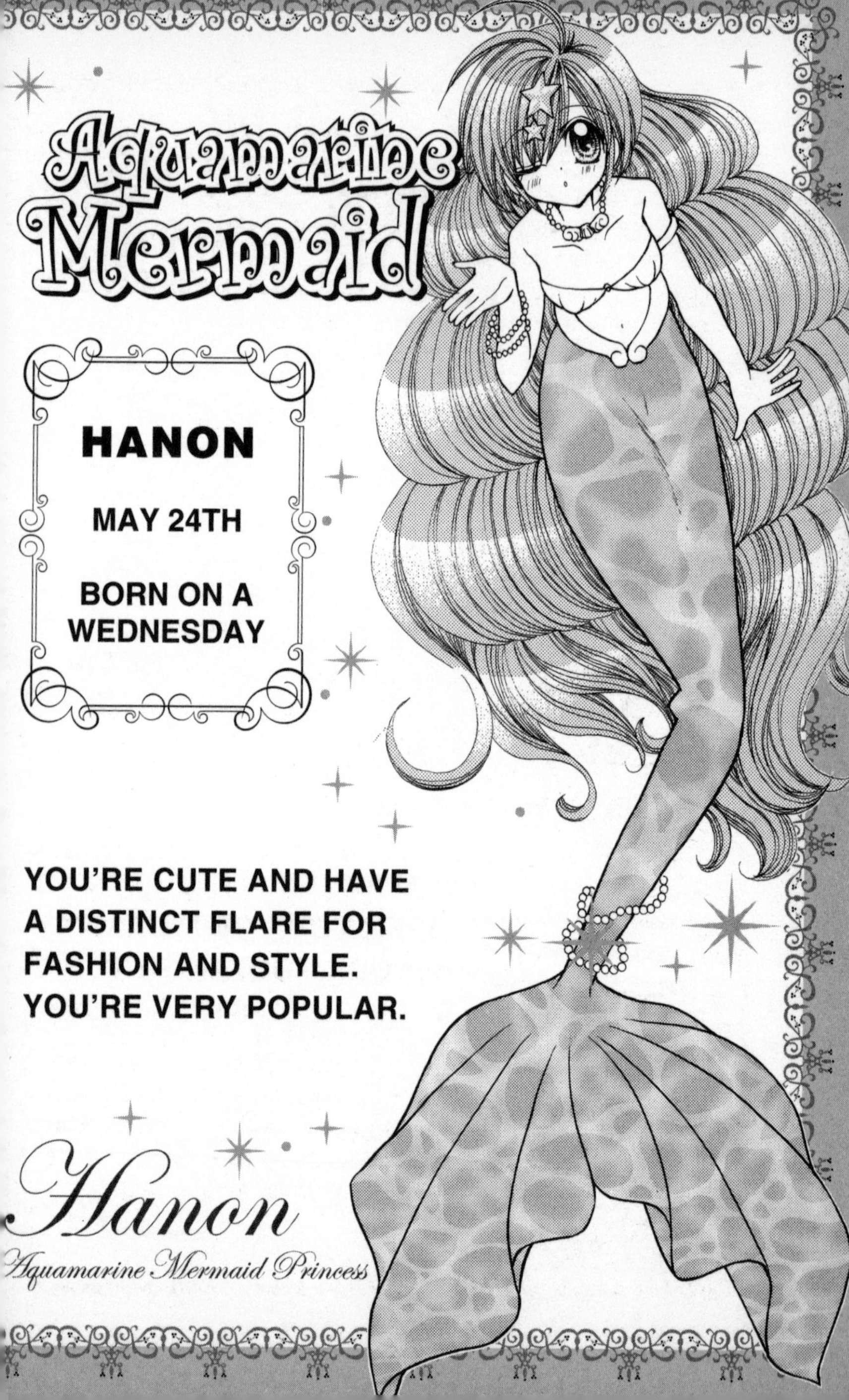

HANON

MAY 24TH

BORN ON A WEDNESDAY

YOU'RE CUTE AND HAVE A DISTINCT FLARE FOR FASHION AND STYLE. YOU'RE VERY POPULAR.

Hanon

Aquamarine Mermaid Princess

BASIC PERSONALITY

YOU KNOW WHAT'S IN FASHION AND HAVE A GOOD SENSE FOR STYLE, SO YOU ARE ALWAYS IN TOP FORM. YOU PULL IN A LOT OF NEW FRIENDS WITH YOUR SKILL OF MAKING FUN CONVERSATION. YOU'RE SMART AND HAVE GOOD HAND-EYE COORDINATION, SO IF YOU TRY, YOU CAN BUILD UP SOME REAL TALENTS. IT ISN'T UNUSUAL FOR YOU TO BE PRAISED AND RESPECTED BY MANY PEOPLE. HOWEVER, YOU'RE A LITTLE CAPRICIOUS, AND DEPENDING ON HOW YOU FEEL THAT DAY, THE THINGS YOU SAY MAY BE WILDLY DIFFERENT. BE CAREFUL OF THAT.

FATE IN LOVE

YOUR SPECIAL TALENT IS TO PICK UP ON OTHERS' FEELINGS, SO NO MATTER WHO IT IS, YOU CAN TURN ON THE CHARM AND MAKE ANYONE YOUR FRIEND. YOU ALSO CAN BECOME VERY CLOSE TO THE GUY YOU LIKE VERY FAST, SO YOU'LL FIND THERE ARE A LOT OF GUYS WHO LIKE YOU. BUT YOU DON'T KNOW THE MEANING OF RESTRAINT, SO YOU FIND IT VERY DIFFICULT TO KEEP A RELATIONSHIP GOING.

WHO MATCHES YOUR AFFECTION

=> GREEN MERMAIDS

=> MEN BORN ON FRIDAYS

SHAPE UP YOUR GOOD POINTS

IF YOU TUTOR THE ONE YOU LIKE IN STUDIES AS IF IT WERE THE MOST NORMAL THING ON EARTH, OR HELP OUT WITH THE STUDENT COUNCIL ACTIVITIES, THE ONE YOU LIKE SHOULD FALL FOR YOU NATURALLY.

BASIC PERSONALITY

YOU'RE A LAID-BACK, BRIGHT, BIG-HEARTED PERSON WHO DOESN'T SWEAT THE DETAILS. YOU'RE BRIMMING OVER WITH CURIOSITY, HAVE MANY DIFFERENT INTERESTS, AND YOU RUSH TO FACE NEW CHALLENGES ONE AFTER THE NEXT. YOU'RE THE TYPE WHO CAN WORK LONG AND HARD ON FULFILLING A BIG DREAM. BUT YOU DON'T LIKE BEING TIED DOWN BY RULES, SO SOMETIMES YOU FIND YOURSELF MOVING INTO THE AREA OF SELFISH WHIMS.

FATE IN LOVE

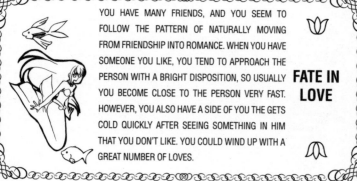

YOU HAVE MANY FRIENDS, AND YOU SEEM TO FOLLOW THE PATTERN OF NATURALLY MOVING FROM FRIENDSHIP INTO ROMANCE. WHEN YOU HAVE SOMEONE YOU LIKE, YOU TEND TO APPROACH THE PERSON WITH A BRIGHT DISPOSITION, SO USUALLY YOU BECOME CLOSE TO THE PERSON VERY FAST. HOWEVER, YOU ALSO HAVE A SIDE OF YOU THE GETS COLD QUICKLY AFTER SEEING SOMETHING IN HIM THAT YOU DON'T LIKE. YOU COULD WIND UP WITH A GREAT NUMBER OF LOVES.

WHO MATCHES YOUR AFFECTION

=> ORANGE MERMAIDS
=> MEN BORN ON MONDAYS

SHAPE UP YOUR GOOD POINTS

YOU'RE GOOD AT SEEING STRAIGHT THROUGH TO A PERSON'S GOOD POINTS, SO ONE THING YOU CAN DO IS PRAISE THE PERSON YOU'RE INTERESTED IN. YOU CAN ALSO GIVE PEOPLE ENERGY AND COURAGE.

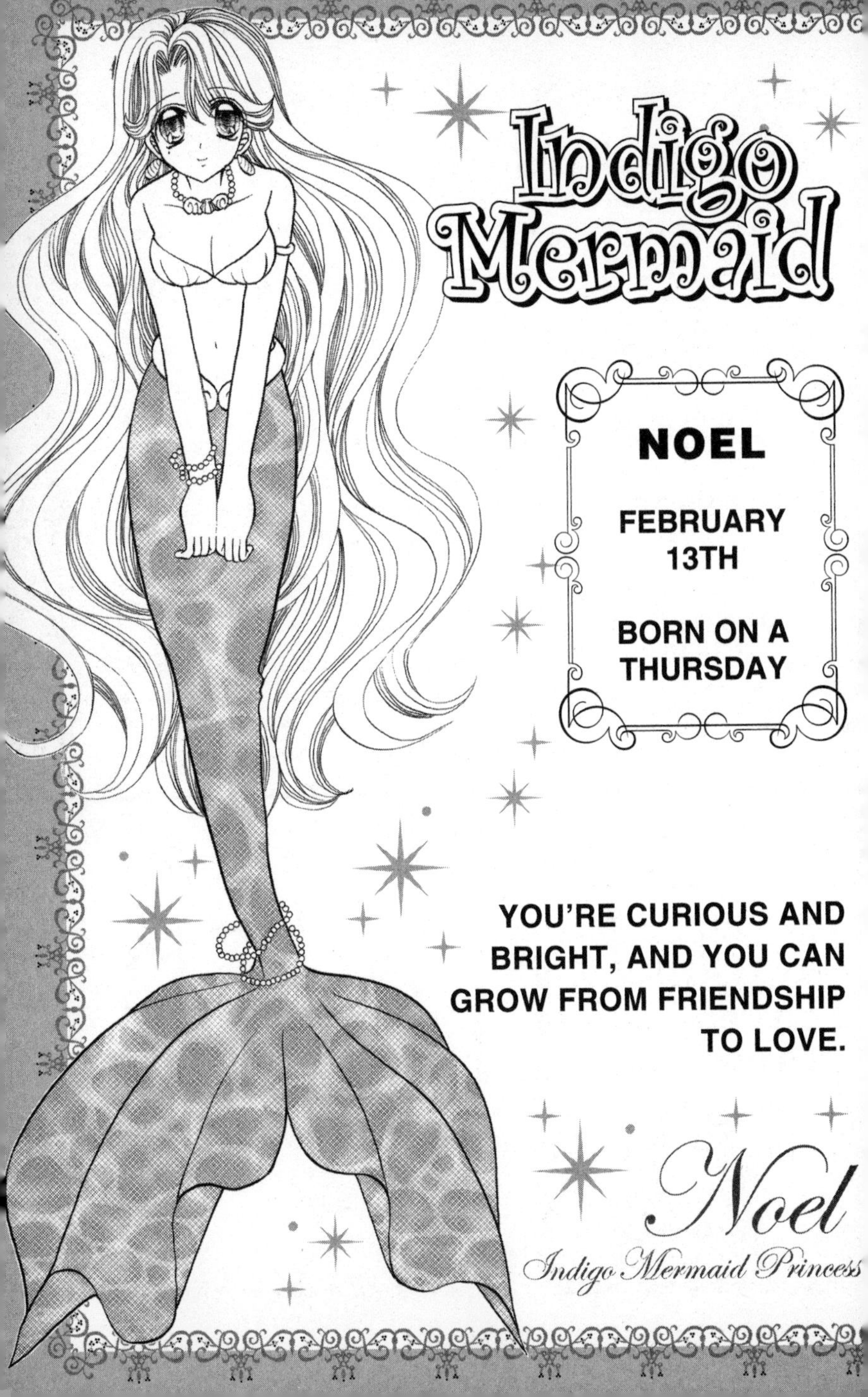

Indigo Mermaid

NOEL

FEBRUARY 13TH

BORN ON A THURSDAY

YOU'RE CURIOUS AND BRIGHT, AND YOU CAN GROW FROM FRIENDSHIP TO LOVE.

Noel

Indigo Mermaid Princess

Purple Mermaid

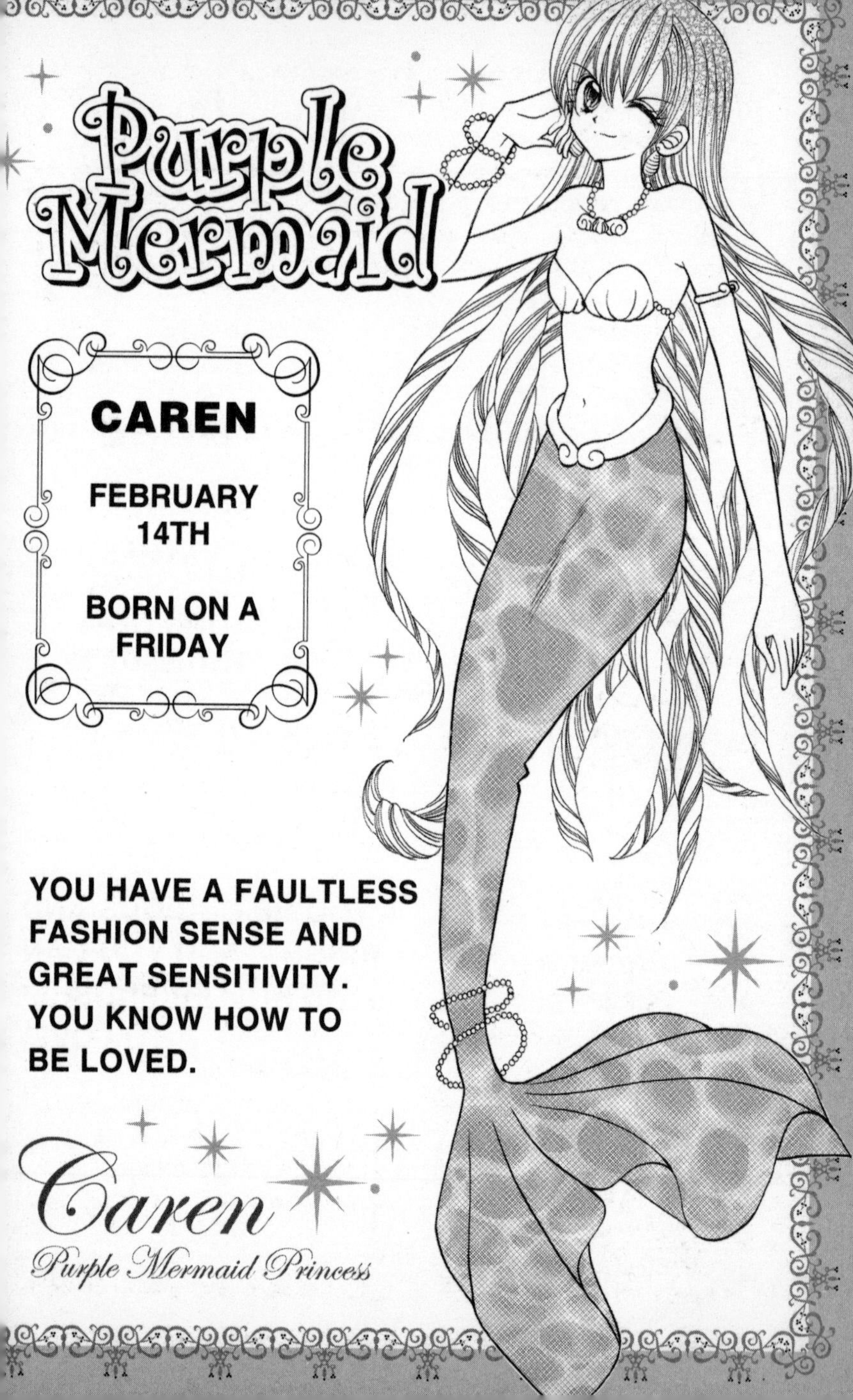

CAREN

FEBRUARY 14TH

BORN ON A FRIDAY

YOU HAVE A FAULTLESS FASHION SENSE AND GREAT SENSITIVITY. YOU KNOW HOW TO BE LOVED.

Caren

Purple Mermaid Princess

BASIC PERSONALITY

YOU'RE GOOD WITH FASHION, AND HAVE A MOOD OF BEAUTY AROUND YOU. YOU ALSO SPECIALIZE IN GATHERING CUTE OR BEAUTIFUL ITEMS AROUND YOU WITH YOUR ARTISTIC SENSE. YOU'RE GOOD AT PLAYING MUSICAL INSTRUMENTS AND DRAWING. YOU FEEL A STRONG DRIVE TO MAKE FRIENDS WITH JUST ABOUT ANYBODY, AND YOU HATE ARGUMENTS AND COMPETITION. BUT YOU'RE RATHER INDECISIVE, AND IT TAKES YOU A LONG TIME TO SETTLE ON ONE THING.

FATE IN LOVE

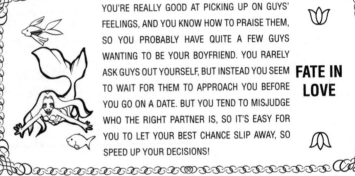

YOU'RE REALLY GOOD AT PICKING UP ON GUYS' FEELINGS, AND YOU KNOW HOW TO PRAISE THEM, SO YOU PROBABLY HAVE QUITE A FEW GUYS WANTING TO BE YOUR BOYFRIEND. YOU RARELY ASK GUYS OUT YOURSELF, BUT INSTEAD YOU SEEM TO WAIT FOR THEM TO APPROACH YOU BEFORE YOU GO ON A DATE. BUT YOU TEND TO MISJUDGE WHO THE RIGHT PARTNER IS, SO IT'S EASY FOR YOU TO LET YOUR BEST CHANCE SLIP AWAY, SO SPEED UP YOUR DECISIONS!

WHO MATCHES YOUR AFFECTION
=> AQUAMARINE MERMAIDS
=> MEN BORN ON SATURDAY

SHAPE UP YOUR GOOD POINTS

USE YOUR BEAUTIFUL VOICE, AND LISTEN WITH A SMILE, AND YOU'LL MAKE GREAT IMPRESSIONS! PUT TO GOOD USE YOUR ABILITY TO CHOOSE YOUR PARTNER'S FAVORITE THING AS A PRESENT!

BASIC PERSONALITY

YOU'RE A SERIOUS, HARD WORKER, AND YOU HAVE A CALM, ADULT DEMEANOR. EVEN IF SOMETHING VERY TROUBLING HAPPENS, YOU NEVER PANIC—YOU ARE THE TYPE WHERE YOU CAN FACE IT WITH LOGICAL REASONING. YOU MAY IMPRESS OTHERS AS BEING A LITTLE COLD, BUT ACTUALLY YOU'RE CONSTANTLY THINKING OF YOUR FRIENDS FIRST. AND DUE TO YOUR SENSE OF RESPONSIBILITY, THE PEOPLE AROUND YOU MAKE A LOT OF REQUESTS ON YOUR TIME. BUT THERE'S A STUBBORN PART OF YOU THAT FEELS THAT YOU'RE ALWAYS RIGHT. BE CAREFUL OF THAT SIDE OF YOU.

FATE IN LOVE

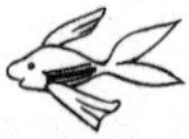

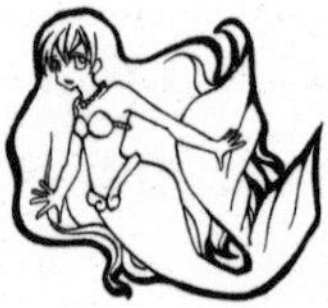

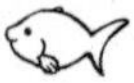

YOU TEND TO INVOLVE YOURSELF IN THE OPPOSITE SEX LATER THAN OTHERS, AND YOU'RE VERY CAREFUL, SO YOUR TYPE TENDS TO FIND IT HARD TO FIND A PARTNER IN ROMANCE. ON THE OTHER HAND, ONCE YOU DO FALL IN LOVE, YOU ARE A PASSIONATE PERSON WHO WILL LOVE THAT PERSON FOR THE REST OF YOUR LIFE. BUT EVEN WHEN YOU DO FIND SOMEONE YOU LIKE, YOU FIND IT HARD TO ADMIT IT TO THE PERSON, SO YOU TEND TO GET HUNG UP IN ONE-SIDED LOVE RELATIONSHIPS QUITE OFTEN.

WHO MATCHES YOUR AFFECTION

=> PURPLE MERMAIDS

=> MEN BORN ON WEDNESDAY

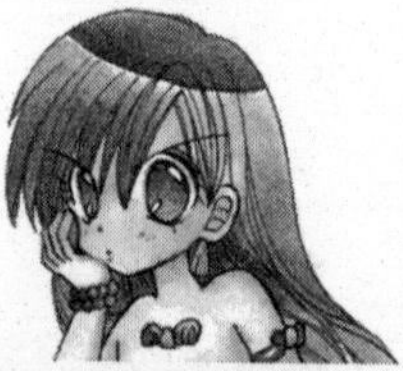

SHAPE UP YOUR GOOD POINTS

IF YOU ARE IN SCHOOL GOVERNMENT OR IN CHARGE OF OTHER FUNCTIONS, IT MAKES IT EASIER TO SEE YOUR GOOD POINTS. IF YOU CAN ADAPT TO FASHION, YOU MIGHT BE ABLE TO SHOW THE WORLD A NEW SIDE OF YOURSELF.

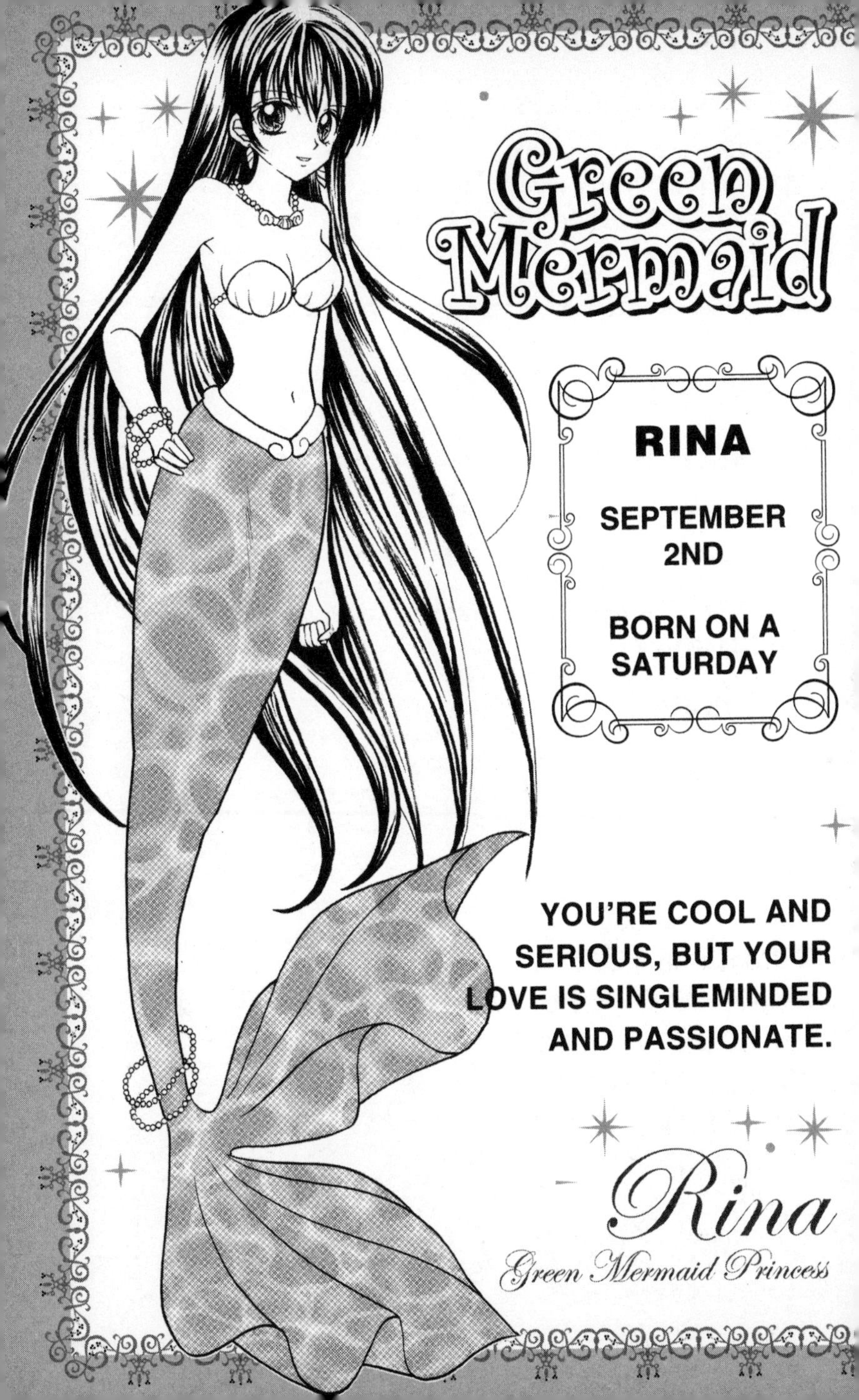
Green Mermaid
RINA
SEPTEMBER 2ND
BORN ON A SATURDAY
YOU'RE COOL AND SERIOUS, BUT YOUR LOVE IS SINGLEMINDED AND PASSIONATE.
Rina
Green Mermaid Princess

Orange Mermaid

SARA

NOVEMBER 22ND

BORN ON A SUNDAY

SEIRA

?

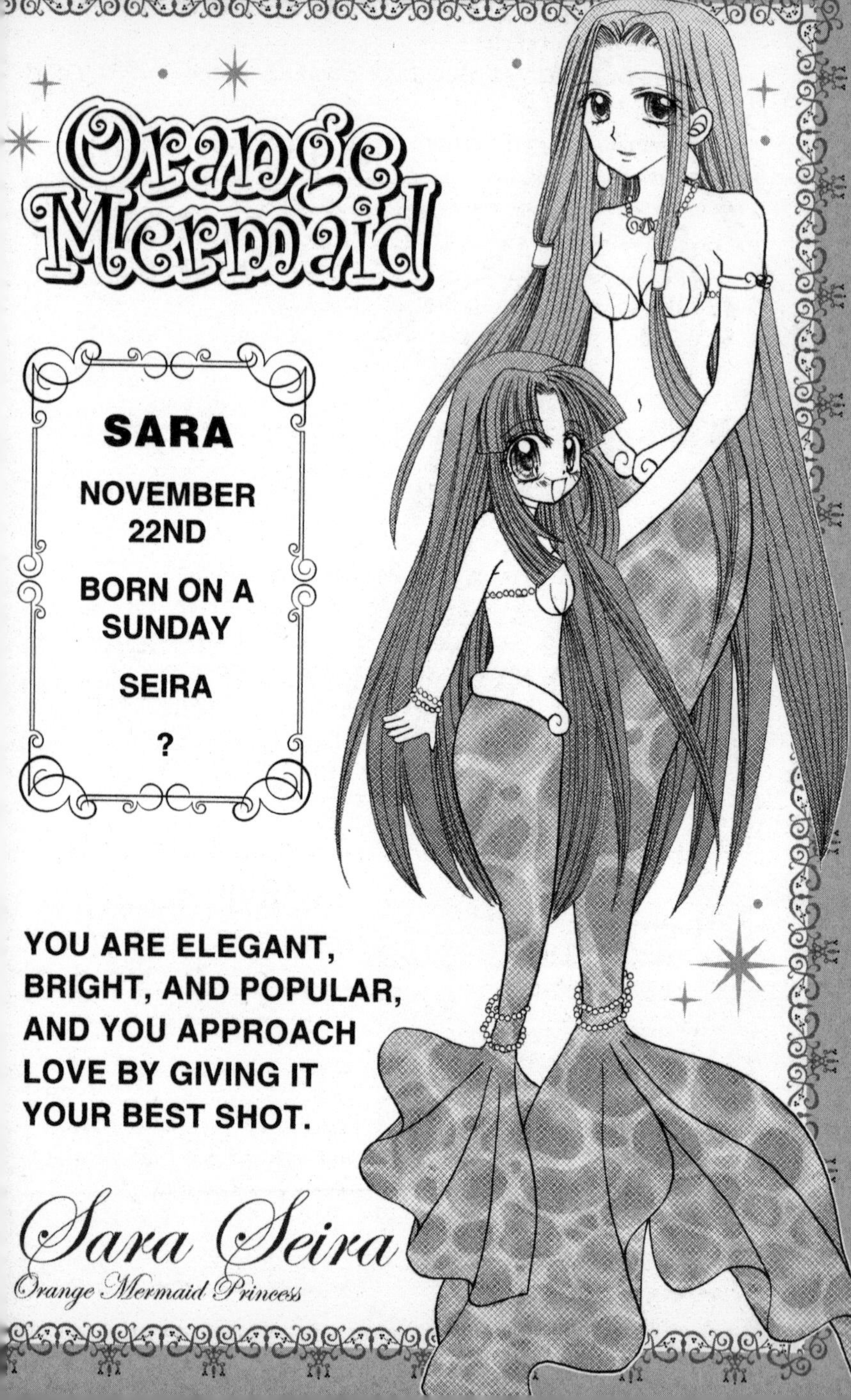

YOU ARE ELEGANT, BRIGHT, AND POPULAR, AND YOU APPROACH LOVE BY GIVING IT YOUR BEST SHOT.

Sara Seira

Orange Mermaid Princess

BASIC PERSONALITY

YOU PROJECT AN ELEGANT BUT CHEERFUL MOOD. YOU LOVE TO STAND OUT IN A CROWD, AND YOU'RE VERY GOOD AT SHOWING YOUR FRIENDS A FUN TIME. OTHERS PROBABLY THINK OF YOU AS THEIR IDOL. YOU LOVE COMPANY, AND YOU CAN TALK ENTHUSIASTICALLY AND EASILY WITH PEOPLE YOU'VE JUST MET, SO YOU CAN BECOME GOOD FRIENDS WITH PEOPLE VERY FAST. BUT THERE IS ALSO A SELFISH SIDE OF YOU THAT GETS ANGRY WHEN THINGS DON'T GO YOUR WAY.

FATE IN LOVE

YOU'RE NOT VERY GOOD AT THE POLITICS OF LOVE, SO WHEN YOU FIND SOMEONE YOU LIKE, YOU TEND TO COME RIGHT OUT AND TELL THE PERSON HOW YOU FEEL. YOU LONG FOR A LOVE WITH A BIT OF DRAMA, AND YOU HAVE HIGH STANDARDS, SO YOU'RE A LITTLE PICKY WHEN IT COMES TO WHAT BOYS YOU LIKE. BE VERY CAREFUL THAT YOU DON'T WEAR YOUR PARTNER OUT THROUGH YOUR SELFISH DEMANDS.

WHO MATCHES YOUR AFFECTION

=> GREEN MERMAIDS

=> MEN BORN ON FRIDAYS

SHAPE UP YOUR GOOD POINTS

YOU'RE FULL OF IDEAS, SO IF YOU CAN RUN A SCHOOL FUNCTION, THAT WOULD BE YOUR CHANCE! IF YOU CAN REMAIN OPTIMISTIC WHEN REAL TROUBLE COMES, IT WILL IMPROVE YOUR POPULARITY.

About the Creator

Pink Hanamori

Born on November 5th in Shizuoka. Prefecture; Scorpio, Blood type AB. Entered the 31st Nakayoshi New Faces contest with the manga *Miss Dieter Heroine* in the year 2000. Her debut work was *Nakayoshi Haru-yasumi Land* (Nakayoshi Spring Break Land) in the year 2001. Her signature work is *Mermaid Melody Pichi Pichi Pitch*. She loves to play with dogs and talk a lot.

Translation Notes

Japanese is a tricky language for most Westerners, and translation is often more art than science. For your edification and reading pleasure, here are notes on some of the places where we could have gone in a different direction in our translation of the work, or where a Japanese cultural reference is used.

Narito Airport, page 14

The name of this fictional airport is intended to recall Narita, or the New Tokyo International Airport. It's called "Narita" after the small town closest to the airport. Situated in the middle of Chiba Prefecture and about an hour by train from the downtown districts of Tokyo, Narita has the most air service to the Western hemisphere of any international airport in Japan. "Narito Airport" is the Pichi Pichi Pitch world's fictionalized version of Narita.

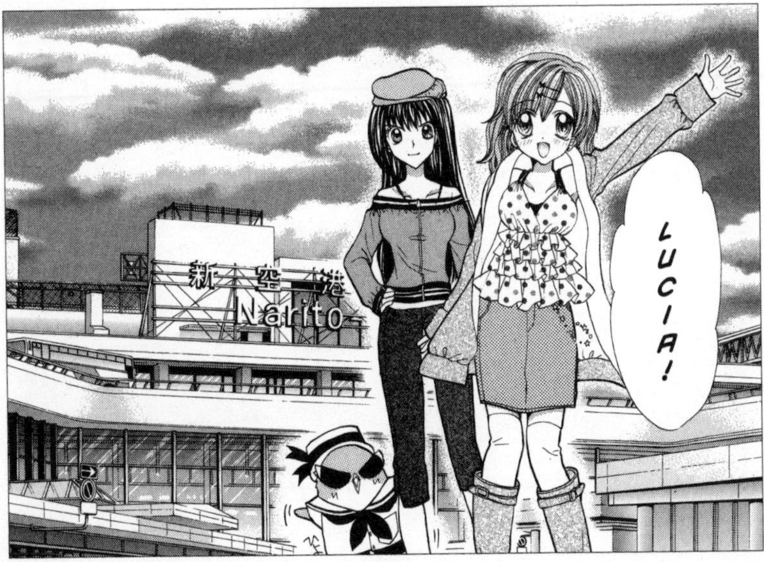
LUCIA!
新空港
Narito

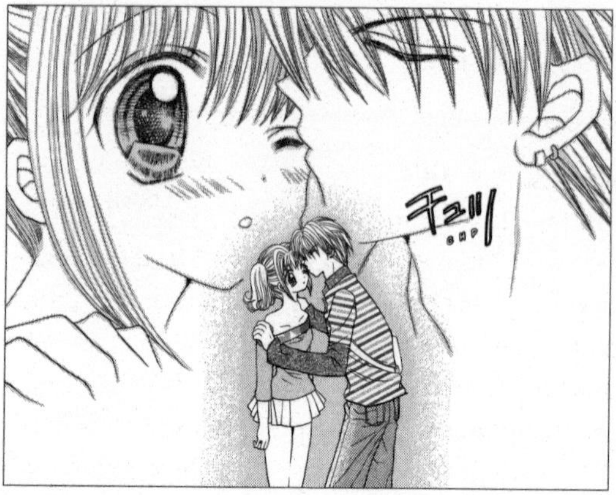
チュッ

Kissing at the Airport, page 18

Kissing at the airport is a treasured Western tradition, but that tradition isn't carried over into conservative Japan. In fact, most public displays of affection are frowned upon in Japan, although many young people flout the the customs of the country. These customs are changing, but it is still rare to see Japanese couples kissing in the airport.

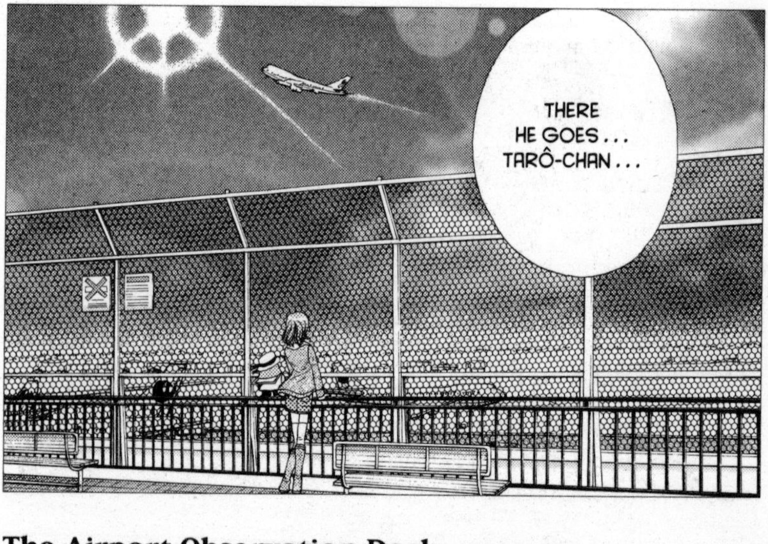
THERE HE GOES... TARÔ-CHAN...

The Airport Observation Deck, page 20

Although most U.S. airports have done away with the outdoor observation deck, Narita Airport still has them on the roof of the terminal buildings. It is sometimes a little smelly, but it does give one a good view of the airliners taking off.

Michel and Michael, page 32

In this book the Japanese pronunciation for Michel's name is Mikeru. This is an obvious reference to the archangel Michael. The Japanese, however, usually pronounce the archangel Michael's name "Mikaeru" or "Maikeru," and I've never seen the pronunciation "Mikeru" used in this context before. But since *Pichi Pichi* often uses slightly different spellings for even well-known names, I decided to render this name as "Michel," which recalls the archangel name without being exactly the same. The girl Michal's name is pronounced "Mikaru" in Japanese, but is clearly intended to be similar to Michel's name. So, as in the Japanese, I spelled Michel's and Michal's names in almost exactly the same way, only altering the *e* to an *a*.

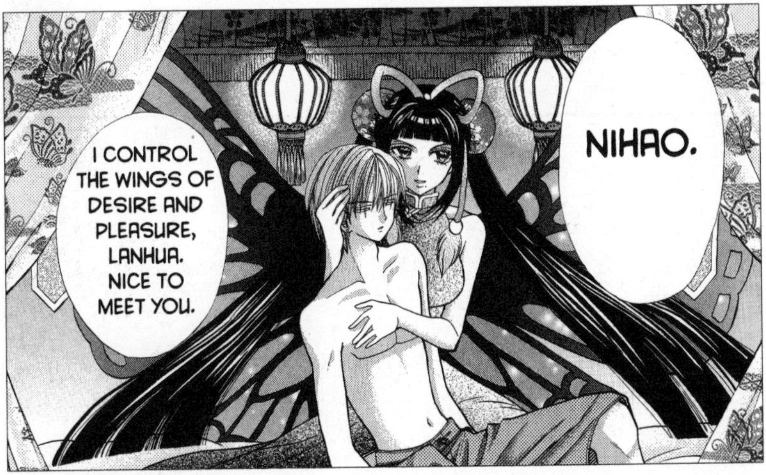
NIHAO.
I CONTROL THE WINGS OF DESIRE AND PLEASURE, LANHUA. NICE TO MEET YOU.

Nihao, page 118

Just as most English speakers know that *bonjour* is a common greeting in French, most Japanese know that *nihao* is a common "hello"-like greeting in Chinese.

Lanhua, page 118

The Japanese pronunciations for the characters that make up her name suggest that her name should be Ranka or Ranhana, but the pronunciation guide next to the *kanji* (the *furigana*) clearly read Ranfua in the foreign-word syllabary *katakana*. The Chinese pronunciation of the characters in her name is Lanhua, and since Japanese makes no distinction between the *L* and the *R* sound, and since the sound *hu* is pronounced as *fu* in Japanese, Lanhua is a reasonable transliteration of the name. (As if her greeting Lucia with the Chinese salutation *nihao* wasn't clue enough.)

Miiin Miiin, page 155

The sound effect *miiin miiin* is one of the onomatopoeia the Japanese use for the sound of cicadas, an insect that can bury itself underground for up to seventeen years before coming out to mate. Summer is when the cicadas come out, so one clue in Japanese entertainment that the scene is set in high summer is the sound of the cicadas' enormously loud and obnoxious chirping

PE Level, page 162

Gym classes are rated from "PE Level 5" to PE Level 1" with a "5" being outstanding and a "1" being the worst classification. Since Lucia is a "1," she must have never shown much athleticism in gym class. It's the equivalent of the failing "F" grade.

Uranai, page 209

Uranai is the Japanese word for fortune-telling or divination. Mermaid *Uranai* is much like Sushi *Uranai* (see the note in Volume 2) in which personality types are divided up into a number of types as decided by the time of one's Birth. Mermaid *Uranai* uses the day of the week.

We're pleased to present a preview of

Pichi Pichi Pitch

volume 6. This volume will be available in English July 31, 2007, but for now, you'll have to make do with Japanese!

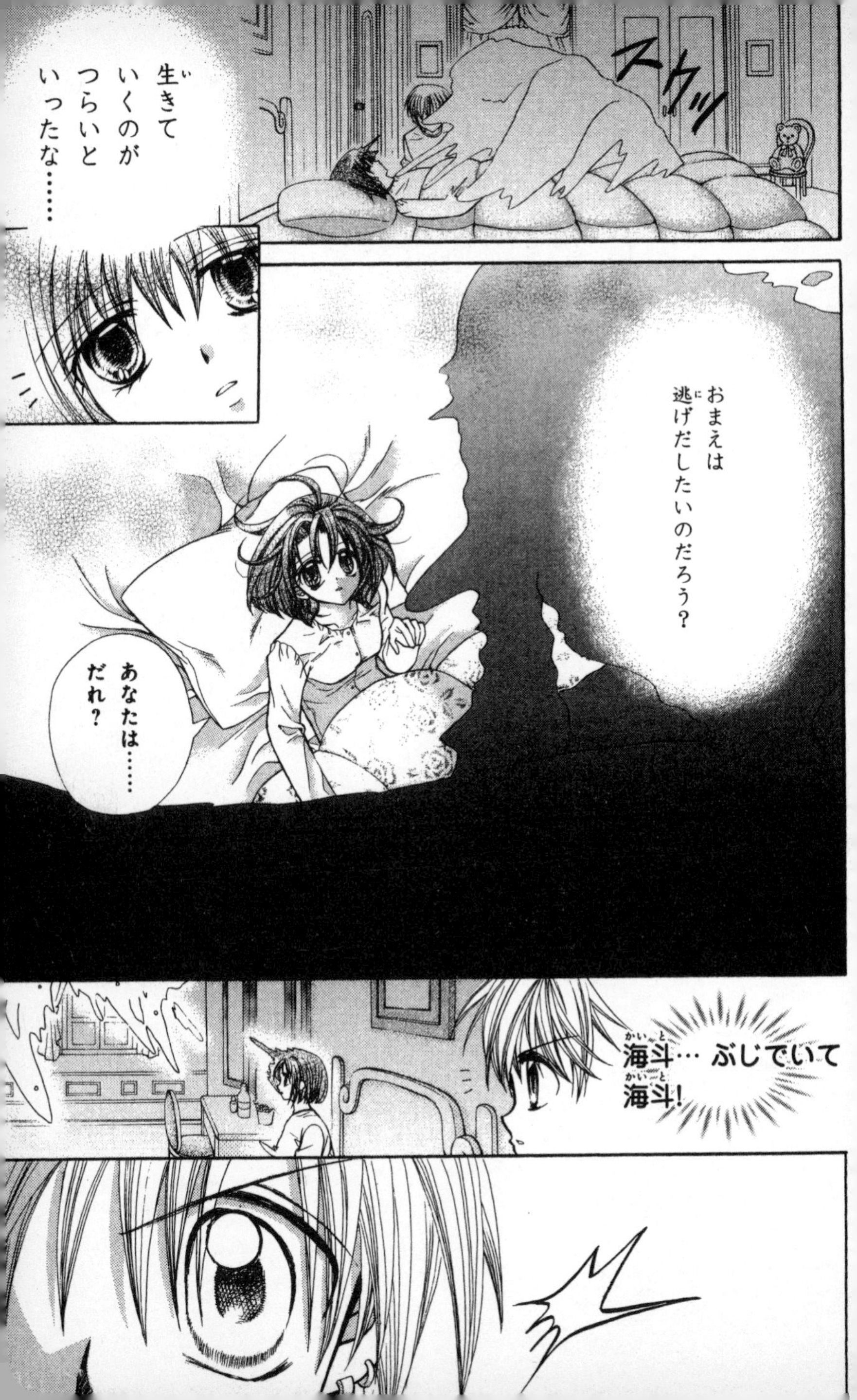
スクッ
生きていくのがつらいといったな……
おまえは逃げだしたいのだろう?
あなたは……だれ?
海斗… ぶじでいて海斗!

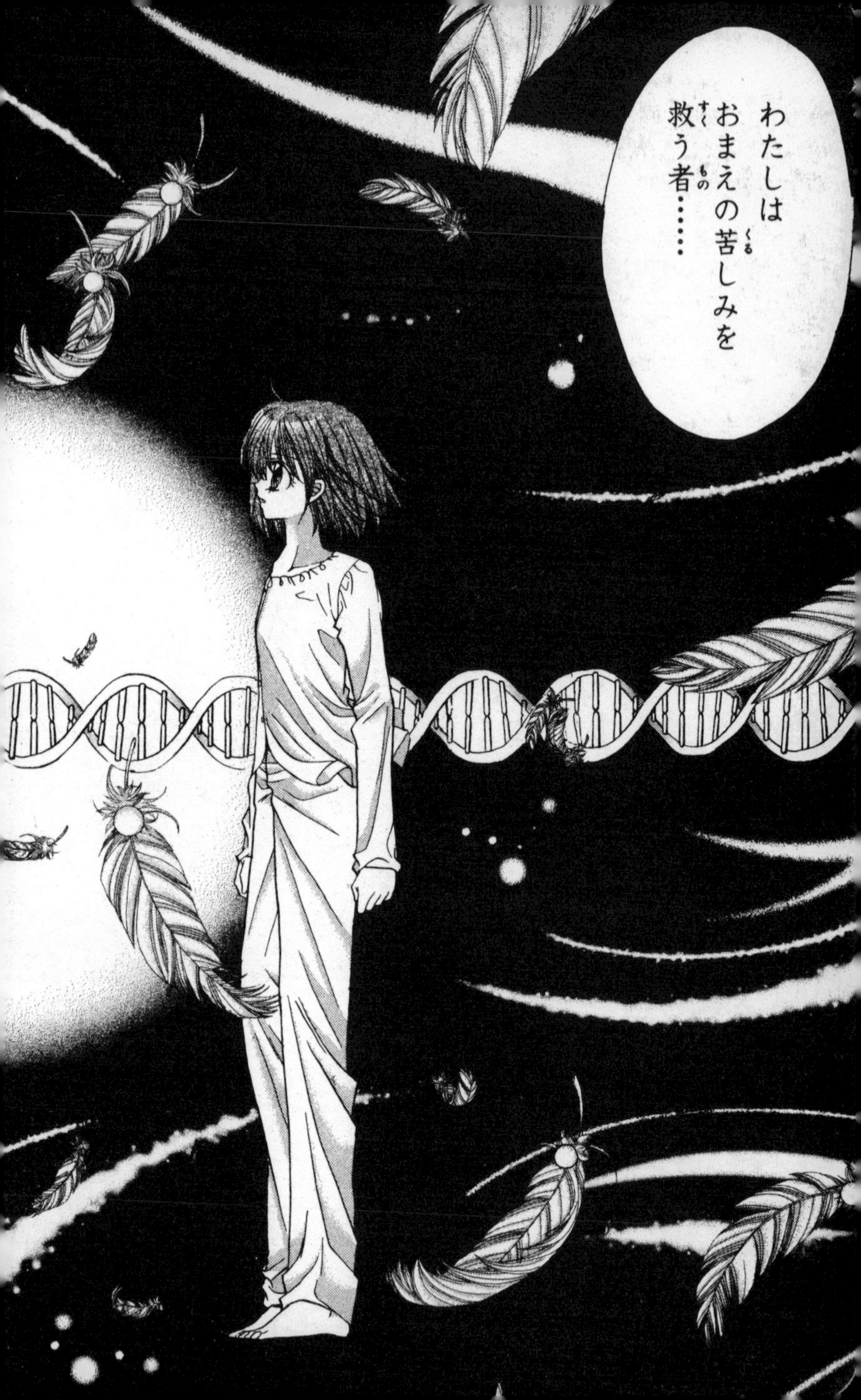
わたしは
おまえの苦しみを
救う者……